UNITY IN DIVERSITY

Essays in religion by members of the faculty of the Unification Theological Seminary

UNITY IN DIVERSITY

Essays in religion by members of the faculty of the Unification Theological Seminary

Edited by Henry O. Thompson

Copyright © 1984
by
The Unification Theological Seminary
Barrytown, New York 12507

Distributed by
The Rose of Sharon Press, Inc.
GPO Box 2432
New York, NY 10116

Printed in the United States of America
Library of Congress Catalog Card Number: 83-051715

ISBN 0-932894-20-8

The editor wishes to acknowledge that Jonathan Wells' article is reprinted with permission from *Parameters and Perimiters in Christology*, ed. Frank De Graeve and Frank K. Flinn (Barrytown, NY: International Religious Foundation, 1984).

DEDICATION

This volume is
dedicated to

Rev. and Mrs. Sun Myung Moon

in appreciation of their
continuous support
of the
Unification Theological Seminary

Table of Contents

On the Human Scene

Unification from Within

Unification and...

Appendix

Bridges of Understanding:
By Way of Preface

Unity in Diversity aptly describes the faculty of the Unification Theological Seminary. We are Eastern and Western. We are women and men. We are European and Asian and American. We come from backgrounds of Judaism, Christianity, Islam, Buddhism and Confucianism. We are Unificationist and United Methodist, Orthodox Jewish and Greek Orthodox, Reformed and Roman Catholic, and "one who submits" (Muslim). Among us are graduate students and triple doctorates. We are full-time and part-time and visitors. We work together in harmony and sometimes disharmony. Someone said, "Work on and do not despair. But if you despair, work on." We are not in despair, but we do work on, sometimes agreeing and sometimes disagreeing but working on. We are a microcosm reflecting a diverse macrocosm that continues to function in spite of its diversity. Some would find this distracting. We find it exhilarating.

A great deal of the exhilaration of teaching at UTS comes from our students. They also are a microcosm reflecting the diversity of the world in which we live. They mix occidental and oriental, black and white, women and men. Some are well-versed in religion while others are still at the introductory stage. A few are special students without degrees while a few have doctorates. All come with inquiring, questioning minds, ready to learn but also to wonder and to ask, to offer perspectives out of their own richly variegated backgrounds. Life is not dull at UTS.

The present collection of essays has grown out of our diverse interests. It surprises people to find that our faculty does not consist entirely of Unificationists. It should not be so surprising, however, that a movement concerned with building bridges of understanding among the diverse peoples of the world should have at the heart of its 'think tank' a similar diversity.

"What is it that ties you together?" We can answer that we are not tied at all but our togetherness is our own shared humanity. The diversity is an enriching stimulus to our own further thought, within our own specialties and, naturally enough, an occasional look at Unification-ism itself. The views expressed are, of course, the authors' own.

We begin like the Bible with the broad human scene. We move from a theology of action to a radical empiricism to the personal experience of faith to the darker side of human nature. Too often we spend our time accusing others of sin when an experience of the mystical oneness which is ours to have in the freedom of democracy would allow us to act together and not only change history but restore it. That is surely a philosophical perspective that is radical enough, though we may all need to be shamans with self-awareness and a willingness to come out of our ethical caves to do good and to stop the vicious cycle of evil that continues to be perpetuated from generation to generation.

From within Unificationism, Wells speaks to the doctrinal concern of Christology. We reprint this very fine study because of the central and crucial nature of its creed. The great debates and councils of the first centuries of Christianity attest to the different understandings of Christ. The record of history suggests that those most concerned about doctrinal purity were those least concerned about practicing what the Christ represented. Jesus came preaching, "Repent, for the Kingdom of Heaven is at hand." He told of a God who longs for his children, suffers with them, calls them to return to him, and offers hope to the oppressed and downtrodden. The call of course is for Liberation Theology's 'praxis,' practicing what we preach. Continuing from within Unificationism, we present the Judaic action side or life style side of religion, in this example of life in the middle years. The Unification movement has been presented in the media in terms of 'children.' These 'children' are in their 20s and 30s but here we share the growing maturity of the movement that never was a teenage phenomenon. In its maturity, the movement offers an alternative to one of the most massive ideologies in human history—David meets Goliath...

New insights have come from looking at Unification and... The foregoing essays do that in a number of ways. Here, we present studies from a biblical perspective by Boslooper and James. The Bible is said to be the best selling and the least read book in America. Some have criticized the Unification movement when it was quoting the Bible; the critics appear ignorant of the source of the quoted material. The Bible's importance in the Western tradition has often been more symbolic than applied. An earlier version of Boslooper's essay circulated in offprint as

"The Character of Unification Theology as a Modern Christian Statement." It is a pleasure to offer this revised version with its additional reflection. As Christianity syncretized the oriental semitic religion of Judaism and the occidental culture of the Greco-Roman Empire, so it has been suggested that Unification thought syncretizes occidental and oriental thought. Dr. Pyun examines some possibilities in this perspective. Lee on his part takes a strictly Western philosopher for comparison. At first glance, this editor would never have thought of Unification and—John Dewey. Yet the paper presented here makes eminently good sense, though readers can judge for themselves. Whether agreeing or disagreeing with the association, however, the issues discussed are an important part of modern history. One of the most volatile issues in modern history has been the relationship of religion and science. Here scientist Kurt Johnson offers a perspective on the Unification Principle and Science. Voluntary association has been an important aspect of modern history. Hendricks points out that it has been a major feature of American life from the beginning of European settlement on these shores. As a voluntary association, the Holy Spirit Association for the Unification of World Christianity fits well with the American scene. But he also points out the pressure to conform as part of our scene from the Puritans unto the parties of the present.

As we cast our bread upon the waters, we acknowledge the help of numbers of people in preparation and presentation, for inspiration and support. A special thanks is due to Lloyd Eby who provided some valuable information on Aristotle for Mr. Kim's essay. We "name in our hearts" as the liturgy goes, but take this opportunity to say "thank you" for the continuing support of John Maniatis, former director of the Rose of Sharon Press. Over the months that this volume has taken shape, his availability for counsel has been neverfailing. Without the determination of Arthur Herstein, this volume might never have seen the light of day. For his 'midwifery' we give thanks and praise. It is a special joy to acknowledge the continuing support of David S. C. Kim, President of the Unification Theological Seminary, for his leadership of the Seminary from seminal thought to reality; from shaky beginnings to the stability of maturity. We gratefully dedicate this book to Rev. and Mrs. Sun Myung Moon for the warm hospitality of their home, for their many gracious kindnesses toward the UTS faculty, for their spiritual guidance and for their continuing support.

Henry O. Thompson
Associate Professor
Religion and Society

Foreword

The Unification movement, along with its unique ideology applicable to many fields of study, has been the subject of much controversy, discussion and interest over the past few years. Though some non-Unificationists have pronounced Unificationism unworthy of serious consideration, a growing number of educated and aware individuals in all fields have been recognizing its viability as a positive new force in world religions and society.

During the last few years books and articles have appeared about the Unification movement, many of them written by prominent professors. Some have had positive things to say, while others have had negative viewpoints. I have been especially eager for the publication of this particular volume, *Unity in Diversity*, a compilation of papers written by professors and other faculty of the Unification Theological Seminary about Unificationism and its movement relative to their own special area of interest. Why have I been waiting so eagerly? Because these professors have had the unique opportunity to study Unificationism firsthand. They have had available to them all the resources for a thorough study of the Divine Principle, as well as the living example of the theology as embodied in their students. During the past eight years the professors at UTS have been able to observe with their own eyes the Unification way of life by working with, living with and teaching Unificationists.

I think these papers in particular are authoritative because they are written on that foundation of personal knowledge as well as their own foundation of academic discipline. The professors at UTS are serious academicians and well-respected in their fields. But even more importantly, perhaps, these papers were written on the foundation of courage. For the most part, the professors are not Unificationists, yet they were willing to step out of the mold of society and study something new and controversial. Even though some of them received severe persecution for their association with Unificationism, they persisted in the face of difficulty for the sake of knowledge and truth. For this they should be highly commended.

In addition to this praise, however, I must also offer a word of caution and a challenge. Being of such high calibre and influence, they now have a responsibility to share their knowledge and experience with others, offering the public a clear view of this movement. I therefore have desired that this book be completed much sooner.

My hope for the future is that this type of work can be published on a continual basis, perhaps annually. I shall fully support that project. I have a very high regard for the UTS professors and other faculty, and I sincerely hope that they will succeed in this great endeavor.

David S.C. Kim
President
Unification Theological Seminary
November 9, 1983

Introduction
Richard Quebedeaux

Korean Missionaries to America

Few movements of any kind in recent American history have provoked more consternation than the Rev. Sun Myung Moon's Unification Church. Ever since his arrival from Korea to take up residence in New York in 1972, Rev. Moon has succeeded in alienating just about everybody. The political left cannot tolerate his unabashed anticommunism, and some of its leaders accuse Moon of having close ties to the Korean CIA through his principal interpreter, Col. Bo Hi Pak. These same individuals also charge him with being a selfish, authoritarian demagogue because of the strict, simple lifestyle he demands of his young followers who often sleep on the floor in communal "centers" while Moon and his family enjoy the comforts of a spacious mansion in Tarrytown and an obedient household staff. They cite the movement's "fund-raising" techniques, by which perhaps 800–1000 youthful adherents sell flowers and candy on city streets in the U.S. for up to 18 hours per day, seven days a week. And they note the fact that Unification fundraisers average about $100 each day— with some making as much as $500 or more—only to see most of the money wind up in New York church bank accounts.

Fundamentalist Christians look at Rev. Moon as a false messiah—anti-Christ, even—bent on seducing their children into a deceptive belief system leading straight to hell. More moderate Christians view him as a dangerous heretic with "another gospel." The Jewish community dis-

cerns in Moon another Hitler, courting intellectuals and religious leaders, and converting young Jews to a sinister ideology and "new family" it
sees as anti-Semitic to the core. Many academics who are invited to the
Korean evangelist's lavish International Conferences on the Unity of the
Sciences and other gatherings of scholars accuse him of wanting to use
their names and presence to legitimize his movement, "buying them off"
by offering to pay all their travel and accommodation expenses—and an
honorarium, if the situation so warrants—even if they live halfway
around the world.

Certain members of the mental health profession have asserted that
Rev. Moon and his lieutenants employ deceptive means to recruit potential converts and subject them—once they can't easily get away—to
"mind control" and "brainwashing" techniques to keep them in line.
Some perceive "glazed eyes" and a "zombie look" on Unification fund-
raisers and their inability (so it would seem) to listen to "reason" when
told what their leader's *real* intentions are. The secular and religious
media, understandably, have sided with the majority in criticizing and
protesting against Rev. Moon and the Unification Church.

Ever since Ted Patrick accomplished his first successful "deprogramming" of cult adherents in 1971, there has grown up a large and influential
anti-cult movement aimed at crushing all high-commitment religious
groups charged with limiting personal freedom. Deprogramming, inci-
dentally, has become a rather lucrative business, especially since Jones-
town. Distraught parents may pay up to $40,000 to have a child "rescued"
from a cult. One major function of this anti-cult movement has been to
provide the media with convincing deprogrammed cultists to tell their
stories, always sensational. And it is interesting to note that, by and large,
the media have not attempted to find and interview the much larger
number of former members who have left the Unification Church and
similar groups voluntarily. Nor have they taken much time to talk to
active members of these movements and others—positive parents, objectively critical academics, and the like—who have a different story to tell.

Finally, there are those white Americans who see in Rev. Moon and the
Unification Church a new "yellow peril," ready to engulf the U.S. at any
moment with waves of Asian nationals. When Korean and Japanese
Unification missionaries came to the U.S. in force with a new message,
they also brought with them their own cultural baggage in the same way
white American missionaries took Christianity to Japan and Korea entan-
gled in the American way of life. When the norms of one culture are

imposed on another for any reason, there is going to be trouble.

By the prevailing social and cultural norms of American life, Rev. Moon and his movement deserve some of the aforementioned criticisms. Others, however, are reminiscent of the unfounded attacks commonly levied against every "new" religious movement by the establishment, be it political, academic or religious. It took centuries for the Jesuits to be accepted in American life. The Mormons suffered persecution for decades, not to mention the Quakers and Jehovah's Witnesses. And the now chic, born-again, tongue-speaking Pentecostals—Pat Boone, Bob Dylan, and Ruth Carter Stapleton among them—were denounced relentlessly and termed "holy rollers" for almost three quarters of a century after the founding of the Pentecostal movement in 1901.

This is all merely to suggest that if the informed, fair-minded outsider examines the Unification Church and its ideology cross-culturally, in the context of its Korean origins, he still may not like what he discovers. But he will almost certainly come up with a far different assessment of the man and the movement than has heretofore been made by the popular mass media and the anti-cult folk.

Sun Myung Moon and His "Korean Connection"

Despite the fact that Korea today is 85 percent Buddhist, Christianity has had a far greater impact there than in Japan or China. The world's largest Pentecostal assembly and Presbyterian congregation are both located in Seoul. But Korean Christianity has also been highly eclectic from the beginning. Many Christians in Korea still affirm some of the basic tenets of Buddhism, Taoism, Korean folk religion—including shamanism—and Confucianism. Confucian ethics, especially, are often practiced within Korean Christianity. Most important in that ethical system are the strong emphases on *jen* ("human-heartedness") and on the Five Great Relationships: kindness in the father, filial piety in the son; gentleness in the elder brother, humility and deference in the younger; righteous behavior in the husband, obedience in the wife; humane regard in elders, reverence in juniors; and benevolence in rulers, loyalty in subjects.

A powerful nationalistic spirit has also pervaded Christianity in Korea. Because of the numerous invasions and occupations perpetrated by its neighbors, "messianic" expectations were already present in Korean culture long before the arrival of Christianity. A national leader would arise and liberate his people from foreign oppression. When Christianity was brought to Korea, with its belief in the second coming of Christ, some Christians came to feel that God was going to make it up to Korea by sending Christ back to *their* land. The messiah would return to earth in Korea, not Jerusalem.

Sun Myung Moon was born in a rural town in North Korea in 1920. The details of his early life related by followers are so hagiographic in character that it is difficult to discern the true facts. Moon himself has said very little about this period publicly, at least, and so inquirers are left with only a minimal amount of reliable information. It *is* known that Rev. Moon's parents converted to Christianity when he was ten and reared him in a Presbyterian home. Sun Myung Moon was a sensitive youth. On Easter morning, 1936, while praying on a Korean hillside, Moon had a vision of Jesus who told him to finish his still uncompleted mission. And for the next nine years Moon studied the Bible, prayed intensely, and —like the early Christian hermits in the desert—had spiritual battles with the cosmic forces of evil. In course of time he discovered the Principle, the basis of the Unification Church's "inspired interpretation" of the Bible.

In 1938, Sun Myung Moon matriculated at Waseda University in Japan to study electrical engineering, but he continued his strict spiritual discipline while a student and worked with the Korean underground in Japan who were seeking to liberate Korea from Japanese occupation. In 1946, he moved to Pyongyang in Russian-occupied North Korea and began his ministry by preaching from the Bible in the streets, gathering disciples. After a few short years, in 1948, Moon was arrested by the Russian-dominated communist authorities—apparently because of the stir his preaching caused—and sent to a labor camp.

During this time in Korea the charismatic street preacher became associated with a variety of eclectic Pentecostal and other enthusiastic Christian sects looking toward the second coming. The main teacher in one group, a peasant woman, came to believe that the promised messiah would return to earth, not glorified "on the clouds" (as in traditional Christianity), and not in Jerusalem, but rather as a baby again, born of woman, in Korea. This was confirmed to her, so the story goes, by the shaking of her belly whenever she preached or taught this doctrine. The "inside the belly church," as it was called, eventually died out, but the present Mrs. Moon was raised with that community.

After United Nations intervention in the Korean War, Moon was liberated by U.N. forces in 1950. Immediately thereafter, he found two remaining disciples, moved south to the refugee town of Pusan in 1951, and began to preach the Principle there. He and a small group of followers lived together in a shack they built from cardboard, while each supported himself by working—Moon, as a laborer on the docks.

In 1954, expelled from the Presbyterian church for heresy, and self-ordained, Rev. Sun Myung Moon and four disciples (only one of whom still survives) organized the Holy Spirit Association for the Unification of World Christianity, still the Unification Church's official name, and he began his ministry once again. The movement grew slowly. By 1955 it had attracted its first theologian, Young Oon Kim, a professor at Ewha University in Seoul, and a Methodist with strong Swedenborgian leanings. Miss Kim later became the first Unification missionary to the U.S. in 1959, preceded a year earlier by Moon's first missionary to Japan. In 1960, Sun Myung Moon was married (the second time) to Hak Ja Han and started his promised family which, his followers believe, is the beginning of the Kingdom of God on earth.

The Principle

Unlike most other new religious movements, the Unification Church already has a highly complex theological and philosophical system, still, however, in the process of formation. Because of its belief in "new revelation" (or "new insight" to the Asian mind), Unification—in contrast with traditional Christianity—accepts the possibility of change, even in its own doctrinal formulations. The Unification system itself is based largely on an allegorical, rather than literal, interpretation of the Bible, informed by Taoism, Buddhism, Confucian ethics and elements of Korean folk religion. Furthermore, the movement's goal is the unification (a popular word in Korea, despite the Korean tendency toward factionalism) not only of fractured Christianity, but also of world religions on the foundation of the Judeo-Christian tradition.

According to the emerging generation of theologically-educated Unificationists, the "Principle" their leader discovered during his early ministry is really an entity within God himself, a metaphysical truth. The book, *Divine Principle* (named by an Australian Pentecostal missionary), did not exist when Moon began preaching. First published in Korea in 1957, it was merely an attempt to systematize his exegesis and interpretation of Scripture, and was written down as a textbook or guide for followers who wanted to communicate Rev. Moon's insights to others. These "discourses on the Principle" were later revised, translated and published in several editions. The present "brown book," the normative edition for now, was published in English in 1973, but it too is currently being revised. This edition is an extremely poor English translation, with some striking historical inaccuracies. It contains some strong anti-Church polemics, responding to a major fundamentalist attack on Unificationists in Korea in 1957, which are inconsistent with current church attitudes and stated goals. And it employs phraseology that the Jewish community interprets as antisemitic, inconsistent with both the movement's belief and practice. Recent study guides to the Principle, notably the standard *Outline of the Principle Level 4* (published in 1980) have shown sensitivity to this issue and removed the most objectionable language. According to the Principle, Judaism, as all religions, continues as a valid path to God up to the present day.

Briefly, the Principle teaches that God is personal and eternal, creator of heaven and earth, whose deepest nature is "heart" and love, and who combines both masculinity and femininity. Man, woman and the universe reflect God's personality, nature and purpose. God created Adam and Eve to respond to his love and thus give him joy, sharing in his creativity.

God's will in calling man and woman into being was that they fulfill "the three blessings": Be fruitful, multiply and have dominion (Genesis 1:28). That is, (1) grow to maturity (i.e., "perfection"), with mind and body united in harmony centered on God's love. Then, (2) when—and only when—maturity is reached, be united as husband and wife, giving birth to children free of original sin (Unification's stress on the primacy of the family derives, in part, from its Korean origins). Finally, (3) take care of the created world by setting up a loving dominion of reciprocal give-and-take with it.

But Adam and Eve, before they had attained maturity, were tempted into illicit love (usually explained as an adulterous "sexual" relationship between Eve and Lucifer, then a "premature" sexual union between Adam and Eve). Thus our first parents turned away from God's will and purpose for them and brought themselves, through this original sin, into spiritual death—and with them, the whole human race. As a result of the Fall, Satan usurped the position of humanity's "true father," so that thereafter all people of Satan's lineage are born in sin and have a sinful propensity.

In due course, however, God sent Jesus Christ, his own son, as the second Adam to become the head of the human race, replacing our first sinful parents. Born without sin as God's messiah, Jesus was to grow to maturity, marry, establish a family and initiate God's intended kingdom of heaven on earth (for which he asked in the Lord's Prayer). But people—Jews and Romans—did not accept him. Rather, the Romans put him to death, making it impossible for Jesus to complete his mission, to initiate the new God-centered, sinless lineage that would restore the world and bring in the kingdom. Nevertheless, by his sacrifice and resurrection, Christ *was* victorious over Satan, and so made possible "spiritual salvation" (i.e., salvation of the soul) for those "reborn" through him and the Holy Spirit. "Physical salvation," however—the kingdom of heaven on earth—must await the Lord of the Second Advent, the third Adam, who will marry, have children, and begin God's long-delayed but promised reign.

The Lord of the Second Advent, whom most Unificationists see as Rev. Moon, with Mrs. Moon, will become the "true parents" of all humanity. By following and obeying them as Father and Mother (without rejecting one's biological parents, however), original sin will be eliminated, and humanity will eventually become perfect. The spreading of true families over the globe, then, will fulfill God's purpose for creation and bring in the kingdom—establishing proper moral standards, uniting all peoples and races, resolving the tension between religion and science, righting all forms of social and economic injustice and overcoming God-denying ideologies such as Marxism-Leninism. In Unification thought, all society will ultimately be organized on the model of these "ideal families" and their loving relationship to God, each other, and the world.

Yet restoration (or salvation) of the world is not easily attained. Those who join the Unification Church must sacrifice, pay "indemnity" for their sins, if not for those of their ancestors (cf. Hebrews 11:39, 40). Indemnity can be understood as a Christianized version of karma, and many Unificationists define it simply as "paying your dues." Since in Unification theology—as in the Social Gospel—self-centeredness lies at the root of all sin, followers of Rev. Moon must lead God-centered lives, expressed "horizontally" by living for others. And because God himself has been *suffering* ever since the Fall, man and woman's first responsibility is to alleviate God's suffering, give him joy, and in so doing, receive joy for themselves—loving God with all their heart, soul and mind, and loving their neighbor as much as themselves (Matthew 22:34–40). But fleshing out this love, making it operative in the lives of believers, is an extremely hard task in the Unification Church. Self-centeredness can be defeated only by self-sacrifice, and the course of this self-sacrifice in the lives of Unificationists is a major reason for the sharp criticisms directed at the movement.

The Unification Church

It should be remembered at this point that Unification is an indigenous *Asian* form of Christianity. Founded and led by a Korean, and utilizing an Asian system of philosophy to express and live out the Christian gospel, the movement is still strongest in Japan and Korea. In fact, only a fraction of its total membership are westerners.

Since its establishment in 1954, the Unification Church in Korea, according to highly inflated official church estimates, has grown to nearly 300,000 members. It has foresaken much of its early spontaneity and communitarianism there in favor of a course that is already rather staid and "organized" and more compatible with traditional Korean family life and culture. In other countries the movement is still made up largely of young people in their 20s and early 30s, the individuals able and willing to fulfill the arduous lifestyle requirements imposed by local and national leaders at this time. But in Korea, with the inevitable routinization and bureaucratization characteristic of an "older" religious movement, the Unification Church now spans all generations. In addition, the Korean church owns and operates a number of highly successful businesses, including Il Hwa Pharmaceutical Co., producers of some of the world's costliest ginseng tea. These businesses, obviously, make the more demanding fund-raising practices unnecessary. Despite moderating trends, however, the Unification movement in Korea is still bitterly opposed, especially by traditional Christians.

In Japan, Sun Myung Moon's church is looked upon, more or less, as just another one of the country's growing "new religions." Membership here (again, according to inflated official church statistics) is in the neighborhood of 400,000, and the Japanese Unification movement— with its increasingly successful business enterprises—shares the growth psychology of the rest of the population. In fact, the church in Japan is the key to the financial growth of the movement worldwide. Often it will underwrite costly projects taken on by the church in other countries, or expensive ventures conceived elsewhere that would benefit the movement as a whole. Until Moon himself took up residence in the U.S. in 1972, his American movement had been tiny and unnoticed. The Unification Church, under a variety of different names, has existed in the San Francisco Bay Area since 1960. During the late 60s and early 70s it fit well into the Berkeley-San Francisco ethos, blooming with a multitude of other "new-age" religious movements. But things changed dramatically when Rev. Moon, who had visited the U.S. on whirlwind tours before, settled in New York and decided to focus his ministry on America. Opposition mounted quickly for reasons having little to do with the essence of Unification theology itself. Rather, it was the curious blend of Moon's own flamboyant Korean messianism and certain cultural traditions—appropriate in the East, perhaps, but scandalous in the West—brought with his Japanese and Korean followers, that constituted the root cause of the opposition soon to arise.

For example, the Japanese introduced new fund-raising techniques to the U.S. church in 1973, and, because of their success, they took over most of the money-raising activities of the movement in America. What appears to casual travelers and shoppers as a sporadic effort by young adults to sell candy or flowers in major shopping centers and airports is actually part of a highly developed computerized national network of Mobile Fundraising Teams (MFT), working key areas of major cities out of vans. Fund-raisers are driven by their captains to the appointed locations methodically, dropped off in the morning and picked up late at night. It has not been uncommon, moreover, for American Unificationists to work three or four years on MFT. While this kind of workaholic drive and commitment which grossed $20 million in 1979 in the U.S. alone is no big deal in Japan, white Americans are horrified when they hear of their children's activities in this regard.

Then the Japanese and Korean followers of Rev. Moon brought another cultural "problem" with them to the U.S., readily apparent both in fund-raising and in membership recruitment. In the Japanese hierarchy of values, loyalty is a far more important principle than honesty. "Heavenly deception" is the term used by opponents to describe Unification evangelistic and money-raising techniques. In the face of harassment and opposition, it has been very common for Moonies not to admit their church affiliation both in fund-raising and in "witnessing." In the San Francisco Bay Area, for instance, they used to invite people on the street to a "workshop" sponsored by the "Creative Community Project," with no indication—in the beginning, at least—that this was an arm of the Unification Church. Today, however, full disclosure is more common.

The Road to Perfection

Sun Myung Moon's church in America is made up, at the present time, almost entirely of highly idealistic young people in their 20s and 30s. According to surveys taken by J. Stillson Judah of Pacific School of Religion in Berkeley in 1976, almost 70 percent of these "full-time volunteers" had completed at least two years of college before joining; 10 percent had been to graduate school. Many are former Marxists, and a high percentage come from a Roman Catholic background. Relatively few are from Jewish homes (less than 5 percent). With all the attention given the Unification Church by the mass media over the last several years, one envisions a rapidly growing American movement "capturing" hundreds of thousands of new adherents. Not so. In fact, 4,000 full-time "core" members in the U.S. might be too high an estimate. It isn't easy to be a Moonie.

"If you follow me, I will make you saints." So goes a line from one of Rev. Moon's rarely quoted in-house speeches. The course of Unification discipleship is much like that followed by novitiates in a strict Catholic order, at least for the first several years. One joins the church simply by accepting the Principle, not by swearing allegiance to the movement's leader. But *living* the Principle is hard work and demands continual self-sacrifice.

Becoming a full-fledged member of the Unification Family, wherever that occurs, usually requires absolute submission to the "parental authority" of the church's leaders and an arduous spiritual and physical discipline. Intense prayer and multiple days of fasting are common practices in the movement as a whole. The reborn Unificationist starts out as a "servant of servants." That usually means fundraising for at least a year, if not two or three. Moon believes that raising money on the streets is itself a spiritual discipline that builds character by demanding humility. Unification fund-raisers can deal with *anyone*.

At the present time most young Moonies sleep on the floor (no problem for the Japanese) in coed centers, often in university towns. With their brothers and sisters, they share in normal household duties, including meal preparation, cleanup, laundry and maintenance. Although most movement leaders encourage six hours of sleep nightly, many

Unificationists get by on less than that. "Sleep deprivation," when it occurs, is usually self-imposed.

The road to maturity—perfection—and marriage is a long one in the Unification Church. But each stage along the way is marked by more freedom and more responsibility. A fund-raiser may soon become an MFT captain, then a center director, state leader and so on up the line. After three years of driving a van, a Moonie may be sent to graduate school on a full fellowship, or asked to start a business—on his own. The greater the responsibility, the greater the creature comforts he may enjoy. Everything the Unificationist does, however, is looked upon as preparation for the divinely appointed role of "true parenthood." (There is a democratization of messiahship in the Unification Church, in that the goal of all Moonies is to become true parents just like Rev. and Mrs. Moon, rearing children without the sinful propensity of fallen nature.)

Marriage can take place within the movement only after a period of preparation lasting at least three years. During this time Moonies live together as "brothers and sisters" and practice celibacy. Yet celibacy and singleness are but temporary norms, for only in "blessed marriage" can man and woman know and serve God fully and fulfill God's purpose of creation. Marriages in the movement are "arranged" by Rev. Moon personally and intuitively. On the Mother's Day weekend 1979, he "matched" 705 couples in New York in 16 hours, and, on the last weekend in 1980, another 843. These "engaged" or betrothed couples will remain apart on their separate missions until the next formal "mass wedding" of perhaps 10,000 couples takes place, probably in 1982. Most blessed couples move into their own apartments, raise their families, and enjoy the independence and responsibility that go with parenthood in the Unification Church. But even in marriage, followers of Rev. Moon must not be self-serving. Marriage itself is not merely for the sake of the partners or their children, it is for the world. Husband and wife, even with small children, are often sent on different missions for extended periods of time, while other Family members take care of the kids. Furthermore, the hospitality practiced by married couples in the Unification Church sometimes exceeds that even of the young singles living in a communal center. There is very little room for privatism in this movement.

Hospitality is the preeminent expression of Christian maturity in the Unification style of life. Even the Moons' mansion in Tarrytown, besides being the home of their twelve children, and a number of administrative and household staff, is a gathering place for church officials and other invited guests throughout the year. The same is true of the other elegant homes presided over by state leaders. Ironically, it is the Unification ideal of self-denial and hospitality—sometimes carried to an extreme—that results in the frequent charge that Moonies "love-bomb" potential converts for some sinister purpose. How could anyone, of their own free will, the critics ask, be so self-sacrificing and so hospitable without having an ulterior motive? There is no such thing as a free lunch.

Of course, hospitality—in true Korean fashion—is the first step in the Unification Church's recruitment process. But apart from the intensity of this hospitality, the movement's evangelistic techniques are essentially no different from those used by many of the more established churches (especially those in the evangelical tradition)—and the courts agree. Guests are invited, initially to dinner and an evening lecture on the Principle. Persons whose interest is kindled here are then invited, generally speaking, to three-, seven- and 21–day workshops in succession (Biblical numerology is very popular among the Moonies.) After this, they may or may not join the church. The lecturing technique itself, another frequent target of criticism, was developed to a high degree in Japan. Lectures are long and, for many people, quite boring. This is why the Northern California movement, the church's most successful recruiting arm, has integrated human potential methods into a greatly simplified lecture program. Thus a complex system of belief, centered more on right action than on correct doctrine anyway, is made understandable. Still, what usually attracts alienated youthful idealists to the Unification Church—at first, anyway—is not just the ideology itself, simplified or in its full complexity. Rather, it is the *praxis* of the community of faith in which the Principle is taught that impresses the hearer, love expressed by hospitality.

Unification Institutions

"Impossible" is a dirty word in the Unification vocabulary. In her extensive study of the British Family, Eileen Barker of the London School of Economics and Political Science found that members, new and old, are anything but the "mindless robots" described by their critics. In her words:

Each member is given considerable responsibility for his work and for other people and often finds that he can do things he would have thought impossible to do before joining the Family. By being thrown in at the deep end with the assurance that he can do it if he trusts in God, the erstwhile introvert is told to go up to complete strangers in the street to ask them about their belief in God or to give a public lecture; the erstwhile city dweller will find himself having to discover how to milk a herd of cows; the erstwhile plumber finds himself in charge of running a large farm and a youth who was never considered responsible enough to be a prefect at school is told to organize a large function involving hundreds of people. And they do it.

Small wonder, then, that the confidence members experience in discovering new capabilities within themselves has enabled them to found and run the movement's numerous enterprises, not only in Korea and Japan, but in America as well. Through fund-raising, the Unification Church has bought a large number of expensive properties in the U.S. during the last several years, including the old New Yorker Hotel in midtown Manhattan, now used as the movement's World Mission Center and as the home of hundreds of Moonies in New York City (where church members also publish two daily newspapers, *The New York Tribune* and *Noticias del Mundo*). A growing fishing industry, with operations in Massachusetts, Alabama, California, Alaska and elsewhere, has been established, with the movement designing and building its own boats; and the church owns restaurants as well, including one of the best Jewish delicatessens in the San Francisco Bay Area.

Since 1975, the Unification movement has operated a graduate theological seminary in Barrytown, New York, enrolling about 120 students who represent the church's *creme de la creme*, 45 percent of whom are women. All but one of the seminary's regularly appointed teaching faculty (Young Oon Kim being that one) are non-Unificationists. Among these are an Orthodox Jewish rabbi, a Roman Catholic priest, a Greek Orthodox church historian, an evangelical New Testament scholar, a United Methodist professor of preaching and a Korean Confucian philosopher. The school allows a high degree of academic freedom for its faculty, and more than three dozen of its best graduates are now pursuing advanced theological studies at some of America's leading universities and schools of theology, including Harvard, Yale, Chicago and Union Theological Seminary in New York City. Like the membership of the movement in the U.S. as a whole, a large percentage of students at Unification Theological Seminary come from a Roman Catholic background. The dean herself is a former Catholic nun.

Most controversial of all Unification institutions created during the last decade has been the International Conference on the Unity of the Sciences (ICUS), held annually in major hotels in the U.S. and abroad. Sponsored and funded entirely by Moon's International Cultural Foundation, these four-day conferences—begun in 1972 with 20 academics—have now grown to large gatherings of more than 850 regular participants, with a number of Nobel laureates among them. Each year physical, biological and social scientists come together with a smattering of philosophers and theologians to discuss world problems from the perspective of their own disciplines. Critics of the church in academic circles are not entirely wrong when they accuse Moon of "courting the intellectuals" through these very posh conferences that cost up to $2.5 million or more (though the same critics are generally silent when the Vatican or the World Council of Churches sponsors similar gatherings).

In the traditional Confucian manner of honoring noted scholars (the concept of "honor" barely exists in the West any more), and with almost unbelievable hospitality, the Unification Church does treat these academics well. Many of the church's seminarians and graduate students in the U.S. and Canada are flown out to help coordinate the proceedings and act as hosts for the guests. And it is probably the case that professors who attend ICUS once wish to return year after year more because of the hospitality shown them and the comradery that develops in the process than because of the interest generated by the papers presented.

Rev. Moon sees himself and his movement as providing a forum, not only for the "search for absolute values" in general—the ICUS theme—but also for the eventual resolution of the longstanding controversy between science and religion. Although ICUS has not yet produced any notable results in this regard, it still remains just about the only place where nuclear scientists and theologians can get together on a regular basis to talk about common concerns. Moon, unlike many other contemporary church leaders, does believe that intellectuals are important. If the mass media constitute the major influence on people's attitudes in the short run, he insists, it is still the intellectuals who will be responsible for changing those attitudes in the long run.

Anticommunism

The growing popularity of ICUS—and of the large number of "theologians' conferences" sponsored by the church-funded New Ecumenical

Research Association (New ERA) each year—may well seem odd in view of Rev. Moon's avowed anticommunism, because the vast majority of academics who attend are anything but anticommunist. Some of them, in fact, are committed Marxists. It can be argued that intellectuals are often gullible. But such an assertion does not adequately explain the situation, because Moon's brand of anticommunism is not quite so simplistic and reactionary as it may seem from the outside.

Unificationists are against communism because of its godlessness and its lack of human-heartedness, not because they want to keep the "fat cats" on top and the poor on the bottom. The alternative to Marxism-Leninism offered by *Divine Principle* is not laissez-faire capitalism. Rather, the Unification counterproposal to communism is "theocratic socialism." And that *is* a problem, because theocratic—"God-centered"—socialism is hard to translate into a workable form in the present order of things. Moonies do believe in hard work, self-sacrifice, and the inherent dignity of the individual—as a child of God—but they are not rugged individualists in the stereotyped American sense of that term. Instead, Unificationists can be described more adequately as the "new puritans," who believe that the U.S.—together with Korea and Japan—has been called by God to be a light unto the nations, a city set on a hill. Many Koreans, in the early days of the movement, accused the Unification Church of being "Neo-communist" because of its communitarian practices and its social idealism. Even Moon's blatant pro-Nixon stance during the Watergate scandal, his followers insist, simply reflects the Korean (and Japanese) reverence for persons in the position of authority. But more than that, Moon's followers say, his statement was an attempt to call *all* Americans—including Richard Nixon himself—to repent, forgive, and unite. This is not to argue that there aren't Reagan Republicans—many of them—in the Unification Church, just as in almost every other church in the U.S. Nevertheless, unlike most conservatives, Moonies have no interest in preserving the status quo. And those who really know Unification theology and the movement's young intelligentsia who are working that theology out also know that Unification is essentially more compatible with the political left than the right.

In an American society dominated by narcissism, where bestsellers read by young and old go by the title *Looking Out for #1, Winning Through Intimidation,* and *The Virtue of Selfishness,* Sun Myung Moon's Unification Church does appear as a threat to the dominant culture and its hedonistic and materialistic values. Self-centeredness is not new. What *is* new is the up-front attempt to make it respectable, to celebrate it as a virtue, and to package and sell it as a new-found cure-all. The Moonies try hard to challenge this narcissism by living lives, by sacrificing all, for others— even if they do it in Asian ways not always appreciated by white, middle-class Americans. Modern American young people, and a few older ones too, join the Unification Church to concretize their frustrated idealism, not a little of which many of them first learned in Sunday or Sabbath school as children—in the same churches and synagogues that persecute them now for trying to *do* something about it. Right or wrong, the Moonies want to change the world. Because of this determination, news headliners and occasionally courts have wondered whether Moon's movement is not really religious but has political goals. The Unification Church is undoubtedly a religion—a religion showing concern for state affairs, but only as these are a background for the spread of religious and familial life or, all too often, a background hostile to new religions. It is easily understandable why the textbook, *Divine Principle*, strongly favors a democratic, pluralistic political environment. The book exalts as the ideal pattern of society "the constitutional political system" of distinct, co-equal legislative, administrative and judicial bodies. Idealistically it looks to the day when these will not be rivals but will work together for the common good. Correspondingly, this doctrinal book speaks against totalitarianism, noting that modern democracy arose precisely to prevent the concentration of power "in a specific individual or organization."

In a review of history, in *Divine Principle*, God is said to have promoted the development of religious, political, economic and scientific freedoms through such developments as the Renaissance, the Reformation, the American and French revolutions, the trend toward socialism, the World Wars and emancipation of colonies, and the contemporary struggles for dignity, rights and equality. Political forms are evaluated "from God's viewpoint," the focal value being freedom of religion.

In addition to seeing America as God's blessed land of opportunity and protection for the new messianic movement, Moonies revere Korea as their "holy land." Surprisingly, *Divine Principle* after its prolonged commentary on Biblical and Western history has no reference to political personalities, regimes or events in post-World War II Korea or America (the only contemporary political leader mentioned being Joseph Stalin). Many cultural reasons are adduced why Korea was essentially prepared for the start of the messianic work, and one ideological reason—Korea's division between the forces of religion and of anti-religion in an already existing "Third World War" between the ideas of "democracy" and "communism." In its religious crusade against communism, Unification urges initiatives only of love, truth and justice in the face of impending violence.

The Moonies claim as their messianic mission the spreading of Godly families. The subsidiary revolutionary goal is for religionists to get together and persuade Marxists and all other materialistic people to bank on spiritual exchange as the only basis for economic prosperity with justice, and for political harmony. Unification seeks a utopia where each person is completely satisfied, living in a loving family with material abundance, and having input into the decisions which affect his or her life. Where else, other than Marxism, can such dedicated idealists go in our society today? Who else really wants them? Jonathan Wells, a Ph.D. student in religious studies at Yale, a veteran Berkeley radical—incarcerated for a year at Leavenworth for draft resistance—and a Unificationist, told his story in the *Yale Daily News* in 1978. His concluding remarks in that article sum up quite adequately the reasons why intelligent and idealistic white American young people are attracted to and follow a "slant-eyed" Korean evangelist with a vision of the kingdom of heaven on earth:

> It's not easy to follow Rev. Moon. In the past four years, I've experienced enough verbal abuse, police harassment, and physical assault to make the time I spent at Leavenworth seem like a vacation. But it's often the case that the best way is not the easiest. When I went to prison, that seemed the best way to uphold high ideals in a messed-up world. I still have high ideals. The times have changed, but the dream has not diminished.

Josef Hausner

Human Action and Theology of Action in Their Philosophical Historical Context

"What Mind can Conceive, Man Can Achieve."

I. INTRODUCTION

The Importance of Human Action

Thoughts and ideas are very important aspects of the activities of the human mind, and we cannot deny their value for the intellectual life and the spirit of man. However, only in *activities* do man's spirit and existence attain their genuine realization and fulfillment, because existence means life and life expresses itself primarily in action. It is on the level of human action "where the action is."

What man thinks and feels is of secondary importance, because feelings and thoughts—even if one were able to share them with others close to him—belong to and remain the exclusive domain of the individual. Most important is how we translate our thoughts and ideas into realities of actions. The relationships between man and man are shaped, not so much in the human heart as on the stage of concrete actions. That is where daily life is consummated, where nations meet in confrontations and bloody wars.

Summarizing his life at the age of only 22 in order to draw conclusions for his future, Soren Kierkegaard, (1813-1855), the father of existentialism, wrote into his diary:

> What I really wish and intend is to clarify for myself what I am to do, not what I shall know, except for that knowledge which is necessary for the progress of any action. I have to understand my purpose, to see what God actually wants me to do. It is important to find a truth which shall be a truth for me, and to find an idea worth living and dying for.
>
> What would be the use of discovering so-called objective truth, of working through all the systems of philosophy? What I am lacking is to live a perfect human life—and not a life of knowledge—to develop my ideas on something real which is connected with the deep roots of my life, my existence. (August, 1835)

This entry into his diary became the leading motif in Kierkegaard's life and later developed into that influential philosophical current which came to be known as existentialism.

From the words of Kierkegaard we hear and feel a desire for the real, the concrete, a longing for a new philosophy, which shall not be alien to the individual, to his life and personality. Disillusioned by the great philosophical systems, Kierkegaard maintained that they do not respond to that important human need. He compared the philosophical systems to a magnificent structure, the architect of which has a little lovely home elsewhere. There is always a gap between the philosophical system and the constructor of that system. The new philosophical system, existentialism, has to be the home in which one lives, because existentialism means and expresses existence, and existence is action. It is in the domain of action where we have to make decisions and where we have to choose between alternatives.

Intention, Action and Responsibility

Action is the result of thought and intention. Intention is the motive of purpose that impels an individual to action. Action is the purposeful performance of a deed. Man's intentions, motives and purposes, whether for good or evil, are of great significance if they result in action. Intention gives meaning to and determines the validity of an act. Intention in itself, if it is not expressed in action, plays almost no role in determining the merit and moral value of an individual. Actions alone determine the moral status of man, and by them alone is he judged and evaluated for good and/or evil.

As long as we only reason with ourselves, and as long as we conceive even the most sublime of our intentions, we do not confront real alternatives. We cannot be made responsible for our thoughts or intentions. Only in the realm of action do we come into a structure of relationships with others, are faced with confrontations, become responsible for our deeds and may be made accountable for our actions.

The Three Dimensions of Human Action

The individual as well as human groups become involved in three dimensional directions:

a. Man acts in the area of creative work, as a producer of goods and supplier of material needs for human existence.

b. Man acts in an area which implies a relationship between man and man. It is here where he acts in an inter-related social-ethical context.

c. Man acts in the historical direction for the fulfillment of goals and purposes for future human generations. Man is telos-oriented.

Aaron David Gordon (1856-1922), a friend of Martin Buber and theoretician of the Palestinian Jewish Kibbutz movement, maintained that *action*, the idea of action is the essential purpose of man. Work is an organic part of man's life. Work in the field is absolutely necessary for the production of the life-sustaining substances. Man's (Adam's) work connects man organically with the soil (Adamah), with nature, with the whole of the Universe.

In action, in his creative and productive work, man becomes a partner in God's Act of Creation, man cooperates in the continuous act of Creation, contributing thereby to the daily renewal of Creation.

In his relationship with others, man establishes the foundations for a *society of man*, for living together and communication between individuals, regulated by norms and ethical principles. Man builds his social environment and creates the conditions which enable him to face the difficulties and vicissitudes of human life and be victorious in his struggle with nature. Man also is able to plan for his tomorrow, for after tomorrow, for his children, for the next and future generations. Without this ability to plan for the future, without the imaginative foresight for future generations, man's life would be lacking the interest for inspiring initiative. He would be limited and unaware of his historical dimension. Only by grasping his essence as a *historical being* is man able to pursue the most imaginative interests and to make intensive efforts for creative actions in the interest of future generations.

II. THE ANATOMY OF ACTION

What is Human Action?

In the word *conduct* we have a general term for human action as such, but, when speaking of a particular instance we usually use the words "act" and/or "actions." The character of human action, as the phrase is ordinarily used, makes the distinction from any other sort of physical action in that that human action is conceived as an expression of consciousness. The human organism exhibits all forms of actions: physical, animal and human actions in the strictest sense. The only physical actions of the organism, however, which are our concern in relation to the concept of human actions—are those actions which depend upon and express consciousness in the form of feeling or purpose. Purposeful action is that action which is performed after being preceded by a conceptualization regarding the thing which is to be executed. The ideas and images which precede the move and which are to be executed, can be based only on some kind of previous experience.

Action, Social Context and Constraint

The actions of the individual depend upon the essentially social character of human life. The actions of the human individual, for the most part, do either explicitly contain or imply a reference to other persons. This social factor in individual action manifests itself not merely in the social context of the action, but mainly in the definite control which social influence exerts over the will of the individual. Man is confronted with social control, which he experiences in the form of commands and prohibitions which continue through his life in various forms as:
a. Constraints upon his desires from without
b. Constraint as an internal factor of his own will.
The external social constraint tends more and more to become internalized, to develop into an internal factor of one's own will and character. It transforms society's law into his own nature. At first it comes to the

individual in the form of particular injunctions to refrain from particular acts, or to avoid particular objects. This obedience is given to particular persons, but it tends more and more to be transformed into impersonal and generalized rules of action to be obeyed as such. It is that which Freud calls suppression, and the sociologist, socialization.

These rules become concrete, and their control reaches out beyond every particular case and pervades the whole practical thinking of the individual. All human action is expressive of consciousness, and to the extent to which it is intelligent and significant to that same proportion is an action voluntary and the expression of character.

Deliberation, Decision, Means and Ends

The individual who seriously is determined to deliberate must come to a decision which is ultimately the option between two or more complex possibilities. Usually, he starts with some sort of decision already vaguely outlined in his mind in the shape of possible alternatives, and the function of deliberation consists in the elimination of those choices which are doubtful, in order to make the proper course of action clear.

Conceptual thinking has long been at work upon the materials which memory always supplies, and which is a level at which the individual usually thinks in terms of generalized purposes, to which he refers, and by which he guides his particular actions. We cannot ignore the desires of the individual, of the adult individual, which are nearly always more or less significant. The more intelligent and reflective the individual is, the more his desires and purposes will be organized in a systematic and structured way, and rendered to that scheme or type of life in which he believes to be able to attain the completest realization of his powers. The more complex and significant the desires are, the less it is possible to imagine their conflict as a mere collision between two forces of different intensities.

One practical relation that must be seen as forced upon the attention of an individual trying to bring about an ideally represented state of things is that of means and ends. And here comes into the entire picture of human action the process of deliberation, in which the individual seeks to discover the means of attaining an end, or to determine which of two or more ways is the best.

The more important a matter for examination and decision is, the more does the choice tend to express, not an isolated desire for a particular end, but the whole character of a human being, or, even more than that, his ultimate and all-inclusive desire for the lifestyle regarded by him as the best. The more ardently and resolutely a man lives, the more will the unity of his character tend to coordinate his plans even in the simplest actions of his daily life. Having deliberated and decided on the proper means, the man who was impatient to act will have removed the obstacles in his way and will act at once. The general purpose of action was present all through, and by the way of the deliberative process the general purpose is finally expressed in the shape of a definitive volition.

The Essence of Action and Moral Activity

Action belongs within the world of existence, to the category of events, processes, and/or changes. An action has a beginning and an end, it occurs in time, it has preceding conditions and subsequent consequences, and it does not occur independently.

A process is always related to a thing or things, a substance or substances, "in" or "to" which it takes place. All changes imply something relatively permanent, as a condition not only of its being known, but also of its *existence*.

Mental activity, being a process, is inherent in a substance, either in the organism as a whole, in the union of mind and body, or in the soul or mind as a reality independent of the body. Neither thinking, nor willing, nor any other form of mental activity occurs without conditions which call it forth, and to which its expression is subject. These conditions may be either mental, bodily, or both. The essence of moral action and activity is to be found in that form of mental activity in which an idea is retained before the mind in spite of its inconsistencies with tendencies or dispositions already present. In other words, the essence of a moral action and activity consists primarily in the fact that we retain in our minds an idea, in spite of the fact that this idea is inconsistent with prevalent tendencies and dominant dispositions. It means that our visions and commitments to change things disregard already opposing conditions and circumstances once we have made up our mind.

III. THE PHILOSOPHY OF ACTION

Arguments Against Hegelian Philosophy

The first representatives of the *Philosophy of Action* and *Existentialism* resulted from the attack against the philosophy of Georg Wilhelm Friedrich Hegel (1770-1831). Two arguments were primarily raised against Hegel's thought:

a. Hegel reflects on the world exclusively from the view of the *spirit* and disregards the real man, and his real problems (Feuerbach, Marx, and to a certain extent also Nietzsche).

b. Hegel transforms religion into philosophy, and prevents man from coming into a direct relationship with God (Soren Kierkegaard).

Based on the philosophical world view of Johann Gottlieb Fichte (1762-1814), the young Hegelian Bruno Bauer (1809-1882) emphasized the paramount importance of a philosophy of action based on a social critique which has the task to reveal and eliminate the unreasonable[1] in the existing conditions of man, and to free the path for reasonable developments.

Joining the Young Hegelians, Moses Hess (1812-1875) maintained that it was the merit of German philosophy that it established theoretically the unity of spirit and the world. However, in opposing Hegel, Hess stressed that Hegel's philosophy connects only in the idea the unity of thought and being, whereas this unity must be realized or fulfilled consciously in the sphere of the spiritual, and translated into reality in social life.

Hess asserted that the starting point should no longer be the conceptualization of abstract thinking, but the conscious will. Speculative philosophy has to be replaced by the Philosophy of Action. Only the *conscious action* as the true synthesis of thought and being will permit man to act independently and creatively in history. Against Hegel, whose philosophical speculation was oriented toward the history of the past, Hess emphasized that it is the task of philosophy to expand its horizons and become future-oriented. Contemplating on the past and the present, philosophy has to elaborate its conclusions for the future. The philosophy of the spirit has to be transformed into a philosophy of action.

Not being, but action, is the most important asset, the first and the last in the scale of human values. Identity is conceived as the content of action. Real life, the living "I" cannot be conceived either as the thinking, or as that which we think of, but only as the fulfillment, or the agent, of action. These three moments together form the "I," which is not something dormant or static, but is conceived as in continuous movement and change—as life itself. The "I" is a spiritual act, an idea which can be conceived only in its change and development and/or movement. As the planets, as everything which we conceive as moving and growing, so man is not only a static and spiritual being, but his self-consciousness is in continuous change and in continuous changing activity which is conceived as life itself. Without that action there is no real "I" and no real identity. Life is activity—creation of an identity, through which the barrier is overcome, and which transforms the "I" from a "non-I" into that state which we regard as activity.

The free, conscious, future creative action is possible because we all are partaking in the Spirit of God, and the future-oriented development tendencies enable us, through the Philosophy of Action, to determine that future.

August Cieszkowski (1814-1894), one of Hegel's disciples and a contemporary of Karl Marx (1818-1883), was a spiritual adherent of the intellectual-cultural school known as Polish Messianism. His philosophy of action was based on the previously already mentioned world view of Fichte and on the concept of the will which influences the changes of the dominant situation, which became the fundamental idea of Cieszkowski, as well as that of the other Young Hegelians. Cieszkowski affirmed that after the "laws of history" were formulated and defined by Hegel, it is time to establish the Philosophy of Action for the future course of human history.

In his writings[2] he stated that history is the evolution of the Spirit on three human levels:
   a. feeling—in the direction of the beautiful
   b. consciousness—in the true, and
   c. action—in the direction of the good.

Action is the domain of the spiritual. The Spirit is action par excellence. Will is preceded by thought, but action is the manifestation of the will. The revelation of truth in action will find its concrete form in life and in social conditions.

The adequate form of life, of the state, of life in the state, of social life, of the true solution of social contradictions, of conscious creation, of autonomous institutions, of the realization in the ethical sphere of law and morality, of the construction of the universal human community—all are the task and the mission for action.

Man's action is Creation, creation of personality, creation of society. Man fulfills himself participating in Divine Providence through his actions. Free and creative action is a form of worship and elevation towards God. Through man's action society becomes the society of man, and through the common effort of man who implements the Will of God in history— man may establish the Kingdom of God on Earth.

IV. THE HISTORICAL CONTEXT OF EXISTENTIALISM

The Crisis of the Twentieth Century

The nineteenth century, especially its second half, was characterized as a period of peace and stability. The dominant ideas of the century were those of rationalism, progress and hope. The confidence in man's rational abilities surpassed all previous expectations. But that was destroyed by the atrocities and convulsions of two bloody World Wars. World War I, and the collapse of all which had been regarded, until 1914, as the unchallenged order and the uncontested values generated new attitudes and a new world view.

Man's previously predominant sense of confidence in his world was lost. He began to feel helpless, surrendering to a chaotic and dismal world—a threatening environment, which overwhelmed him socially, politically, morally and economically, and which invaded all aspects and manifestations of his life.

The shock produced by the European conflagration of the years 1914-1918, with its accompanying symptoms: the Russian Revolution and the rise of bolshevism, fascism, nazism and economic depression, were the signs of the time of an era of crisis and turbulence, violent confrontation and bloodshed.

The road to decline and decadence was virtually opened with the anti-Christian writings of Friedrich Nietzsche, and with them their demoralizing and disintegrating influences: *Die Genealogie der Moral, Der Wille zur Macht, Der Antichrist.*

The intellectual doctrinarian of decline after World War I was the German historiosopher Oswald Spengler, the author of the bestseller: *Der Untergang des Abendlandes* and the mythological theory of "Blut and Boden," (Blood and Soil), the veneration of the myth of the Aryan race, deepened the moral, social and religious crisis of the world, and especially that of its shortsighted leaders.

World War II, in its totality and cruelty was the logical consequence of the neo-pagan anti-Christian spirit which dominated Europe and the world between the two Wars.

The world situation in the 1950s, 1960s and 1970s was marked by political instability, social confrontations, youth revolts, psychological fear and economic depression. It was a world which lived, and still lives, in the shadow of a thermo-nuclear war, under the permanent threat of destruction and the peril of the extinction of western civilization, if not of the entire human race. This is the "Sitz im Leben" of the new philosophical current known as modern Existentialism.

What is Existentialism?

The philosophy of existence, as a current which developed in Germany at the end of the 1920s, attracted large segments of the German public. Its most important representatives in Germany were Karl Jaspers and Martin Heidegger. During the 1930s existentialism was suppressed by the leaders of the Third Reich. In the 1940s and especially after World War II the philosophy of existence flourished in France, and came to be designated with the name of Existentialism. Its main representatives in France were Gabriel Marcel and Jean Paul Sartre. Existentialism may be considered as a link in an all-inclusive cultural-historical continuity, with influences in philosophy, poetry and scientific thought.

In the theological field it was the dialectical trend which was to a great extent influenced by existentialism. There are close connections between Bultmann and Heidegger.

Existentialism, more than a philosophical system, is the expression of the tragic sense of man's existence. Existentialism is not a formulated sytematic philosophy but the interpretation of man's "Dasein" as an existence towards death, and the anxiety of man before death. Existentialism is the interpretation of a period in human history dominated by dangers and despair. Existentialism is also the literary expression of a pessimistic view of life, of a tragic "Weltgefuhl" and of a "Gotterdammerung" (decline of gods).

V. CONCLUDING REMARKS

Theology of Action

Anxiety and despair can be overcome solely by the restoration of faith in God, confidence in man and his destiny, and in the acceptance of the concept that "the world, even though tormented, can be changed."

What we must do, in order to attain a world which can be considered as good, is to follow God's Commandments, to walk in His Ways and to act in accordance to His Will.

The tragic destiny of man, the pessimistic "Lebensgefuhl," fear and despair, can be defeated only by purposeful human action. Elements for such a theology of action we find in the thought of Gabriel Marcel, but even more explicit and clear in the thought and writings of Nicolai Berdyaev (1874-1948). According to Berdyaev, existence is a permanent and continuous struggle between good and evil, between the spiritual and the material, between freedom and enslavement. Evil is expressed in the struggle for life, in suffering and death. Even though he thinks the world to be evil, Berdyaev does not teach resignation. On the contrary, he emphasizes the importance of the fight and struggle against reality, against the evil manifestations in the individual, in society, in nature. The problem of man is at the core of Berdyaev's thought. His religious philosophy is anthropology more than theology. His teachings contain four positive concepts: Personality, Spirit, Freedom and Action (Creation).

The foundation of the "Imago Dei" in man is hidden and resides in his spirit, in his individuality, his "I," his personality. The individual is more important than society, but the individual cannot live alone, without others. Isolation means death. The "I" is and finds itself only in the relationship with others, with the "Thou." The individual, belonging to nature, is under the rule of the laws of enslavement and death. "Personality" is a spiritual phenomenon and in it resides the element of man's freedom.

Freedom is the dominant factor in the Kingdom of God. In our life, freedom reveals itself from time to time in our struggle against nature and enslavement. Original sin resides in nature more than in man. In man there is an inherent continuous struggle against nature, against enslavement, against death.

There is a relationship between man and God. Without God man is powerless and without purpose. God acts in reality through man. The Kingdom of God, the final ideal, is the realization not by God alone, but through man's action. Man is the telos of salvation and redemption. Man will be redeemed and saved not by renunciation, asceticism and self-abnegation, but through and by action (Creation), since the power of action (Creation) comes to man on behalf of God who created man for the satisfaction of His Creative Spirit.

In Plato's theory, the ideas, as the ultimate and only realities, have movement and life, soul and intelligence. The soul is most active when detached from the body, in the ecstatic union with the infinite and eternal idea of the good. According to rabbinic thought, however, "Ayn ha'Midrash ha'Ykkar ela ha'Masseh" ("The act, not the doctrine, is of paramount importance"), especially in the rabbinic doctrine of the "Zaddik" (the Righteous), where one single individual can by a single action, either good or evil, determine the existence of the entire world. Every human being, every individual, must therefore weigh each of his daily actions, not only for their effect on him, but mainly for their effect on the well-being and restoration of the entire world.

NOTES

1. Blind determinism is the conception which is able to find a ready acceptance with those who look upon human action and conduct from a biologistic-evolutionary perspective, or from a point of view of a philosophy like that of Schopenhauer or Von Hartmann's, which sees in blind will the ultimate principle of all existence. According to those views—the true forces which generate human actions lie in the strong instinctive tendencies of man's nature which shape his desires and feelings. The *calculating intellect* to which the reflection of the individual naturally but mistakenly attributes the direction of his life, are only superficial activities. In reply to such a blind deterministic conception, it can be maintained that such a conception of human life may have an appearance of profundity, but that it conveys no real insight. To appeal to instinctive tendencies means to involve ourselves in empty mystery, which obstructs the work of scientific analysis and explanation.

2. Cieszkowski wrote: *Prolegomena Zur Historiosophie, Gott und Palingenese "Ojcze Nash"* (Our Father).

Joseph McMahon

William James and Religion

I. RADICAL EMPIRICISM

What is philosophy?

In *Some Problems of Philosophy* James says that philosophy is only man thinking about generalities rather than particulars.[1] There is no special way of thinking involved in philosophy. All of our thinking incorporates observing, discriminating, classifying, analyzing, looking for causes, and developing hypotheses. But what do we think about or what data falls within the scope of philosophy? James replies that philosophy embraces all experiences actual and possible, and furthermore, it looks for a system of completely unified knowledge. In short philosophy is metaphysics.

> One may say that metaphysics inquires into the cause, the substance, the meaning, and the outcome of all things. Or some may call it the science of the most universal principles of reality (whether experienced by us or not), in their connection with one another and with our powers of knowledge.[2]

When James applied his definition of philosophy to the problem of being, he placed the emphasis on the question "what" rather than "why." This emphasis, without doubt, is a key factor which accounts for the particular direction found in his radical empiricism.

The question of being is the darkest in all philosophy. All of us are beggars here and no school can speak disdainfully of another or give itself superior airs. For all of us alike, fact forms a datum, gift, or *Vorgefundenes*, which we cannot burrow under, explain or get behind. It makes itself somehow, and our business is far more with its What than with its Whence and Why.[3]

Percept and concept

Now that James has defined philosophy in the framework of empiricism, he proceeds to analyze the problem of percept versus concept. His emphasis on the question "what" orients his approach to this problem. He stresses the importance of percept insofar as through perception we are directly in touch with external reality while he views the value of concept in a functional role. Such concepts as God, justice, etc., result from some sort of practical experience. Certainly, they are not innate. These concepts do have significance, but only as they relate to perceptual particulars. James can be considered a realist since he says, "The intellectual life of man consists almost wholly in substitution of a conceptual order for the perceptual order in which his experience originally comes."[4] In the following passage James explains the relationship that exists between the percept and concept.

Perception is solely of the here and now; conception is of the like and unlike, of the future, of the past, and of the far away. But this map of what surrounds the present, like all maps, is only a surface; its features are but abstract signs and symbols of things that in themselves are concrete bits of sensible experience.... Who can decide offhand which is absolutely better: to live or to understand life? We must do both alternately and a man can no more limit himself to either than a pair of scissors can cut with a single one of its blades.[5]

Although James recognizes the value of conceptual knowledge, he is ready to point out its shortcomings. Reality consists of existential particulars and here conceptual knowledge finds itself inadequate to capture the fullness of reality which can be grasped only in the perceptual flux. Consequently, the concept must be put to the pragmatic test to determine whether or not it has any meaning.

The pragmatic rule is that the meaning of a concept may always be found, if not in some sensible particular which it directly designates, then in some particular difference in the course of human experience which its being true will make. Test every concept by the question "What sensible difference to anybody will its truth make?" and you are in the best possible position for understanding what it means and for discussing its importance.[6]

Again, in another place, James subscribes to empiricism as the way of arriving at meaning.

I am happy to say that it is the English-speaking philosophers who first introduced the custom of interpreting the meaning of conceptions by asking what difference they make for life. . . . The great English way of investigating a conception is to ask yourself right off, "What is it known as? In what facts does it result? What is its cash-value, in terms of particular experience? And what special difference would come into the world according as it were true or false . . . ? For what seriousness can possibly remain in deviating philo-sophic propositions that will never make an appreciable difference to us in action?[7]

Suppose a concept does make an appreciable difference in action. What assurance does one have whether the concept is true or false? Or in other words, by what criterion does one judge the truth or falsity of a concept? Satisfactoriness is proposed by James as the touchstone for the validity of concepts. James is aware of the objections to his position and endeavors to answer his critics.

Humanism says that satisfactoriness is what distinguishes the true from the false. But satisfactoriness is both a subjective quality, and a present one. Ergo (the critics appear to reason) an object, qua true, must always for humanism be both present and subjective, and a humanist's belief can never be in anything that lives outside of the belief itself or antedates it. Why so preposterous a charge should be so current, I find it hard to say. Nothing is more obvious than the fact that both the objective and past existence of the object may be the very things about it that most seem satisfactory, and that most invite us to believe them.[8]

In the foregoing passage he fails to answer the objection concerning the truth of the concept referring to the future. Yet, he does offer an answer to this problem when he discusses the chief satisfaction of a rational crea-ture. That which pleases us most is to know that what we believe is true. This so-called solution compounds the problem because truth seems now to be prior to satisfaction. James handles the issue by avoiding the problem of the prior and posterior in relation to truth and instead he approaches truth by appealing to the experience of consistency.

> Are they (experiences) not all mere matters of consistency and emphatically not of consistency between an Absolute Reality and the mind's copies of it, but of actually felt consistency among judgments, objects, and manners of reacting, in the mind? And are not both our need of such consistency and our pleasure in it conceivable as outcomes of the natural fact that we are beings that develop mental habits—habit itself proving adaptively beneficial in an environment where the same objects, or the same kind of objects, recur and follow "law"?⁹

Simply put, James rejects the theory of truth as being an *"adaequatio mentis et rei."* Such an outcome in his philosophy is inconceivable in the light of his definition of radical empiricism according to which the percept is the measure of the truth. Therefore, the satisfaction which he is talking about is not a return to hedonism but is a satisfaction of accord which pertains to all of man's experiences.

> Theoretic truth is thus no relation between our mind and archetypal reality. It falls within the mind being the accord of some of its processes and objects with other processes and objects—"accord" consisting here in well defin-able relations. So long as the satisfaction of feeling such an accord is denied us, whatever collateral profits may seem to inure from what we believe in are but dust in the balance—provided always that we are highly organized intellectually, which the majority of us are not.¹⁰

The Jamesian problem

Although James has an affinity for the percept, yet, he is aware of the danger of succumbing to materialism. And, aware that the rationalist could fall victim to monism, he sets out to melt into one system the qualities of the tender-minded and the tough-minded philosopher. According to the empiricist or tough-minded philosopher, all that is, are experienced, possible or actual, while according to the rationalist or tender-minded philosopher there is a sense of the "more" or the "beyond." James tries to solve the problem without surrendering individualism or the reality of the here and now. He pursues his objective by opting for what he calls the graft theory which claims as its prototype of reality the here and now. Also it optimistically maintains that in the process of experimentation order is being won. The following is an account of James' theory.

> His "program", James continues, is to solve these puzzles "by the principle of nextness, conterminousness, which is defined as "outer relation with nothing between." There follows a long argument for community of objects between two or more minds; and for an externality or adventitiousness of relations that shall permit of the growth of unity, without the need of assuming a preexisting and "absolute" unity of the monistic sort... "The essence of my contention is that in a world where connections are not logically necessary, they may nevertheless adventitiously 'come'."[11]

Here there seems to be a paradox in James' approach to future events. He shies away from the Absolute which robs us of our personal initiative. He holds to a theory about the future based on evolution. In this theory there is no guarantee that the 'more' or 'beyond' of experience is any more than a bare possibility. If this is so then man is caught up in determinism. The development featured in his system is without purpose. Belief in a non-existent 'more' or a bare possibility could not leave us satisfied. However, put the 'more' or 'beyond' already in our hands and the problem vanishes. The 'more' or 'beyond' is now being developed by us. There is only one world. "The world exists only once, in one edition, and then just as it seems. For the usual philosophies it exists in two editions, an eternal edition... and an inferior temporal edition...."[12]

Therefore, James solves his problem by adopting the method of pragmatism and expounding the doctrine of panpsychism. He explains the unity of the world and avoids subjectivism by arguing for the coterminousness of minds which is their convergence in or towards the same experiences. By holding to the above tenets he fosters empiricism, personalism, democracy, and freedom. James describes his radical empiricism in his own words.

> My philosophy is what I call radical empiricism, a pluralism, a "tychism", which represents order as being gradually won and always in the making. It is theistic, but not essentially so. It rejects all doctrines of the Absolute. It is finitist; but it does not attribute to the question of the infinite the great methodological importance which you and Renouvier attribute to it. I fear that you may find my system too bottomless and romantic. I am sure that, be it in the end judged true or false, it is essential to the evolution of clearness in philosophic thought that someone should defend a pluralistic empiricism radically.[13]

Radical empiricism and religion

In *The Varieties of Religious Experience* James puts religion to the test of radical empiricism. In *Varieties* "James is not trying to prove that God exists or that religion is true; he is only trying to prove that we have a right to believe that God exists and to act as though religion is true."[14] His purpose in *Varieties* is to show that experience is the essence of the religious life, and that the life of religion is man's most important function. In a letter to Miss Frances R. Morse, James professes invincible belief in his purpose for writing *Varieties*[15]

In keeping with his method James searches for the data of religion which is to be put to the test of empiricism. According to James, religion has its own direct and independent data which are not ideas but facts.

> We may now lay it down as certain that in the distinctively religious sphere of experience, many persons (how many we cannot tell) possess the objects of their belief not in the form of mere conceptions which their intellect accepts as true, but rather in the form of quasi-sensible realities directly apprehended.[16]

James' position concerning quasi-sensible realities has its basis in his psychology. "According to the general postulate of psychology... there is not a single one of our states of mind, high or low, healthy or morbid, that has not some organic process as its condition."[17] Religion gives man a sense of well-being and a feeling of security which is an added dimension of emotion. Consequently, man is filled with enthusiasm and a spirit of freedom which eases the former tension produced by the conflict with evil. No doubt, certain effects are produced by belief. However, what assurance is there that the object of one's belief is true or has any meaning? Perhaps belief itself extends no further than the sensible effects it produces. Or is it a matter of sensible effects producing the belief? Does belief have meaning? The following excerpt sheds some light on James' theory of meaning.

> A statement is meaningful if either (a) it has experiential consequences, or (b) it has no such consequences, but belief in it has experiential consequences. In case (b) there is no explanation of what constitutes the meaning and we are left with the bare criterion of meaningfulness. This is the tender-minded view.[18]

Therefore, belief brings about certain consequences which produces saintliness in the person. How is this saintliness to be put to the test in order to judge the validity of the belief? The only possibility at hand will be human working principles which are consonant with moral demands and the voice of human experience within us. In short, the norm for saintliness will be common sense.[19] Although he employs the empirical method, he by no means sets out on a course of wanton doubt. All beliefs must be submitted to the twist of human ideals lest in pretending to possess the truth without trial one may lose it. Consequently, the empirical method proposes no set order of beliefs.

> But in our Father's house are many mansions, and each of us must discover for himself the kind of religion and the amount of saintship which best comport with what he believes to be his powers and feels to be his truest mission and vocation.[20]

One problem lingers on. James himself states it. "How, you say, can religion, which believes in two worlds and an invisible order, be estimated by the adaptation of its fruits to this world's order alone? It is truth, not its utility, you insist, upon which our verdict ought to depend."[21] In brief, the answer to the question is in mysticism. People in this state see the truth in a special manner. James cites numerous cases in which a sudden and almost indescribable experience accounts for an unparalleled religious insight into the truth of one's belief.

> The kinds of truth communicable in mystical ways, whether these be sensible or supersensible, are various. Some of them relate to this world— visions of the future, the reading of hearts, the sudden understanding of texts, the knowledge of distant events, for example; but the most important revelations are theological or metaphysical.[22]

While discussing the question as to whether or not mysticism is authoritative, he at the same time outlines the general traits of the mystic range of consciousness. "It is on the whole pantheistic and optimistic, or at least the opposite of pessimistic. It is anti-naturalistic, and harmonizes best with twice-bornness and so-called other-worldly states of mind."[23] Can such a state commend itself to us as a criterion for truth or just remain authoritative for the mystic alone? Although the mystical states wield no authority by simply being mystical states, nevertheless, they do have value for the non-mystic.

The mystical states offer us hypotheses, hypotheses which we may voluntarily ignore, but which as thinkers we cannot possibly upset. The supernaturalism and optimism to which they would persuade us may, interpreted in one way or another, be after all the truest of insights into the meaning of this life. [24]

Philosophy and religion

What are the criticisms James levels against philosophy in relation to religion? By philosophy James means the rationalistic approach as opposed to his own empirical approach. Throughout the *Varieties* James becomes more adamant in his stand on viewing religion as an experience based on feelings which are definite perceptions of fact needing no support from intellectual processes. No intellectual process can produce a religious experience. In fact, "Philosophy... is thus a secondary function, unable to warrant faith's veracity... " [25] Again, he criticizes the brand of intellectualism in religion which precedes experience and which shuts the door to the possibility of a science of religions.

> The intellectualism in religion which I wish to discredit pretends... to construct religious objects out of the resources of logical reason alone, or of logical reason drawing rigorous inference from non-subjective facts. It calls its conclusions dogmatic theology, or philosophy of the absolute, as the case may be; it does not call them science of religions. It reaches them in an a priori way, and warrants their veracity. [26]

James spells out clearly what philosophy cannot do and what it can do. In speaking of philosophy's limitations he says, "In all sad sincerity I think we must conclude that the attempt to demonstrate by purely intellectual processes the truth of the deliverances of direct religious experience is absolutely hopeless." [27] On the positive side philosophy can be a contributing factor in the study of religion if it abandons metaphysics and deduction in favor of criticism and induction. In so doing philosophy can sift out what are the common facts of religious experiences and eliminate doctrines that are scientifically absurd. She must then content herself to deal with what is left as hypothesis. [28] According to James, "Philosophy lives in words but truth and fact well up into our lives in ways that exceed verbal formulation." [29] If the object of religion is God, he must be more than a word for us; he must be more than a concept; he must be experienced.

> What keeps religion going is something else than abstract definition and systems of logically concatenated adjectives, and something different from faculties of theology and their professors.... What the word "God" means is just those passive and active experiences of your life.... They need not be infallible. But they are certainly the originals of the God-idea, and theology is the transaction; and you remember that I am now using the God-idea merely as an example, not to discuss as to its truth or error, but only to show how well the principle of pragmatism works.[30]

II. PERSONALISM

The concept of man and the needs of man

James' notion of personalism finds its expression in his notion of man which he constructs from observing man as he searches to satisfy his individual needs. In keeping with his radical empiricism he does not divide man into two parts but accepts him totally as a unit who undergoes a variety of experiences that reveal his deepest spiritual needs. No ready-made theology can forecast these unique experiences. An a priori approach to man's needs is inconsistent with the origin of these needs which spring from an ultra-rational region in man. In notes made while preparing the Gifford Lectures he speaks about the ultra-rational in the following way.

> Yet I must shape things and argue to the conclusion that a man's religion is the deepest and wisest thing in his life. I must frankly establish the breach between the life of articulate reason and the push of the subconscious, the irrational instinctive part, which is more vital.... In religion the vital needs, the mystical overbeliefs...proceed from an ultra-rational region. They are gifts. It is a question of life, of living in these gifts or not living...[31]

Therefore, a person's religious needs are peculiarly his own. We come alive as individuals by responding to these felt needs. Religion in the context of individualism means the personal response to one's experiences. Religion concerns "the way an individual's life comes home to him, his intimate needs, ideals, desolations, consolations, failures, successes!"[32]

Obviously, religion is individual and non-rational. Religion is not God-centered but man-centered and more particularly emotion-centered

since feelings are the immediate given religious experiences of the individual. James' basis for religion calls for a personalism which may be readily
identified with individualism. Perhaps it might be better to say that his
ardent desire to preserve his individuality dictated the foundations for his
religion. Then again in keeping with his radical empiricism it can be said
that whatever experience is first will determine the course of developments. For example a strongly felt need for an ideal will impose a demand
to believe in an ideal, and man will believe because he wants to believe.
The core of James' personalism is to be found in the individual's will
which frees a man by allowing him to believe that which he believes will
make him free.

How a man's needs are known

Although we secure freedom in willing, how do we know what to
will? Evidently, what we will will be determined by our needs. These
needs are made known to us by way of intuition and feeling. For example,
if James were alive today what needs would correspond to his intuitions
in the matter of religion? No doubt he would experience the coldness of
the 'technopolis', the tension among nations, and the struggle for men's
sentiments in the world forum. Consequently, there is need for brotherhood among us to bring security to our minds and to enable us to
construct a better world. Once we have experienced this feeling we may
then express our feelings in rational terms so that brotherhood becomes
an ideal which demands belief. "Articulate reasons are cogent for us only
when our inarticulate feelings of reality have already been impressed in
favor of the same conclusion."[33] Therefore, the depth of one's religion
will be revealed by the quality of one's feelings.

The meaning of religion

The meaning of religion is discovered in the interest of the individual
in his private, personal destiny. If we find a trysting place with the divine,
we do so only in the area of our personal concerns. However, is the divine
always present in personal concerns? Do we call the divine or does the
divine call us? If the divine calls us through our feelings what assurance
do we have that this call is authentic and not merely subjective? According to James we deal with realities when we deal with private and
personal phenomena.[34] When we deal with the cosmic and the general we

deal with symbols of reality. Therefore, the answers to the above questions can be given only by those that have experienced the answers in a mystical state. Even then these answers may be incommunicable to the rest of us. The true meaning of religion is experienced; afterwards we try to talk about it.

The veracity of religion

James examines the veracity of religion in the context of personalism. At the expense of being redundant he points out again the limitations of philosophy. Can philosophy stamp a warrant of veracity upon the religious man's sense of the divine? James answers with an emphatic 'no.' The reason given is clear to him since religion is individualistic and private, whereas philosophy deals with the general. Any sort of theological formula is secondary. The core of religious convictions or the fact of religious experiences have their residence in the subliminal.

> It (the subliminal) contains, for example, such things as all our momentarily inactive memories, and it harbors the springs of all our obscurely motivated passions, impulses, likes, dislikes, and prejudices. Our intuitions, hypotheses, fancies, superstitions, persuasions, convictions, and in general all our non-rational operations, come from it. [35]

Philosophy, therefore, cannot attest to the veracity of religion but must yield to radical empiricism. The veracity of religion is determined by its fruits in the individual since its origins reside in the individual's subliminal, which is impervious to philosophy. From an examination of a number of people who have experienced mystical states it may be safe to claim the following beliefs as characteristics of an authentic religious life:

1. The visible world is part of a more spiritual universe.
2. Union with a higher universe is our end.
3. Prayer is a process wherein the work of bringing about a better world is accomplished.
4. New zest takes the form of lyrical enchantment or appeal to earnestness or heroism.
5. One experiences security, peace, and love. [36]

III. FREEDOM

A person's main concern

As mentioned before under the topic of personalism, man's major concern is his private destiny. The struggle encountered in one's personal concerns reveals to the individual the call to freedom or the call to be born again. Through his individual feelings a person experiences a need for redemption which is especially evidenced in the emotion of forlornness. Simple reflection enlightens a person as to his needs.

> To ascribe religious value to mere happy-go-lucky contentment with one's brief chance at natural good is but the very consecration of forgetfulness and superficiality. Our troubles lie indeed too deep to that cure. The fact that we can die, that we can be ill at all, is what perplexes us; the fact that we now for a moment live and are well is irrelevant to that perplexity. We need a life not correlated with death, a health not liable to illness, a kind of good that will not perish, a good in fact that flies beyond the Goods of nature.[37]

However, the importance and value of the need of redemption seize a person through emotions. If a person's emotional life is suppressed, then he is poor in value, meaning, and character. The individual simply does not exist without emotions. Emotions or feelings are the facts, the given, and need no further explanation.

> And as the excited interest which these passions put into the world is our gift to the world, just so are the passions themselves gifts—gifts to us, from sources sometimes low and sometimes high; but almost always non-logical and beyond our control.[38]

Therefore, the gift of passion makes us vividly aware of our need for redemption from our present state of affairs for a better life. Our uneasy state will lead us to examine the significance of our feelings.

Emotions and values

The value of emotions surfaces when considered in relation to man's main area of importance; namely, religion. The common elements in all religions are conduct and feeling. All religions have their peculiar dogmas, but people of various faiths are similar in conduct. Consequently, feeling and not thought accounts for action which leads to the conclusion that the value of emotions is determined by the difference they make in our lives. The emotions pertinent to religion may be designated as the "faith-state" which in general is an enthusiastic and optimistic feeling about life. An optimistic feeling concerning one's private destiny produces fruitful results in daily living wherein is found the value of the emotions under the label of the "faith-state."

Conversion

The full realization of redemption is experienced by us in the conversion from the sick-minded state to the state of saintliness. Our anxiety about our private destiny vanishes in our self-surrender to an ideal or over-belief. For the most part conversion is a psychological transformation. Any renewal attributed to a transcendent power is left open as a possibility but escapes the tests of radical empiricism.

Now the question may be asked, conversion and redemption from what? We are oppressed by evil. We desire freedom from this oppression. If we hold a monistic view of the universe, we must maintain that evil has its foundation in God. On the other hand we cannot live according to a naive optimism and dismiss the fact of evil while at the same time claim that our system is complete. Therefore, the burden of the solution to the problem of evil is placed totally before us. We must seek an adequate answer from the concrete situation. James provides us with the examples of Bunyan and Tolstoy.

> The fact of interest for us is that as a matter of fact they could and did find something welling up in the inner reaches of their consciousness, by which such extreme sadness could be overcome. Tolstoy does well to talk of it as that by which men live; for that is exactly what it is, a stimulus, an excitement, a faith, a force that reinfuses the positive willingness to live, even in full presence of the evil perceptions that erewhile made life seem unbearable.[39]

The fruit of conversion is a new found freedom which occurs as the result of energy in the individual. According to James, there is no explanation for this change.

> Now if you ask of psychology just how the excitement shifts in a man's mental system, and why aims that were peripheral become at a certain moment central, psychology has to reply that although she can give a general description of what happens, she is unable in a given case to account accurately for the single forces at work. Neither an outside observer nor the

Subject who undergoes the process can explain fully how particular experiences are able to change one's centre of energy so decisively, or why they so often have to bide their hour to do so.[40]

Although he cannot account for the change, he does propose reasons which inhibit the change.

Such inaptitude for religious faith may in some cases be intellectual in its origin. Their religious faculties may be checked in their natural tendency to expand, by beliefs about the world that are inhibitive, the pessimistic and materialistic beliefs, for example, within which so many good souls, who in former times would have freely indulged their religious propensities, find themselves nowadays, as it were, frozen; or the agnostic vetoes upon faith as something weak and shameful, under which so many of us today lie cowering, afraid to use our instincts. In many persons such inhibitions are never overcome.[41]

Complete freedom is attained through the efforts of the subconscious. At this particular point it seems as if James has negotiated the full swing of the pendulum. He escapes the determinism he attributes to the Absolute, but he surrenders to an optimistic determinism inherent in human nature. Perhaps his position may be accounted for as a reaction to his Calvinistic background. He emphasizes the power of the will, and maintains that it concerns itself with the imperfect self. Complete conversion is experienced in complete self-surrender to the forces of the subconscious. "When the new center of personal energy has been subconsciously incubated so long as to be just ready to open into flower, 'hands off' is the only word for us, it must burst forth unaided!"[42]

Consciousness does figure into conversion but the weight of attention is given to the subconscious or subliminal which stands just outside primary consciousness. The subliminal in no way precludes the operations of a higher power within our religious experiences. On the contrary, exclaims James, "If there be higher powers able to impress us, they may get access to us only through the subliminal door."[43]

The authenticity of these higher powers at work can be judged by their results which are the signs of a state of saintliness.[44] The person experiences a feeling of being in a wider life which results from his self-surrender to subliminal forces. If the whole emotional center is shifted toward loving and toward embracing existence in a spirit of elation and freedom, then, enough evidence is at hand to validate the presence of higher powers.

Faith-state

The faith-state, the basis of conversion and, consequently, freedom, is a natural psychic complex. By surrendering to its demands we experience the jubilation of being alive as our self-centeredness fades into the shadows. In the lengthy quote which follows, James describes the abandonment of self-responsibility which results from the faith-state.

> The transition from tenseness, self-responsibility, and worry, to equanimity, receptivity, and peace, is the most wonderful of all those shiftings of inner equilibrium, those changes of the personal center of energy, which I have analyzed so often; and the chief wonder of it is that it so often comes about, not by doing, but by simply relaxing and throwing the burden down. The abandonment of self-responsibility seems to be the fundamental act in specifically religious, as distinguished from moral practice. It antedates theologies and is independent of philosophies. . . . Christians who have it strongly live in what is called "recollection", and are never anxious about the future, nor worry over the outcome of the day.[45]

No one can doubt the effects produced since they are approved by the critical eye of the empiricist. The effects produced are real, and, consequently, that which produces them is real even though the cause is in another reality.

> We and God have business with each other; and in opening ourselves to his influence our deepest destiny is fulfilled. The universe, at those parts of it which our personal being constitutes, takes a turn genuinely for the worse or for the better in proportion as each one of us fulfills or evades God's demands. As far as this goes I probably have you with me, for I only translate into schematic language what I may call the instinctive belief of mankind: God is real since he produces real effects.[46]

IV. DEMOCRACY

What kind of a universe does man inhabit?

Man is neither pessimistic nor optimistic in his view of the world, but rather he is determined to improve his situation. The kind of a world we inhabit is largely up to us to decide. This type of universe may be called melioristic, that is, it can get better. There is no preordained order that the universe obeys. In fact, the world is in the course of developing according to the direction that man charts out for it. According to James the meaning of the term "world" embraces all the areas which are significant to man's personal concerns and to the social order. The challenge ahead is to perfect the world.

> "If we do our best, and the other powers do their best, the world will be perfected"—This proposition expresses no actual fact, but only the complexion of a fact thought of as eventually possible. . . . The original proposition per se has no pragmatic value whatsoever, apart from its power to challenge our will to produce the premise of fact required.[47]

The meaning of God

James is not about to relinquish the challenge of perfecting the world by surrendering his responsibility to a God who is the almighty and omniscient Lord of the universe. What is left for us to do in the presence of such a God? James rejects the Absolute but he does not abandon the objectivity of God. Good emotions are facts which must have an objective significance. After all, religious experiences like perceptions are experiences of something.[48]

Therefore, the meaning of God must be discovered in the human challenge. Both man and God will labor together in developing a better world. In this spirit of democracy God becomes the superhuman consciousness of our own ideals. Indeed the meaning of God for James himself is rather hazy. However, he is not indecisive about the ideality and actuality of God. His position is clearly affirmative on this matter. James, essentially a man of faith, reveals his meaning in a letter to Professor Leuba.

> My personal position is simple. I have no sense of commerce with a God. I envy those who have, for I know that the addition of such a sense would help me greatly. The Divine, for active life, is limited to impersonal and abstract concepts which, as ideals, interest and determine me, but do so but faintly in comparison with what a feeling of God might effect, if I had one. . . . I recognize the deeper voice. Something tells me: "thither lies truth"—and I am sure it is not old theistic prejudices of infancy . . . Call this, if you like, my mystical germ.[49]

What is man's relation with the "more"?

The deeper voice that James recognizes may be termed the 'more' or the 'beyond.' Our connection with the 'more' blends with our concept of unity as continuity. Fundamentally, the universe is pluralistic and is in the evolutionary process of achieving unity. Enclosed within the universe of man's experience is the unity of continuity which is the absolute nextness of one part to another which we find in the minutest portions of our inner experiences.[50] The preceding thoughts are found in the Introduction II of James' unfinished book *The Many and The One*. These ideas certainly reflect his mature thought. James does away with the dualism of object and subject and extends his theory to the field of religious experience when he claims that the beyond is part of the same continuum. He explains his position in notes he prepared for his lectures.

> Remember that through a certain point or part in you, you coalesce and are identical with the Eternal... The more original religious life is always lyric—"the monk owns nothing but his lyre"—and its essence is to dip into another kingdom to feel an invisible order... au prix duquel the common sense values really vanish.[51]

In answer to our question concerning our relations with the 'more' it seems that we are in communion with the 'beyond' in the very core of our being. However, the communion takes on the aspect of dialogue in mysticism. Such communication confirms us in our personal initiative and preserves the democratic approach to the divine, since such conversation makes us more aware of our individuality.

We elect the God with whom we converse. The type of God will be chosen according to the value he represents, that is, according to whether or not he advances human progress which in turn is determined by the experimental method. There is no fixed meaning of God for all ages, a fact which can be verified from history. God must meet the demands of the day, but since the demands of the day change, so does the meaning of God.[52]

Beyond the subjective need

In concluding the lectures in the *Varieties* James comes to grips with the problem concerning the merely subjective utility of religion. He claims that there is a common nucleus in which all beliefs concur.

It consists of two parts:

(1) an uneasiness; and (2) its solution.
1. The uneasiness, reduced to its simplest terms is a sense that there is something wrong about us as we naturally stand.
2. The solution is a sense that we are saved from the wrongness by making proper connection with the higher powers.[53]

Do we identify our real being with the wrongness we experience or is identification discovered in the germinal higher part of ourselves?

He becomes conscious that this higher part is conterminous and continuous with a MORE of the same quality, which is operative in the universe outside of him, and which he can keep in working touch with, and in a fashion get on board of and save himself when all his lower being has gone to pieces in the wreck.[54]

V. CONCLUSION

The foregoing exposition endeavored to explain why James chose the type of God that must be if he is. The God of personal experience is the God defined by James' own personal experiences. Passionately, he labors against determinism which he attributes to a God of reason only to subscribe to another determinism, namely, the one of emotion or passion. Happily, an optimistic approach to our instincts enables us to achieve freedom and individuality by self-surrender to the germ of higher powers which are conterminous with the 'more.'

There is much value in James' approach to God. He clearly indicates man's need for redemption, and he asks for a God who is meaningful. However, if James is to be faithful to his philosophy of radical empiricism, the God that he must propose is discovered in a mystical experience, which is the only type of experience that can satisfactorily bear witness to the validity of God. James found himself wanting in mystical experience, and, consequently, he never experienced the 'more' in any intense degree.

In criticism of James it must be said that the ordinary man is left with a possible God of some indescribable nature. Furthermore, he seems to be too optimistic about man's emotions as the basis for religious belief. Suppose a man's emotion for the most part is one of apathy or enthusiastic concern for material goods; what feeling does such a person have for redemption? If the basis for God is our sentiments, and we do not care about religion, how does one tell us that God cares?

NOTES

1. William James, *Some Problems of Philosophy* (New York: Longmans, Green, and Co., 1911), p. 15.

2. *Ibid.*, p. 31.

3. *Ibid.*, p. 46.

4. *Ibid.*, p. 51.

5. *Ibid.*, p. 74.

6. *Ibid.*, p. 60.

7. William James, "Philosophical Conceptions and Practical Results," in *Philosophy in America,* Paul Anderson and Max Fisch (New York: D. Appleton-Century Company, 1939), p. 40.

8. William James, *Essays in Radical Empiricism* (NY: Longmans, Green, and Co., 1912), p. 253.

9. *Ibid.*, p. 261.

10. *Ibid.*, p. 264.

11. Ralph Batton Perry, *The Thought and Character of William James* (Boston: Little, Brown and Company, 1935), Vol. II, p. 382.

12. *Ibid.*, p. 384.

13. *Ibid.*, p. 373.

14. Edward C. Moore, *American Pragmatism* (NY: Columbia University, 1961), p. 129.

15. Perry, *op. cit.*, p. 326.

16. William James, *The Varieties of Religious Experience* (NY: The New American Library of World Literature, Inc., 1958), p. 65.

17. *Ibid.*, p.29.

18. Paul Henle, "Introduction", *Classic American Philosophers,* ed. Max H. Fish (NY: Appleton-Century-Crofts, Inc., 1951), p. 126.

19. James, *The Varieties of Religious Experience,* p. 259.

20. *Ibid.*, p. 290.

21. *Ibid.*, p. 291.

22. *Ibid.*, p. 314.

23. *Ibid.*, p. 323.

24. *Ibid.*, p. 328.

25. *Ibid.*, p. 346.

26. *Ibid.*, p. 331.

27. *Ibid.*, p. 346.

28. *Ibid.*

29. *Ibid.*, p. 347.

30. William James, "Philosophical Conceptions and Practical Results," *Philosophy in America*, p. 536.

31. Perry, *op. cit.*, p. 328.

32. *Ibid.*, p. 329.

33. James, *The Varieites of Religious Experience,* p. 73.

34. *Ibid.*, p. 376.

35. *Ibid.*, p. 366.

36. *Ibid.*, p. 367.

37. *Ibid.*, p. 121.

38. *Ibid.*, p. 129.

39. *Ibid.*, p. 155.

40. *Ibid.*, p. 162.

41. *Ibid.*, p. 168.

42. *Ibid.*, p. 122.

43. *Ibid.*, p. 195.

44. *Ibid.*, p. 216.

45. *Ibid.*, p. 228.

46. *Ibid.*, p. 389.

47. James, *Some Problems of Philosophy*, p. 230.

48. Perry, *op. cit.*, p. 348.

49. *Ibid.*, p. 350.

50. *Ibid.*, p. 379.

51. *Ibid.*, p. 331.

52. James, *The Varieties of Religious Experience,* p. 258.

53. *Ibid.*, p. 383.

54. *Ibid.*, p. 384.

55. *Ibid.*, p. 386.

BIBLIOGRAPHY

Anderson, Paul R. and Fisch, Max H. *Philosophy in America.* NY: D. Appleton-Century Company, 1939.

Bixler, Julius Seelye. *Religion in the Philosophy of William James.* Boston: Marshall Jones Company, 1926.

Blau, Joseph L. *Men and Movements in American Philosophy.* NY: Prentice-Hall, Inc., 1952.

Fish, Max. H., ed. *Classic American Philosophers.* NY: Appleton-Century-Crofts, Inc., 1951.

James, William. *Some Problems of Philosophy.* NY: Longmans, Green, and Co., 1911.

———. *Essays in Radical Empiricism.* NY: Longmans, Green, and Co., 1912.

———. *The Varieties of Religious Experience.* NY: The New American Library of World Literature, Inc., 1958.

———. *Pragmatism.* NY: Meridian Books, Inc., 1955.

———. *Essays on Faith and Morals.* NY: Longmans, Green and Co., 1949.

———. *The Will to Believe and Other Essays in Popular Philosophy.* NY: Dover Publications, Inc., 1956.

More, Edward C. *American Pragmatism.* NY: Columbia University, 1961.

Morris, Lloyd R. *William James: The Message of a Modern World.* NY: Scribner, 1950.

Perry, Ralph Barton. *The Thought and Character of William James*, Vol. II. Boston: Little, Brown and Company, 1935.

Riley, W. *American Thought.* NY: Henry Holt and Company, 1923.

Smith, John E. *The Spirit of American Philosophy.* NY: Oxford University Press, 1966.

Young Oon Kim

Mysticism, Shamanism, Spiritualism

In her classic book entitled *Mysticism*, Evelyn Underhill warned bluntly that in the condition of psychic instability which is characteristic of the religious man's movement to higher states of consciousness, man is at the mercy of suggestions and impressions he receives from the spirit world. Hence, in every period of true mysticism there appears also an outbreak of occultism, illuminism or other perverted forms of spirituality. Underhill is especially wary, she says, of the even more dangerous and confusing borderland region where the mystical and psychical meet. Occultism accompanies mystical activity but should not be confused with it, for this feeble, deformed and arrogant mystical sense does not attain the Absolute, this author maintains.[1]

Since the New Religions these days are often criticized as examples of such wild occultism, I think that it is now necessary to re-examine and re-assess Underhill's argument. This is not to deny the value of her study of mysticism. Under the guidance and inspiration of her teacher, Baron von Hügel, she was attempting to assert the objective existence of a transcendent realm and refute the subjectivist, rationalistic and reductionist explanations of mystical phenomena espoused by modernist theologians like James Bisset Pratt, Rufus Jones, and Dean William R. Inge as well as psychologists such as James Leuba.[2] However, one can ask if she did not go too far in her fear of the mysterious, the parapsychological and the so-called "occult."

In the following article, I propose to revise Underhill's blanket condemnation of the borderland where the mystical and psychical meet. First, we shall look at the oldest sources of mysticism, seen in the archeological remains of Paleolithic and Neolithic cultures. Next we shall briefly note the continuation and elaboration of this ancient shamanism, notably in the traditional religion of Korea, prior to the importation of Buddhism and Confucianism from imperial China. Then we shall highlight the parapsychological dimension of Christian mysticism from Saint Teresa of Spain in the Counter-reformation to the present day. Thus I hope to provide enough material to make a positive case for the reality of the spirit world and the need for recognizing our continuous relationship to it.

I.

In his lectures on the history of religion, Mircea Eleade has reminded his students at the University of Bucharest, the Ecoles des Hautes Etudes in Paris and the University of Chicago that there is a real unity to the spiritual history of humanity which originates at least as far back as Neolithic and even Paleolithic times. The roots of religious experience, thought and practice are clearly evidenced by 30,000 B.C. because of artifacts discovered in Spain, France, the Ukraine, southern Italy, the Ural Mountains of Russia and elsewhere.

Eleade cites a remarkable example of such Paleolithic religious art discovered deep in a cave at Lascaux, France. This painting shows a wounded bison thrusting its horns toward an apparently dead man lying on the ground. The fallen hunter's pike-like weapon is pressed against the animal's belly. Near the man is a bird on a perch.

At first glance this caveman art looks like the picture of a common hunting accident. But why would a prehistoric artist take the time and labor to portray such a typical event, especially deep within a cave which is difficult to reach? In 1950 Horst Kirchner gave a profoundly religious explanation for this Paleolithic art. This was not the picture of a prehistoric hunting accident but depicted an ancient shamanic seance. The speared bison represents a sacrificial animal, and the prostrate man is in a deep trance. The bird nearby symbolizes the soul of the believer and the man is travelling to the spirit world to ask for a blessing in some tribal hunting expedition.[3]

For many years anthropologists and historians of religion have labored to rediscover the world view of primitive peoples. This "religion of the caves," as scholars term it, is deciphered from a painstaking analysis of prehistoric engravings, paintings, cult objects, statuettes and the contents of ancient burial sites. While such artifacts by themselves cannot provide the whole story, their meaning is illumined to some extent by similar items in later cultures as well as the myths and rites of remaining aboriginal tribes in isolated regions of the present world (Australian primitives, African Pigmies, Latin American Indian tribes, etc.).[4]

What then was humanity's oldest religion? Paleolithic man performed sacred dances. He engaged in special ceremonies for the dead. He put on sacred robes—a deer skin, a horse's tail and deer antlers, for example. He worshipped a god of the wild animals, the Lord of Wild Beasts, so to speak; and as numerous statuettes reveal, he also revered a goddess of fertility, a divine Earth Mother. Paleolithic peoples believed in a mysterious kinship of themselves and certain wild animals. They were convinced of the immortality of the soul and the need for worship of ancestral spirits. They invoked the aid of supernatural powers for success in food-gathering activities, recognized a sacred dimension in acts of procreation, established special sanctuaries and honored those who possessed the supernatural power of communicating with the spirit world (shamans and shamanesses).

This ancient religion persisted and was undoubtedly developed for tens of thousands of years prior to the Neolithic age when men and women turned from a hunting society to an agricultural economy. Humans became farmers gradually between 9,000 and 7,000 B.C.—a momentous revolution in the whole lifestyle of men and women. As archeologists have discovered, in Thailand by 9,000 B.C. villagers were cultivating peas, beans and roots of certain tropical plants. Scientists also now know that sheep, goats, pigs and dogs were domesticated in various parts of the world from 8,000–6,500 B.C.

Inevitably, the change from a hunting society to an agricultural one altered and deepened ancient man's religious concepts and practices. During the Paleolithic age, hunters naturally emphasized their mystical oneness with the animals. However, during the subsequent Neolithic age they supplemented this awareness with "the mystical solidarity between man and vegetation," to use Eleade's phrase. [5]

What were some of these new concepts of humanity's relationship to the divine? For one thing, an analogy was discovered between the fertility of the earth and feminine fecundity. As men and women mated to produce children, so the sky above mates with the earth beneath to produce an abundant harvest. This idea led to belief in the importance of a cosmic marriage between the masculine deity of heaven and the feminine divinity of earth. Yin/yang theology and many cultic practices grew out of this concept. Secondly, the role of the woman as mother and priestess was stressed. A woman was seen as one who knows the mystery of creation. As no man can ever realize, a female understands the secret of birth, death and resurrection. And thus from an awareness of the sanctity of motherhood it was natural to develop religions of the dying and risen god who transcends the pain and terror of mortality. Thirdly, Neolithic religion gave birth to the notion of a cyclical view of life. As the moon has its cycle and nature passes through four seasons, so humans are subject to a continuous circle of life, death and rebirth.

Neolithic religion possesses several clear features. It revolves around cults of fertility indicated by countless statuettes of pregnant goddesses and belief in the storm god symbolized by the sacred bull. Agricultural religion created various rituals connected with the mystery of vegetation. Also quite naturally, Neolithic farmers pondered the secrets of the sun, moon, stars, producing the occult art of astrology and the beginnings of the science of astronomy.[6] According to the anthropologists, all subsequent faiths are derived from this primordial religious worldview and built upon its Paleolithic-Neolithic foundations.

Against the background of such a many millennia-old understanding and experience of spiritual phenomena, it becomes easier to appreciate the true relationships which exist among separate topics like mysticism, the occult, spiritualism and shamanism. From the very dawn of religious consciousness these different elements have been intertwined in a single spiritual philosophy of life. Every one of them goes back to the beginnings of human awareness.

Of course, in the onward course of history, these aspects of authentic religion have taken on new and varied forms. At times they have degenerated into mere folklore or superstitions. At other times they have been revived and revitalized with amazing inspiration or intensity. As the biblical prophets pointed out, there is a vast difference between the exalted worship of the God who demands a religion of justice, mercy and humility and the syncretistic Hebrew-Canaanite practices of many kings of Israel and their unenlightened subjects. Similarly, there was in Christendom an unbridgeable gulf between the mysticism of a St. Bernard of Clairvaux or St. Francis and the superstitious folk-Catholicism of the average peasant. Even so, it would be foolish to ignore the inspiration and profound validity of these basic religious beliefs and practices.

II.

The ancient faith of Paleolithic hunters and Neolithic farmers survives to the present day. It is at the core of Amerindian tribal rites, Haitian voodoo and traditional Japanese Shinto. In Korea we call this original religion shamanism or "Sinkyo" (belief in spirits) or the faith and practices of the Mudang (female mediums and exorcists).

When Protestant missionaries started preaching in Korea in the late 19th century, they denounced and ridiculed this widespread folk religion as superstition and "demon worship." For example, Presbyterian missionary James S. Gale in his book *Korea in Transition* (1909) describes shamanism as follows:

> The whole land of Korea is plagued by demon-worship as Egypt in Moses' time became infested with locusts. Spiritualist mediums, exorcists, fortune-tellers, astrologists, believers in hill gods and dragons exist everywhere. Koreans believe that earth, air and sea are peopled by invisible demons. These spirits haunt certain trees, springs, lakes and mountaintops. They live on the roof of every home, the fireplace, the chimney, the doorway. Spirits infest earth, sky and water. By the thousands these demons waylay the traveller as he leaves home. They are beside him always, behind him, dancing in front of him and whirring over his head.

Gale goes on, saying that spirits of the dead who passed from earth under some wrong keep tormenting the living until their wrongs are avenged a thousandfold. Many spirits have found no resting place and so remain at large, more dangerous than even a tiger. Gale therefore concludes, belief in spirits surrounds Koreans with indefinite terrors and keeps them in a perpetual state of nervous apprehension.[7]

In recent years such a derogatory picture of Korean shamanism has been gradually replaced by a more objective interpretation. Eleade's book entitled *Shamanism* (1964) was of enormous benefit in educated circles. And more recently Korean and other Asian scholars have published positive evaluations of "Sinkyo," shamanic folk dances and folk art, the rituals of the Mudang and their roots in the distant past. For English readers, Jung Young Lee's *Korean Shamanistic Rituals* (1981) is a good sample of recent re-evaluation.

According to J. Y. Lee, the contemporary practices of the Mudangs may involve over 80% of the South Korean population. However, these present-day rites should be viewed as "a deteriorated form of traditional faith."[8] Traditional Korean shamanism originated long before the introduction of Confucianism and Buddhism and was for many centuries the national faith. As such, it contained some basic elements which persist in shadowy form to the present day. First, Mudangs are not simply members of a traditional priestly class: they exercise power because they are able to make direct contact with the spirit world. Second, Korean shamanism claims to be closely connected to the founding of the Korean nation, symbolized by the Tangun myth. Thirdly, the Mudangs have always believed that divine powers should be worshipped in mountain-side or mountain-top shrines. Fourthly, women take the highest priestly role in Korean shamanism, which indicates its close relationship to the fertility religion of the very ancient Neolithic society. Finally, at least in its oldest forms, the religion of the Mudangs is based on worship of the one supreme God of heaven and earth, "Hananim." In other words, there is a strong monotheistic element in ancient shamanism, so it was natural for the first Korean Protestants to identify the God of the Judeo-Christian tradition with Hananim, the high-god of the Mudangs.

III.

In her study, *Mysticism,* Underhill shows how the experience of immediate contact with spirit world has been an outstanding feature of the Christian tradition from apostolic times to the opening decades of the 19th century. Especially in the chapters on "Voices and Visions" (part 2, chapter V) and "Ecstasy and Rapture" (ibid., chapter VII) she gives striking illustrations from the writings of the mystics of their personal contacts with supernatural beings and discarnate spirits.

According to Underhill, St. Teresa d'Avila (1515–1582) let her life be completely governed by voices she heard from the spirit world. They told her when and where to go on a journey. They advised her which houses to purchase for nunneries and monasteries for the Carmelite order. Sometimes the spirits commanded her not to found a community in a certain place which she had thought would be favorable, and just as often they ordered her to begin work in an area which appeared to be impossible. In small things as in great ones, Teresa relied upon such spiritual guidance—even when such supernatural advice involved her in great hardships, ran counter to her personal judgement or interfered with her carefully laid-out plans.[9]

By listening to spiritual voices, this Carmelite nun revitalized Catholicism during the troubled years of the Protestant Reformation. She also greatly improved the state of monastic life in western Europe. Most importantly, she gave birth to the magnificent school of Spanish mysticism which was carried on by her talented disciple, St. John of the Cross (1542–1591). Like few others, Teresa and John proved that Christian mystics could be exceptionally talented organizers and practical administrators as well as profound contemplatives.[10]

But earlier Catholic mystics experienced the same kind of guidance and inspiration from the spirit world. The Dominican monk Henry Suso (circa 1295–1365) was a trained philosopher and theologian who often heard voices from above. In fact, he claimed that his book of one hundred meditations on the Passion of Christ were dictated to him by a spirit speaking not in Latin but in German. Two centuries earlier, the Benedictine saint Hildegarde of Bingen (1098–1179) claimed that her prophecies came directly from the spirit world, so she prefaced her writings with the words, "Thus saith the Living Light."[11]

The Bible contains many examples of visions of discarnate spirits: Abraham is visited by three angels, Jacob wrestles with a supernatural spirit at the river Jabbok, Stephen and St. Paul experience a vision of the risen Jesus, etc. Similar events continued to occur throughout Christian history to the present day.

Blessed Angela of Foligno (1248–1309), a Franciscan nun whose writings greatly influenced many later mystics, repeatedly saw visions of Jesus. Once she saw a vision of him as a child 12 years old while she took Holy Communion. Another time she declared, "I saw Him most plainly with the eyes of the mind... first living, suffering, bleeding, crucified; and then dead upon the cross."[12]

Particularly memorable was St. Catherine of Siena's experience of holy betrothal to Jesus in 1366 A.D. One day he appeared to her, saying that he was ready to espouse himself to her. Suddenly she saw with him the Virgin Mary, St. John, St. Paul, King David and St. Dominic, the founder of the Dominican order she belonged to. While David played nuptial music on his harp, Mary took Catherine's hand and extended her finger toward Jesus. Jesus placed a diamond ring on Catherine's finger, saying, "Lo, I espouse thee to Myself and this will preserve thyself ever without stain until thou dost celebrate thy eternal nuptials with Me in Heaven." Then he and the others vanished. But Catherine claimed that the engagement ring remained on her finger forever, even though it was invisible to everybody else.[13]

Histories of the Christian saints also contain numerous anecdotes about the extraordinary mystical powers with which these holy men and women become endowed. In many cases contact with the spirit world enables one to possess gifts of faith healing, extrasensory perception, prophecy of future events, out-of-body experiences and trance communications or actual travel to spiritual realms. Various theories have been worked out by theologians and philosophers of religion to explain such strange phenomena. But the facts of mystical phenomena and psychic powers are really beyond reasonable doubt.

IV.

Let me give four interesting examples from the post-Enlightenment modern world.

A. The late 18th century poet William Blake was a baptized member of the Church of England who strayed far away from the conventional path of Anglican orthodoxy. Blake (1757–1827) is unique in British artistic life because he has won great posthumous fame as a painter, engraver and poet. His books, like *The Marriage of Heaven and Hell* (1793), reveal how his elaborate mystical symbolism and metaphysical poetry were expressions of his unusual visionary powers. In 1788 the spirit of his brother Robert (who had died at age 21) came to Blake and showed him an entirely new method of printing from etched copper plates.[14] The poet's mind was also greatly stimulated by Swedenborg's writings which had appeared for the first time in an English translation.[15] But by temperament and in his faculty for seeing visions while fully awake, Blake had a natural ability to experience the spiritual world.

For one thing, he possessed an unusual gift of seeing at first glance the basic character and future fate of people he met. At age 14 his father introduced him to a painter who was to have been the boy's art teacher. But Blake stubbornly refused to become the man's pupil, telling his father that such a wicked individual was fated to become a criminal and be sentenced to die. In later years the man was hanged as a crooked business-man and forger.[16]

Like St. Teresa, Blake said that his books were dictated to him by spirits. Of his poems, "Milton" and "Jerusalem," he reported that he wrote them from immediate dictation, twelve to thirty lines at a time, without premeditation, study or labor and sometimes even against his will.[17] At age eight he saw a vision: a tree was filled with angels whose wings sparkled like the stars, Blake told his parents.[18] His father threatened to spank the child, to teach him not to tell lies to his elders. The warning was to no avail. When he was a grown man, Blake insisted that he acted under explicit direction of "Messengers from Heaven," daily and nightly.[19] On his deathbed, he told those around him that he was not the real author of any of his books and paintings; they were the works of his "celestial friends."[20]

B. Padre Pio (1887–1968) was a Capuchin friar in southern Italy who became world-famous because he bore on his body the five wounds of the crucified Jesus (the stigmata).[21] From early childhood, this sickly son of a peasant family was subject to visionary experiences, but he didn't tell anyone about them until he was a grown man. At age 15 he joined the Capuchin order of Franciscans and four years later he took his final vows as a life-long friar. Throughout his life, Padre Pio suffered terribly from asthma and acute bronchitis. He also indulged in extreme ascetic practices, depriving himself of sleep, starving his body and whipping his back. In 1910 he was ordained a Catholic priest, and that same year the wounds of Christ suddenly appeared on his hands, feet and side.

Padre Pio's unusual condition naturally attracted the attention of the church authorities. Father Agostino, his provincial superior in the Capuchin order and later his spiritual director, wrote in his diary in November 1911 that he personally witnessed Padre Pio assaulted by the Devil and then going into ecstasy to meet Jesus, Mary, his guardian angel and St. Francis. These ecstatic trances usually lasted for an hour or more. First Satan would appear as a wild beast, a naked woman or sometimes a Capuchin friar. After an agonizing struggle, Padre Pio would banish these demonic powers by invoking the name of Jesus and then he would see visions of good spirits, like Christ, the Madonna or his guardian angel.[22]

There are many carefully documented accounts of Padre Pio's abilities to perform faith healings. On February 15, 1949, an admirer of the friar was badly hurt in a dynamite explosion. All the skin on his face was torn off and his right eye was blown out of its socket. While the victim was lying in the hospital, he felt that somehow he had been visited by Padre Pio. After ten days in the hospital, the patient had his bandages removed and discovered that the skin had grown back on his face and his right eye was back in place and in good working order.[23]

Padre Pio possessed other rare qualities. For twenty-one days he lived off nothing but the nourishment derived from the communion wafer and sips of holy wine. His body and anything he wore gave off a strong odor of sanctity, a perfume-like aroma of violets and honeysuckle. He could read people's hearts and tell them of their sins or problems when they went to him at the confessional. He also had an uncanny knowledge of the future, more than once predicting the death of a fellow-priest or friar.

More significantly, Padre Pio seems to have possessed the ability to be in more than one place at the same time. Out of several such incidents, let me cite only one told by Cardinal Barbieri of Uruguay. Monsignor Damiani had expressed the wish to live near Padre Pio but was told he was needed in his own diocese. However, Padre Pio promised to be with him when he died. In 1941 in Uruguay, Cardinal Barbieri awoke one night because of a loud knock on his door. He looked up to see a Capuchin pass down the hall toward the room where the dying monsignor was staying. He got up and rushed to the dying man's room. He found on the desk a note which said in the monsignor's handwriting, "Padre Pio came."[24] Yet it was well-known that Padre Pio never left his little village in southern Italy.

C. The experience of Saint Teresa in the 16th century and William Blake in the 18th century has reoccurred in our own time. Rob and Jane Roberts of Elmira, New York, are an example. Rob is a painter and his wife, Jane, is a novelist and poet. In the autumn of 1963 they began playing with a ouija board their landlady found in the attic. After a few experiments, they started receiving messages from a man in Elmira who had died about twenty years earlier.

But the big event in their lives took place on December 3, 1963. The couple started to get messages from an entity who called himself "Seth." By the 15th of the month Mrs. Roberts was able to go into a light trance and become the direct medium for extensive and carefully worked-out messages from Seth, which her husband writes down.[25]

Their first book, *The Seth Material*, was published in 1970 and contained the beginning of an elaborate philosophy about the nature of the spirit world dictated word for word from a discarnate entity through Mrs. Roberts to the world at large. Continued communication with this remarkable spirit personality has produced additional books entitled *Seth Speaks, Adventures in Consciousness, The Nature of Personal Reality*, etc.

For our purposes there is no need to elucidate or evaluate the contents of the Seth material. We refer to Mrs. and Mrs. Roberts merely as contemporary illustrations of the fact that from Paleolithic times to the present, men and women have experienced direct contact with a world which transcends the conventional framework of space and time.

D. My final example of psychic experiences comes from contemporary Korea: the astonishingly successful Pentecostalist preacher, Dr. Paul Yonggi Cho. His biographer aptly sums up his career with the title of her book, *Dream Your Way to Success*.[26]

Dr. Cho was born in 1936 during the harsh occupation of Korea by the Japanese imperialists, but he is now the pastor of the Full Gospel Central Church in Seoul which has over 150,000 members, making it the largest single congregation in the entire world. He was hospitalized at age 18 with a seemingly fatal case of acute pulmonary tuberculosis. While in the hospital, a teen-age girl visited him, tried to convert him to Christianity and left him a Bible. Having been warned that he had less than a month to live, Cho was ready to try anything to stay alive. Reading the Bible and praying for help, he was soon healed. But by becoming a Christian, the teenager infuriated his parents and was disowned as their son.

Cho next attempted to enter medical school. Since he had not been able to graduate from high school because of his illness, he purchased a forged diploma and was accepted. However, the authorities discovered his deception and promptly expelled him. Still determined to be a doctor, Cho became a hospital orderly in Pusan and read medical books loaned him by the resident doctors. But as a result of overwork, he took sick again and had to live with his grandmother. Fearful of a reoccurrence of tuberculosis, Cho again sought help. This time the novels of Hermann Hesse, the Nobel Prize winner, revived his determination to live. He returned to the hospital staff and lived in the dormitory.

Soon he was attracted to the preaching of a young American ex-Marine at the YMCA. The man invited Cho to live with him and take his big meal every day at the home of an American missionary. Cho then gave up his hospital work and became the clergyman's interpreter.

One night he tried to test the efficacy of the prayers which the Christians were always preaching about. Feeling hungry, he prayed for food. Immediately, someone knocked at his door and offered him a box of noodles and kim chi from a nearby restaurant. After the delivery boy left and Cho had eaten his meal, he suddenly saw someone else in his room. It was Jesus, dressed in a white robe and wearing a crown of thorns. Jesus urged him to become a preacher for his kingdom.

When he told the American missionary about this experience, arrangements were made for him to enroll in the Full Gospel Institute in Seoul. In 1958 he graduated and joined an older student, Mrs. Choi (his future mother-in-law) in starting a new church in the city. For 12 years Pastor Cho preached an evangelistic message based on three points: "hereness," "nowness" and love. During this same period he also discovered that he possessed the gift of faith healing which naturally attracted many members to his church. But there is no need to elaborate further on Cho's successes and his present international reputation. Like St. Teresa, Swedenborg, Blake and Padre Pio, Yonggi Cho is proof of the reality of a spirit world which we can depend upon for unusual power, truth and love.

NOTES

1. Evelyn Underhill, *Mysticism* (1955 ed.), p. 149.

2. Contrast Underhill with J. B. Pratt, *The Religious Consciousness* (1920); R. Jones, *Studies on Mystical Religion* (1909); W. R. Inge, *Studies of English Mystics* (1906); J. Leuba, *A Psychological Study of Religion* (1912).

3. M. Eleade, *A History of Religious Ideas* (1978) vol. 1, pp. 18–19; this art is depicted in E. O. James, *History of Religion* (1957).

4. E.O. James, "How Religion Began," *History of Religion* (1957), pp. 1–30.

5. Eleade, *op. cit.* , p. 40.

6. *Ibid.*, pp.40–55.

7. James S. Gale, *Korea in Transition* (1909), pp. 82–88; cf. G. Underwood, *The Call of Korea* (1908), 84–99.

8. Jung Young Lee, *Korean Shamanistic Rituals* (1981), p. 25.

9. Underhill, *op. cit.*, p. 276.

10. *Ibid.*, p. 468.

11. *Ibid.*, p. 276.

12. *Ibid.*, p. 288.

13. *Ibid.*, p. 291.

14. *Encyclopedia Britannica* (1968), vol. 3, p. 756.

15. June K. Singer, *The Unholy Bible* (1970), p. 21.

16. *Ibid.*, p. 17.

17. Underhill, *op. cit., p. 66.*

18. Michael Davis, William Blake (1977), p. 14.

19. Underhill, *op. cit.*, p. 294.

20. *Ibid.*

21. John A Schug, *Padre Pio* (1976); also Oscar de Liso, *Padre Pio* (1960).

22. Schug, *op. cit.*, p. 36.

23. *Ibid.*, pp. 172–175.

24. *Ibid.*, pp. 201–202.

25. Jane Roberts, *The Seth Material* (1981 ed.), pp. 16–24.

26. Nell Kennedy, *Dream Your Way to Success* (1980).

SOME ADDITIONAL READING

Boyer, Louis. *et al. The Spirituality of the Middle Ages.* NY: Desclee Co., 1968, vol. 2.

Castaneda, Carlos. *The Teachings of Don Juan: A Yaqui Way of Knowledge.* Berkeley: University of California Press, 1968.

———. *A Separate Reality: Further Conversations with Don Juan.* NY: Simon and Schuster, 1971.

———. *Journey to Ixtlan: The Lessons of Don Juan.* NY: Simon and Schuster, 1972.

———. *Tales of Power.* NY: Simon and Schuster, 1974.

Cloutier, David. *Spirit, Spirit: Shaman Songs, Incantations.* Providence: Copper Beech Press, 1973.

Ducasse, C.J. *The Belief in Life after Death.* Springfield: C. C. Thomas, 1974.

Eliade, Mircea. *Shamanism: Archaic Techniques of Ecstasy.* NY: Pantheon, 1964.

Halifax, Joan, ed. *Shamanic Voices: A Survey of Visionary Narratives.* NY: Dutton, 1979.

Hardinge, Emma. *Modern American Spiritualism.* NY: University Books, 1970.

Hardy, Alister. *The Biology of God.* NY: Taplinger, 1975.

———. *The Spiritual Nature of Man.* NY: Oxford, 1979.

Harlow, S. Ralph. *A Life After Death.* NY: Doubleday. 1961.

Harner, Michael. *The Way of the Shaman*. NY: Bantam, 1982 (Harper and Row, 1980).

Hultkrantz, Ake. "A Definition of Shamanism." *Temonos* 9 (1973), 25–37.

———. *The Religions of the American Indian*. Berkeley: University of California Press, 1979.

Inge, W. R. *Mysticism in Religion*. Westport: Greenwood, 1976.

Kelsey, Morton. *Afterlife*. NY: Paulist Press, 1979.

Lewis, I. M. *Ecstatic Religion*. Harmondsworth; Penguin, 1971.

Louth, Andrew. *The Origins of the Christian Mystical Tradition*. Oxford: Clarendon Press, 1981.

Maloney, George A. "Mysticism and Occultism," *Inward Stillness*. Denville, NJ: Dimension Books, 1976, pp. 213–228.

Moore, E. Garth. *Try the Spirits: Christianity and Psychical Research*. Oxford: Oxford University Press, 1977.

Perry, Michael. "The Hereafter: How Will You Survive?" *Spiritual Frontiers*. Fall, 1981.

Reinhard, Johan. "Shamanism and Spirit Possession,"pp. 12–18 in *Spirit Possession in the Nepal Himalayas*, ed. John Hitchcock and Rex Jones. Warminster: Aris and Phillips, 1975.

Rose, Mary Carmen. "Some Fruits of the Mysticism Survey," *Spiritual Frontiers*. Fall, 1982.

Jan Knappert

What Every Religion Needs

The history of religion shows that religions have a number of aspects, qualities or properties in common, which help them to survive. When examining these common qualities I discovered that they were numerous and complex. I will here discuss a number of them briefly. I have started from a wide base, drawing on not only the history of some of the Christian churches, but also Islam, Hinduism and Buddhism, as well as the African and Indonesian religions that I have studied.[1] We shall end with the question: what does a religion require in the future of the modern world, where there is strong competition from secular ideologies? I believe that the militant attitudes of old religions now work against them.

A. First and foremost, all religious leaders must keep in mind that religion is for man as well as for God. In other words, the leaders must not rule their community as if only God needed to be pleased. Men are no longer slaves. They can vote with their feet in a religion where there is too much discipline and not enough communication. Churches have to be more careful than in the days when men of different opinions could be burned at the stake. Only a few can still defy public opinion in the world by executing apostates.

B. Religious leaders often hope that their religion will become a world religion. By sending missionaries to the far corners of the world they hope to achieve this, often even before their nuclear community has been consolidated. In the past, great numbers of converts were often made by conquest and by high birthrate. Modern religious groups should rely rather on the zeal of their members and the good example of their leaders.

1. THE GENESIS OF A RELIGION

A new religion may be born from contact between the deity and the man (on rare occasions a woman) who has been chosen to receive and divulge the first knowledge of the new religion. Thus Yahweh spoke to Moses, Allah to Muhammad,[2] and Vishnu to Manu in early India.[3] In each of these cases the initiative was taken by the deity, the prophet was chosen as worthy and capable of the task, and the contents of the revelation were entirely determined by the deity. In these cases also, the revelation resulted in laws, a code of behaviour for the society in which these prophets lived. There was also a nation in *statu nascendi* although the Jewish, Arabian and Indian tribes might not be described as nations in our sense of the term today. The prophet rallied disparate fragments of tribes and created a nation by means of a new religion, law and political structure. Moses and Muhammad, at least, were political leaders who created and maintained the unity of their respective groups. All three of these prophets were also law-givers, with rules for life, of which the ten commandments may be the best known. In those days, law had to be divinely formulated and ordained.

God may take the initiative by calling (the Arabic word originally meant 'awakening') his prophet to fulfill his mission. The Lord showed a sign of his revelation on the persons of some of his prophets. Moses, Muhammad and Guru Nanak are said to have radiated the divine light, so that all men could see that the light of God had come to dwell among them.

2. THE FOUNDER'S IMAGE

The founder of a religion may never forget that his followers will believe him to be their own channel of information from God to themselves on earth where they are walking in darkness. He should be seen and heard every day by his followers for whom he is the only 'window to Heaven,' and that not only for as long as he walks on this earth. Moses and Aaron were amidst their people day and night. Jesus could be seen, heard and touched by the multitudes and he let the children come near him. The Prophet Muhammad could invariably be found in his mosque at Medina, praying, preaching or explaining the word of God to the circle of his followers who would always be there listening and memorizing. Thanks to this, many followers of Muhammad knew his teachings by heart and could recite them 20 years later when the Koran was finally compiled in writing. The *hadith*, the tradition of Muhammad's sayings (*sunna*) was also compiled entirely on the basis of what followers remembered. The Christian Gospels were composed from the reports of those who had seen and heard Jesus and memorized his words, according to modern scholars. Confucius traveled widely, teaching in many towns of China, after which he returned to his native Lu in Shantung, to teach until he died in 479 B.C. His writings are believed to have been preserved in the Chinese classics in which he set out his philosophy.

The Buddha preached in the populous city of Benares. He was usually followed by a crowd of listeners. To have a following, leaders must be heard and seen, and that applies to religious leaders as well as to political leaders. Hermits have found admirers, even imitators, but they never founded a religion. No missionary can make converts without teaching and preaching, and giving people a feeling of togetherness.

A modern example of such religious leadership is Mahatma Gandhi, the creator of India as a modern nation. He was always ready to speak with friends, to receive visitors, to mingle even with the humblest of his followers for he considered himself as one of them. In addition, he wrote numerous articles in which his philosophy can be found, set out very clearly in English as well as his native Gujerati, and in Hindi.[4]

3. PREACHING AND TEACHING

When a prophet has received a revelation, he tells it to his people. Confucius, Buddha, and Guru Nanak traveled around their countries, preaching and teaching. The messages of Confucius and Buddha were exceptions to the above in that they were not inspired by any divine revelation, nor does a deity function in their doctrine. In the case of Jesus, many Christians believe that he was himself an incarnation of the divine spirit, like Rama and Krishna whom their followers believe to be incarnations of Vishnu. The question is a crucial one since the justification of their authority may stand or fall with the belief in their inspiration. Buddha's philosophy and that of Confucius were to be accepted purely on the basis of merit. To aid their work, several founders chose amongst their followers a man or a number of men who would act as their deputies and successors. Buddha and Jesus were surrounded by an inner circle of disciples who carried their teaching to distant peoples. This was vital for the survival of their religions, for neither religion survives on a large scale in the founder's native land.

For preaching and teaching, a good command of language is vital and several of the languages of the world's prophets have become classical and are studied by theologians today, especially Hebrew, Arabic, Sanskrit, Pali, Gurmukhi (the language of the Sikh scriptures), Avestan, (the language of the Parsee scriptures), and classical Chinese, the language of the ancient philosophers of China, such as Confucius. One of the important instruments for the survival of Christianity was the diligence of its translators. Before the end of the Roman Empire, translations of the Gospel existed in Latin, Syriac, Gothic and Coptic. But better than any tools are the builders of the church, for they are the workers whose edifice will stand for centuries. They are the apostles, the disciples who themselves became masters and taught His word to the nations.

4. PRIESTS, PREACHERS AND PEOPLE

A religion is destined to be embraced by the broad masses of the people, rather than being a philosophy for scholars alone. The founder of the religion, the one who had the original inspiration for it, does not want it to die with him. He will then have to think of and prepare in time, three things: a successor, or a group of disciples, a method of training them, and a textbook. The Prophet Muhammad did not prepare any of these, and the effect was nearly disaster: three of his successors were assassinated (Omar, Uthman and Ali) and the text of the Koran was almost lost before it was committed to writing nearly twenty years after the Prophet's death. The training of the 'spreaders of the faith' was a problem that took even longer to solve. However, Islam spread mainly through military conquests and the travels of Muslim merchants and through migration. Islam is now the third largest religion in the United States, largely the result of migration. There are over 20,000 Muslims in Korea. The faith there stems from Turkish soldiers in the armies of the United Nations in the Korean war. Guru Nanak (1469–1539 A.D.) appointed a successor, Guru Angad. He gave Angad the manuscripts of his writings, including prayers, hymns and rules for life. He had already made converts across the width of India. His community, the Sikh Khalsa, needed a good organization in the years of persecution in the Moghul Empire (1526–1857 A.D.) which had only just been founded. The Sikh community is well organized in local committees supervised by a *manji* or episcopal court in provincial headquarters.[5]

A religion may require a special class of priests, recruited by birth like the Brahmins of Hinduism, or by training and ordaining, like the Catholic priests. They function in a ritualistic religion as the ceremonial intermediaries between their flock and the deity. They call the faithful to prayer and remind them of the teachings.

5. THE PREACHERS, THE PILLARS OF THE CHURCH

The young Methodist Church was successful because it provided spiritual uplift to the uneducated poor in the squalid cities of England. More than a century later, the young socialists were successful with the same methods: preaching to the lowest classes, giving them new hope, a sense of purpose and a feeling of their own worth. This could be done through education. Earlier the Dutch Reformed Church in the Netherlands realized at its foundation in the 16th Century that it needed many ministers and so it organized their education at the highest available level. Still today, its ministers are true scholars. Earlier still the Christians had been successful in the Roman Empire because the lowest classes, the slaves and proletarians, were won over with new knowledge. Teaching the masses to raise their spirit can be done through a group of preachers and teachers who combine dedication to the cause of the underprivileged with a very high standard of education. The Islamic preachers that I have met are all real scholars. The same is true for most of the many Christian missionaries I met in Africa. Socialist and Communist propagandists that I have heard are all highly educated.

In order to preach to the masses, teach the new converts, educate their children, debate with opponents, argue with the authorities, the leaders of the church need the highest level of education, the most sophisticated form of scholarship. I have seen simple people in small towns reach in their own pockets, add penny to penny, in order to send one of their sons to a university so that he might come back and become their spiritual leader, explain the Scriptures to them, and enlighten his fellow townsmen. That is the best method to further the cause of one's religion. The success of a religion depends on the organization of its local and supralocal communities, and good organization depends on devoted, well-educated leaders, the preachers and pastors who must maintain contact between themselves, their parishes and each other.

6. THE BOOKS: DOCTRINE, LAW AND THE COMMUNITY

New religions often fix rules of conduct or establish a philosophy for their community. These may be written down as texts in a codebook. Frequently it is the community, the believers themselves, who ask their leaders what they must do. How to pray and how to marry, how to conduct a funeral service and how to divide an inheritance are but a few of their questions. Are all people equal in the sight of God, even His chosen prophet? Should all share in the decision-making process? Is it a good thing to earn money? If so, should a father not bequeath his wealth to his children, or else what does he work for? If not, how will the community live? There are literally thousands of questions that followers have asked their religious leaders ranging from "is smoking and drinking bad?" to "how often should a man embrace his wife?"(three times a week, according to Luther; twice a night, according to the Rabbinical literature).

These questions can be divided into four categories, viz.:

1. Rules of conduct for daily life: diet, trade, relations with other people.

2. Rules for religious ritual: baptism, interment, prayer, fasting, thanksgiving.

3. Rules for right thinking and speaking: theology, philosophy, doctrine.

4. Rules of law.

Some religions have fixed these rules down to the minutest details properly recorded in textbooks. Whenever this was not done by the founder of the religion, there has arisen dissidence, e.g., in both Islam and the Christian Church over the question of who has the right to rule. Disputes have arisen over any point that was not settled explicitly by the founder, for a man will disagree with his own brothers, even over the food they eat. Ideally these matters should be settled and put in writing and the answers distributed by the founder himself during his lifetime so that his disciples can ask him yet more questions before he dies. He owes his followers precise and complete instructions for the correct way of thinking and acting, for he is their guide on the path to Heaven or Nirvana.

7. THE COMMUNITY AND ITS LEADERS

People are contradictory creatures: they want leadership, but at the same time they want to be independent; they want freedom but no responsibilities. Leaders need to sail between these two rocks. If their course is too dictatorial, they will lose members, but if they leave too much freedom to their members, they will be accused of not having enough confidence in their own authority. The pope has been accused of the former, the leaders of certain liberal protestant churches of the latter.

In the early days of Islam, the prophet Muhammad and his successors united and ruled Arabia where there had not been a state previously. The Christian bishops of the early fifth century saw the western Roman Empire collapsing, so they had to became secular rulers. They were ill-prepared for this rule. Yet, until the establishment of the Carolingian empire almost four hundred years later, they ruled their dioceses with remarkable success, unity and harmony. In modern societies though, there is no place for religious leaders in political power. Still, in the tolerant states of the western world, they have a large leeway to rule their flocks as they think fit. They can raise untaxed money, set rules for marriage and divorce and in many other ways control the behaviour of their members. As soon as the members' numbers inside a given state rise to several percent of the population, the leaders may form a political party which, if they are determined and purposeful, may exercise influence far beyond the effect their numbers would cause one to expect.

8. THE COMMUNITY AS NUCLEUS OF LIFE

Many men want immortality. One way to find immortality in this world is to create great works made with stone and mortar, or with pen and ink, or with brush and canvas. The commonest way to perpetuate one's name is by creating a family, the larger the better. The family is biological ordinarily, but in religion the family is spiritual. The prophet Muhammad had no son to survive him. He called his followers collectively in Arabic *ummati* which we translate as 'my community' but originally the word meant 'my family,' from *umm* 'mother', and Muslims call each other 'brother.' 'Father' is the term of address for all priests in the Roman Catholic and Anglican churches, whose parishioners are their children, spiritually.

An almost perfect model for founders of new churches are the Wesley brothers who found their field of mission in the neglected urban populations of England and Wales. They preached eloquently wherever they went; like St. Paul, wrote numerous letters to friends of kindred spirit; composed hymns for their liturgy; and most of all, showed a remarkable talent to organize groups of new converts into parishes.

Religions which have to survive on conversion alone do not do so well today. The religious family expands biologically as well. Buddhism, which once covered most of the south-eastern corner of Asia, has lost most of that territory to Islam and Communism, and India itself to Hinduism. I attribute that to the strong monastic tradition of Buddhism. Many religious leaders oppose birth control. The continuity and growth of the movement depends on children.

9. WILL THE NEW RELIGIONS BE SUCCESSFUL?

By extrapolation from a comparative study of the history of the Christian churches, the religions from the Middle East, India and other parts of the world, it is possible to sketch a few outlines for the future. We assume that there will not be any rapid and world shaking changes in the culture of mankind, such as a new world war (read holocaust) or a complete computerization of our lives.

We can already see the inexorable impact on the Western mind of the continuous progress of scientific thinking, crowding out the poetic thinking of myth and belief. In that spiritual climate, any new religion has to row upstream, even the "big" churches may become minority communities (which, as one theologian remarked, may be salutary for them). To be successful in spite of that adverse climate, religion must have more than good leaders, good organization, good family life, good community structure and devoted members. For a religion to survive it is essential that it be a living religion. A living religion is one in which the members participate in the ceremonies and have a large amount of freedom in their organization. Rigidly prescribed ceremonies in which the members do not participate will die out.

The essence of the religion of the future will no longer be its attractive mythology, its system of beliefs, the colorful beauty of its ritual processions, nor, at least to a much lesser extent than before, the assertiveness of its priestly hierarchy based hitherto on their believed superiority. The religion of the future will in the first place be the protective spiritual framework for a social structure, like the beehive for the honeycombs in which the bees live.

It is therefore possible to foresee that the young religions of the world, which emphasize social activities rather than ritualistic precision, will gain the upper hand, much against the expectation of the leading authorities in the present established churches. They cannot imagine the day in which the sun will not shine upon their buildings full of worshippers. Yet that day may well arrive, earlier than many priests think. Many church buildings are empty in France, the Netherlands and England, as are many temples in Asia. We do not realize how powerful the gods of the Romans, with whom those of the Celtic and Germanic tribes were identified, once were over all of Western Europe and North Africa, where the ruins of their temples can still be seen. Yet who worships them today? Nothing is eternal in this world, not even a religion, since all human institutions are perishable. The religions of antiquity have all been crowded out by the newer religions, Islam and Christianity, in Europe and the Middle East. Only in remote parts of Africa, India, and the Indian reservations of America, can the old religions still be observed. Buddhism spread over most of the Far East, though the autochthonous religions of China, Japan and Indonesia are still alive.

Of the now powerful religions like Islam and Christianity, the early history is well known. We know that their beginnings were as threatened and uncertain as those of the new religions today. The same was true of Protestant Christianity when it started in the 16th century.

Times change and so do human beings, changing their cultures as they go along the paths of their lives. Nothing remains the same. What was once important is now negligible and vice versa. There is thus every reason to assume that today's persecuted minority groups will one day be the established groups in the world, whereas the 'old' bodies will survive only if they adapt themselves drastically to the changing ideology of the times. Social consciousness seems to be the essential quality for a modern religion.

EDITORIAL NOTES

1. Dr. Knappert's many published studies include such works as: *Bantu Myths & Other Tales*. (Nisaba Series No. VII); Leiden: E.J. Brill, 1977.

   Fables from Africa. London: Evans Brothers, 1980.

   Malay Myths & Legends. Heinemann Educational Books, 1981.

   Myths & Legends of the Congo. Heinemann Educational Books, 1971.

   Myths & Legends of Indonesia. Heinemann Educational Books, 1977.

   Myths & Legends of the Swahili. Heinemann Educational Books, 1970.

   Namibia: Land and Peoples, Myths and Fables. (Nisaba Series, No. 11); 1981.

"The Religions of Africa," pp. 223–233, in *The Global Congress of the World's Religions: Proceedings 1980–1982,* ed. Henry O. Thompson. New York: Rose of Sharon Press, 1982.

2. Dr. Knappert notes here that whether Allah spoke directly to Muhammad or through the intermediary of his angel Jibril, is not the relevant point. The point is the revelation.

3. For a general introduction to these and other world religions, cf. Young Oon Kim, *World Religions,* 2nd ed.; New York: Golden Gate Publishing Co., 1982.

4. Cf. K. L. Seshagiri Rao, "Mahatma Gandhi's Experience in Interreligious Dialogue," *World Faiths Insight,* New Series 6 (Jan. 83), 2–10, and literature cited there. Cf. also Rao's "Mohandas Gandhi and the Hindu Vision of Religious Co-Existence," pp. 50–63, in *Towards a Global Congress of World Religions,* ed. Warren Lewis; New York: Rose of Sharon Press, 1979.

5. For recent developments in this tradition, cf. Mark Juergensmeyer and N. Gerald Barrier, eds., *Sikh Studies: Comparative Perspectives on a Changing Tradition;* Berkeley: Graduate Theological Union, 1979.

Yaqub Zaki

The Concept of Revelation in Islam

Revelation (*wahi*) is the act by which God, having created the world, proceeds to disclose Himself to His own creation, acting in His capacity as *hadi* (Guide). As such the term embraces any act of self-disclosure, beginning with God's addressing our First Parents in the Garden, and proceeding through a series of disclosures to prophets of both categories, i.e., *rusul* and *anbiya'*, culminating in a final definitive act of disclosure known as *khatm an-nubuwwa*, or Seal of Prophethood. With the exception of the first, all these acts have made use of intermediaries, and the use, throughout history, of certain lineages forms an essential part of the divine plan. Thus the Qur'an tells us that God has preferred the families of Abraham and 'Imran over all others (3:33). The Abrahamic Prayers in the *darud*, or concluding portion of the Muslim liturgy, have the specific function of bracketing Abraham and Muhammad together. In this connection, the Prophet Muhammad as true heir of Abraham, the Prayer of Abraham (*du'a' Ibrahim*) in sura 2, vv. 127–9 takes on special significance:

127. And when Abraham was raising the foundations of the House and Ishmael [also, he prayed:] "Our Lord! Accept [this work] from us, [for] you are the Hearer, the knower.
128. "Our Lord! And make us submissive unto You (*muslimaini laka*) and our seed a nation submissive unto You (*ummat muslimat laka*), and show us the rites by which we may worship You, and relent towards us, [for] You, only You, are the Relenting, the Merciful.
129. "Our Lord! And raise up amongst them an envoy from amongst

themselves who shall relate unto them Your revelations (*ayatika*) and shall impart to them scripture and wisdom and shall purify them, [for] You, only You, are the Mighty, the Wise."

At this moment Isaac had still to be born so "our seed" must refer to the seed of Abraham as transmitted through the loins of Ishmael, progenitor of the Arabs, but the relationship is even closer, as we shall see. This passage should be taken in conjunction with another (38:100–8), the sacrifice of Abraham. Since Ishmael was at this moment the Patriarch's sole progeny the sacrifice demanded of Abraham was that of his whole posterity. The dramatic intervention at the last moment in vv. 104–5 whereby Ishmael was reprieved is an instance of divine providence; God provided for the future by sparing Ishmael so that from his seed—the Prophet was descended of Kedar, second son of Ishmael—a prophet could be born who would bring Abraham's work to a triumphant conclusion (*khatm an-nubuwwa*—Seal of Prophethood). Thus the Covenant of Abraham was fulfilled in the person of his descendant with the restoration of the elder line. Abraham's prayer is answered in 3:164; and God's dispensational formula as found in the lineage of Abraham is comprised within the centuries which elapsed between the prayer's utterance and its fulfillment 2,400 years later in the very same place where it was uttered. Were it not for this, God's salvific plan, whereby man is enabled to overcome the effects of the Fall, would have been inoperative.

The temporal nature of revelation embodies the concept of progressive disclosure as well as periodical reaffirmation. We do not propose, however, to go into the details of this doctrine, the Seal of Prophethood, as these belong rather to prophethood than revelation. Prophethood and scripture are the twin vehicles of revelation: one is the impermanent life, the other the permanent record. Both testify to the truth, which is why the Muslim creed is known as the Shahada, or testimony, and the centrality of prophethood is evident from the fact that it forms the content of the second clause of the Shahada:

I testify (or bear witness) that there is no god but *the* God and that Muhammad is His envoy (*rasul*).

The first clause affirms (a) the existence of God, (b) His ontological unity, and (c) His unicity; whilst the second affirms Muhammad's special role as chosen (*mustafa*) medium through whom God, having created Man, discloses Himself to His own creation, i.e., having created, in Man, a rational being capable of apprehending Him, God reveals Himself, using for the purpose those faculties with which He has endowed him. The *modus operandi* of revelation is variable; revelation can be either oral or written: the Qur'an is written revelation, the Hadith oral revelation. In the first God addresses Man directly, using the first person plural; the second is more akin to inspiration except that the Qur'an refers to Muhammad as "an excellent model (*uswat hasanat*)" without venturing to affirm that his every action or statement is inspired. Exception must of course be made for the *hadiths* which are *qudsi*, i.e. *hadiths* in which God speaks in the first person, but these *hadiths* only amount to six out of the thousands which exist.

Islam discriminates between various categories of revelation all comprised under the generic *wahi*. There is a lower category of revelation known as *ilham*, which is the kind poets, artists and saints are accustomed to receive. This latter kind equates with inspiration and is fallible of its nature. Satanic inspiration is known by the onomatopoetic *wiswas* (whispering) and al-Tabarī instances two verses in the Qur'an whose source was recognized as satanic and were in consequence struck out immediately. The two verses in question came directly after 53:20.[1] By contrast with *ilham* the *wahi* of the Qur'an is infallible, and to make this clear the Qur'an uses the term *inzal* (sending-down) which since it comes from a transitive verb (*anzala*) presupposes an object. What is sent down therefore is the text of something already in existence, a procedure intended to preclude the possibility of error. Grammatically the term is a *masdar* (verbal noun) of the fourth measure of the verb (from the root *nzl*: to descend). In this measure the verb is causative: if *nazala* means "to descend" *anzala* means 'to make to descend,' the subject behind God and the object a Qur'anic text (*tanzil* is used for an instance of its occurrence). The notion of descent is crucial to a proper understanding of Islam, for it is the correlative of transcendence. As God transcends His own creation the Qur'an can only come down from wherever He transcends it to. The two notions are inseparably linked. Also implicit in the concept of descent is the notion of hierarchy. God stands at the apex of a hierarchy of being (*wujud*), with man at the opposite remove in the capacity of recipient. Included on this lower plane are the Animal Kingdom (*'alam al-hayawanat*) and the Demonic Order (*al-jinn, al-jann*) as likewise beneficiaries of revelation. The form of revelation the brute creation receives is not entirely clear, although the Qur'an affirms its existence implicitly and in one case ("Then your Lord revealed unto the bee...." 16:68) explicitly; but we can take it that animals have an instinctual apprehension of reality, *al-Haqq*, the Real, being one of the 99 names of God, and thus live in a world of total albeit limited certitude. This much at least is clear from the interesting fact that only man can be a non-Muslim. Much clearer is the position with regard to the Demonic Order, although they pertain to an altogether different category of being, ontologically distinct from man and beast. The Prophet is the prophet to both mankind and jinn ("a mercy for the worlds"); and the Qur'an notwithstanding its terms of reference are human is addressed to both categories. The equality of both the human and demonic orders in respect of their ultimate destiny is clear from the numerous passages in which the Qur'an classes them together: "*Ya ma'ashir al-jinn wa al-ins . . . .*" ("O assembly of jinn and humankind . . . ." 6:130). It is recorded that the Prophet preached to the jinn; and the jinn, who understand human language and sometimes intrude into our world, listened to the recitation of the Qur'an and exclaimed in admiration (72:1). Muslim jinn of course read the Qur'an all the time.

Returning to the downward movement of *inzal*, concomitant with God's transcendence (*mukhalafa*), it is with this doctrine that Islam demolishes all notions of immanence, in-dwelling or pantheism. Likewise, incarnation (*hulul*): any religion predicated on the basis of incarnationism runs the risk of eroding the ontological boundaries that separate man from God. Pantheism is the negation of all hierarchy and, ultimately, of all worth. By defining *wahi* as *inzal*, a descent from a higher plane on to a lower, Islam wishes to signal to us that here is a basic pattern of movement in the universe, on the basis of which much can be predicated, not least politics. Politics is in fact no different from religion: truth comes from on top and moves down. Thus, in the state, power emanates from the top and on the way down it is met by responsibility moving up. Society is regulated by law, and in the Islamic state the source of law is divine. Thus *wahi* taking the form of descent provides us with a paradigm for the structure of both society and state, since the state is nothing but a function of society:

Allah   (God)
↓
Rasul Allah   (God's Envoy)
↓
Khalifat Rasul Allah   (Deputy of God's Envoy)
↓
Umma   (Nation, Community)

The meaning is clear: the Caliph is the guarantor of the legality of the state, for he holds his authority in virtue of its transmission from the Prophet to his successors. Obedience to him is therefore mandatory equally as in the case of the Prophet. This is not to be confused with state absolutism on the European model; it does not involve either deification of the state (Marxism) or of its head (monarchism); the Caliph is not a monarch but a mere executive whose function is to uphold the Law (*shari'a*) and provide a visible focus for the authority of the state. Since, at its ultimate source, the Law is divine the Shari'a is, strictly speaking, infallible. The paradigm just outlined sanctions the state as an apparatus for the enforcement of Shariya, enabling man to live under justice (*'adl*). Just as God and man confront one another from opposite ends of the ontological scale so do theocracy and democracy stand at opposite removes from one another, democracy being an inversion of the natural order of things, or hierarchy.

Although the Qur'an is only one of the four sources of law in orthodox (Sunni) Islam, the reason the Law must be accounted infallible is because it partakes of the infallibility of its source. The textual infallibility of the Qur'an derives from its being a transcript of a *princeps*, the *lauh al-mahfuz*. This term is one of those gripping metaphors in which the Qur'an abounds; it means "the Preserved (or Guarded) Tablet." The Arabic admits of both constructions, both *preserved* (from, and for, all time) and *guarded* (against textual corruption). What is referred to here is the same as what Horace meant when he spoke of having erected a monument more enduring than bronze or marble. Inscriptions on marble or consisting of bronze letters on a marble slab were the Roman way of perpetuating a decree or historic document, e.g., Augustus' will.

Thus the Qur'an affirms that it is but the transcript of a celestial archetype, which is why the Prophet is adjured to add or subtract nothing but to adhere strictly to the text that is given him. *Inzal* therefore refers to the sending-down of a text, its vesture in sounds and words. The *lauh* is referred to in 85:21–2:

21. Nay, but it is a glorious Qur'an
22. On a tablet guarded.

And again in 43:3–4:

3. We have made it an Arabic Qur'an that you might understand,

4. And in the Source of the Book (*umm al-kitab*) present (here) with us, it is indeed sublime, decisive.

The Tablet may only have a metaphorical existence—and to this we shall return later—but the nature of *wahi* is that it is essentially a disclosure of things otherwise unknown or at least hitherto unclear. As the source of *wahi* pertains to the suprasensible world it is evident that we are dealing here with an order of things unseen, for which Islam uses the term al-Ghaib, the Unseen. Sura 3, v.44 juxtaposes the two terms *wahi* and *ghaib*: "This is information from the Ghaib. We reveal it to you (O Muhammad)..." More details are given in 45:51:

> And it was never given to any mortal that God should speak to him but by revelation or from behind a veil or by sending an envoy to reveal whatever He wills. He is Sublime, Wise.

This is to say, God speaks both directly and indirectly, directly to the recipient of the *wahi* and indirectly to others through him. To be totally effective it is necessary for the resultant text to be unassailable from the standpoint of literary or textual criticism. Thus the Prophet is commanded to adhere strictly to the text of what is revealed to him, that is not to add, substract or otherwise embellish (43:43). Consequently, the Qur'an is described as "an unassailable scripture" which "Falsehood cannot come at from before or from behind, a disclosure (*tanzil*: a sending-down) from the Wise, the Laudable" (41:42). When the Prophet is invited by his critics to produce another reading (*qur'an*) or alter the existing one, he replies that "It is not for me to alter it of my own accord. I follow only that which is revealed to me. I fear if I disobey my Lord the punishment of an Aweful Day" (10:15). Reproduction of an archetype precludes the possibility of error, save in the course of subsequent transcription, due to the fallibility of the human medium or the deficiencies of the Arabic script before al-Hallaj's orthographic reforms; and, clearly, the mechanism of revelation ties in with the doctrine of finality, for a definitive revelation requires a definitive text as foundation. The thrust of all these doctrines—Qur'anic inimitability, abrogation, and the one just considered, the *lauh mahfuz*—is toward the establishment of a text of unimpeachable integrity such as shall serve as the secure cornerstone for a new world order. This marks the transposition of Islam's message from a metaphysical plane on to a socio-political one with the inception of the Umma, a revolutionary conception of nationhood in which the criterion of belief replaces the genetic accident of birth as the determinant of nationality. The concept of finality is therefore central to Islam's way of viewing the world.

The Qur'an not only issues from a source stated to be divine (27:6):

As for you (O Muhammad), you receive the Qur'an from the presence of One Wise, Aware,

but as we have seen reproduces a celestial archetype, the *lauh al-mahfuz* that may in fact be a metaphor for the mind of God. As a literal transcript it cannot be altered in any way, even by translation. The instant the Qur'an is "translated" into another language it ceases to be the Qur'an and the resultant book is not the Qur'an but an interpretation—one amongst many possible—of its meaning. This is why there can be no such thing in Islam as an Authorized Version, and a translation has neither theological nor liturgical status. The author of the Turkish national anthem, Mehmet Akif, had to flee to Egypt to save his life when Atatürk ordered him to translate the Qur'an into Turkish. He knew the dictator's intention in having it translated was to vernacularize the liturgy, as indeed had already happened in the case of the *adhan*. Since God has chosen to communicate with His creation in the tongue of "the mother settlement" (*umm al-qura*) Arabic constitutes a sacred language, consecrated as the vehicle of communication between the higher and the lower planes; and it functions as the medium in which the dialogue is carried on, with God addressing man in the Qur'an and man replying through the liturgy, using, to do so, both the prayer of praise and the prayer of supplication. A careful translator like Pickthall recognizes these pitfalls, and by entitling his version *The Meaning of the Glorious Qur'an* neatly evades the trap. People without theologically trained minds, a Dawood, a Zafrullah or a Yusuf Ali, either do not hesitate to use the word "Qur'an" or else blasphemously associate the text with the translation so as to infer that they are somehow the same things. Adding insult to injury, an apologetic commentary is sometimes added at the foot by way of directing the mind along approved channels.

"Qur'an" means 'a reading' and comes from the very first word of the first revelation to Muhammad, when the angel exhibited to him a piece of brocade into which these words were woven (96:1–5):

1. *Read* in the name of your Lord Who created,
2. created man from a viscosity.
3. Read! for your Lord is the most beneficient,
4. (He) who taught man that which he (formerly) knew not,
5. taught him by means of the pen.

"Qur'an" therefore means a reading, or recitation, from an already existent text which is published through revelation, and the inclusion of the reed pen (*galam*) refers to the means of its transmission, i.e. the recording process as well as its subsequent dissemination. This passage also adumbrates a whole theory of knowledge but the question of epistemology does not concern us here. The recording was done by Zaid ibn Thabit, the Prophet's secretary, on an odd assortment of writing surfaces from all of which the Qur'an was subsequently put together. The passages making up the Qur'an were dictated on the Prophet's emerging from a tranced condition during which the *wahi* took place, chiefly by audition (75:17–18). Very little is known about the physiology of revelation and still less about the psychology of revelation. The latter in any case does not concern us here since the Qur'an as the literal word of God does not admit of human admixture, although for other religions with a belief in an inspired scripture the question of filtration through a human mind and the degree to which the message is affected by the human filter are matters of transcendent importance. The signals which heralded the onset of a *tanzil* were various. Bukhari refers to the reverberation of bells, which was the most painful.[2] Tirmidhi alludes to a sound like the humming of bees close to the face just before Sura 23 was revealed.[3] Observers noted, and Bukhari records, that even on cold days sweat would appear on the Prophet's face.[4] He would change colour, turn red, sometimes livid; he snored or—delicious detail—rattled like a young camel, before falling into a lethargy.[5] Such details are very vivid and bear the impress of authenticity. Although the parallel with shamanism is close these revelations differ from shamanism in that they come unbidden; they would come on him suddenly with no more warning than the excruciating sound of bells. The Fifth Sura was revealed when he was on top of a camel and as the poor beast could not support him any longer, he was obliged to dismount. At 'Arafat during his last pilgrimage the Prophet used his she-camel Qaswas as a pulpit from which to preach the Farewell Sermon, and at the moment the concluding portion (5:3) of the Qur'an was revealed,

> This day I have completed your religion for you and perfected my grace upon you and chosen for you as religion the Surrender (*al-islam*),

Qaswas sank to her knees under the impact of the *wahi*.

As a work whose authorship is divine it is only to be expected that the Qur'an should surpass stylistically books whose authorship is merely human. Much of the impact of the Qur'an resides in the way in which the genius of the Arabic language is wrought to the height of its potential; and it is precisely an aesthetic criterion that is held to be the proof of its divine origin. This teaching, formalized in a doctrine known as the dogma of inimitability (*i'jaz al-Qur'an*), is derived from those passages where it challenges "the two dependent categories" (53:31) to which the Qur'an is addressed, i.e., humankind and jinn, to produce its like, or, failing that, then ten suras or even just a single one that is comparable in style (17:88, 11:13 and 2:23). This challenge has never seriously been taken up, and the Qur'an's position as the supreme work of Arabic literature and the unsurpassable model of Arabic prose remains unchallenged.

Another doctrine bearing directly on the question of revelation, because it involves its progressive nature, is the dogma of abrogation (*naskh*). It has been said that the Qur'an is unique in that alone amongst scriptures it supplies rules for its own interpretation. One of these is the distinction between allegorical and literal matter (3:7). Another is the doctrine stated in 2:106 giving the rules for abrogation. An abrogation (*tansikh*) involves two parts, the *nasikh* and the *mansukh*, respectively the active and the passive participles of the same verb: in other words, the passage which abrogates and the passage which is abrogated. Briefly what is entailed is that if there be a discrepancy between two texts bearing on matters of legislation the subsequent text cancels out the earlier one. By extension, the Qur'an abrogates all previously revealed scriptures just as Muhammad's prophethood supersedes the missions of all previous prophets, which are now rendered otiose in virtue of his universality. Thus the doctrine of abrogation links up with another, the Seal of Prophethood, which works both forward and backward in time: retrospectively, by annulling the claims of previous dispensations; and forward, by invalidating those of any future claimant to the title of prophet. This is why there was never any question in Islam of reference back to previous scripture, the way that in Christianity the Old Testament is used as a support system for the New. Equally, anyone coming after Muhammad is demonstrably a fraud, like Baha'ullah or the lying prophet of Qadiyan. This is one of the reasons why the search for the sources of Islam has been so futile; the question of antecedents is irrelevant in the same way that the question of Judaic sources is irrelevant to Christianity, when we reflect that the structure of Christianity was from the start distinct fron Judaism.

It should come as no surprise therefore that the theology of revelation in Islam involves concepts foreign to both Judaism and Christianity. Thus the Qur'an is not only the literal word of God but uncreated (*ghair makhluq*) and coeternal with Him. As the thought of God the Qur'an may be said to form part of the divine ipseity. As divine utterance (*kalam Allah*) it transcends, as we have seen, all human speech and partakes of the *dhat* (essential nature) of God. An-Nasafi, whose creed (*'aqida*) is one of, if not the most famous in Islam, states:

> And He whose majesty is majestic, speaks by means of speech (*kalam*). This speech is an attribute from all eternity (*azali*), *not belonging to the genus of letters or sounds*,[6] an attribute that is incompatible with coming to silence and knows no weakness.

> God Most High speaks with this speech, enjoining and prohibiting and narrating. And the Qur'an is the uncreated work of God, repeated by our tongues, heard by our ears, written in our copies (*masahif*), preserved in our hearts, yet not simply a transient state (*hal*) in these [tongues, ears, copies, hearts]."

This sums up the orthodox position. Just before this point in his *'Aqa'id*, in reference to the key Islamic doctrine of the *mukhalafa* (*'al-mukhalafa min al-hawadith*, God's difference from originated beings, i.e., that God is essentially different from and other than all that we can know), an-Nasafi distinguishes between a thing originated (*muhdath*) and an originator (*muhdith*):

> Further, the world in the totality of its parts is a *muhdath* in that it consists of substances (*a'yan*) and accidents (*a'rad*) . . . .

> The *muhdith* of the world is God Most High, the One (*al-Wahid*), the Eternal (*al-Qadim*), the Living (*al-Hayy*), the Powerful (*al-Qadir*), the Knowing (*al-'Alim*), the Hearing (*as-Sami'*), the Seeing (*al-Basir*), the Desiring (*ash-Sha'i*), the Willing (*al-Murid*). He is not an accident or a body, nor a substance (*jauhar*), nor a thing formed, nor a thing bounded, nor a thing numbered, nor a thing divided, nor a thing compounded, nor does He come to an end in Himself; and He is not described by quiddity (*mahiya*), nor by modality (*kaifiyya*), and He does not exist in space or time, and there is nothing that resembles Him and nothing that is without His knowledge and power.

> He has attributes which are from all eternity (*azali*), resting in His Essence (*dhat*). They are not He nor are they other than He.[7]

Thus the *mukhalafa* (otherness) of God differentiates the *kalam* (speech) of God: unlike other speech it has no origin in time and thus does not end in time. Since the *dhat* (essential nature) of God is inapprehensible to a being such as man whom He so totally transcends God can only be known through His Attributes (*sifat*). The Attributes represent the modalities of God's operation within the world He has created. The 99 names, the Attributes they connote, (*e.g.*, *rahma*, compassion, from *ar-Rahman ar-Rahim*, the Compassionate, the Merciful, or, more likely, the Merciful Compassionator) and certain other deducible *sifat* form the only means by which God can be apprehended. The Attributes are the clue to the Islamic understanding of God, for a god that was completely transcendent would be an agnostic god. Therefore the Attributes provide the *analogia entis* otherwise supplied in Christianity by the Incarnation. But the most important of the Attributes are hypostatized ones pertaining to the *dhat*, such as priority (*qidam*) and continuance (*baqa'*), transcendence (*mukhalafa*) and *tanzih* (independence of substrate or termination). The remainder, such as the one just quoted, compassion (*rahma*), are relationships only. It is in fact several of these hypostatized Attributes which explain the creation of man, because when God took the inert clay and breathed into it of His spirit (32:7–9), thereby animating it, He effected thereby the transference of seven of His own Attributes. These are the Rational Attributes (*as-sifat al- 'aqliyya*):

Life   (*hayat*)
Knowledge   (*'ilm*)
Will   (*irada*)
Power   (*qudra*)
Hearing   (*sam'*)
Seeing   (*basar*)
Speech   (*kalam*),

the totality of which makes up a rational being, i.e., one open to revelation in a way not possible to the brute creation, who intuit the existence of God. By endowing man with this faculty (*kalam*) God thereby renders him capable of recognizing divine *kalam*, or revelation, which, apprehended by the other faculties, hearing, seeing, *etc*, becomes *'ilm* (knowledge), knowledge of one's Creator, one's duties in respect of Him, etc. It is the reciprocral nature of *kalam* that constitutes the basis of the revelatory process, and this solely because in the act of transmission God created, through the combination of these seven faculties, a creature distinguished by the possession of *'aql*, the faculty of discursive reasoning.

   Kalam of course must, of necessity, pre-exist creation if it is to be imparted to it. The Qur'an therefore as *kalam Allah*, or divine utterance, is the Logos, the fertile intersection of the two planes, both cross and swastika. Clearly the uncreated nature of the Logos cannot refer to the physical book or no less physical sounds produced by the larynx since both of these had and have their origin in time. An-Nasafi stresses that God's *kalam* being *azali* does not partake of the characteristics of human speech, it does not belong "to the genus of letters and sounds," rather it is "an attribute that is incompatible with coming to silence and has no weakness." Precisely the same point is made by al-Ghazali in somewhat more detailed form in the *Ihya'*. When we say that the Qur'an is uncreate and co-eternal with God this obviously cannot refer to the written book, for which Arabic reserves the term *mushaf* (copy), or articulated sounds (*qira'a*, reading, repetition or recitation) but to something distinct from either. Al-Ghazali says that the term "Qur'an" embraces three levels of meaning: *lugha wa natq* (language and utterence), *huruf wa kitaba* (letters and writing) and *ruh wa ma'na* (spirit and meaning). It is only in the last sense that the Qur'an can be said to be uncreated and co-eternal with God. The first two act reciprocally one upon the other but both go back to the third and are but attempts to concretize or embody something in itself ineffable. The precise nature of God's *kalam* like the precise nature of God Himself eludes definition. God, of course, is constrained by the limitations He imposes upon Himself, one of which is that in addressing man he has perforce to use anthropological language, with all that that implies (grammar, logic, terms of reference, etc.). Not only is there no single human tongue but even the terms of reference must operate within the framework of human and sometimes even local experience. If, instead, the Qur'an had been revealed to dolphins—and who is to say it has not been?—its terms of reference would have been altogether different. We revert to the mystery of the bee.

NOTES

1. See trans. in A. Guillaume, *The Life of Muhammad*, pp. 165–167. OUP, 1955. Cf. *sira* of ibn Hisham ed. Mustafā's-Saqqā, Ibrāhīm al-Ibyārī and 'Abd al-Hafīz Shalabī, 2nd. ed.; Cairo: 1375/1955, I, 364–365. The story is rejected by Caetani (*Annali*, I, p. 278ff.)

2. Bukhārī, *Sahīh*, sect. *wahī*, bāb 2: "Al-Hārith ibn Hishām asked God's Apostle: 'O Apostle of God, how does the *wahī* come to you?' God's Apostle replied, 'Sometimes it comes to me like the ringing of bells, and this form is the hardest for me, and then it passes off after I have grasped what was said; and sometimes the angel appears as a man, who speaks to me

and I grasp whatever he said.' "

3. *Tafsīr*, sūra 23.

4. Bukhārī, *ibid.*: " 'Ā'isha added: 'I saw him when the *wahī* descended on him on an extremely cold day and when it passed the sweat would be coursing from his forehead'."

5. Muslim, sect. *Hudūd*, trads. 13, 14. Bukhārī, sect. *Hajj*, bāb 17.

6. Our italics.

7. This sentence is the famous formula, *Hiya lā huwā wa lā ghairahu.*

ADDITIONAL READING

Arberry, Arthur J. *Revelation and Reason in Islam.* London: Allen & Unwin, 1957.

Crollins, Ary A. Roest. *The Word is The Experience of Revelation in Qur'an and Hindu Scriptures.* Rome: Universita Gregoriana, 1974.

Sadr-ud-Din. *The Holy Prophet's Revelation and it's Nature.* Lahore: Ahmadiyya Anjuman Isha'at-i-Islam, 1969.

Wielandt, Rotrand. *Offenbarung und Geschichte im Denken moderner Muslime.* Wiesbaden: F. Steiner, 1971.

Henry O. Thompson

A Study in Antisemitism

Israels In Divine Principle[1]

The subtitle does not contain a typographical error. There is not one Israel in *Divine Principle* (hereafter DP). There are three. This essay is primarily concerned with the first. A major concern is whether DP is antisemitic, in the traditional sense of anti-Judaism.

The references to the first Israel cluster in two main areas: the historic Hebrew-Jewish people from Abraham to Ezra, and, the Jewish people in the time of Jesus of Nazareth. The people are called "The Chosen People" in both periods, in the DP. They began with Abraham. He was both successful and a failure. He failed ritually and symbolically in the way he offered the sacrifice in Genesis 15. He cut part of the offering in half but not the dove. In his willingness to sacrifice Isaac, however, Abraham succeeded, according to the DP. He laid the foundation for his family to become the channel for God's redemptive activity.

DP claims Abraham's successful accomplishment continued with Isaac, who was willing to be sacrificed; with Jacob who victoriously wrestled with the angel and was reconciled with his brother Esau; with Joseph and later with Moses. The Bible says Moses also failed. For this disobedience, he was not allowed to enter the promised land. However, the DP indicates he faithfully laid the Foundation of Faith. According to the Bible, the people under Moses failed by worshipping the Golden Calf and by accepting the majority report of the spies. The latter said they could not conquer the land of Canaan. For their faithlessness, most of this generation was condemned to the Wilderness Wandering. However, the next generation entered Canaan.

In the DP, the story of the Hebrew people continues with the failure of Saul and the kings and priests of Israel. Yet, according to DP, the Chosen People and their leaders in each era had the option of obedience. Their faithfulness would have set the stage for the Messianic Age and the Redemption of the world. Even at that, they *did* set the stage for the Messiah, though imperfectly. Their obedience in the Exile, and subsequently in the reform of Ezra, prepared the way for Jesus.

THE CHARGES

A listing of the Israelite failures noted in DP has led some to accuse DP of being antisemitic.

A Problem

Antisemitism itself is something of a problem while the charge is even more so. Antisemitism has many faces.[2] At times, the faces are so many that one could despair of being anything but antisemitic. There is a danger here, represented by Jaroslav Pelikan[3] as he talks about dialogue:

> The trouble with most fad words is not only that they obscure the meaning of language and serve as a substitute for thought, but also that they articulate inadequately a need that is deeply felt; this is, indeed why they become fads.

For example, at various times in American history, it has been fashionable to label "Communist" anyone with whom you disagreed. A neighbor did not like college students parking in front of her house. "Obviously,"she said, "they are all Commies." The red-baiting of the 1920's in the United States, and the McCarthyism of the 1950's, is seen by some as a smear on our national honor. Others point out that the hysteria hid the very real danger which Communism is to the free world.

Thus it seems to me that words like "Communist" and "antisemite" should not be used casually or indiscriminately, without clear and careful thought.

In my view, antisemitism is one of the most vicious aberrations in history. It is totally counter to the essence of democracy, human decency, and the Judeo-Christian tradition. To label someone antisemitic is a serious charge indeed. Glazer politely says it thus: "...the way Jews are treated is an important index—sometimes the chief index—of a country's spirit of freedom and good will... Thomas G. Masaryk of Czechoslovakia, put it: 'A nation's attitude toward Jews is the measure of its cultural maturity'."[4] To put it another way, antisemitism is a measure of a society's health. The presence of antisemitism represents sickness in a society's soul, a fatal flaw in its being. Unless this illness is cured, even the most technologically advanced nation will slide into the darkness of barbarism, as Nazi Germany so horribly illustrated.

Introducing *The New Anti-Semitism*, Seymour Groubard notes that this is "in the larger sense, a book about the wrongs people do people in the twentieth century... We hope it will prod the reader into awareness of what is hurting his neighbor, his country—and, ultimately, himself."[5]

I write with the awareness that what hurts my neighbor, sooner or later, hurts me.[6] Martin Niemoeller explained:

> In Germany the Nazis first came for the Communists, and I didn't speak up because I wasn't a Communist. Then they came for the Jews, and I didn't speak up because I wasn't a Jew. Then they came for the trade unionists, and I didn't speak up because I wasn't a trade unionist. Then they came for the Catholics, and I didn't speak up because I wasn't a Catholic (I was a Protestant). Then they came for me, and by that time there was no one left to speak for me.

So I write out of vital personal concern rather than mere academic curiosity.

But I also write with this awareness: "Challenging another's faith goes against the American grain and the First Amendment."[7] It is too easy to slip back into the pre-American Europe of the Thirty Years War or the Crusades where religions were busily trying to destroy each other. The pluralism of America requires that all religions be free to believe. There have been too many examples where this was not true. Antisemitism is but one of these examples. It and all other "anti-isms" such as the discrimination experienced by Catholics, Jehovah's Witnesses, Mormons, and others, as well as racism and sexism, are all blights on democracy.[8]

One temptation in facing these blights is to "fight fire with fire."

There may be some value in that but it also perpetuates the very evil with which one is supposedly concerned. It also violates an old tradition illustrated by Rabbi Hillel: "Do not do unto others that which is hurtful to thyself."[9] Further, if we continue doing what we accuse others of doing, we may simply project onto others our own fears, anger and sin, instead of constructively solving problems. An alternative is to seek understanding rather than subjugation, openness rather than oppression, dialogue rather than the trading of accusations.

Iris Cully's words are meaningful in the midst of such uncertainty:

...it is the provincial mind that wants to close debate, keep ideas circumscribed by a prescribed fence, ultimately have everyone subjected to a 'standard,' which very often turns out to be one person's prejudice, or even a rationalized commercial objective.[10]

Commenting on *The Myth of God Incarnate*,[11] Trevor Beeson notes:

There seems to be plenty of material here for useful debate, and it is to be hoped that those who are afraid of the authors' approaches or who disagree with their conclusions will keep their heads sufficiently to enable a constructive discussion to take place. There are few signs of such dialogue at the moment...[12]

When asked for his support in burning Jewish books and eliminating Jews, Erasmus suggested they all read the Jewish books and then sit down and have a discussion with Jewish scholars and learn something. Abraham J. Heschel notes the:

clash of doctrines is not a disaster but an opportunity... The world is too small for anything but mutual care and deep respect; the world is too great for anything but responsibility for one another.[13]

This is good advice for anti-semites, anti-Unificationists, the ACM. With these preliminary remarks, let us take a closer look at the issues.

The American Jewish Committee

In December '76, the AJC published a report, "Jews and Judaism in Rev. Moon's *Divine Principle*."[14] The report claims that the DP shows unrelieved hostility to the Jews. It is pejorative, stereotyped, and accuses the Jews of collective sin and guilt. It describes them as reprobates. Their intentions are seen as evil (often diabolical). Their religious mission is eclipsed.[15] The report does not refer to the faithfulness DP ascribes to Hebrews and Jews. Rabbi Rudin is upset because the DP describes the Israelites of the Hebrew Bible (Old Testament) as faithless.[16] In similar fashion, DP refers to the attitude of the Jews towards Jesus as hostile.[17] Rudin objects to the DP statement:

> As a matter of fact, Satan confronted Jesus, working through the Jewish people, centering on the chief priests and scribes who had fallen faithless, and especially through Judas Iscariot, the disciple who had betrayed Jesus. Nevertheless, due to the Jewish people's rebellion against him, the physical body of Jesus was delivered into the hands of Satan as the condition of ransom for the restoration of the Jews and the whole of mankind back to God's bosom; his body was invaded by Satan.[18]

Rudin sees the anti-Jewish thrust continuing into our own time. These references in DP he claims are viciously anti-Jewish, the worst of traditional Christian displacement, viewing the persecution of Jews as punishment for sins.

> God's heritage (has been) taken away from the Jewish people.

> Israel has been punished for the sin of rejecting Jesus and crucifying Him.

> Jesus came as the Messiah; but due to the disbelief of and persecution by the people he was crucified. Since then the Jews have lost their qualification as the chosen people and have been scattered, suffering persecution through the present day.

Rudin is concerned that there is only one mention of the Nazi Holocaust.

> Hitler imposed the strict primitive Germanic religious ideology by concluding a pact with the Pope of Rome, thus founding a national religion, and then tried to control all Protestantism under the supervision of bishops throughout the country. Therefore, the Catholics as well as the Protestants were strongly opposed to Hitler. Furthermore, Hitler massacred six million Jews.[19]

Rudin goes on to sketch the history of Christian antisemitism, acknowledging that UC teachings have their parallels. However, he notes that in recent years, Protestants and Roman Catholics have repudiated antisemitism. Among other examples, he quotes the Presbyterian Church in the United States as saying: "We can never lay exclusive claim to being God's people as though we have replaced those to whom the covenant, the law and the promises belong. We affirm that God has not rejected His people, the Jews. The Lord does not take back His promises." Rabbi Rudin neglects to note that the DP was developed prior to 1954 and that all the Catholic and Protestant statements to which he refers have only been made in recent years. He ends his pronouncement with the observation: "One can only speculate on what negative and anti-Jewish impact *Divine Principle* may have upon a follower of Rev. Moon." This is of course not true since one does not need to speculate at all. One could talk with these followers and ask how they feel. Of the 3,000 Unificationists, fewer than 200 are of Jewish background, including the current president of the UC in America. Several of these *have* been asked. They claim the UC and DP have deepened their appreciation of their Jewish heritage, a thought echoed by Unificationists of other backgrounds. Obviously we need some dialogue here in the spirit of Erasmus, Cully, Beeson and Abraham Heschel.[20] To repeat Cully's observation, it is the provincial mind that closes debate often for prejudices of the person's own or even for a rationalized commercial objective.

Rudin's report notes another report, then in preparation, by a committee of the Faith and Order Commission of the National Council of Churches. The report has since been published.[21]

The Commission on Faith and Order

Under presuppositions, the CFO report notes the responsibility of Christians and Jews for the restoration of fallen humanity.[22] It quotes DP: "the history of the Israelite nation is the central focus of the providential history of restoration."

That is a high status for Israelites but the committee report does not focus on the high esteem. It goes on to quote DP statements on Israelite faithlessness and that Christians who fail to acknowledge the Lord of the Second Advent will be like the Jews who failed to recognize Jesus as the Messiah. The Committee claimed to be concerned with antisemitism. They claim a recurrent emphasis in DP on the responsibility of the Jews for the failure of the mission of Jesus. They say the attitude expressed toward the Jews is consistently and unrelievedly negative though on p. 6 they acknowledge the positive appreciation of Jews. They see DP as condemnation of an entire people which results in an inevitable antisemitism. Antisemitism, of course, is what their denominations have been, and continue, practicing. They admit that in the past, Christians have been antisemitic. That is not completely gone but is openly regretted by Christians, they claim. The Gospel of Jesus Christ is not helped by any discrimination, whether of race, color, creed, sex or economic status. Apparently discrimination against the UC is alright. They claim that the antisemitism of DP is incompatible with a real Christian teaching and practice. They fail to note that most of their own constituency is part of this antisemitism and that it is present and on-going. The AJC *has* noted this and has also accused the entire NCC of antisemitism but has promised to continue dialogue anyway.[23]

The UC and Rev. Sun Myung Moon

The following advertisement[24] was published in *The New York Times*, 19 December '76:

Jewish Brethren:

On September 18, 1976, at our God Bless America Festival at the Washington Monument, in the presence of 300,000 people, we stated:

"Judaism, Christianity and the Unification Movement are indeed three brothers in the Providence of God. Then, Israel, the United States and Korea, the nations where these three religions are based must also be brothers. Because these three nations have a common destiny representing God's side, the Communist bloc as Satan's representative is trying to isolate and destroy them at the U.N.

Therefore these three brother nations must join hands in a unified effort to restore the United Nations to its original purpose and function. They must contribute internally to the unification of world religions and externally to the unification of the world itself."

(Cf. our advertisement in *The New York Times*, Sept. 24, 1976)

And yet, in spite of this clear and explicit statement, we were attacked repeatedly and accused of anti-Semitism. Our views were distorted, our struggle, its meaning and objectives misrepresented.

On the occasion of these Hanukkah Days, the Festival of Light and commemoration of your victory over the forces of darkness and evil, we wish to clarify our genuine convictions and express our honest and sincere feelings toward you, Jewish Brethren.

Towards this end and purpose we publish herewith and bring to your attention the document signed on August 10, 1976.

In the course of their history the people of Israel and Korea have experienced suffering and persecutions by neighboring enemies and expanding imperialistic powers.

As a son of the Korean people, living in this blessed by God land of America, I extend to you, Jewish Brethren, my hand of friendship and wish to state the principles which are guiding the activities of our Movement, especially those regarding the problems and difficulties confronting the Jews of the World and Israel at this crucial juncture of our common human history.

1. The Unification Movement categorically condemns antisemitism, the most hideous, abject and cruel form of hatred. We regard the murder of six million Jews in Europe the result of political short-sightedness and lack of moral responsibility on the part of Germany's political and religious leaders, and statesmen from among other nations, in the period between the Two World Wars. Ignoring the basic teachings of the Scriptures, they acted too late to block Hitler's ascent to power, they postponed the action for his downfall, and they did nothing to rescue the victims who were the captives of his satanic plans and designs. Only a unified front of all Christian and Jewish forces, inspired by the principles of the Divine Commandments and guided by the concept of human brotherhood, would have been able to prevent the Holocaust, the implementation of the "Final Solution,"—a Cain-inspired action, carried out by the Nazis between 1933 and 1945.

2. The Unification Movement recognizes the divine and natural right of the Jewish people to physical survival and preservation of its specific religious traditions, the marks of its distinctive historical entity. These fundamental human rights must be secured everywhere, especially for Jews living in the lands of the Diaspora.

3. The Unification Movement regards the Land of Israel as a haven for the Holocaust survivors and sanctuary for all those individual Jews who are trying to escape physical persecution and religious, racial or national oppression. The demand for free emigration—the undeniable and inalienable right of every human being—must become the stated policy of the United States in her dealings with foreign countries, and particularly in her relations with the Soviet Union.

4. The Unification Movement, in its efforts to resolve conflicts among nations and harmonize antagonistic social-economic and political interests, will work toward the creation of political conditions necessary for an acceptable accommodation between the Arabs and Jews, and to achieve a genuine and lasting peace in the Middle East, one of the most important corners of the world.

5. The Unification Movement believes that religious and free people

throughout the world must cooperate in building a spiritual and organizational unity among nations which will be capable to contain Soviet imperialism, which continues to inflict hardship and suffering upon its own people and is spreading the poison of hatred and dissension among nations of the world, with the ultimate purpose of political global subjugation and enslavement.

6. The Unification Movement is grateful to God, to His true and righteous prophets and saints of our common spiritual tradition who prepared the foundations on which we stand and organize our struggle. We consider ourselves to be the younger brother of our Jewish and Christian brethren, all of whom are children of our Heavenly Father. We regard it as our duty to respect and serve the elder sons of our Father, and it is our mission to serve Judaism and Christianity by promoting Love and Unity among all the children of God.

7. The Unification Movement teaches the Principle and strives toward the establishment of a Unified World Family of Nations guided by the concepts of Unity and Brotherhood expressed in the Divine Commandments, the foundations of our common spiritual heritage. It is our conviction that we must unite in order to attain this Divine and Sublime Historical Objective.

> Reverend Sun Myung Moon
> Belvedere,
> Tarrytown, New York
> December, 1976
> Hanukkah, Kislev 5737

A Response

Responding to this, Rabbi Tanenbaum commented:

We trust that the Rev. Moon's declaration... will result in concrete actions that will demonstrate that he means what he professes. A comprehensive and systematic removal of negative and hostile references to Jews and Judaism which abound in his *Divine Principle*, the basic teachings of the Unification Movement, would be one such demonstration that his statements are serious and are made in good faith and are not simply public relations pieties.

The *NY Times* quoted him as saying Rev. Moon's statement "represented only 'public relations pieties'." Rabbi Tanenbaum went on to say "that all major Christian bodies... from Vatican Council II to the World and National Council of Churches to Dr. Billy Graham to the Southern Baptist Convention—have unambiguously repudiated these anti-Jewish canards." In the light of this "we call upon Rev. Moon not to be guilty of planting these poisonous weeds which so many faithful people have labored for decades to uproot." He added that the American Jewish Committee was also concerned about proselytizing, reputed mind-conditioning methods of indoctrination, and what appeared to be justification of oppressive regimes.[25]

COMMENTARY

Rabbi Tanenbaum's response is in one sense confusing. Rev. Moon published to all the world his condemnation of antisemitism and his support for the state of Israel (in contrast to the NCC), and Rabbi Tanenbaum calls upon Rev. Moon to repudiate antisemitism. If I say antisemitsm is bad and then someone turns around and demands that I say antisemitism is bad, either this someone has not heard me, or something else is happening. It is perhaps then in this second sense that Rabbi Tanenbaum's remarks are to be understood.

The war that fizzled

In 1963, Bernard E. Olson published his epoch-making study of antisemitism in Protestant texts and teaching materials.[26] Since then, the Second Vatican Council (1962–1965) as well as several groups have issued statements favorable or even friendly to Jews and Judaism. Some of these are a bit curious. "In Catholic Spain—stronghold of the Inquisition for three centuries—a pamphlet issued over the imprimatur of the Bishop of Madrid asserts: 'In no way can a Christian reproach the entire Jewish people for the assassination of Christ.'" At first glance this Roman statement seems positive, but what it really says is that *some* Jews, though not all, *can* be reproached for the assassination of Christ. Fortunately the booklet is entitled "We the Jews" and talks about "the God-chosen people." It was, of course, the Romans who executed the historical Jesus, and thousands of other Jews as well.[27]

This is quoted in an article titled, "The Christian War on Anti-Semitism." The article is dated 1964, the year *after* Olson's publication. The tone of the article is optimistic. "We're on our way... Not a war so much *against* anti-Semitism as *for* freedom—freedom to live in the kind of world Pope Paul prayed for in the Holy Land, a world of 'true, profound concord among all men and all peoples.'"[28] Olson, himself, writing the following year, was a bit less optimistic.[29] "The purification of the Gospel is going to take some time!"

Common sense agrees. Antisemitism has been built up and carried on by Christian churches for centuries. It's not apt to disappear in a decade. Gerald Strober's study suggests it has by no means disappeared.[30] His study was not as extensive as Olson's and concentrated on antisemitism in a selection of denominational educational materials. He found a few slight improvements and many of the old problems still present. The one outstanding change for the better was an example from the Missouri Synod Lutheran material.[31] Since this Protestant denomination is not otherwise noted for its liberalism, we are reminded here that the problem of antisemitism cuts across the traditional liberal-conservative spectrum.

It is appalling to point out that the people being quoted in 1964 in the war on antisemitism and in Olson's 1965 treatment of "a lively skeleton," belonged to denominations that Strober's 1972 studies show as contining to have an inaccurate portrait of the elder brother. These are people in power, in key positions (curriculum editors for example) in Protestant and Roman Catholic hierarchies, the very groups publicly repudiating antisemitism. Some of these groups belong to the NCC, apparently overlooked by the CFO committee. In the decade following Olson's monumental study pointing out what they were doing to prejudice children's minds against Jews and Judaism, these key people and their religious groups made relatively little progress in presenting a more accurate portrait. Rabbi Tanenbaum has good reason for wanting to see concrete results. After many years of pious statements, concrete results appear to be few and far between. Strober noted in 1972 that while the various groups had made their statements or resolutions, "none of the denominations surveyed has even one staff member devoting full time to Christian-Jewish relations, and neither has the National Council of Churches."[32]

The second sense

This leads me to the observation that the CFO might want to take very seriously a suggestion Rabbi Tanenbaum makes regarding Christian efforts to evangelize Jews. He defends the fundamental right that we have, "to proclaim one's truth in the marketplace of ideas." That includes the right to seek converts to one's cause. Presumably, that right belongs to the UC as well. But then he notes: Given the self-evident fact that there are millions of baptized Christians whose association with Christianity is nominal, and the uncounted others who are Gentiles and/or domestic heathens, it would seem that evangelical fervor and money would be far more rationally and legitimately employed in converting Christians to Christianity than in the relatively fruitless proselytization of Jews, with its consequent affront to the dignity of Judaism and its potential for serious intergroup discord.[33] According to a study by Rabbi Allen Maller, those converts cost $3,000 to $4,000 per capita and amount to only a few hundred a year in contrast to the seven or eight thousand Christians who convert to Judaism every year, for free.[34]

Not only does this suggest (to me at least) that the CFO might want to try spending its time with its own constituency to deal with Protestant antisemitism.[35] It suggests that proselytizing is a bigger problem for the AJC than the official statements suggest. Tanenbaum's foreword to the above quoted report says, "It has been estimated that nearly thirty percent of the Moonies today are Jewish young men and women..." Rabbi Rudin is quoted elsewhere as suggesting a figure of 10%. The UC says it is 5.3%.[36] We are talking about less than 200 people. There are over 7 million Jews in America. The figures are less important than the concern, a concern that also appears in relation to "Jews for Jesus" (most of whom are Jews), The American Board of Missions to the Jews, Hare Krishna (12% Jews), and other such groups. Still, one wonders why the protest is aimed at the UC while there is no objection to Jews becoming witches (11%—3,000–4,000 Jews), Muslim Sufis (15%) or Zen Buddhists (25%).[37] Why is the protest aimed at a group with only 5–6% Jews but groups with 2–5 *times* as many Jewish converts receive no press conferences, and little or no criticism?

The very title of the Rudins' article suggests that they (and others too) feel the threat is greater than Rabbi Allen Maller's study concludes. The writers note there are an estimated 60 groups of Hebrew Christians trying to convert Jews. They note that "...irate public responses by Jewish and Christian leaders to Hebrew Christian publicity tactics have unwittingly given them free and extensive exposure." A similar thought echoes in "The Many Faces of Anti-Semitism": "Anti-Semitic propagandists still burst into the headlines from time to time. What is the best way to deal with them? Attempts to silence them only transform them into martyrs for free speech. And running debates actually help them by providing the publicity they thrive on. But it is not incumbent on the community to provide them with a platform... the best answer, wherever possible, is...the 'silent treatment'."[38] One wonders about this policy in relation to the Unification Movement. One wonders why they continue to publicize the UC. It seems doubtful they would do it on purpose to aid the growth of the UC; still, perhaps the UC can be appreciative of the free publicity.

It is perhaps wise to put in a reminder here of Judaism's own proselytizing efforts. These have been low key over the centuries. In the time of Jesus, they were widespread and very active. The New Testament reflects this in several places (Matthew 23:15, Acts 2:10, 6:5, 13:43). The Proselytes of Righteousness were those who were circumcised and observed the law of Moses. The Proselytes of the Gate (Exodus 20:10), were not bound by circumcision. These Godfearers were attracted to Christianity in some numbers, perhaps because circumcision was not required. Christianity was a Jewish sect. Jesus and all his early followers were Jews. He said he came only to the house of Israel (Mt. 15:24). But after his death, the Christian movement spread out to include Gentiles as well. As a sect of Judaism, Christianity grew well in the seedbed so well prepared by earlier Jews.[39]

Non-Christian Jewish proselytism may have slowed because of the inroads of Christian proselytism. The former certainly declined after Christianity came to power and laws were passed against it. As Christians had already found when these were used against themselves, one rather effective way to slow a missionary movement is by murdering both proselytes and those who attempt to proselytize. That it was a violation of everything Jesus taught didn't seem to bother them. It also violated Rabbi Hillel's teaching. But Jewish proselytes/proselytism has never stopped completely in these nineteen centuries, as Rabbi Maller's study testifies for the present day. Reform Judaism has announced resumption of active public proselytism.

Love thy neighbor

It is appropriate here to note Rabbi Rudin's analysis of the threat of Rev. Moon's proselytism.[40] Rudin claims people do not join the Unification Church for its theology or politics. Rather the Unification Church is able to give its followers a "sense of belonging, warmth and community." This is an interesting comment. Most of us need this. He goes on to say it is "a new family run by a rigid code of standards." Young people "tumble for the companionship, the appreciation, the sense of belonging—and the rigidly clean living—of a cult like the 'Moonies'."[41] "Black and Hispanic young people are usually too busy trying to 'make it' in society to have the leisure for getting involved with the Moon group..." Thus "most of Moon's followers are white, middle class, educated young people who are looking for a 'sense of warmth and security.' " Personally I think we need more clean living, warmth and love rather than less. But Rudin says they are alienated and disaffected young people who are vulnerable because they do not have a deep faith on the one hand, while on the other hand they "find in the authoritarian figure of the Rev. Moon a father image to direct them toward a more emotional, spiritual life." "And joining the group gives kids a chance to kick their parents very hard—and get a new parent, Rev. Moon... And they don't have to do it alone. It's very convenient and very warm." "The Unification Church," Rabbi Rudin said, "offers the best and the brightest young people a sense of belonging, a sense of purpose. They are taught they have natural parents who bring them into the world, but Rev. Moon is their true parent." However, "This is not child's play. People act out their theology. It sometimes takes political and social action," Rabbi Rudin said, calling the Nazi attempt to exterminate the Jews such an example. From a Muslim perspective of course, Jews act out their theology. Some Muslims believe the Jews are planning to exterminate the Arabs.

Elsewhere, Rabbi Tanenbaum notes, "The troubling question cannot be evaded: why are Rev. Moon and his political backers resorting to the Nazi model of exploiting anti-Semitism for ideological purposes?" He feels that "the American people must be alerted to the emergence of the Moon phenomenon of an ideological campaign whose antecedents trace back to the Nazis and to Stalinist Communism. Those totalitarian movements consciously and cynically employed anti-Jewish hatred as a major vehicle for realizing their apocalyptic goal of undermining the Biblical and democratic values of Western civilization."[42] Both Rudin and Tanenbaum extended their criticism to an alleged involvement of the Unification Church with the Korean CIA and called for Congressional investigation of this.[43]

Rabbi Rudin is well aware of the challenge all this presents to traditional Judaism and Christianity. It says the traditional groups are cold and insecure. It seems to me that similar things are being said about white, middle class families, both Christian and Jewish. In other words, the question of warmth and belonging, a sense of purpose, a deepening of faith—all this is a judgment upon present structures. Rather than condemning Rev. Moon and the Unification Church for responding to these human needs, organized religion might rather commend him for it, and if they wish, seek ways to go and do likewise. Rabbi Rudin strongly urges synagogues and churches to do the latter.[44] What is not clear is why the UC should be condemned for doing this—for showing the love which the rest of us are supposed to be showing to one another. Nor is it clear why Rudin's and Judaism's love should not include the UC. The Hebrew Scriptures urge Jews to love their neighbors.

Rabbi Rudin makes an unexamined assumption in saying the appeal of the UC is only psychological. My own contacts with Unificationists suggest that while they appreciate and practice the loving warmth cited above, many of them genuinely believe the DP is true. Joseph Fichter, the Roman Catholic sociologist, says the overwhelming majority of the people who join new religions do so freely because it makes sense to them. While the secularist is embarrassed by the concept of a personal relationship with God, others find that it gives meaning and purpose to the rest of life. Even without that meaning and purpose, the encounter is an end in itself.[45]

One might note that there are those triumphalists in both Jewish and Christian circles who insist their religion is doctrinally superior and who will continue missionary efforts. But I suspect they will find less and less support for their position. What many people have not realized over the centuries of missionary activity is that Jews and Christians have been disrupting families all over the world whenever they converted an individual. This is especially true in cultures with close-knit family structures as in India and China. Exceptions might be places like Borneo where whole villages have converted, or the Indian pastor who told me that when an individual came for conversion, he or she was instructed to go back and bring their family with them into their new faith. But perhaps now that some American families have experienced the upset of having someone join a new tradition, they will be even less willing to support the proselytizing of the missionary enterprise than presently.

A secular society

It needs to be noted that organized religion may be fighting the times. Rev. Moon, then, may be just the scapegoat for the frustration these groups feel in the face of the paradox Rabbi Tanenbaum describes in the study cited earlier.[45A] He notes that humanity is both more unified and more fragmented. On the one hand, we live in a global village. On the other hand, the "globalization of the human consciousness has led to the undermining of dependencies on the more limited local loyalties, such as the nation-state." "By and large we do not dominate the structures (of society), rather they control us." "In the pursuit of personal meaning, there is a desire for wholeness, and for clarity about one's identity. It is no accident that there has emerged in recent years such a spontaneous growth of youth communes, encounter and human potential movements." He quotes Anton C. Zijderveld: "... societal control is no longer characterized by a family-like authority but dominated by bureaucratic neutrality and unresponsiveness. The individual often seems to be doomed to endure this situation passively, since the structures of society vanish in abstract air if he tries to grasp their very forces of control. No wonder that many seek refuge in one or another form of retreat... As a result, many modern men are turning away from the institutions of society and are searching for meaning, reality and freedom elsewhere."[46] The Unification Church, of course, offers a "family-like authority" within the context of a global organization, one of many parallels with Roman Catholicism. Why the UC should be condemned for responding to this human need is not clear.

Rudin emphasizes that legislation is not the answer. "I'm very fearful of a government agency defining for me what is religion." He adds that violating civil liberties (kidnapping and deprogramming) is not the answer either. The answer, as noted above, is for synagogues and churches to educate people in the context of a warm, accepting, genuinely caring community. This is commendable, from my perspective of civil liberties. His call then for congressional investigations is an aberration from this stated position, as are legal attempts to repress the UC. Unfortunately, his aberrant call, and the accusations of Nazism and Communism relate to the larger issue of discrimination and prejudice.[47]

PREJUDICE

Who is loyal?

Antisemitic literature abounds with such accusations. While accusing Jews of being Nazis and Communists, antisemitic literature also accuses Jews of loyalty to a foreign power, world Jewry, the state of Israel. The loyalty issue is an old one used against Jews. One could see it in Exodus

1:10. They were suspect in Rome because of the 'revolts' in 66–70 and 132–135 A.D. Jews have proven over and over again that they are loyal citizens.

The loyalty issue was used against Catholics in Reformation England. It was not settled until the Spanish Armada attacked in 1588. English Catholics fought loyally for Protestant England against Catholic Spain. That issue remains in this country and effectively helped block a Roman Catholic from the presidency until John F. Kennedy. The first Methodists were accused of being spies for the French against Mother England. Jesus was executed as a political figure, according to some Christian and Jewish interpreters. Christians have often been accused of disloyalty—by the Romans (it was an illegal religion) and by communist and third world countries. The latter know full well that when the missionaries arrived they had the Bible while the local people had the land. In short order, the local people had the Bible and...

In a recent lecture on the persecution of Jehovah's Witnesses, Dr. James Penton noted:

> As a prominent "come outer" church, at times even militantly depicting government, economics and existing churches as evil, Dr. Penton characterized the Jehovah's Witnesses as persecuted more than any other group outside of the Jews. Difficulties with flag saluting (idolatry for JW's) and their refusal to serve in WW I precipitated brutal reprisals in the United States during the 1920's according to Dr. Penton. The first organization banned under Hitler in Germany, many Jehovah's Witnesses were sent to their death in concentration camps during WW II. Most recently, Jehovah's Witnesses have suffered miserably in communist countries where, in Dr. Penton's words, "they hate us like poison."[48]

Who has the power?

The loyalty issue is not the only one used in the anti-movements. The power issue mentioned above is common. Anti-Catholicism sees Catholics gaining power to deal with heretic Protestants and for financial advantage, all of it on behalf of the Pope. Antisemitic literature frequently hints ominously at powerful Jewish interests who control the press and the government.[49] Orthodox Jews have believed the world will some day submit, voluntarily or otherwise, to a messianic dictatorship in Jerusalem. A recent publication referred to "the American Jewish Committee and other powerful Jewish groups..."[59] It was an early charge against

Christianity. Those who insist that we take the power issue seriously point out the explicit statements the various groups make regarding their world wide interests. These include Old Testament statements about all nations coming to Zion, New Testament statements about overcoming the world, Israeli statements that all Jews everywhere are citizens of Israel, the labor movement's call for workers of the world to unite, as well as the more well-known communist slogans, Nazi slogans, British Imperialism, the United States' Manifest Destiny, and other movements of yesteryear and today. All this is not to say that loyalty issues and power issues are to be ignored. The world did that to its sorrow with Hitler. But such a common accusation might be taken with a grain of salt.

Who has the money?

One extension of the political power issue is the question of economic power. Rev. Moon is accused of having a very high tax-free income, derived mainly from exploited members of the Movement. The source of the "information" is not given. In this connection, his personal lifestyle is attacked as being unseemly for a religious leader. The Pope, of course, has been accused of this for centuries. I assume the income of the Roman Catholic Church is high. I do not know what it is, nor do I know anyone else who knows. Jews are commonly accused of being wealthy. It will be a surprise to some to find that one of the main problems in American Jewry is helping the Jewish poor. I find people unwilling to believe there is such a problem. Sociological surveys indicate that Jews have the highest income in the U.S., with Catholics second and Episcopalians third.[51]

A controversy arose over the Billy Graham organization. A newspaper investigation revealed a $23 million fund which the paper said had not been previously revealed. The Graham organization denied secrecy but the Council of Better Business Bureaus noted that the Graham organization had never submitted to their willingness to audit it, along with 10,000 other non-profit groups the Bureau audits. The Oral Roberts Evangelistic Association is another Protestant group the Bureau had not been able to audit.[52]

The Mormons are said to have an income of $1 billion a year. The Mormon Church was once reviled and persecuted but has become one of the most respectable of U.S. religions. Its members include highly placed figures in the political, business and entertainment worlds.[53]

A report noted church and synagogue income in America to be $11 billion in a year when three major sports grossed only $221 million. The report says that in the '60's, church construction exceeded a billion dollars a year. A minister wrote to his congregation, urging their concern for the ill-housed of the nation. He wrote from an air-conditioned office in a church costing several million dollars.[54]

If Rev. Moon or the Unification Movement has money, this would not appear to be all that different from other religious groups except that the others have a great deal more.

Brainwashing children

We can note here, also, Tanenbaum's concern with reputed brainwashing and Rudin's fear that "they're out to get our kids." This reflects yet another ancient problem. Pogroms against the Jews were started on the pretext that a lost child had been taken by Jews. Christians are reported to have taken Jewish children and forcibly baptized them. Cardinal Newman said, "Give me a child until he's 8 and he'll be a Catholic for life." My mail includes an appeal for funds from a Protestant group for the evangelization of grammar school children, especially Catholics and Jews, with no protest from the AJC. Various other groups, such as gypsies, from time to time are also accused of being "out to get our children."[55] One should note that the "children" in the Unification Movement are old enough to vote. Their average age is reported to be 28. The group includes older people such as the 80 year old woman converted at age 78. But the point here is that once again an antisemitic charge against the Jews has been diverted to the UC.

Miscellaneous charges

In addition to the issues of loyalty, power, money and children, the "out-group" is accused of being liars (especially common against Jews, Jesuits and Japanese). It comes as no surprise that the same charge is levelled against the UC. Sexual aberration is another common theme. Both reputed excessive sexuality and abstinence are a source of condemnation. One excuse for imposing the ghetto on the Jews was Christian fear of Jewish sexuality. This also appears in hate literature against Blacks, Mormons, Catholic priests, Japanese, and others.[56] These traditional charges are now diverted to the UC.

Cast a wide net

Thus, the accusations that the UC is antisemitic and non-Christian are set in a wider context. An insurance advertisement referred to the Egyptian Pharoah Akhenaton and his monotheism.[57] After Akhenaton's "death, the 'good old days' of multiple gods returned and it was left to the Hebrews, Christians and Moslems to develop this concept. Akhenaton was obviously a man born too soon, about 1400 years too soon." Whether Moses was a monotheist or not is debated in scholarly circles. Many scholars admit there was definitely monotheism by the sixth century B.C. To imply that monotheism did not arrive until Jesus can be taken as antisemitism. It denigrates the achievement of pre-Jesus Hebrews and Jews in the 1400 years between Akhenaton and Jesus.

"Six United Methodist executives have urged President Carter to consider applying human rights criteria to foreign aid to Israel, based on reports of torture of Arab prisoners there.... The report... charged that torture has been regularly used against Palestinians during the 10 years of the Israeli occupation of the West Bank, to pacify the population and obtain information.... The U.M. executives declared that 'despite the denials by the Israeli government, the fact remains that no open and independent inquiry into the matter has been permitted'." Is this antisemitism? Some say yes.[58] It should be noted that American Jews historically have been largely on the side of civil rights, a position Rabbi Rudin affirms for himself. It should be noted also that Israeli civil libertarians have also protested their government's actions. It will be recalled that Rev. Moon has stated unequivocally that he supports the state of Israel.

THE HOLOCAUST

"The Unification Movement regards the Land of Israel as a haven for the survivors and a sanctuary for all those individual Jews who are trying to escape physical persecution and religious, racial or national oppression."[59] It's an odd twist, if the above is true, that physical persecution and oppression has now fallen on the Arabs. At any rate, Rudin noted, "the sole mention of the Nazi Holocaust" in *Divine Principle*. He adds, "Moreover, the Holocaust, when one-third of the Jewish people was murdered by the Nazis, is gratuitously mentioned by Rev. Moon, and nowhere in *Divine Principle* do we find any calls for repentance or for self-examination in the face of six million dead. The United Methodist Church (UMC), in a 1972 statement, expressed 'clear repentance and a resolve to repudiate past injustice and to seek its elimination in the present. But not Rev. Moon."[60] But the UMC is one of those cited in Strober's study as continuing to have antisemitic elements in its educational material for little children and the UMC sided with the NCC in claiming human rights for Arabs, along with Israel's right to exist, which is antisemitism according to the AJC.

In his "The ambiguity of vision," Clyde A. Holbrook notes that without vision, the people perish. But "with certain kinds of visions the people do in fact perish...(for example) the vision of Hitler, with his chatter of Lebensraum, blood and soil, and a solution to the Jewish problem. That was a vision which engulfed most of the so-called civilized world in its horror. Millions died because of that vision."[61] Some 29 million died from 1933–1945, according to the Anti-Defamation League of B'nai B'rith.[62] The six million Jews were slaughtered because they were Jews. The gypsies were slaughtered because they were gypsies. The mentally ill and physically handicapped were slaughtered because they were. The slaughter of Jehovah's Witnesses was mentioned earlier. The incredible evil of Hitler and the Holocaust cannot be overemphasized. Is Rev. Moon antisemitic for slighting the Holocaust?

Rev. Moon did not in fact slight the Holocaust in his 18 December 1976 statement. Whether DP should be expected to show similar sensitivity is highly questionable. It originated prior to 1954, being supposedly a compendium of, or a systematic presentation of, the thought of Rev. Moon, as compiled by Eu Hyo Won, one of his disciples.[63] At that time, the persecution and murder of Christians by Japanese and Communist occupation forces was a major, recent and present issue. It is hardly surprising that the torture and murder of Korean Christians gets more space than the Holocaust. But it is not simply that this volume originated prior to 1954, before the Holocaust became popular. It's that great numbers of Christian works do not deal adequately with the Holocaust, even *since* 1954. Even numbers of Jewish works are silent or inadequate on the Holocaust. Are these *all* guilty of antisemitism?

The Eisenberg article cited above was published in 1964, *ten years* after DP. The authors quote Augustin Cardinal Bea as saying, "It would be impossible for the Council to be quiet after the holocaust of the war years. Six million people cannot be wiped out and the Church be silent." This of course was *20 years* after the Holocaust and 23 million other dead are not even gratuitously mentioned! The same article noted that "Many U.S. Catholics eagerly await a directive." Why wait for over 20 years? This is not to downgrade Catholic reaction to the Holocaust or Catholic efforts on how to relate to the Jews. It's to emphasize that the new climate of Christian detente or rapport with Judaism is largely a post-World War II phenomenon, even though it has pre-war roots. And it is largely since 1960 that many of the statements heralding a new day have been produced. Holocaust theology is a "Johnny come lately." Perhaps it has to be that way. It has taken time to contemplate and absorb the monumental evil, let alone to make an adequate response, which still has not been made. An adequate response may be simply impossible.[64]

Many of Ulrich Simon's relatives died in concentration camps. His father died in Auschwitz. He himself got out of Germany in 1933. In England, he became a priest. His book, *A Theology of Auschwitz* (Atlanta: John Knox Press) was not published until 1967. He notes the need is *not* felt by all. He talks about it as "facts which the human eye finds too repulsive to see and which the mind cannot fathom." He found no answer for the deep destructive force which wills its own and everyone else's enslavement. Borowitz claims that American Jews did not come to terms with the Holocaust until 1967–1973. Sophie K. Black has only now come to terms with it (1981). She and her family got out of Germany eleven days after "Kristallnacht."

If Jews and Christians who have experienced the Holocaust first hand need so much time to come up with "no answer," it seems absurd and even bizarre to expect Koreans in 1954, fresh out of a Communist torture camp and only a few years out from under the Japanese yoke, to deal adequately with the Holocaust only nine years afterwards. In fact, it is amazing that DP mentions the Holocaust at all. Borowitz says American Jews knew what was going on and silently accepted the decision of Allied leaders to do nothing when something might have been done to prevent, slow or stop it. Perhaps Rudin's real quarrel is with American Jews. They, we, are currently allowing Ethiopian Jews to die like flies, according to news reports. Israel, the supposed refuge for survivors of the Nazi death camps, will not let these Falashas, who are Black, enter Israel in any significant numbers. The Holocaust of 50 years ago is trivialized while the genocide of today is ignored.

Of course, it is a commonplace of ethnocentrism that we expect others to be supersensitive about our concerns while we are totally insensitive to others. That's probably one reason Rabbi Hillel found it necessary to say, "Do not do unto others that which is hurtful to yourself." "Do you know what hurts me?" Now we *all* need to *practice* Hillel's wide ethical standard. We might begin by allowing the Falashas to enter Israel and the U.S.[64A]

We can of course still honestly ask if Moon's statement is sufficient. The Rudins quote, "Arthur Robins, 22, a Jewish former 'Moonie,' (who) says he was taught that Hitler had to kill six million Jews as 'indemnity' because they did not accept Jesus as the Christ. Robins ominously warns, 'Moon is building an army, not a church.' "[65] The concept is hardly novel. Lincoln's Second Inaugural Address reflected the idea that "the Civil War was a divine judgment intended to purge the nation of slavery."[66] Both Christians and Jewish leaders have suggested the Holocaust was punishment for the sins of the Jews.[67] These leaders have not been condemned for antisemitism.

I have problems with all of these concepts. They reflect a concept of God which appears in the Bible, both Hebrew and Greek Scriptures. Personally, I find the idea of God as one who slaughters millions of people, an abhorrent concept whether we are considering the Genesis Flood, Hebrew wars, the final Revelation, or for that matter "The War Between the Sons of Light and the Sons of Darkness" (the Dead Sea Scrolls), the Crusades, or the War to make the World Safe for Democracy (World War I). That it is a common Christian and Jewish concept does not make it any more palatable. On the other hand, I'm not sure my own concept of the evil of mankind is any more adequate, and, apart from the free action of the laws of nature, my concept of "evil" in nature and the death and loss from natural disasters is even less adequate. I'm not sure an adequate Holocaust theology is possible, though it has stimulated much thought and writing.[68]

On the other hand, I see Rev. Moon's unequivocal statement on the Holocaust and its victims as a major sensitization. If Robins presents an accurate picture of what happens within the Unification Movement, the Movement has its work cut out for it, for it has not yet caught up with its leader's opinion. While not questioning Robins' veracity, I'm aware that I would not go to an antisemite, or to the antisemitic hate literature, for an accurate understanding of Judaism. If we rely on antisemites to give us an accurate picture of Judaism, Jews could justifiably question our motives. Relying on ex-Moonies and antisemites may produce more hate literature but it will not give honest understanding.

In the meanwhile, both Christians and Jews need a deeper sensitivity to the Holocaust and to the larger issue of genocide. While the Bible does indeed contain the concept of "cherem," the ban, the *total* destruction (holocaust) of people (Joshua 6:17; I Samuel 15:3), I believe that this denies and contradicts the fundamental basis of the Judeo-Christian tradition which says, "Do not do unto others that which is hurtful to thyself," and "love thy neighbor as thyself." For example, the genocide which has been historically practiced against the American Indian, should call forth a "clear repentance and a resolve to repudiate past injustice and to seek its elimination in the present." We should be concerned about this murderous discrimination whether it is practiced against Jews, Indians, Blacks, Arabs, Latvians, Tibetans, Vietnamese, Armenians, or Moonies.

COLLECTIVES

The indemnity theme is also objectionable to Jorge Lara-Braud. In the preliminary release of the CFO paper, he noted that "*Divine Principle* contains a legalistic theology of indemnity in which grace and forgiveness play little part. The central figures of providence fail even when they are not believed—a vicarious failure is certainly not central to Christian affirmation. That is, Christ failed because the Jews did not believe in him, and put him to death. That is double indemnity indeed, and its penalties are continuing anti-semitism and the requirement that another savior come to complete the salvation of Jesus Christ."[69] S. Mark Heim believes that the *Principle's* "whole scheme of history is built around the concept of 'indemnity'—that is, around humanity's struggle to fulfill its portion of reparation for the Fall. The debt humanity owes God cannot be paid in full. But if an individual can, through complete devotion, discharge 5 per cent of his or her portion of the debt, God will wipe out the rest." He goes on to claim the two world wars, including the Holocaust, to be a necessary part of "God's plan for restoration" according to the *Principle*.[70]

Heim's analysis suggests there is a rather considerable amount of grace involved in the *Principle's* scheme of restoration. The ransom theory is an old interpretation of the crucifixion (Matt. 20:8; Mark 10:45; I Tim. 2:6). Regarding our human efforts, Lara-Braud's spiritual ancestors, the Scotch Presbyterians, worked as though everything depended on them while they prayed as though everything depended on God. This is a rather neat solution to the paradox. But the point is that indemnity is an old problem in Christian theology. We are called to work out our salvation in fear and trembling (Phil. 2:12). According to Protestant interpretations, Catholicism was sunk in works of righteousness, of which indulgences were only a part. Protestantism itself has not avoided the problem. The Puritan work ethic may be seen as part of this issue. A major concept in Judaism has been the long held belief that if Jews everywhere were to obey God completely for only one day, the Messiah would come. Classical Jewish tradition demands man exert himself to the full even while relying on God for the final fulfillment.[71] A major strand of biblical thought is that suffering is the result of sin (John 9:2). The call for repentance by the Hebrew prophets and in the New Testament and throughout the Judeo-Christian tradition, has often carried the corollary that sin brings destruction (Num. 16). Where present sin does not seem adequate to explain the suffering, it is often ascribed to the parents or ancestors of the sufferer (Ex. 20:50, John 9:2). That includes collective guilt for sin, a biblical concept that has also been carried into the present day. Scores of examples are at hand. WASPS, Jews, Blacks, Catholics, Hispanics, and many others have been accused of collective guilt. Both ancestral guilt and collective guilt were already being called into question by Ezekiel (18:20) as well as in the Johannine (9:2) literature. Yet it is common knowledge that the Israelis have taken actions against families and whole villages in their attempts to stem what they call terrorism. Arab reprisals indiscriminately kill and maim Israeli civilians and military, little children and tourists. It was commonplace a short time ago for at least some Americans to say that the only good Indian is a dead one. Europeans came to this area, stole Indian land, and then slaughtered the Indians when the Indians objected. Double indemnity indeed. The whole sorry record is certainly inhuman and reflects man's inhumanity to man.[72] If those condemning the UC for double indemnity are actually opposed to double indemnity, they have many examples to deal with, including their own constituency. I wish them well but suggest they clean up their own house as Tanenbaum suggests Christians begin their proselytizing by first converting their own people.

The use of the collective is very common in literature (which of course does not make it right). It often violates the niceties of historical accuracies. Writing on "The Living Faith of Judaism," Roman Catholic scholar John B. Sheerin recognizes that "the church began as a Jewish religious group. Early Christians thought of themselves as true Jews but did not want to be identified with the Pharisees, the Sadducees or some other Jewish group. Eventually they ran into difficulty because they admitted Gentiles into their ranks without requiring them to observe Jewish laws. *The other Jews* feared that this nonobservance would dilute or corrupt

Judaism." The result was mutual hostilities.[73]

We don't really know whether observance was any more strict then than now. Probably only a minority were observant, then as now. To treat non-Christian Jews as a block is historically questionable.

The Jewish scholar Geza Vermes does the same in explaining why the Gentile Church retained the title of Christ.[74] It was for polemical value in fighting the Jews who refused "en bloc" to be impressed by the messianic claims of Christianity. Yet he himself notes that the disciples were all Jewish. The truth is, we do not have accurate records of how many Jews accepted those messianic claims. Some did, some did not. Keep in mind that only a minority of Jews even lived in Palestine. The Diaspora had been under way for over 600 years. Without mass media or TV, only a minority of the minority even knew Jesus existed.[75] At what point in the ensuing centuries would a majority of non-Christian Jews have come to know of Jesus' existence? Even then, or now, there is no "en bloc" in Judaism or Christianity, either one! There never has been and I doubt there ever will be. The "en bloc" is another myth that Cox might well add to his deep structures of religious persecution.

A similar problem appears in David Singer's study in which he notes that "throughout this whole period, needless to say, Jews have steadfastly rejected Christianity's Messianic claim."[76] As an historical absolute, this is inaccurate. One could similarly question his, "Jews, therefore, have no other choice but to reject the Christological Jesus." At least some Jews have thought otherwise. Some (perhaps many/most) Christians do also.[77] They reject Singer's Christological (divine) Jesus and see Jesus as a quite human teacher, with or without messianic status. Christologically speaking, liberal Christians and liberal Jews have much in common. But the point here is that "The Jews" is almost always an historically inaccurate designation, for neither Christian Jews (spiritual semites if you will, to quote Pius XII's 1938 statement[78]) nor non-Christian Jews (whether Orthodox, Conservative, Reform, Reconstructionist, atheist, agnostic, secular, or something else) are an "en bloc," a monolithic entity, and never have been.

Historically speaking, "The Jews" did not, and do not reject Jesus. To say it is historically inaccurate, whether the person saying it is Jewish or Christian or neither. If this historically inaccurate statement is antisemitism, then that charge is laid against some Jews as well as some Christians. It is laid against the New Testament as well as DP, and parenthetically it must be said again that the Tenak or the Old Testament has *numerous* statements on the failure of Israel. If accusing the ancient Hebrews of failure is antisemitism, then the Hebrew Scriptures are antisemitic. Now there may be some value in labeling so many antisemitic, but I wonder. It is, of course, instructive to keep in mind.[79]

WHO FAILED?

The World Council of Churches urged its member churches to resist antisemitism. "In Christian teaching, the historic events which led to the Crucifixion should not be so presented as to fasten upon the Jewish people of today responsibilities which belong to our corporate humanity and not to one race or community. Jews were the first to accept Jesus, and Jews are not the only ones who do not yet recognize him."[80]

Speaking at Madison Square Garden on Sept. 18, 1974, Rev. Moon noted that Jesus came to his own people. "Then what happened? History is the witness. We did not know him. We rejected him, rebelled against him and finally crucified him on the cross... It was in ignorance that we crucified Jesus Christ. It was God's will that His people accept the Messiah. But we crucified him instead. And then Christians 'passed the buck' by saying that was the will of God."[81]

In my view, this kind of historicizing is an appropriate way to interpret Scripture. The prophets denounced the sins of the first Israel. These sins have a striking similarity to the sins of the second Israel. Instead of using the prophets for antisemitic purposes, it is appropriate to appropriate their message for our time. This is in fact what Rauschenbusch and the Social Gospellers have done.[82]

In ascribing the crucifixion to us, Rev. Moon stands in that tradition. This understanding of history goes back to the Hebrew Scriptures themselves where over and over again, the word is that such and such did not happen to our fathers who came out of Egypt, but to us. Rev. Moon is quite biblical.

Early in the Christian tradition, Christian interpreters understood themselves to be the new Chosen People, the new or the second Israel. DP focuses on Christianity, the second Israel, in two major areas—the historical period from Jesus to the modern era, and the present. The historical period parallels the Abraham to Ezra period of the first Israel. The second Israel also suffered persecution. The second Israel also had the option of obedience and faithfulness, says DP. The second Israel also 'blew it,' especially in the medieval period. Kings and priests and other leaders have failed in the second Israel as in the first. Incidently, Jesus failed, as had Abraham, Moses and John the Baptist. Jesus' failure differed from theirs in that he did not do something rebellious, according to DP. Rather, his failure was caused by John the Baptist (in some passages) or the Jewish people (in other passages). The result of Jesus' failure was that his resurrection brings spiritual salvation but not physical or material salvation.[83] This has been the Christian message for 2,000 years. Anyone who says the physical world is already saved has obviously not been out in the world.

Today, DP says we have come to the time of the Second Coming or the Age of the Lord of the Second Advent. The *Principle* contends that the Lord of the Second Advent will come as the first one did. The first one is Jesus. He did not come on Clouds of Heaven. He was born in human form. The Lord of the Second Advent will also be born in human form. The Lord of the First Advent was rejected by the first Israel. The Lord of the Second Advent will be rejected by the second Israel. This paves the way for the advent of the third Israel, identified with the Korean people. This time there will be no failure, for God is determined that His will shall be fulfilled.[84]

Virtually nothing is said in DP about the continuance of the first Israel since the time of Jesus.[85] Christian theologians have wrestled with this question for centuries. DP doesn't deal with it directly. Similarly, virtually nothing is said about the continuance of the second Israel after the arrival of the Lord of the Second Advent. What is said, is that God wants all of His children to be saved (II Peter 3:9). This takes in the first and second Israels, the rest of mankind, and even the devil.

If all people are to be saved, what's the purpose or the role or function of the Israels of mankind? They are or were to be channels of God's saving grace. Salvation is not only the spiritual brought by the faithfulness of Jesus, on the foundation of Jewish faithfulness. It is also material. So through the Third Israel and the Lord of the Second Advent, God will bring His Kingdom on earth. The physical and material world will also be saved.

Earlier, and continuing coterminous with Israel's failure, is the failure of all mankind. DP presents the Fall of Man and the entrance of Satan into human existence as the interpretive focus of the Bible, and of all human enterprise—philosophy, history, politics, science. There is strong agreement here with a major segment of Christianity, including Lara-Braud's Presbyterianism. If the interpretive concept here is considered 'anti-', it is anti-humanity rather than antisemitic. DP however, insists that man has the capacity to obey God, an insistence in agreement with a major segment of Judaic thought as well as a mainstream of Christian thought (Pelagius, Arminius, Wesley). Some Presbyterians stand in the Augustinian-Calvinist tradition that man is incapable of obeying God... condemned to sin and condemned because he sins. Double indemnity? As noted earlier, DP also states that God has predestined all to be saved, in contrast to Presbyterian or Calvinist doctrines which claim God has predestined (many or most?) people to be damned.

My own orientation to Christianity does not emphasize The Fall. I note in passing that neither the Hebrew Scriptures nor Judaism emphasizes this doctrine. It might be called an invention of Christianity except for the uncertain authorship of such works as "The Life of Adam and Eve."[86] But even here, with this doctrine, we are concerned with *some* Christians rather than all of them. The Fall has received much more emphasis from the tradition of Augustine and Calvin than from Pelagius and Arminius. Through Methodism, I stand closer to the latter tradition within Christianity. I suspect that Rev. Moon stands closer to the former through his Presbyterian antecedents, Jorge Lara-Braud's antecedents as well.

In this paper, the origins of Rev. Moon's thought or of the ideas expounded in DP are of concern only as they relate to the Israels of the *Principle*. However, the concern with The Fall, it seems to me, influences the subsequent interpretation of biblical data. It brings an emphasis on failure, for example. In a way, this is a logical outgrowth of the millennialism represented by Rev. Moon's concern with the End time at hand. One can explain the arrival of the End at this time by reviewing the failure of all previous history, including the first and second Israels. And indeed, while not myself a follower of Rev. Moon, I can see where one could objectively ask, if either the first or the second Israels had been obedient and faithful, would not the world be in better condition? Maybe it's time for a third Israel... Note, however, that Unificationism itself is positive. The failure is humanity's—the glory is God's. He *will* restore his creation. Unificationists believe in a better world tomorrow. That better world will include all three Israels and not just some people but all humanity.[86A]

THE SOURCE OF CONTEMPT

There are two other issues that must be dealt with. One is the question of whether Christianity is inherently antisemitic. In some places, Rev. Moon claims to be Christian. If all Christians are antisemitic, he presumably is, too. If all Christian groups are antisemitic, and if the UC is Christian, then it presumably is antisemitic. The CFO committee said the UC was non-Christian. If this be true, it and its parent NCC are antisemitic while the UC is not! In her book, *Faith and Fratricide: The Theological Roots of Anti-Semitism*,[87] Rosemary Ruether claims that Christianity is inherently antisemitic. It is in the very soul of Christianity and one cannot say Jesus is Messiah without implicitly or explicitly also saying "and the Jews be damned." I noted earlier that antisemitism in a society means that that society is suffering from a sick soul. If Ruether is right, Christianity is really sick, perhaps what the Danish philosopher, Soren Kierkegaard called a sickness unto death.

Others suggest that "the source of Christian anti-Judaism, is not Christian thinking per se, but the political purposes to which it is put. Doctrinal formulation (or reformulation) will not end anti-Judaism, much less anti-Semitism. History shows both to be complex phenomena which depend heavily on political, social and economic factors, as well as the intellectual and theological developments which give expression to them."[88]

Both studies point to the New Testament as part of the problem. This collection has been labeled antisemitic on other occasions. A segment of the issue turns on the Gospel of John. Christians have long been guilty of using John and other portions of the New Testament for antisemitic purposes. This is a misuse of the New Testament. In my view, however, if the antisemites did not have the New Testament to quote, they would have quoted something else, as they have invented other rationalizations for their activity. There's abundant evidence for this in pogroms and in Nazi ideology.

The New Testament is a collection of Jewish writings on and by a branch of Judaism. When John or others refer to "the Jews" not accepting Jesus as the Messiah, we are dealing with a family fight. The authors are Jews talking to other Jews. So too Markus Barth in his *Jesus the Jew*. The phenomenon is well known in ethnic history. The commonest example is the Americans who damn the foreigners coming into the United States. Historically, *all* Americans are foreigners, i.e., immigrants. Historically, *all* the early Christians were Jews. So "the Jews" in the New Testament are actually "other" Jews who have not joined the Jewish movement which was later called Christianity. This is quite clear in the writings of Paul, who emphasizes his own Jewishness. However, he wanted so much that his people, "the Jews," should accept his brand of Judaism, i.e., Christianity, that he was willing to be damned himself, if that would help swing the vote. Some Jews had accepted Christianity while most of the Jews did not know it existed. But Paul's attitude contrasts strongly with the Jews of Qumran who, as noted earlier, planned to exterminate *all* other Jews *and* all Gentiles in the War Between the Sons of Light (them) and the Sons of Darkness (others). If the Qumran sectarians had won instead of the Jesus sectarians, there would only be Qumranites. The entire human race would be killed except for them.

Olson notes that at first all the Christians were Jews. Then they expanded to include Godfearers. The third expansion was to Gentiles. The last brought in pre-Christian and anti-Christian antipathy toward the Jews. Olson's scheme may be a bit too neat, since history doesn't usually function so succinctly. But he is "right on" when he says: "The Hebraic prophets, among them the apostles, spoke self-critically as Jews to fellow Jews. The Gentile Christians misused these strictures as anti-Jewish polemic in the same way that they twisted Jesus' dispute with the Pharisees. As Jocz puts it, the *internal* conflicts within Judaism were *externalized* as conflicts between Jews and Gentiles."[89]

Idinopulos and Ward, among others, see the development of antisemitism as coming especially after 70 A.D., when it was politically expedient for Christians to distinguish themselves from other Jews. One thrust of this argument is that if antisemitism is historically conditioned (e.g., by power politics), it can change. If it is endemic, Christianity can only avoid antisemitism by committing "hari-kiri." Some indeed see this as the honorable thing to do, though it is not likely to happen. It would not, of course, make antisemitism disappear.[90]

Speaking of origins, it is worth noting that contempt for others is not limited to Christian writers. The Greeks thought all others to be barbarians. There's a Jewish tradition about waking up and thanking God you were not born a "Goy" (that's all the rest of us), a slave (some versions say "a dog"), or a woman (that's half of humanity).[91] The Judeans looked with contempt upon the Galileans.[92] "Glossolalia is the road to senility and loss of reason," may be one man's opinion alright. Putting it in print may represent contempt for 60 million charismatics.[93]

Even the newspapers seemed surprised by the vituperous attack on the Unification Church by Catholics, Protestants and Jews.[94] It has been observed that "eclesiastics have always had a certain penchant for vitriolic language... Fortunately latitudinarian views have accompanied the birth of the ecumenical movement... and heresy hunting has been increasingly confined to the ignorant, the bigoted and the backward remnant of the clergy. By and large the motto has become: 'In essentials, unity; in non-essentials, liberty; in all things charity.' What else would be appropriate for a religion whose..." core is love? Jesus has been "accused of being an antichrist, an immoralist and a blasphemer."[95] His People the Jews likewise. His People the Unificationists likewise. How sad.

Nationalities, races, tribes, families, and individuals have been holders of and recipients of, contempt. Perhaps it's endemic in humanity. But to believe that would lead *me* to have contempt for humanity, so I decline. As the song in "South Pacific" put it, "you have to be carefully taught to hate." Scientific studies show that "prejudice, like any social attitude, is *learned*."[96] Like contemporary Jews, I tend to be an optimist in regard to human nature.[97]

BROTHERHOOD, OR...

Rev. Moon describes the Unification Movement as the younger brother of Christianity and Judaism. This has led some to call him arrogant for assuming his movement of 30 years is equal to one of 2,000 and another of 4,000 years of age. Others have noted the curious twist that this self-identification makes the Unification Church non-Christian, or at least something other than Christian. This is supported by the description in *Divine Principle* of the three Israels with Korea (*not* curiously enough, the Unification Movement) as the third Israel. Self-identification, of course, is an old problem. Jews continue to struggle with the issue of who is a Jew.[98]

The Christian struggle in recent decades has been muted. One implication of the CFO document is that the CFO determines who is Christian, and the Unification movement falls short. It would have been convenient to have such a body around these last 2,000 years and thus to have avoided the murderous infighting of the ecumenical councils, the wars, the Inquisitions, heresy trials, the Reformation, and so forth. Of course, those who have struggled against such authorities over the centuries will decline the convenience.[99]

The concept of "brother" is widespread. The Strober work cited earlier is titled, *Portrait of an Elder Brother*. The elder brother of course is Judaism.

Those who know the story of the prodigal son, will remember the elder brother as stiff-necked and unforgiving, which is not my experience with Jews. Ruether's title also implies brotherhood. "We are siblings," says Episcopalian Lawrence M. Coombe.[100] So Rev. Moon is not alone in this concept. I was taught that both Christianity and Judaism grew out of an earlier Hebrew religion, so the two groups are indeed siblings of one mother. There is some historical accuracy in this if one sees Pharisaic Rabbinic Judaism and Christianity as the two forms of Judaism to survive the devastations of 70 and 135 A.D. My alternative is to see Judaism as the mother and Christianity as the daughter. The Freudian use of the Electra complex thus becomes a useful way of understanding antisemitism. The daughter wishes to possess the father (God) and thus must displace the mother. Since the mother declines to go away and die, the daughter's wishes become murderous.[101]

The analogy fails of course, because God is a spirit and not a sexual partner. Because he (or she) is spirit, Jews, Christians, or anyone else can worship him. That, of course, includes the followers of Rev. Moon.

The *Divine Principle* sees mankind's failures predominating over humanity's successes. But now the end is at hand. The millenium is here and with it God's Restoration of the original Paradisical bliss of Eden, which God intended all along for us, His children. What's more, this time, there will be no failure. And what's more, all God's children will be saved.

I deeply appreciate this messianic vision and fervently hope the final apocalypse will be the symbolic one Rev. Moon describes rather than a physical Armageddon which he recognizes as possible. As we await this blessed (I hope) event, there are two writers who speak to our condition. One is Marc Tanenbaum. He notes that:

> ... a vast yearning for human-size communities in which the individual can relate to another person... face-to-face... in an environment of caring, shared concern and mutual confirmation...[102] Never before in human history... have Judaism and Christianity had an opportunity such as the present one to translate their Biblical theologies of Creation—and the unity of mankind under the fatherhood of God—into actual experience... the Biblical theology of redemption contributed to a messianic conception of history, which conditioned Biblical man to responsibility for the events of history...[103] Thus a primary issue on the agenda of the human family is helping build a united human community that respects diversity and difference as a permanent good, quite clearly as a God-given good... The second priority concern... (is) the role of religious educators in helping our people to create and experience genuine community... The conscious efforts to

restore an appreciation of the sacred and the transcendent in the lives of individuals and communities in the face of dehumanizing bureaucracies[104] might well become one of the most important tasks of religious education... (We) must delve... into the core questions of existence. There we confront the mystery of existence, of the marvel of the earth and mankind calling to new modes of selfhood with integrity, and of fellowship with compassion. Within this limited terrestrial enterprise, we sometimes glimpse and feel the all-embracing mystery.[105]

Rabbi Tanenbaum notes further that:

... if Jews and Christians want to consider seriously their mutual relationships, it is not sufficient that they declare generalized sentiments of reciprocal regard. Genuine caring between groups, as between individuals, presupposes a willingness to enter into the life situation of the other, and to be present with concern and support at the moment when the other person or group is hurting.[106] As human beings, Christians and Jews share a universal agenda... They are both concerned about eliminating wars and establishing peace; about overcoming racial injustices and ending the scourges of poverty, illiteracy, and disease; about ecology and preserving the quality of life; about nation-building and economic development in the Third World; about closing the gap between the "have" and the "have-not" nations...; about reordering our national priorities... The "Judeo-Christian" value system... orients Jews and Christians in a special, distinctive way toward the universe... The biblical ground of these monotheistic faiths unite their adherents in a theology of creation which affirms the unity of the human family under the sovereignty of a transcendent Creator-God; a shared reverence for the prophets of Israel who require justice and righteousness and therefore impose an obligation of respect for the dignity of every person and of building a society based on caring and compassion." Why? To the end "that all the people of the earth may know that the Lord is God, and that there is none else." (I Kings 8:60) [107]

The second person is Dr. Young Oon Kim, Unificationist theologian. Speaking to the students of the Unification Theological Seminary, she said:

First, let me emphasize the crucial importance of seminary training as an intellectual disciple... Having said this, I must insist on something even more important. I want you to have an epoch-making experience in your life meeting the living God face-to-face, a heart-warming experience of the truth of *Divine Principle*. (Note that "The divine principle is the principle of creation. Creation is the reality of existence and its movement toward perfection.")[108] This kind of experience will be the fountain for a passionate desire to share God's love and truth with others... Only through spiritual development based on direct confrontation with God and only through your magnetic personal quality can you get your "heart strangely warmed" and keep it warm... The eagerness to help others, a genuine concern for people, a sensitivity to others' needs and a readiness to serve others—these are the ingredients which create a magnetic personality. All these are derived from one's deep experience with God and passionate love for Him. If you really feel what Schweitzer calls "reverence for life" and if you have a burning desire to love others, you will have discovered the secret of radiant living.[109]

It would seem that a Jewish theologian and a Unification theologian have the same aims, goals and purposes. They might sit down and discuss them. They might find they have more in common, more on which they agree, than on which they disagree. One of the things on which they *agree* is the evil of antisemitism. They also agree on the evil of denigrating the religious faith of another.[110] Do not do unto others that which is hurtful to thyself, said Rabbi Hillel. Rabbi Tanenbaum surely does not want to do unto others that which is hurtful to himself.[111] Let the dialogue begin...

NOTES

The following have been abbreviated in the text:

ACM—Anti-Cult Movement, also known as the Anti-Religion Movement

B&S—David G. Bromley and Anson D. Shupe. *The Moonies in America*. Beverly Hills: Sage, 1979.

CC—*Christian Century*

CFO—Commission on Faith and Order

CHE—Chronicle of Higher Education

DP—*Divine Principle*

IB—*Interpreter's Bible*

IDB—*Interpreter's Dictionary of the Bible*

LCMS—Lutheran Church—Missouri Synod

NB—Jacob Needleman and George Baker, eds. *Understanding the New Religions*. NY: The Seabury Press, 1978.

NCC—National Council of Churches of Christ in America

S&B—Anson D. Shupe, Jr. and David C. Bromley. *The New Vigilantes: Deprogrammers, Anti-Cultists, and the New Religions*. Beverly Hills: Sage, 1980.

UC—Unification Church

UMC—United Methodist Church

UMR—United Methodist Reporter

WSI—Bryant Wilson, ed. *The Social Impact of New Religious Movements*. NY: Rose of Sharon Press, 1981.

1. The references here are to the Second Edition (1973) of *Divine Principle* in English translation. It is published by the Holy Spirit Association for the Unification of World Christianity, commonly known as the Unification Church (hereafter UC). The UC was founded in 1954 by Rev. Sun Myung Moon. The movement and DP stem from a revelation in 1936 in which Jesus Christ appeared to him and told him to finish his (Jesus') work on earth, and Rev. Moon's subsequent thought and experience. DP was compiled by a disciple, Eu Hyo Won and extensively revised by, among others, Dr. Young Oon Kim. It is currently being revised again. While DP might be said to represent Rev. Moon's thought or the core of the revelation, the book is not literally his words though it might have been closer to being that in the original Korean language in which it was compiled.

2. *The Many Faces of Anti-Semitism* (NY: The American Jewish Committee, 1967).

3. Foreword, p. 5, Gerald S. Strober, *Portrait of the Elder Brother*, NY: AJC and the National Conference of Christians and Jews, 1972. Jacques Barzun once referred to the vogue words that almost always mean nothing but a temporary vacancy of the mind. On "patterns of excess" and the resulting faulty reasoning, cf. Rabbi Marc H. Tanenbaum, "Some Current Mythologies and World Community," *Theology Digest* 19 (Winter '71), 325–333.

4. *The Many Faces...*, p. 6. I would personally prefer to state this: "The way the powerless are treated..." whether the powerless are Jews or goyim, European or Asian, Black or White, etc. The last comment on antisemites is from T. W. Adorno, *et al.*, *The Authoritarian Personality* (NY: Harper & Brothers, 1950), p. 2. Applied to our present study, this hypothesis says the clue to anti-Unificationism is in the anti-Moonies rather than the Unificationists. On p. 42, the Adorno text refers to an antisemitic ideology. His subject spoke of Jews as if they were all alike and they are to assimilate but the subject won't accept them if they do. Unificationists are described as look-alike robots. When they try to be like others, they are accused of trying to legitimize the UC. The Adorno study (p. 971) comments on the contempt the authoritarian personality has for whatever is relegated to the bottom. Contempt is a common attitude of the anti-Moonies.

5. Arnold Forster and Benjamin R. Epstein, *The New Anti-Semitism* (NY: McGraw-Hill, 1974), p. xii. It is often the powerless who are wronged and hurt. My neighbors include Jews, Unificationists and many others. I would prefer that none be hurt.

6. Marc H. Tanenbaum, "Do You Know What Hurts Me?," *Event* (Feb '72), 4–8. Maurice Ogden's poem, "Hangman" makes the same point: "First the alien, then the Jew... I did no more than you let me do." Lest the reader consider this old hat, take note that a liberal American theological seminary had a debate in 1982 (*not* 1942). The issue was whether we should support the civil rights of those with whom we disagree theologically. Niemoller's attitude is still with us and Roger Williams' fight for religious freedom must continue.

7. Abe D. Jones, Jr., "Cults hold lesson for religious faiths," *The Greensboro Record*, 12 Feb '77, A5. This is not a unanimous opinion. A friend claims that Americans love to challenge one another's faith. The history of persecution because of one's religion runs from Roger Williams to this morning's newspaper. This suggests many challenges to other people's faith. "Religious Persecution in America" by Denis Collins, 22 Feb '82, unpublished.

8. Lincoln said a nation cannot exist half slave and half free. Justice Learned Hand said, "To keep our democracy, there must be one commandment: Thou shall not ration justice."

9. This silver or golden rule has been called the bedrock of ethics, the minimum of human, social, Christian and Jewish ethics. So many fail to live up to this simple standard that one is tempted to say people live under the bedrock, as ethical troglodytes, ethical cavemen. Antisemitism is an example of this. So is the

anti-cult movement (ACM) described by S&B cf., also Bromley and Shupe, *Strange Gods*; Boston: Beacon Press, 1981.

10. "Sparks of Contact," *The New Review of Books and Religion* I, No. 9 (May '77), p. 2.

11. *The Myth of God Incarnate*, ed. John Hicks (London: SC, 1977).

12. "Debating the Incarnation," CC, XCIV, No. 27 (31 Aug-7 Sept '77), 740–742.

13. Foreword, p. vii, James W. Parkes, *Prelude to Dialogue* (NY: Schocken Books, 1969).

14. Copies are available from the AJC. The foreword is by Rabbi Marc H. Tanenbaum, Director of National Interreligious Affairs for the AJC. Rabbi Tanenbaum notes the report is the first systematic study of DP. The report is by Rabbi A. James Rudin, Assistant Director of the Interreligious Affairs Department.

15. Such charges are fairly standard practice in the internecine warfare of religion. It is said that Jews talk this way about Christians. George W. Buchanan, *Revelation and Redemption: Jewish Documents of Deliverance from the Fall of Jerusalem To The Death of Nahmaides*; Dillsboro, N.C,: Western North Carolina Press, 1978. The ACM sees the UC as diabolic and charges the UC with sundry related charges— the standard myths of religious persecutors throughout the ages. Cf. Harvey Cox, "Deep Structures in the Study of New Religions," pp. 122–130, in *NB*. These stagnant myths are used to accuse the Jews, all new and different groups, and now the UC. We might note too among numerous examples, that Jehovah's Witnesses' literature often refers to "Christendom" as belonging to the devil. Rabbi James S. Diamond suggests the modern state of Israel "may have as much demonic as it has redemptive potential." "Making Sense Out of Israel," CC, XCVII, No. 39 (3 Dec '80), pp. 1205–1206. No doubt there are Arabs who would agree that Israel is demonic. See further later.

16. As noted earlier, DP also emphasizes Israelite success. Any reader familiar with the Tenak, the Old Testament, will of course recognize the origin of the faithlessness theme. It is all there in the Bible and the DP is quoting the Jewish Scriptures. DP notes a similar record of failure and success for Christianity. It is of interest to note that the language of DP is quite mild compared to that of the biblical prophets who called the Hebrews whores and rotten fruit whom God would wipe off the face of the earth with only the tag of an ear and a bit of fur left to show his sheep ever existed. Andrew C. Tunyogi, *The Rebellion of Israel* (Richmond: John Knox Press, 1969), p. 11, points out that from the time of her election, Israel repeatedly rebelled against God. There is no parallel like it in any other religion. Compare also George W. Coats, *Rebellion in the Wilderness: The Murmuring Motif in the Wilderness Traditions of the Old Testament* (NY: Abingdon Press, 1968). If talk about the failures of biblical Hebrews is antisemitism, then the biblical prophets were antisemites, and the Hebrew Scriptures, the Jewish Bible, is antisemitic. And presumably the Presbyterians and Methodists are antisemitic for publishing the books cited. Cf. further later.

17. Readers familiar with the New Testament will recognize the origin of these

descriptions. I believe these Jews of the Jewish sect commonly called Christians were talking to other Jews in a style familiar to them all. From my perspective, the style is inappropriate, then and now, for both Judaism and Christianity. The Talmud says peasants are unclean animals, their wives are reptiles, their daughters beasts. Jesus and his disciples were Galileans. "Galilean" is also synonymous with a cursed, lawless rabble. So the New Testament hands out to the rabbinic Jews what the rabbinic Jews dumped on the Jesus Jews. Its not clear which came first—the chicken or the egg. *Cf.* Vermes, *Jesus the Jew* (NY: Macmillan, 1973), pp. 54ff. Unfortunately, mutual contempt has continued. Antisemitism is well known. Jewish contempt for Christians has been documented by Buchanan, *op. cit.* and remains common in the literature. See further later.

18. DP, pp. 357, 510, etc. Note that the concern here is *restoration of the Jews*, and of all humanity, a standard theme in the Jewish Bible. Many Jews in Jesus' day hoped for the restoration of Israel. I'm told that some still do. Those people who believe in the devil commonly see him working through people as in I Chronicles 21:1. He even quotes Scripture. The Judas reference is Luke 22:3. Emil Fackenheim relates Christianity to the devil as he asks, ". . . has Christian theology even in its most saintly and profound character played into the devil's hands?" Quoted by Thomas A. Idinopulos and Roy B. Ward, "Is Christology Inherently Anti-Semitic? A Critical Review of Rosemary Ruether's *Faith and Fratricide*," *Journal of the American Academy of Religion* (hereafter JAAR) XLV, No. 2 (June '77), p. 211. Here is a modern Jew accusing Christianity of being a tool of the devil, what the AJC objects to in the DP. Cf. further, Theodore H. Gaster, "Satan," IDB 4 (1962), 224–228. Vermes, *op. cit.*, notes the belief in Jesus' day that the devil caused illness and sin. The UC theologian, Young Oon Kim, states flatly and explicitly that "the Jews were not overwhelmed by Satan. No matter how often they had to walk through the valley of the shadow of death..." p. 219, *Unification Theology and Christian Thought* (NY: The Golden Gate Publishing Co.). This was published in 1975 before the current flap arose.

 The ransom theory is a common one in the history of Christian doctrine. It is the doctrine of the Atonement in Judaism. *Cf.* Mark 10:45 in the New Testament. It is of course a Jewish doctrine well known in Yom Kippur, the Day of Atonement. Biblically it is the entire story of the Exodus, the origin of Israel in the view of some, that is, the belief in God as the Redeemer. Cf. Deuteronomy 7:8 and G. Ernest Wright, "Exegesis" of the Book of Deuteronomy, IB 2; (1953), 380–381. Hopefully, Rudin is not objecting to the restoration of the Jews. Some Jews and Christians do not think they need restoration.

19. DP, pp. 519, 226, 147, 485, etc. Cf. further later, on the Holocaust. The view that Jews suffer for their sins is common in Jewish thought. It is biblical. That they suffer for "crucifying Christ" is common in Christian thought. In my view, it should be repudiated. Historically it was the Romans who crucified Jesus as well as thousands of other Jews. For Christians to use this psychological "club" of the crucifixion of Jesus the Jew, against Jews, is a denial of everything that is Christian.

20. During the Nazi era, Christian attitudes were traditionally antisemitic. Robert R. Ross, *So It Was True: The American Protestant Press and the Nazi Persecution of the Jews* (Minneapolis: University of Minnesota Press, 1980). Morris C. Katz, "Canadian Record," CC 100, No. 10 (6 Ap '83), 325. For a contribution to Jewish-Unification, see Andrew Wilson, "Israels in the Divine Principle: Implications for Jewish-Christian Dialogue," unpublished manuscript, 25 Oct 77. Wilson denies any antisemitism in the DP and suggests Rudin read DP more carefully. See also Wilson's "A Unification Position on the Jewish People," *Journal of Ecumenical Studies* 20, No. 2 (Sept '83), pp. 191–208.

21. "A Critique of the Theology of the Unification Church as set forth in *Divine Principle*," June '77, available from the CFO. The statement as published is not signed. A covering letter from the then Commission Ch., Jorge Lara-Braud (Presbyterian), notes his own involvement in the report; the basic text was done by Sister Agnes Cunningham (Roman Catholic); she was assisted by Robert Nelson (United Methodist) and William L. Hendricks (Southern Baptist). The document as a whole is interesting as an example of "One person's orthodoxy is another's heresy" ("Take a Moonie to Lunch," *The Philadelphia Inquirer*, 5 Jan '77). The CFO orthodoxy as reflected in this paper is very close to my own. It is of interest to note that neither the Roman Catholic Church nor the Southern Baptist Convention belong to the NCC. For them, by their *traditional* standards, the NCC and its constituent members are *not* Christian. They are heretics. The hypocrisy of this process is mind boggling. On Southern Baptist antisemitism, cf. n. 25 later. On Roman Catholic antisemitism, cf. n. 27. On Methodist and Presbyterian antisemitism, cf. Strober, *op. cit.*

    Dr. Lara-Braud released excerpts from the working paper on 28 Dec '76. The report concludes that the UC is not Christian. That includes antisemitism. The Romans accused the Christians of heresy. The Catholics accused the Protestants of heresy. Now they get together in order to accuse someone else of heresy. And on and on it goes...

    For further comments on the CFO document, see Frank K. Flinn, "Preface," pp. vii-xi in Frank Flinn, ed., *Hermeneutics & Horizons: The Shape of the Future*, (Barrytown, NY: Unification Theological Seminary, 1982).

22. Cf. Isaiah 42:6 and 49:6 on Israel's responsibility to the nations. DP, pp. 283, 298, 315, 535, etc. On p. 6 of the CFO report, the authors note their awareness of the DP interpretaton of the *success* of Abraham, Moses, etc., through faith*ful*ness. Their statement interalia that the failure was total seems to falsify their own report. Questions about inconsistencies in the report and the action that led to it brought no answers on either. In DP, Christianity is called the Second Israel while the Hebrews/Jews are the First Israel. Not only have both failed in complete obedience, so has all humanity. DP is largely based on the Fall and God's Plan of Restoration. Until now, everyone has failed (Psalm 14:1; Roman 3:9). But God wants everyone to be saved, says DP and the Bible (II Peter 3:9). It is curious that the CFO committee is not interested in this nor particularly upset by the DP catalogue of Christian failures. Speaking as a Christian, I would say the catalogue has more truth than poetry, in it, though my own approach to the matter differs from that of DP. The data on Christian failure is

ubiquitous. Perhaps the most imfamous failure is antisemitism. If this committee or the NCC is genuinely concerned with antisemitism, they ought to do something about their own constituency. Cf. A. Roy Eckhardt, "Recent Literature on Christian-Jewish Relations," JAAR XLIX, No. 1 (Mar '81), 99–111. "'Liberal' Christian view said to obstruct Jewish ties," UMR, 129, No. 20 (22 Oct '82), p. 3. The report quotes an investigation which claimed a Methodist bookstore was selling literature with anti-Jewish images. Cf. Carl D. Evans, "The Church's False Witness Against the Jews," CC 99, No.16 (5 May '82), 530–533. When the *Reader's Digest* reported that the NCC and WCC were supporting Marxist groups, numbers of people accused the *Digest* of false witness. The Commandment says, "Thou shalt not bear false witness against thy neighbor" (Exodus 20:16). If we bear false witness against our neighbor, on what ground do we object if we think someone is doing it to us? They are doing to us as we have done unto others. That is of course a perversion of the Golden Rule, a Rule up to which ethical troglodytes do not yet measure. "Bishop Deplores Attack Against Interfaith Effort," UMR 129, No. 25 (26 Nov '82), 4. Paul Abrecht, "Ecumenical Illiteracy in the 'Reader's Digest'," John A Lovelace, CC 99, No. 37 (24 Nov '82), 1195–1198. "NCC and Digest battle on," UMR 129, No. 34 (28 Jan '83), 4. Cf. further later n. 42.

23. The vast majority of Christian Church members exhibit an affinity for antisemitic beliefs and nearly half frankly admit to antisemitic feelings, say Charles Y. Glock and Rodney Stark, *Christian Beliefs and Anti-Semitism*; NY: Harper & Row, 1966, p. 146. In 1981, acts of antisemitism more than doubled in the U.S. according to the Anti-Defamation League. "Anti-Semitism in the U.S.," CC 99, No. 2 (20 Jan '82), 49. Eugene J. Fisher, "Anti-Semitism," CC 99, No.12 (7 Ap '82), p. 425. Cf. Ernest Volkman, *A Legacy of Hate: Anti-Semitism in America* (NY: Franklin Watts, 1982). It is ironic that the AJC and other Jewish groups have issued angry denunciations of an NCC report on Israel. Jews boycotted preliminary hearings to prepare the NCC statement. Their prepared denunciations were handed out the moment after the NCC vote, i.e., the denunciations were prepared in advance. The NCC statement called for negotiations with the Palestine Liberation Organization (PLO). So on the one hand, Jewish groups condemn the NCC, and then get together with the NCC to condemn the UC. Jean Caffrey Lyles, "No Peace Without the PLO?," CC XCVII, No. 38 (26 Nov '80), 1147–1148. Dan Louis, "UMs support council's new mid-East policy," UMR 8, No. 49, p. 3. Presumably this means the UM Church is condemned as antisemitic along with the NCC. Cf. also Allison Rook and Jay Vogelaar, "National Council of Churches Adopts New Comprehensive Statement on the Middle East," *The Link* 13, No. 5 (Dec '80), pp. 1–13. Tracy Early, "Mideast statement: no lasting damage?," *The News World*, 29 Nov '80, p. 1A. While protesting, Rabbi Rudin is quoted as assuring the NCC, "We will continue to work with you." The NCC is called antisemitic but the dialogue goes on anyway, without removal of the offensive passages. Cf. further later, footnote 58. Eckhardt, *op. cit.*, p. 100, says the NCC and the World Council of Churches are both antisemitic. The irony is deepened by those who point out that Zionism was a Jewish heresy and is still thought to be such by some Jews. It is

only in the past few decades that Jews and Jewish organizations opposed to Zionism have become proponents of Zionism. Such total switches in opinion could be called brainwashing. Cf. I. F. Stone, "Confessions of a Jewish Dissident," *The Palestine Forum* (Mar-Ap '78), p. 3.

24. Cf. also Rev. Moon, "America and God's Will," *The New York Times*, 24 Sep '76, pp. A14–15. Moon called for brotherhood and unity among Jews, Christians and the UC.

25. Release by the AJC, 20 Dec '76. "News Release" by the AJC, 28 Dec '76. William Claiborne, "3 Major Faiths Mount Harsh Attack on Moon," *The Washingtion Post*, 29 Dec '76. David F. White, "Rev. Moon Strongly Criticized by Religious Leaders," *The New York Times*, 29 Dec '76. "Interreligious Newsletter," 1, No. 3 (May '77), p. 5. Considering his statement about the Southern Baptists, it is ironic that the president of the Southern Baptist Convention was in the news in 1980. In August, the Rev. Bailey Smith said, "God doesn't hear the prayers of a Jew." In September, he said, "Why did (God) choose the Jews? I don't know why he chose the Jews. I think they got funny looking noses, myself." In December, he is reported to have apologized, though a personal communication reports he did not repudiate his words. Jean Caffrey Lyles laconically remarks, "There's no record that he's ever actually retracted the remark." Smith was re-elected in 1981. Southern Baptists have had a long standing program to convert Jews, which is antisemitic, according to the AJC. One is tempted to suggest that Southern Baptist Hendricks might want to do something about antisemitism in his own communion. The practice of pointing at someone else to cover one's own sin is a common psychological phenomenon called projection. "No Comment Department," CC XCVII, No. 38, p. 1150. Lyles, "Southern Baptist Detente," CC LCVIII, No. 22 (1–8 July '81), 694–695. UMR 9, No. 4 (2 Jan '81), 2. Jacob Gartenhaus, "The Jewish Conception of the Messiah," *Christianity Today* XIV, No. 12 (13 Mar '70), 8–10. It is of interest that Rabbi Tanenbaum did not call upon Christians and Jews to remove the offensive passages from the Bible as a demonstration of their good faith. "Public Relations pieties" is an interesting phrase. We note in passing that the CFO committee that objected to antisemitism has not offered their services for such effort.

The "canards" are still quite useful. They are applied (projected?, diverted?) to the new religions. James and Marcia Rudin, *Prison or Paradise: The New Religious Cults* (Philadelphia: Fortress Press, 1980). S&B, *op. cit.* Cox *op. cit.* NB, *op. cit.* WSI. The old antisemitic canards, or the deep structures of religious persecution, to use Cox' phrase (he calls them myths used by the persecutors against the persecuted), are used to accuse the new religions. Sexual irregularities (both too much and too little), power, wealth, politics, involvement with foreign governments, heresy are all here. Only here, they are directed from the Jews to others. The sources of the information are often the enemies of the new religions, ex-members who have now turned on their former compatriots, just as antisemites in the past have used ex-Jews who have turned on Judaism. A book on Judaism drawing only on antisemites would be quite sure to produce the same old tired canards. Would the use of such antisemitic sources produce an honest understanding of Judaism? It seems doubtful, very doubtful indeed. So a book like the Rudins drawing on ex-Moonies and others produces what one would expect.

26. *Faith and Prejudice* (New Haven: Yale University Press, 1963). The study covered other religious prejudices and racism, as well as antisemitism.

27. Arlene and Howard Eisenberg, "The Christian War on Antisemitism," *Look*, 2 June 64. The Roman Catholic Declaration on non-Christian Religions (1965) is also a bit curious. It says, "... the Jews should not be presented as rejected or accursed by God, as if this followed from Holy Scripture." The antisemite can say, "Fine. They are accursed as long as we don't use the Bible." The Covenant is forever. They are not rejected or accursed at all in my understanding. To reject or curse the Jews is a mockery of Jesus the Jew who said we are to love our neighbor and we are to do unto others as we would have others do unto us. Cp. the Presbyterian statement quoted in the AJC report by Rudin. Andrew M. Greeley noted Roman Catholic antisemitism in a column, "Vatican on Anti-Semitism." He cited insensitivity and resistence by the Curia to the Vatican Council's statement on the Jews. *San Antonio Light* (12 Jan '83), 5J. The Roman Catholic author of the CFO committee report claimed antisemitism was in the past in 1976. Greeley apparently does not see it as past in 1983 in *her* church.

On Jesus' crucifixion, cf. Leonard C. Yaseen, "The 2,000th Year," *Together*, (July '73). Yaseen presents another curiosity in terms of motive. He quotes the United Methodist document (1972) against antisemitism. Its purpose is to continue Jewish and Christian efforts for the common cause of mankind. He himself says we can't afford the luxury of discrimination because of the danger of nuclear war. I appreciate the pragmatic approach, but one could simply say that antisemitism is wrong. It is un-Christian. That should be reason enough for Christians to stop it, even if there were no danger at all of nuclear or any other kind of war.

28. Note that the Eisenbergs agree with Rev. Moon on the hope for concord. Perhaps we should all be hoping and working toward that end.

29. "In the Church's closet... Anti-Semitism: a lively skeleton," *The Christian Advocate*, 22 Ap '65.

30. *Portrait of an Elder Brother*, op. cit.

31. The Rudins, however, note that while some Christian groups repudiate the proselytizing of Jews, there are close ties between "Jews for Jesus" and the Lutheran Church—Missouri Synod. In July '77 the LCMS planned to have half their people become effective witnesses to the Jews whom they depicted as agnostic materialists. Cf. A. James and Marcia R. Rudin, "The Jews for Jesus (and others too) are out to get your kids," *Present Tense* 4, No. 4 (Summer '77), p. 23. Balfour Brickner, "Christian Missionaries and a Jewish Response," *Worldview* 21, No. 5 (May '78), pp. 37–41. In the ACM, the primary target was the UC.

The ACM never succeeded in becoming a national organization say S&B. They think one reason is that the ACM could not agree on what is a religion that needs to be repressed. The AJC wanted to so designate Jews for Jesus as a new religion, a cult, but others in the ACM thought converting Jews is legitimate business. S&B, p. 114. "Shall We Evangelize the Jews?", *Christianity Today* XIV, No. 12 (13 Mar '70), 33–34, is an editorial which answers the question positively.

32. Strober, *op. cit.*, p. 55. CC (24 Sep '80), p. 873, reported that Rufus Cornelson of the Lutheran Church in America had been appointed Director of the NCC Office of Christian-Jewish Relations and staff assistant to the NCC Commission on Regional and Local Ecumenism. Issac Rottenberg was chairman for five years as of 1978. He accused the NCC of being anti-Israel. CC XCVIII, No. 9 (18 Mar '81), p. 289.

33. "Religious Education in the Future Tense," *Religious Education*, (Mar-Ap '73), pp. 157–169. This is a superb article which I highly recommend to anyone interested in religious education or simply the current scene. For a Christian study that comes to a similar conclusion, see Rottenberg, "Should there be a Christian Witness to the Jews?," CC XCIV, No. 13 (13 Ap '77), pp. 352–356. Roderick Campbell, *Israel and the New Covenant* (Philadelphia: Presbyterian and Reformed Publishing Co., 1954), p. 223, says that because of the unfaithfulness of the church, many who are born in supposedly Christian families are almost as ignorant of the true nature of the Christian faith as pagans. We can note in passing a key word in Tanenbaum's statement. "Proselytization" is in disrepute these days. Leslie Newbigin said, "Evangelism is what I do, proselytization is what other people do." Quoted by J. Richard Peck, "The Comfortable Pigeonhole," *The Circuit Rider* 2, No. 4 (Feb '78), 2. Cf. also Gaylord Noyce, "The Ethics of Evangelism," CC XCVI, No. 32 (10 Oct '79), 973–976. It is an interesting problem. The AJC has raised no objection to a New Jersey group whose stated aim is to convert grammar school children. Catholics and Jews are primary targets for this effort. On the other hand, some would say Tanenbaum's words come back to him with the observation that most American Jews are non-observant and many are secularists. Perhaps it would be more objective to say that we all need to work on the depth and consistency of our faith and its practice.

34. The Rudins, *op. cit*, p. 22. Brickner, *op.cit.*, p. 37, notes that "Judaism has lost more Jews to apathy or assimilation than it ever has—or probably ever will—to the blandishments of Christian missionaries." Estimations of Unification membership vary widely. One figure is 30,000 which is actually the membership *goal* in the U.S. Actual core membership is closer to 3,000. The first U.C. missionary arrived in the U.S. in 1959. In 24 years, that is less than 200 per year which compares in an interesting way with the Jews' "take" of seven or eight thousand converts per year. Every year the Jews get twice as many converts as the UC's entire membership after 24 years of effort. In the same period, a *single* Presbyterian church went from a membership of 22 to over 4500. The Mormons have increased by one *million* in this same period.

For another perspective, see David A. Rausch, "The Messianic Jewish Congregational Movement," CC 99, No. 28 (15–22 Sep 82), 926–929. He notes that "Jews for Jesus" (led by Martin Rosen) grossed nearly $2.5 million in the previous year. Susan Perlman writes that is the figure for 1979. She has a different perspective than Rausch. "Messianic Jews," CC 99, No. 31 (13 Oct '82), pp. 1028–1029.

35. It is of course, not unusual for a group to denounce another group for something the first group is doing. At a meeting of a psychological association, ostensibly called to discuss the psychology of the cults, the group in charge of the meeting denounced the UC for not allowing freedom of choice. They allowed no freedom of discussion. They gave details (one is tempted to say they were quite proud of their activities) of kidnapping their children (who were in their 20's and 30's), and forcibly holding the "kids" against their will and deprogramming them. Freedom of choice? Cf. also Robert H. Tucker's discussion of "Jewish Yellow Pages" which urge Jews to buy Jewish. The Anti-Defamation League took the "Christian Yellow Pages" to court for antisemitism. In war, it is common to condone actions by our troops while denouncing the other side for doing the same thing. One curious side point in deprogramming is the way in which it is tolerated when practiced against a religious group. No one to my knowledge has deprogrammed pushers, prostitutes, pornographers, members of organized crime, or other criminals. When "behavior modification" was used on convicts to help them to acceptable behavior, there was a great hue and cry that this violated the civil rights of the convicts. People accept adults who choose to be alcoholics and all these other things but a choice of religion is not acceptable. In my personal opinion, this is a very warped, a really bizarre sense of values.

36. James A. Franklin, "Sense of belonging is magnet for Moon group, says Rabbi," *Boston Globe*, 16 Feb '77, p. 26, 2nd section. The article actually quotes Rudin as saying 10–12%. In a personal communication, he used the figure of 10%. He notes that target groups of UC evangelism are college freshmen and seniors. Substantial numbers of these appear to be indifferent to their Jewish heritage. Cf. Thomas Piazza, "Jewish Identity and the Counterculture," pp. 245–264, *The New Religious Consciousness*, ed. Charles Y. Glock and Robert N. Bellah (Berkeley: University of California Press, 1976). Brickner, *op. cit.*, p. 37. In a press release on 29 December '76, Dr. Josef Hausner confirmed the point. UC members of Jewish background were "lost" to Judaism in the drug culture and alienated radical groups before they came to the Movement. Dr. Hausner is a Rumanian survivor of the Holocaust who teaches at the Unification Theological Seminary and who remains committed to his orthodox Jewish tradition. Numbers of UC members of Christian background claim they were inactive and non-religious before coming into the UC. They are grateful to the UC for helping them appreciate their ancestral faith. The same inactivity appears in the background of adherents of other new religions as well. Cf. James V. Downton, Jr., *Sacred Journeys: The Conversion of Young Americans to Divine Light Mission* (NY: Columbia University Press, 1979). Some members of the UC are and

were active members of their parental religious group or were active seekers of religious truth. Some UC members who had dropped out of their parental religions are grateful to the UC for reviving their interest in their ancestral group.

Eugene B. Borowitz says American Jewry as a whole has been largely secularized. Agnosticism and atheism are endemic. "Most Jews are far from being... observant or pious." Cf. his "Judaism in America Today," CC XCV, No. 36 (8 Nov '79), 1066–1070. If he is right, Jews in general "do not have a deep faith." It is not surprising then that young adults of a Jewish background "do not have a deep faith." The less than 200 in the UC did not, but they do now. Personally, I see that as a gain. My personal value system says it is better to have a strong faith in God than none at all. I find it difficult to understand those parents and others who prefer no faith, dope addiction, alcoholism, sexual promiscuity, etc., because these are "normal" in today's world. Parenthetically, if Borowitz is right, the LCMS is at least partly right in its estimate of American Jews though they have been accused of antisemitism for this.

37. J. Gordon Melton and Robert L. Moore, *The Cult Experience* (NY: Pilgrim Press, 1982), pp. 30, 134. Again, proselytism is an interesting phenomenon. The Rudins offer no objection to 7–8,000 Christians converting to Judaism, only to the 400 Jews who convert to Christianity. Dow Kirkpatrick watched "tens of thousands of Cubans" parading for May Day in Havana. "I thought that if Methodism could mount an equal demonstration, we would call it 'successful evangelism.' " UMR. 22 Jul '77, p. 2.

38. *Ibid.*, p. 37.

39. Alexander Cruden, *Complete Concordance* (Philadelphia: John C. Winston, 1949), pp. 518–519. Tanenbaum, "Religious Education...," p. 162. Olson, "In the Church's closet...," Rosemary Radford Ruether, *Faith and Fratricide* (NY: The Seabury Press, 1974), p. 26.

40. Greg Lewis, "Rabbi Calls Moon Church 'Ominous,' Cautions Parents," *Greensboro Daily News*, 10 Feb '77, p. C7. John Roberts, "Rabbi: Moon slurs Jews," *Greensboro Record*, 11 Feb '77. Jones, *op. cit.* Franklin, *op. cit.* Dan Frazier, "Moon hit for bigotry, distortions," *Fort Worth Star-Telegram*, 8 Mar '77. Mike Anderson, "Rabbi Says Unification Church Harmful," *Pittsburgh Press*, 29 Mar '77. Berkeley Rice made a similar judgment: "Moon's Family, a warm womb, shuts out care, responsibility, and the need to think for oneself." Cf. his "Honor Thy Father Moon," *Psychology Today* 9, No. 8 (Jan '76), 26–47. Like Rudin too, Rice notes parental objections to the young joining the UC but Rice adds that other parents approve, feeling it is better than drugs or drifting aimlessly around the country. Neither commentator offers sources or evidence for this view. It might be supported by Robert N. Bellah who notes the inability of America's utilitarian individualism to give meaning to existence. The religious fallout of the '60s is a demand for immediate religious experience and face-to-face community, which the churches cannot fulfill or at least do not for some. The new religious movements provide this plus a sense of stability after the instability of the '60s.

Eastern Religions have the added attractiveness of a sharp contrast with western materialism. Cf. his "New Religious Consciousness and the Crisis in Modernity,' pp. 333–352, in *The New Religious Consciousness, op. cit.* See also Tanenbaum, "Religious Education...," pp. 157f. Cf. further B&S. WSI. NB. What is not clear is why the new religions should be condemned for providing what the world needs.

Personal observation indicates that the UC does not shut out care and responsibility but just the opposite. Some of the dropouts from the UC have indicated they just could not "hack" the high standards. Instead of a warm womb, Unificationists are required to think and plan and produce in a context that more resembles the Puritan work ethic than today's extended babyhood that excuses responsibility on all sides of America.

41. Judaism and Christianity were once attractive for some of these same reasons in the pagan world of Rome. It must be emphasized again however that many Romans came to these religions because they really believed (Matt. 8:5, 27:54; Acts 10:1) and many members of the UC come because they think the Principle is true. They believe among other things that Rev. Moon has overcome the dichotomy between science and religion. The DP is a rational interpretation of history that makes sense where other interpretations are less satisfactory to them. Brickner, *op. cit.*, p. 39, suggests we might try correcting the system that failed instead of "snatching" the convert.

42. Claiborne, *op. cit.* AJC report, *op. cit.* The irony here may not be apparent to the reader. Rev. Moon sees western democracy as the epitome of civilization and communism as the world's greatest threat to human well being and to God's will. The AJC is accusing the pro-democracy, anti-communist UC of being undemocratic and pro-communist. Antisemitism has long accused the Jews of being undemocratic and communist as well as being Nazis loyal to the foreign nation of Israel. Anti-Zionists claim Jews have acted out their theology by conquering Arab Palestine. Rev. Moon supports the present state of Israel. He is pro-Zionist. Parenthetically, we can note the NCC has been called communist. "'Fortune' Accuses NCC," CC XCVII, No. 27 (27 Aug-3 Sep '80), 815–816. So has the World Council of Churches. Joseph A. Harries, "Karl Marx or Jesus Christ," *Reader's Digest* 121, No. 724 (Aug '82), 130–134. The charge has been angrily repudiated. Cf. Albrecht, *op. cit.* It is hard to say whether these charges and counter-charges are just thoughtless (brainwashed?) remarks or if it is a way of diverting old age attacks onto another. One would like to think the chargers are sincere but when the same old tired canards appear again and again, one wonders. I trust the irony here is also obvious. When *we* accuse others, that's one thing. When others accuse *us*, we get mad.

Protestants have commonly accused Catholicism of being authoritarian and totalitarian though some Protestants are more rigid than the Pope. Catholicism is currently going through an upheaval in its authority structure. Cf. Andrew M. Greeley, William C. McCready and Kathleen McCourt, *Catholic Schools in a Declining Church* (Kansas City: Sheed and Ward, 1976), p. 32, only 32% think the Pope is infallible; p. 35, 83% approve of artificial contraception in spite of the

Pope's words against it. Piazza, *op. cit.*, p. 245 notes, "traditional Judaism was authoritative in defining social roles, patterns of behavior, and a system of belief for Jews." He adds that this traditional authority has been declining for many years. So the AJC and others accuse the UC of being authoritarian, just what they were and in some quarters still are. It is as though they are saying to the UC that what we used to be and do is wrong and you can't be like us. Within the UC, both members and non-members report greater freedom than in many other groups. This is not a freedom for immorality but freedom of thought and practice in promoting high ideals such as obedience to God which also used to be an ideal in Judaism and Christianity. I have Jewish and Christian friends for whom high ideals are still important even if Borowitz and others see this in decline.

43. Such an investigation was begun in 1977 (CC XCIV, No. 30, p. 841). It was part of a larger study, the *Investigation of Korean-American Relations*, published in a series of Reports of the Subcommittee on International Organizations of the Committee on International Relations, U.S. House of Representatives; Washington, D.C.: U.S. Government Printing Office, 31 Oct '78. Various volumes were published for stated portions of the hearings. The UC responded through Bo Hi Pak, *Truth is My Sword* (NY: Unification Church in America, 1978), and, through a volume titled, *Our Response* (NY: Holy Spirit Association for the Unification of World Christianity, 1979). Both are available from the HSA-UWC, 4 West 43rd St., New York, NY 10036. The former is available through the committee, Congress or the Printing Office. The Congressional Committee failed to prove any connections between the UC and the KCIA. One wonders if others groups would fare as well, say in terms of connections with Israel, or the Vatican, or the CIA in missionary quarters. While living in the Near East, I was accused several times of being with the American CIA. This is not an unusual occurrence. Jeffrey Pickard, "Hey—Are You with the CIA?," *The Rising Tide* VII, No. 15 (10–24 Oct '77), p. 5.

45. Cf. n. 41. The refusal to take doctrine seriously is of course a form of discrimination. Jews are accused of not believing anything. In Puritan New England, Quakers were condemned because they were Quakers. They were not asked what they believed. S&B and B&S make it clear that the condemnation of the UC is sociological rather than theological. Cf. also Cox, *op. cit.* "War on the Moonies," *Human Behavior* 6, No. 9 (Sep 77), 37. Fichter, "Youth in Search of the Sacred," WSI-21–41.

45A. The human need for a scapegoat is an entire study in itself. Robert Coles has suggested that "We crave scapegoats, targets to absorb our self-doubts, our feelings of worthlessness and hopelessness." See his "Psychology and Armageddon," *Pschology Today* 16, No. 5 (May '82), 13–14, 88. Sydney Harris speaks of a psychological drive, as yet unidentified, that seems to compel us to divide rather than unite. "Mankind's seductive trait that may be the undoing," *Detroit Free Press*, 2 Aug '82, p. 78. His "unidentified" and the scapegoating process may be the repetition compulsion which makes abused children become abusing parents. See Ashley Montague, "Poisonous Pedagogy," *Psychology Today*, 17, No. 5 (May '83), pp. 80–81.

46. "Religious Education...," pp. 157f. Numbers of commentators have compared this description of our era with that of Jesus' day. As the pagan world was "ready" for Jewish missionaries and the Gospel ("in the fullness of time God brought forth His Son"), our world is "ready for...." Perhaps this explains Rev. Moon's "success." It needs to be noted though that estimates of the numbers of his converts are a fraction of those converting to Judaism which is not exactly a "new religion." To me, Judaism *is* a religion while others disagree. Cf. Diamond, *op. cit.*

47. Michael Mewshaw calls this "grotesque parodies of exorcism." He is intrigued as I am with the fact that dope dealers and pornographers are not kidnapped and deprogrammed. Nor are Protestant seminary students, Catholic nuns or Orthodox Jews. So why are "born again Christians singled out?" Cf. his "Irrational Behavior of Evangelical Zeal," *The Chronicle of Higher Education* (hereafter CHE) XV, No. 7 (18 Oct '76), 32. The professional deprogrammer Ted Patrick has a list of 5,000 cults including Catholics, Protestants and Eastern Orthodox. Cf. "Houston (Episcopalian) church on 'Cult' List," CC XCIV, No. 29 (21 Sep '77), 809. William C. Shepherd, "The Prosecutor's Reach: Legal Issues Stemming from the New Religious Movements," *The Journal of the American Academy of Religion* L, No. 2 (1982), 187–214. Anti-cult legislation has been used against Jews, Christians and religionists in general. Melton & Moore, *op. cit.*, p. 95.

48. Tony Martinez, "Dr. James Penton," *The Cornerstone* 1, No. 11 (May '77), p. 6. Hundred of thousands of JW's were slaughtered in Africa with no protest from the West. While JW's may not be hated like poison in the West, there's not much love or concern. On the loyalty issue as one of the standard myths used by religious persecutors throughout history, cf. Cox, *op. cit.* On Christianity as disloyal, cf. Ruether, *op. cit.*, p. 29. The antisemites normally charge the Jews with disloyalty.

49. The Forster and Epstein study, *op. cit.*, effectively deals with the myths of Jewish control of the media and of government. They also cover Zionism, which has been called a political ideology masquerading as a religion. Rabbi Rudin claims the UC "is nothing less than a 'political movement dressed in religious garb.'" Once again, an antisemitic barb is transferred to the UC. Cf. Roberts, *op. cit.* On a Jewish dictatorship of the world and the destruction or enslavement of Christians, cf. Buchanan, *op. cit.* One Arab view of Zionism is that it is a political movement dressed in religious garb. A news report said the Ayatollah of Iran claimed the Baha'i faith is not a religion but a Washington-backed political party. The Baha'is are now outlawed in Iran. Cf. CC 100, No. 21 (6–13 July '83), 642, and, CC 100, No. 29 (12 Oct '83), p. 898.

50. Campbell, *op. cit.*, p. 23. Jean Caffrey Lyles, "Charismatics: Beyond 'Sloppy Agape'," CC XCIV, No. 17 (17–24 Aug '77), 708. Lyles defends the right of personal choice even when others such as parents disapprove. "Letting Go:

Everybody has the Right to be Wrong," CC XCIV, No. 17 (11 May '77), 451–453. Rudin says the First Amendment freedoms include the "right to screw up your own life" (Anderson, *op. cit.*). That should mean one has a right to choose to be a Jew or a Moonie or even a Methodist.

51. Greeley, *et. al.*, *op. cit.*, pp. 8, 43, 51, 57, 73 "the standard of comparison for ethnic success has always been the Jews—a standard that derives from one of the most outstanding success stories in all human history." Antisemites deride this success while others applaud success, whether of Jews or Moonies. See also Gerald Krefetz, *Jews and Money: The Myths and the Reality* (NY: Ticknor & Fields, 1983). Glock & Stark, *op. cit.*, p. 110, note how in the Dark Ages, Christians forced Jews to become money lenders and thus created the myth of Jewish economic power. While Jews are systematically excluded from the banking industry, the myth teaches that international banking is dominated by Jews. Antisemites conjure up images of Jews as munitions manufacturers who profit from both sides of a war. Rumors persist that Rev. Moon's wealth comes from munitions factories— another antisemitic myth diverted to the UC.

    One criticism of Rev. Moon is that he lives in a big house, i.e., expensive. The cost of housing for leadership is a fascinating question whether one considers religious leaders, labor union leaders, or others. A recent report said t cost $440,000 merely for the renovations of a university owned president's home. Total costs, including moving, furnishings and other expenses were listed at 1.2 million dollars. Note that the property was already owned and this is in excess of the original purchase price. Cf. John McMillen, "Hackneys Move Into Renovated Eisenlohr," *The Daily Pennsylvanian* XC VIII, No. 67 (15 Sep '82), pp. 1, 9. Steven K. Ludwig, "The Shadow Knows," *Daily Pennsylvanian* XCVIII, No. 74 (24 Sep '82), p. 4.

52. UMR 9, No. 9 (6 Feb '81), 1, reports the annual income of Oral Roberts to be $60 million, Billy Graham $38 million, the Armstrongs $65 million, Robert Schuller $58 million, Jerry Falwell $33 million, the 700 Club $30 million, Rex Humbard $18 million, PTL Club $25 million, Christian Broadcast Network $58 million. The United Methodist Church's income is 1.6 billion a year.

53. Bruce Russell, "Persecution to prosperity: the Mormon Saga," *News World*, 29 Aug '77, p. 1B. Rudin is also concerned with the UC acquisition of property. Residents of Clearwater, Florida were upset when the Church of Scientology acquired $1.85 million worth of hotel and office buildings. An upstate New York county has more land in non-profit (tax free) hands than there is land on the tax rolls. There has been much discussion in recent years about the possibility of taxing churches and synagogues. Religion controls property that runs into billions of dollars in value, according to conservative estimates. The debate continues with cogent arguments on both sides. Cf. D. B. Robertson, *Should Churches be Taxed?* (Philadelphia: Westminster, 1968). Dean M. Kelly, *Why Churches Should Not Pay Taxes* (San Francisco: Harper & Row, 1977). Rudin did

not say how much property is owned by Jewish or other religious groups nor did he suggest they give up their tax free status.

54. O. Dillon Neal, "Is self-interest an enemy among the clergy, or just among others?," UMR 5, No. 46 (28 Oct '77), p. 2.

55. Glock & Stark, *op. cit.*, pp. 139f, note that Hitler believed Jews seduced unsuspecting German girls and removed them from the bosom of their people. "Child stealing" is an old charge against Jews and others, and now the UC. The deprogrammers publicly admit and "brag" about stealing 'children'—kidnapping people. Borowitz, *op. cit.*, points out that American Jews are expected to support Israel, no matter what. Support for the Zionist cause is now the "raison d'être" of American Jewry. Such 'party line' and 'toe the line' expectations are common in adult circles. We do not call it brainwashing but I at least find it difficult to distinguish the two. If we are not free to think for ourselves and have our own opinion about things, including the modern state of Israel, are we not brainwashed or subjected to thought control? The brainwashing charge is a variant of the evil eye or the hex or the vampire myth which Cox, *op. cit.*, sees as one of the deep structures of religious persecution throughout history.

The concern for children may be a reflection of America's extended babyhood by which we keep people out of the job market. A century ago, the average age of people having religious conversions was 16. Today it is 22. More and more parents are assuming responsibility for their children into the 20's in addition to paying for college expenses. The kidnapping and deprogramming of people may be seen as an extension or continuation of this parental control. Parents do not always readily accept the growing up of their children.

56. Christianity was said to be immoral and disloyal in its early centuries. Cf. Ruether, *op. cit.*, p. 29. E. P. Sanders, ed., *Jewish and Christian Self-Definition*, Vol. 1: *The Shaping of Christianity in the Second and Third Centuries* (Philadelphia: Fortress Press, 1980). Hans von Campenhausen, *The Formation of the Christian Bible* (Philadelphia: Fortress Press, 1977). Hitler's antisemitism included a sexual element. See n. 55. The dissimulation myth and the orgy myth are two of the deep structures Cox, *op. cit.*, sees throughout the history of religious persecution.

57. "Life Line," published by *Ministers' Life*, Aug '77. The statement is debated but in my view, Akhenaton was not a monotheist.

58. "Church leaders call for human rights in Israel," UMR 5 Aug '77, p. 3. They based their call on a series of articles in *The Sunday Times* of London. The charges and Israel's denial are available as a reprint booklet, *Israel and Torture*, from Americans for Middle East Understanding. Forster and Epstein, *op. cit.*, p. 17, state that "Of course one can be unsympathetic to or oppose Israel's position on specific issues without being anti-Jewish . . . but many statements carry an undeniable anti-Jewish message . . ." They give examples of this new antisemitism (pp. 83ff; 309ff) and include Michael Novak's comment, "To be a Zionist is now virtually identical with being Jewish—and the difference between the two

is not for a Christian to adjudicate." See also Volkman, *op. cit.* Perhaps it is equally difficult to distinguish between legitimate criticism of Israel and anti-semitism, but in the present context, it is worth repeating that the UC and Rev. Moon are pro-Israel. If it is antisemitic to be anti-Zionist, it would seem to follow that to be pro-Zionist would be at least some kind of evidence for being pro-Jewish and not antisemitic. The UC and Rev. Moon are *allies* of the AJC in this cause.

Roman Catholics and 20 Protestant denominations urged President Reagan to cut foreign aid to Israel until she recognizes the human rights of the Palestin-ians. "Middle East petition has UM signers," UMR 9, No. 7 (23 Jan '81), 4. "Clergy Call for Cut in Aid to Israel," CC XCVIII, No. 2 (21 Jan '81), 40. The World Jewish Congress claims Jews have a right to think for themselves and criticize Israel if they wish. "Jewish Study Criticizes Israel's Affairs," *The Miami Herald*, 22 Jan '81, p. 2A. Progressive Jews from all over America organized the "New Jewish Agenda." The agenda includes opposition to Israeli government policies and a re-affirmation of Jewish values like Justice and Peace. "Progressive Jews Organize," CC XCVIII, No. 5 (18 Feb '81), 161. Are these all antisemites? William Ward, "Semantics of Anti-Semitism," *The Middle East Newsletter* III, No. 4 (May-June '69), pp. 2–3. The Jews of the New Jewish Agenda were ex-communicated for criticizing Israel, in Nov 82. Cf. "Liberal Jews excommuni-cated," *The News World* (27–28 Nov '82), p. 1B. The Shalom Network is an organization dedicated to the survival of Israel but they do not excuse every-thing Israel does. Network Jews are also committed to self determination for the Palestinian people. *The Shalom Network Newsletter* 2, Nos. 8–9 (Oct/Nov '81), p. 1.

Cf. n. 23 earlier. The double standard of morality is an old one. It has been used against Jews, women, Blacks, Catholics and other out-groups. The State of Israel is, however, a problem, along with the Zionism that gave it birth. As Diamond, *op. cit.*, has noted, when Zionism was born 90 years ago, religious Jews condemned it as a heresy. Even today there are orthodox Jews who are anti-Zionists. They consider Israel the ultimate in rebellion against God. Dia-mond sees Israel as having demonic as well as redemptive potential. But the real thrust of his article is that Christians do not understand Israel, *nor do Jews!* We need dialogue and discussion to answer our ambiguities and questions. One of the question is whether a Christian can be anti-Zionist without being antise-mitic. For some, the two are still separate issues. The irony remains that the AJC and the UC support Israel and the NCC does not. The AJC condemns the NCC but does not *commend* the UC. The AJC dialogues with the NCC which has not removed "the offensive passages" while refusing to dialogue with the UC which supports the Zionist cause.

59. *The New York Times*, 18 Dec '76, *op. cit.*

60. The AJC report, p. 5.

61. *Oberlin Alumni Magazine* 73, No. 4 (July/Aug '77), pp. 8–10.

62. "The Holocaust: 1933–1945," no date.

63. Cf. n. 1. Jane Day Mook, "New Growth on Burnt-Over Ground. III: The Unification Church," *A.D.* 3, No. 5 (May '74), pp. 30–36.

64. The "Jewish Declaration" (*Nostra Aetate*), was produced in 1965. The Vatican Guidelines for Catholic-Jewish Relations in 1975. That is, it took 10 years just to develop the guidelines, some *30 years* after World War II. Rome in Italy and the Catholic Church in Germany were rather close to the whole Holocaust. The UC did not even exist and Rev. Moon was half a world away. In 1977, the U.S. Catholic Bishops' Committee on Liturgy recommended the "Reproaches" be dropped from the Good Friday services 32 years later and over 40 years after Hitler began his evil. Cf. the *Interreligious Newsletter* 1, No. 3 (May '77), 1. The article seems positive though it took almost 2,000 years after the Romans killed Jesus for the Roman Catholic Church to get around to removing the reproaches against the Jews for what the Romans had done. In the *same* year as the Declaration, Olson reports a first grade primer used in Spain, showed Jews crucifying Spanish Christian children on a wall. The text asked, "Of what biblical incident does this remind you?" It is an ongoing and continuing phenomenon. Protestant antisemitism was noted earlier. In this context, note that world Lutheran leaders repudiated Martin Luther's antisemitism. They did this in the summer of *1983*, a mere 450 years later. The news report did not quote the Jewish delegation on public relations pieties nor the 40 years that have passed since the Holocaust. CC 100, No. 25 (31 Aug 83), 770. The Protestant Church of the Rhineland was as close to the Holocaust as Roman Catholics. It took a Synod of this group until January, 1980, to confess guilt for the Holocaust. See Franklin H. Littell, "Lest We Forget: Holocaust Well Planned, Supervised by Universities," *The Jewish Times of the Greater Northeast* (1 July '82), p. 14.

The irony of it all is demonstrated by a personal experience. A Jewish book published in 1967 had been checked out of the library at least a dozen times. Several articles had been read. Jacob Robinson's had not. I slit the pages and read of his concern for the apathy people had about the holocaust. The uncut pages suggest the apathy is still with us. "Research on the Jewish Catastrophe—Where Does it Stand Today?," pp. 15–20, *Fourth World Jewish Congress*, vol. 1; Jerusalem: World Union of Jewish Studies, 1967.

A new report claimed a study commission broke up without finishing its study of American Jews on the Holocaust. Could American Jews have saved Jewish victims of the Nazi regime? Some Jews say yes while others deny this. "Look Back in Anger," *New York Times*, (9 Jan '83), p. 8E.

64A. Simon, pp. 11, 13, 15. There is a burgeoning Holocaust literature. Eckhardt, *op. cit.*, reviews the main material of the 1970's. Cf. Michael D. Ryan, ed., *Human Responses to the Holocaust* (NY: Mellen Press, 1981). Borowitz, *op. cit.* Black, "Traumatic Sojourn: A Jewish Refugee Re-encounters Europe," CC XCVIII, No. 21 (17–24 June '81), pp. 668–670. If one is honestly concerned with the Holocaust, instead of condemning literature produced before 1954 as inadequate, one might look at the current scene. Eckhardt claims Germany is as antisemitic as ever. The Holocaust has had little if any impact on leading theologians like Moltmann, Pannenberg, Rahner and Küng. He goes on to say that

America is hardly the Kingdom of God in sensitivity to the Holocaust. *Op. cit.*, p. 101. One is tempted to suggest it is an insult to the holy dead of the Holocaust to be fiddling with pre-1954 Korean literature when we ourselves are so inadequate and gratuitous in our sensitivity to the Holocaust. Nahum Goldman says, "To use the Holocaust as an excuse for the bombing of Lebanon, for instance, as Menachem Begin does, is a kind of 'Hillul Hashem,' a banalization of the sacred tragedy of the shoah, which must not be misused to justify politically doubtful and morally indefensible policies." *The Shalom Network Newsletter, op. cit.* I repeat, such use of the Holocaust is an insult to the holy dead.

65. A. James and Marcia B. Rudin, "pied pipers and would-be messiahs" *keeping posted* Feb '77, pp. 20–22, offprint. It may be appropriate here to note that Robins with his Jewish background may not be familiar with the extensive use of military language by Christian groups. It is very extensive for example in hymnology, *e.g.*, "Onward Christian Soldiers," "Soldiers of Christ Arise," "Battle Hymn of the Republic," *ad infinitum*. The Roman Catholic Society of Jesus (Jesuits) has had a military type organization for centuries. The Protestant Salvation Army is organized along military lines. Jean Caffrey Lyles, "New Battle Plan for Booth's Army," CC XCVII, No. 27 (27 Aug–3 Sep '80), pp. 811–812. William Booth, the founder was a Methodist. From a Jewish perspective, Christian militarism has indeed been a threat over the centuries. From an Arab perspective, Zionist military power appears threatening. Arabs would perhaps wholeheartedly agree that Zionists have built "an army, not a church." "Religion and Warfare were constantly linked in the Middle East in 1980..." UMR 9, No. 4 (2 Jan '81), p. 1.

The Rudin article does not say Robins is an ex-Jew. If he is Jewish, he is oddly unfamiliar with the Tenak, the Hebrew Scriptures, the Jewish Bible, the Protestant Old Testament. It contains extensive wars and rumors of war. This includes The Holy War(s). Holy War is quite pervasive in the text. The Holy War is a holocaust, at least for the enemies of the Hebrews or Jews. This ban or "cherem" was extended to the apocalypse by Jewish writers of the Dead Sea Scrolls. Among the latter is one called "The War of the Sons of Light and the Sons of Darkness." The Jewish Qumranites of course were the sons of light. Everyone else will be killed in a holocaust. If the Qumranite Jews had won, there would be neither rabbinic nor Jesus Jews left alive. There would be no one left alive except the Qumranite Jews. On holy war, cf. Lawrence E. Toombs, "War, Ideas of," IDB 4 (1962), pp. 796–801. Norman K. Gottwald, "War, Holy," IDB Supplementary volume; Nashville: Abingdon Press, 1976, pp. 942–944. Gerhard von Rad, *Der Heilige Krieg im alten Israel* (Zurich: Zwingli, 1951). Rudolf Smend, *Yahweh War and Tribal Confederation* (Nashville: Abingdon, 1970). Millard C. Lind, *Yahweh is a Warrior: The Theology of Warfare in Ancient Israel* (Scottsdale, PA: Herald Press, 1980). The common idea in the Hebrew Scriptures is the "herem" or "cherem", the ban or "devoted", which involved total destruction of whole peoples (genocide) and indeed destruction of everything that could be destroyed. However, there is some question about how often it was actually practiced. Marvin H. Pope, "Devoted," IDB 1:838–839, Exodus 22:20; Numbers 18:14;

21:2–4; 31:7–12, 17–18. Leviticus 27:31. Deuteronomy 2:34; 7:1–3; 13:17; 20:16–18; 21:10–14. Joshua 2:10: 6:17, Isaiah 34:2. Micah 4:13. In view of the Zionist claim that the Bible promises Jews the Holy Land, the Arabs might with some correctness be concerned about the Holy War talk of the Bible. The ban or cherem in subsequent centuries was transmuted to a kind of excommunication. In the middle ages, Jews excommunicated each other so often, the process lost much of its effectiveness. Cf. Joseph Hausner, "Ban and Excommunication: The Meaning, Usage and Purpose of the Herem," unpublished manuscript.

In our present discussion, however, our concern is simply the odd silence of the Jewish informant who claims the UC is militaristic without saying anything about the militarism of his people or that of the Christian society in which he lives. That could be called deception. Without questioning Mr. Robins' veracity, one could note that anyone who wrote a book on Judaism and relied on antisemites for information might legitimately be suspected of antisemitism. One could question their motives and at least be permitted a doubt or two that the writer wanted an honest understanding of Judaism. Are we permitted to reverse that reasoning? If someone relies on ex-Moonies for information, may we wonder if they are seeking an honest understanding of the UC? Or, are they merely diverting the old antisemitic canards onto a new victim?

66. Bicentennial God Bless America Festival Statement of Purpose.

67. Rabbi Richard Rubenstein, public lecture, Drew University, Feb 77. Fackenheim notes that in 1942, "Rabbi Israel Shapiro of Grodzisk was telling his flock about to die at Treblinka that their ashes would purify Israel and help redeem the world" (quoted by Idinopulos and Ward, *op. cit.*, p. 211). In Shapiro's place, I doubt that I would be able to offer anything better. Note that the Hebrew prophets, not quoted in DP, rather continuously decry the sins of Israel, in the most degrading terms. The Israelites were totally evil. God was going to crush them to powder and destroy them, almost. I realize here and regarding the Holocaust, it is one thing for someone Jewish to say Jews have failed or sinned. It is another matter for a non-Jew to say it. (Cf. the discussion later on the use of "the Jews" in the New Testament). But does it then become antisemitic? "What (is required) of the Christian is not better theology but better deeds. One hopes that Christians will cease using their cross as a battle-axe against Jews. Or as the Jewish theologian Eliezer Barkowitz puts it, "All we want of Christians is that they keep their hands off us and our children," Idinopulos and Ward, *op. cit,* p. 210. The reversal of course should also be true that the star of David should not become a weapon against Christian and Muslim Arabs, and that Jews and others should keep their hands off the Moonies.

The reversal is also true in who says what. My reaction differs when a Catholic or Protestant says Jesus' messiahship was invented by the Church and when Jews say it or when they call Christianity an ersatz religion or a pseudo-messianic movement. Cf. David Singer, "The Jewish Messiah: A contemporary Commentary," *Midstream* May '73, p. 5. Vermes, *op. cit.*, p. 155. It would be understandable if the Holocaust now becomes a battle-axe. Yet, when cross or Holocaust is so used, it degrades the faith that claims to remember for it shows the users have forgotten what that faith is all about. They make the good into evil and the evil they call good. They fail the minimal ethic of "Do not do unto others that which is hurtful for thyself," substituting the more common standard of the world of "Do unto others as others have done unto you." Unfortunately this is not simple revenge but taking it out on innocent people and perpetuating the evil through the generations. It is time to stop the evil and start practicing our Jewish and Christian faith such as the Jewish Bible's suggestion that we love our neighbor.

68. Leslie D. Weatherhead, *The Will of God* (NY: Abingdon Press, 1972), distinguished God's intentional will from his circumstantial will from his ultimate will. The intentional and the ultimate will are for good. Circumstantial will is God's will in the face of evil. Like Rev. Moon, English Methodist Weatherhead did not believe God intended that Jesus should die on the cross (p.12).

69. *Op. cit.* He overlooks here the Second Coming, a prominent doctrine in various periods of Christian history, including the present. The First Coming was somehow incomplete, *i.e.*, a failure, or there would be no need for a Second. The idea that the Jews did not accept or agree with the messiahship of Jesus is common Christian and Jewish doctrine. Historically of course, *all* of the first followers of Jesus were Jews.

   Lara-Braud is Presbyterian. The Presbyterian or Calvinist doctrine of double predestination has been called double indemnity. This doctrine says God has predestined who will go to Heaven and who will go to Hell. There is no choice; there is nothing we can do about it. I've not met a believer in this doctrine who did not know where *he* was going to as well as where all the rest of us were going. Double indemnity indeed. If Lara-Braud is sincere in his concern, he is condemning his own tradition. If I may be permitted an unscholarly remark, I say it's about time. But why now divert this evil doctrine and blame the UC for it? While it's true that Rev. Moon's family converted to Presbyterianism when he was ten years old, his teaching is that *all* will be saved. Ultimately no one will be able to withstand the wonderful love of God forever, not even the anti-Moonies. It is universalism rather than Presbyterianism's traditional eternal damnation of all the rest of us. Lara-Braud appears to be refusing to take responsibility for his own tradition. Were non-Anglo-Saxons ever included among the Elect? Personally I believe God loves all people. We should also. To hate others, whether Moonies or Hispanics or Presbyterians is a denial of our Judeo-Christian heritage. Some Hispanics are Moonies and some are Presbyterians.

70. "*Divine Principle* and the Second Advent," CC XCIV, No. 17 (11 May '77), pp. 448–451.

71. Singer, *op. cit.*, p. 11. Islam is another tradition that insists on man's responsibility.

72. *The Many Faces of Anti-Semitism, op. cit.*, p. 35, also sets antisemitism in the context of this larger evil and notes, "Man now has the means to destroy himself; if he is to keep from doing so, he must learn quickly to restrain his destructiveness and strengthen his humanitarian instincts." I can agree with this pragma-

tism as with Yaseen, *op. cit.*, even while maintaining quite simply that antisemitism and similar evils are wrong. They violate human decency and the heart and soul of the Judeo-Christian tradition.

73. *The Lamp.* Strober, *op. cit.*, pp. 30–31, notes an interesting phenomenon. "Conservative Protestants lay particular stress on the individual's relationship to Jesus; yet . . . cannot perceive the Jewish response to Jesus as a matter of individual decision." That is, neither the 'Jews' nor the 'other Jews,' but simply individual Jews, individual people, are involved.

74. Vermes, *op. cit.*, p. 155.

75. Strober, *op. cit.*, p. 29. Yaseen, *op. cit.*

76. Singer, *op. cit.*, pp. 6–7. This article is also interesting for its claim that Jesus appears as most decidedly "un-Jewish" while Vermes, *op. cit.*, fits Jesus neatly and merely into the Jewish charismatic movement. One assumes the CFO would have difficulty with both of these views of Jesus.

77. Cf. Rodney Stark and Charles Y. Glock, *American Piety* (Berkeley: Univ. of California Press, 1968), p. 209.

78. The Eisenbergs, *op. cit.*

79. The TV program "All in the Family" has bigoted remarks about many groups, apparently with the implication that that makes it alright. Others disagree. Cf. Forster and Epstein, *op. cit.*, pp. 114ff., and John Slawson, "How Funny Can Bigotry Be?," *Education Broadcasting Review*, Ap '72. Reprint. For the Hebrew Scriptures as antisemitic see Israel Zangwill's remark quoted by Louis Jacobs, *A Jewish Theology* (NY: Behrman House, 1973), p. 273.

80. Quoted by the Eisenbergs, *op. cit.* Note that it would be more accurate to say "The first individuals to accept him were Jewish." The implications of the "yet" is that some day "the Jews" will or should. Some Jews might take issue with this. Note also the collective judgment in "our corporate humanity," which echoes in Rev. Moon's statements below, and in Strober, *op. cit.*, p. 33. To repeat, Jesus the Jew was crucified by Roman soldiers under Roman authority. Such authorities crucified thousands of Jews.

81. *The New Future of Christianity* (Washington: Unification Church International, 1974), pp. 87f.

82. Olson points out also that Christianity picked up all the Old Testament heroes for Christianity while all the villains were ascribed to Judaism.

83. Note that "mainstream" Christianity also believes Jesus "failed." From within the faith, I would say the Christians in general have failed. Instead of diverting their sins or projecting their sins onto others, Christians might rather repent and reform.

84. *The New Future . . .*, p. 111 notes that "American Christianity today is in the

spiritual position of Israel 2,000 years ago. America is destined to serve as the Messiah's landing site for the 20th century . . . America's role is parallel to that of the Roman Empire of 2,000 years ago." On p. 42 he notes, "America herself can be heaven." America must "realize God's ideal here on earth." On p. 126 he says, "This New York shall be His Kingdom, too." This would appear to restrict the Second Israel in the present age to American Christianity. The failure of this Second Israel is not yet a foregone conclusion. Korea and the Third Israel are not mentioned in this text.

There are reflections here of America and the Promised Land. Rice, *op. cit.*, p. 36 claims this is why Rev. Moon came to the U.S. The idea is at least as old as the Puritans. It surely appeared that way to many of America's immigrants. The concept lies behind 19th century Manifest Destiny doctrine and the present day Civil Religion. Cf. further Robert N. Bellah, *The Broken Covenant: American Civil Religion in Time of Trial* (NY: Seabury Press, 1975). American Indians have a different perspective.

While the CFO report, *op. cit.*, p. 10, objects to facile identification of nations as good or bad (an objection with which I agree), the practice is as old as nationhood and more. In the Near East, some Zionists claim God has given them the land. They characterized their actions as defensive while the Palestinians are terrorists. Some Palestinians see *their* activities as defensive while the *Israelis* are the terrorists.

85. On p. 147 of DP is the statement that since the time of Jesus, "the Jews have lost their qualification as the chosen people and have been scattered, suffering persecution through the present day." Historically, the Diaspora began over 600 years before Jesus and pre-Christian antisemitism is well attested. Note too that this statement does not explain the continuance of the Jewish people or the Jewish faith. According to some Christian interpreters, both should have disappeared with the arrival of the Messiah. However, the biblical covenant is forever.

86. Bernard J. Bamberger proposes Jewish authorship. Cf. his "Adam, Books of," IDB I (1962), pp. 44f.

86A. Eileen Barker, "Who Would Be a Moonie?," WSI, *op. cit.*

87. Ruether, *op. cit.* Cf. the similar thought of Glock and Stark, *op. cit.*, p. xvi, "historically it is clear that the heart and soul of anti-Semitism rested in Christianity." Cf. also Charlotte Klein, *Anti-Judaism in Christian Theology* (Philadelphia: Fortress, 1978).

88. Idinopulos and Ward, *op. cit.*, pp. 193–214. Strober, *op. cit.*, p. 52, says the negative view of Judaism can be traced back to "the infant church. It was solidified between 240 and 450 A.D. and continuously expanded and elaborated in each of the subsequent centuries. Its formation probably was influenced by New Testament concepts and phraseology. However, in its substance it would seem to stem, not from Scripture itself, but from interpretations of scripture by authoritative spokesmen of the nascent Church."

89. "In the Church's closet..." (his italics). Barth, *Jesus the Jew* (Atlanta: John Knox Press, 1978).

90. They note that antisemitism was in the world before Christianity appeared, as noted above. Cf. also Ruether, *op. cit.*, ch. 1. On the New Testament, cf. also Samuel Sandmel, *Anti-Semitism in the New Testament?* Philadelphia: Fortress Press, 1978). He answers his own question, "Yes!"

91. S. Scott Bartchy, "How Much Freedom Can You Stand?," *Radix* 9, No. 1 (July-Aug '77), 22–23. This may be background for Paul's Galatians 3:28.

92. Vermes, *op. cit.*, pp. 54–55. Yaseen, *op. cit.*, notes that "Christianity has no need to degrade any other religion in order to validate itself." Christian antisemitism suggests some Christians have not yet learned this. The very existence of an ACM suggests the same, expanded to include Judaism. Heim, *op. cit.*, p. 448, takes note of the urgency with which mainliners have rushed to cast aspersions on the devotion of UC members, though it does not appear overly different from a traditional Jesuit seminary or a charismatic community. He sees something wildly ironic about Christians protesting UC members turning over their worldly goods to the Church as though this were something sinister. He sees it as a fear by mainliners that UC theology may be true. I agree wholeheartedly on the irony. Once upon a time, devotion was considered good. I disagree with Heim that DP must be rejected on theological grounds. To reject DP en toto is to reject a great deal of the Bible and Church history. What we must do is learn to "live and let live" with UC doctrine even as we have the hundreds of other religious groups in our pluralistic society. As Tanenbaum points out, we are all free to express ourselves in the marketplace of ideas (cf. n. 33 earlier). That freedom should include the freedom of the UC. I suspect also that the devotion of UC members is felt as a judgment by traditional Jewish and Christian groups. The bulk of our members do not exhibit such devotion to God or to our groups.

Of course, degrading others is a common human trait. It is an ersatz way of claiming superiority or company in one's misery, i.e., "I may not be OK but you're not either!" Cf. Thomas A. Harris, *I'm OK-You're OK* (Old Tappan, NJ: Fleming H. Revell, 1973). Harris' title indicates the healthy perspective. Cf. the earlier discussion on our sick society and our sick religions.

93. The Rudins, "The Jews for Jesus...," p. 19. Lyles, *op. cit.*, p. 707.

94. Claiborne, *op. cit.* White *op. cit.* My historical mind reflects on the Reformation. Catholics and Protestants were busy fighting each other but they stopped, formed an alliance, slaughtered the Anabaptists—and then went back to killing each other... A report from Uganda says Catholics and Protestants have stopped fighting each other. They stand together against the Muslims. Abraham M. Murray suggests "There must be a better road to Christian unity." "A View of the World," *Worldview* 21, No. 5 (May '78), 33–34. So Christians and Jews stop fighting each other long enough to fight the UC. How sad... Robert Ellwood, Jr., suggests a lack of even a rudimentary sense of history among many of the

studies of new religions. NB, p. 270. Those attacking new religions are often attacking their own history.

95. Kim, *op. cit.*, pp. 284, 286.

96. Marie Jahoda, "What is prejudice?," *Look* (24 May '60). Offprint. Gordon W. Allport, *The Nature of Prejudice* (Garden City: Doubleday Anchor Books, 1958). Harris, *op. cit.*

97. Singer, *op. cit.*, p. 10. This contrasts with the talmudic emphasis on human sinfulness, a reflection of the biblical concept that all have sinned and come short of the glory of God. By the standards used to judge DP, the Talmud could be accused of being antisemitic, along with the Jewish Bible.

98. Cf. Piazza, *op. cit.* James Parkes' "Verdict on Father Daniel," explores some of the issues, p. 78–91, in Parkes' *Prelude to Dialogue, op. cit.* Father Daniels was the son of a Jewish mother so he applied for citizenship as a Jew under the Israeli "Law of Return." The Israeli Supreme Court denied him citizenship because he had converted to Christianity. American Black Jews were also denied citizenship. Cf. Diamond, *op. cit.* So too the Falashas, the Black Jews of Ethiopia. Here is a horror story that matches the Nazi Holocaust or at least Leon Uris' novel, *The Exodus.* As the British kept Jewish survivors of the Nazi death camps out of Palestine, so news reports say the Zionists now keep out the Jewish survivors of Ethiopia's wars and starvation. What an incredibly brutal repetition of man's inhumanity to man. As the song, "Where Have All the Flowers Gone?" asks, "When will we ever learn?" Cf. Susanne Jackson Levy, "The Falashas of Ethiopia: God's Lost People." CC XCVIII, No. 22 (1–8 July '81), pp. 704–706. Note that this holocaust is not something that happened 40 or 50 years ago. It is going on now. Israel and America could open its doors wide to these poor people. Their black skin is irrelevant. The horrors of history are being repeated by Jews and Christians alike. Antisemitism indeed. Racism indeed. Double indemnity indeed.

99. One humorous response to the CFO declaration was that of course when the Protestants got a pope, it would be a committee!

100. Quoted by the *Interreligious Newsletter*, 1, No. 3 (May 77), 8.

101. Cotton Mather said "Religion brought forth prosperity and the daughter destroyed the mother." Quoted by Lawrence A. Cremin, *Traditions in American Education* (NY: Basic Books, 1977), p. 23. Personally, I think the economic and political power theory makes more sense for the origins of antisemitism. It started out as a family feud with both sides violating their essence as a faith and a people. When the daughter got power, she (Christianity) used it against her mother (Judaism). Economic greed, rape and scapegoating were strong contributing factors. As Lord Acton noted long ago, power tends to corrupt and absolute power tends to corrupt absolutely.

102. This of course is what Rudin accuses the UC of providing.

103. This is UC doctrine which Lara-Braud's committee finds objectionable.

104. On the threat of bureaucracy, cf. Richard L. Rubenstein, *The Cunning of History*; (NY: Harper & Row, 1975).

105. "Religious Education...," pp. 159–161. 166–167, 169. Harvey Cox has "warned against a 'too easy tolerance' trivializing important differences among traditions... Cox called for a theory of unification that 'accepts without relativizing' other traditions." *The Cornerstone* I, No. 10 (Ap '77), p. 3.

106. UC members feel hurt from the attacks of others, including Tanenbaum's.

107. "Do You Know What Hurts Me?," *op. cit.*

108. The CFO report, *op. cit.*, p. 2.

109. "My Dream Concerning Seminary Education," *The Cornerstone* I, No. 8 (Feb '77), pp. 5–6.

110. Kim, *Unification Thought...*, *op. cit.*, p. 284.

111. "Do You Know What Hurts Me?," *op. cit.* Tanenbaum and Kim are not the only ones who share common concerns. As noted earlier, the UC believes God is planning the Restoration. He calls the UC and all his people to work for this cause. Stanley N. Rosenbaum says we "Jews accept the impossible task of redeeming" the world. Cf. his "What to Do Until the Messiah Comes: On Jewish Worldliness," CC 99, No. 39 (8 Dec '82), pp. 1251–1254. It is time to work together. Let us begin.

Jonathan Wells

Unification Christology

The primary purpose of this essay is to provide an exposition of Unification Christology. In theory, such an exposition could be presented without any reference at all to traditional views; but since Christology is a central topic in most discussions between Unificationists and traditional Christians, some comparisons are in order. Of particular interest is the question of whether Unification Christology is consistent with Christian orthodoxy, so my secondary purpose is to address that issue.

Christological discussions invariably raise a host of epistemological and hermeneutical questions. For example: How can one arrive at knowledge of the "true" Jesus, given only the biblical text and the internal testimony of the Holy Spirit? How did the original Christians come to their conclusions about Jesus; would witnesses of the Second Coming arrive at their conclusions in the same way? To what extent does any theological position, traditional or modern, grow out of scripture; and to what extent does it interpret scripture from the perspective of unscriptural presuppositions? How can one test the validity of a text which claims to contain revelations from God? Such questions are fundamentally important, but they are not the topic of this paper, and I will largely ignore them here.

Likewise, I will not dwell on specifically trinitarian issues, i.e., those which deal with the relation between the divine in Christ and the divine in the Father. Although it seems to me that Unification theology affirms that the divinity manifested in Christ is "equal" (to use Pelikan's terminology [1]) "with the Creator and Lord of heaven and earth," and therefore that it avoids Arian heresy, this is a trinitarian question which is beyond the scope of this paper.[2] Instead, I will confine myself primarily to specifically Christological issues, i.e., those which deal with the relation between the divine in Christ and the human in Christ.[3]

The question of norms also deserves some introductory comment. Determining what is normatively "Christian" is, to put it mildly, a complex problem. The history of Christian doctrine reveals that the arguments of heretics have often been just as scriptural as the arguments of orthodox believers, so the New Testament alone is not sufficient to establish Christian orthodoxy. On the other hand, the same history, with its theological disputes and denominational schisms, points out the danger of confusing particular theological positions with "Christianness" in general. It seems to me that the best solution is to rely on the doctrinal statements of the ecumenical councils, in conjunction with the Old and New Testaments. Christologically, this means primarily a reliance on the Definition of Chalcedon. Needless to say, this proposal is not a perfect solution, since the Definition of Chalcedon has been rejected or ignored by some who consider themselves Christian, and since its interpretation is itself something of a problem. Nevertheless, we have to start our discussion somewhere.

Finally, in this paper I will assume that the normative text for Unification doctrine is *Divine Principle* (New York: HSA-UWC, 1973), which presupposes the authority of the Old and New Testaments. The use of *Divine Principle* as a norm is questionable, since Unification doctrine is still undergoing development, and no single text has been officially identified as the permanent and sufficient standard. However, *Divine Principle* is the most comprehensive text available in English, and I believe that it offers the best starting-point for our discussion.

I will begin my exposition with Unification anthropology, and will then proceed to discuss the person and work of Christ, the Unification view of the life, death, and resurrection of Jesus, and the Christological implications of the Unification view of Rev. and Mrs. Moon. I will then argue that Unification Christology falls within the bounds of Christian orthodoxy in its description of Jesus Christ, and that Christian orthodoxy does not exclude or proscribe the less traditional aspects of Unification Christology.

UNIFICATION ANTHROPOLOGY

According to *Divine Principle*, human beings were created to be the "perfect object for God's joy." God's joy is "produced in the same manner" as ours; and just as we experience the greatest joy when the object of our love reflects the best aspects of our own nature on as many levels as possible, so "God feels joy when He feels His original character and form objectively through the stimulation derived from His substantial object."[4] (Although Unification theology explicitly affirms that God has both masculine and feminine characteristics,[5] it follows traditional usage in referring to God as "He." For convenience, I will follow that usage in this paper.) Therefore, we were created in God's image and likeness (Genesis 1:26), reflecting on God's dual characteristics (which include internal character and external form, masculinity and femininity, and positivity and negativity, but *not* evil). However, in order to reflect God's nature fully, human beings must "inherit God's creatorship and participate in His work of creation." Thus, before creating human beings in His image God created the world in *their* image, so that they could exercise a god-like "dominion over all creation" as God's children.[6]

In order to "qualify" for such a role, human beings must first fulfill their "portion of responsibility," which consists of establishing a "four-position foundation" with mind and body centered on God. This is accomplished during a period of growth by directing one's love toward God until a state of "perfection" is reached. In Unification theology, "perfection" does not imply absolute infallibility, but refers to a complete "union with God's heart," in which limitations and mistakes are possible, but sin and evil are not (cf. Augustine's *non posse peccare*). A "perfect" individual is one who "feels all that God feels, as if God's feelings were his (or her) own. Consequently, he (or she) cannot do anything which would cause God grief," and thus would never sin.[7] Yet perfection is not merely relational, since Unification ontology is based on relationality. The "reciprocal base" formed by the "give and take action" of mind and body, which is initiated and sustained by God's "Universal Prime Energy," produces a "foundation of existence in an individual self." The four-position foundation thus constitutes existence, and a perfected individual is ontologically united with God.[8] Just as the body is "the substantial object to the invisible mind, which it resembles," so a perfected individual is "the substantial object to the invisible God, taking after His image," and is said to be "one body with God." Such a person becomes the "temple" of God, assumes "deity," and acquires the "divine value of God."[9]

However, perfected individuality is not enough. *Divine Principle* interprets Genesis 1:26–28 to mean that individual perfection is only the first of the "three great blessings" which God wants all human beings to fulfill. Once an individual has reached perfect unity with God's heart, the second blessing is to marry and raise sinless children. A God-centered family then becomes the foundation for a God-centered society, the Kingdom of Heaven on earth, in which people would "not perform any act which would hurt their neighbors, because the whole society would experience the same feeling toward those in trouble as God would feel in His grief over them."[10] The third blessing is to exercise God-centered "dominion" over the creation, such that perfected people would "subdue" the natural world "through highly developed science" and establish "an extremely pleasant social environment on earth." The fulfillment of all three blessings would represent the realization of "the ideal of creation," and would "return joy to God."[11]

God's ideal should have been realized in the family of Adam and Eve, our first human ancestors. However, Adam and Eve failed to fulfill their responsibility to direct their love toward God during their growth period (cf. Irenaeus' claim that Adam and Eve fell before reaching maturity). They lost faith, violated God's commandment, and fell into an illicit love relationship centered on the archangel, Lucifer, who thereby became Satan. Instead of forming a four-position foundation centered on God, they formed one centered on Satan, becoming ontologically united with him. Their children were thus, in a sense, children of Satan rather than of God; and *Divine Principle* calls this familial relationship, inherited by all the descendants of Adam and Eve, "original sin."[12] Since fallen people are *born* into this relationship with Satan, they cannot eliminate original sin by themselves. Only Christ can accomplish that task.

The Person and Work of Christ

Since the fall proceeded from Lucifer and Eve to Adam, salvation begins with a new "Adam," reversing the process. Christ comes as the "perfected Adam," the sinless man who succeeds where Adam failed (cf. Irenaeus' "recapitulation").[13] As "perfected Adam," Christ is ontologically united with God, and all of the predicates applied above to perfected individuals can be applied to him. Thus, Christ is "one body with God," the "temple of God's constant abode," and "the incarnation of the Word."[14] Therefore, Christ "may well be called God." Nevertheless, "he can by no means be God Himself," since the relationship between God and the human nature of Christ "can be compared to that between the mind and the body," and "the body can by no means be the mind itself."[15]

It seems to me that the Unification view of the work of Christ can best be understood as (1) the fulfillment and (2) the restoration of the three great blessings. In other words, Christ comes (1) to realize in his own person and family the ideal of creation which should have been realized in the first human family; and (2) to provide a way to eliminate original sin and its consequences for the descendants of Adam and Eve. Although the following schema does not appear in *Divine Principle*, it seems to me to be a helpful summary of the Unification view of the work of Christ.

The Work of Christ

(I) Fulfillment	(II) Restoration
1. First Blessing:	
To Achieve individual perfection.	To eliminate original sin in fallen individuals.
2. Second Blessing:	
To establish a God-centered family which becomes the foundation for a god-centered society (the Kingdom of Heaven on Earth).	To eliminate Satan's dominion in human society (manifested as immorality, atheistic Communism, etc.)
3. Third Blessing:	
To establish a God-centered dominion over the creation (manifested as scientific progress and economic well-being).	To eliminate suffering due to ignorance, misapplied technology, and economic abuses.

Since I.1 is a prerequisite for I.2 and I.3, and since II. is in every case dependent on I., the work of Christ is inseparable from the person of Christ. Nevertheless, it should be noted that upon fulfillment of I.2 the messianic office is assumed by a couple, the "True Parents." Just as God's image is both masculine and feminine (Genesis 1:27), and just as Adam and Eve together should have fulfilled the three great blessings, so the work of Christ needs to be completed by a True Father and a True Mother who can give birth to sinless children as well as re-birth to the descendants of Adam and Eve.[16]

However, fallen people cannot be saved unless they fulfill their portion of responsibility, which is to establish a "foundation to receive the Messiah." Only by having faith in the Messiah and by uniting with him completely can fallen people be separated from Satan, cleansed of original sin, and re-born into God's lineage.[17] Thus, Unification soteriology is consistent with the relational emphasis of Unification ontology and Christology. Since a four-position foundation centered on Satan constitutes original sin, our salvation requires the establishment of a four-position foundation centered on the True Parents, who themselves have established a four-position foundation centered on God. As more and more people follow the True Parents and fulfill the three great blessings, the work of Christ will be shared by more and more "true parents," until sin and evil are finally eliminated from the world and God's ideal is established.

Jesus

In the Unification view, Jesus was not merely an outstanding prophet or saint whom God chose for a special mission. Although *Divine Principle* neither affirms nor denies the virgin birth of Jesus, it clearly affirms what many Christian theologians have considered to be the principal content of that doctrine, i.e., that Jesus was born as the direct Son of God, without the original sin which all other human beings had inherited from Adam and Eve. Fallen people are of Satan's lineage, but "Jesus came as the Son of God, without original sin, from God's direct lineage," specifically to be the Christ.[18]

According to *Divine Principle*, Jesus, as the "second Adam," followed the course Adam should have followed. He obeyed God's will in spite of temptations and became "perfect," in the sense that "he knew God's heart completely and experienced His feeling as if it were his own."[19] Having established a four-position foundation centered on God, Jesus was "one body with God," the "incarnation of the Word." All of the predicates applied above to a perfected individual (and thus to Christ) are applied to Jesus.[20]

Jesus came to save fallen people and to establish the Kingdom of Heaven on earth as well as in the spirit world.[21] To accomplish this task, he did his best to inspire in people the faith to follow him, but he could not compel anyone to do so. It was the responsibility of fallen people "to believe in him whom He (God) has sent (John 6:29)," and to unite with him him completely; but people never fully accepted Jesus, and even his closest disciples eventually deserted him in his hour of need. Jesus should have been welcomed and honored, but instead he was rejected and crucified.[22]

However, the crucifixion was not without salvific value. According to *Divine Principle*, "we can never deny the magnitude of the grace of redemption by the cross." Although the crucifixion was not God's original plan, it became an alternate plan in the face of disbelief and rejection.[23] By rejecting Jesus, the Jewish people abandoned the foundation they had inherited from their faithful ancestors, and placed themselves completely under Satan's dominion; but by voluntarily surrendering his life to Satan on the cross, Jesus "ransomed" those who had rejected him. Thus, *Divine Principle* explains that God "handed Jesus over to Satan . . . in order to save the whole of mankind, including the Jewish people, who turned against Jesus, and were now on Satan's side."[24] Therefore, the value of the crucifixion is seen primarily in terms of rescuing those who rejected Jesus from the consequences of their disbelief.

The resurrection also had salvific value, though in the Unification view the benefits are due less to the resurrection itself than to the subsequent activities of the resurrected Jesus among his followers. *Divine Principle* interprets the biblical resurrection narratives to mean that Jesus' "spiritual body" appeared to his disciples (cf. I Corinthians 15:44)—i.e., it was a *bodily* resurrection but not a *physical* resurrection. Since even fallen people have spiritual bodies, and since spiritual appearances occurred even in the Old Testament, the significance of Jesus' resurrection goes beyond the mere fact that he appeared to his followers after his death. Jesus had entered a new and higher spiritual realm, and as a "divine spirit" he assumed the position of "spiritual True Father" (with the Holy Spirit in the position of "spiritual True Mother"). Since Jesus had defeated Satan by his sacrifice on the cross, it then became possible for Christian believers to be subsequently re-born spiritually (through the "spiritual True Parents") into "a sphere inviolable by Satan."[25]

However, the crucifixion had prematurely severed the connection which the incarnation had established between the spiritual realm and the physical realm, so the salvation offered by the resurrected Jesus was *only* spiritual. Thus, in traditional Christian piety we find the expectation of salvation in the "next life" or the "next world." Furthermore, children are still born with original sin, which indicates that our physical bodies have not been liberated from Satan's dominion. Just as Satan claimed Jesus' earthly self, so he continues to claim our earthly lives; and God's ideal has yet to be established physically on the earth. In preparation for the eventual completion of the work of restoration, the Christianity which Jesus established through his followers became the "second Israel," providing a foundation for the Second Coming.[26]

Rev. and Mrs. Moon

Divine Principle does not mention Rev. or Mrs. Moon, except to assert in its "General Introduction" that Sun Myung Moon is God's "messenger," sent to "resolve the fundamental questions of life and the universe." The same introduction characterizes *Divine Principle* itself as a record of "what Sun Myung Moon's disciples have hitherto heard and witnessed."[27] Beyond this the book is silent. Therefore, if we take *Divine Principle* as our normative text for Unification doctrine, there is no Church doctrine which claims messianic status for Rev. or Mrs. Moon.

However, it is no secret that most (and perhaps all) Unification Church members believe that Rev. and Mrs. Moon are the instantiation of the True Parents, the new Adam and new Eve, the messianic figures for the present age—in other words, the Second Coming of Christ. Indeed, I cannot imagine that anyone would long remain a dedicated member of the Unification Church who did not share this conviction in some form. Nevertheless, having laid epistemological issues aside, the relevant point here is not the question of whether Reverend and Mrs. Moon really are the True Parents, but rather the fact that Unificationists regard two living human beings, neither of whom is the historical Jesus of Nazareth, as messianic figures.

Having said that, I must point out that Rev. and Mrs. Moon are not thought of as functioning in isolation from Jesus of Nazareth. Unificationists are familiar with the account of how Jesus Christ appeared to Reverend Moon in 1936 and asked him to complete the work which Jesus had begun 2,000 years before. According to this account, Jesus not only commissioned Reverend Moon in the first place, but has also continued to communicate with him and guide him to the present day. It seems to me that this continuity between Jesus and Rev. Moon is providentially and soteriologically essential in the context of Unification theology, and therefore that it would be incorrect to say that Unificationists see Rev. and Mrs. Moon as competitors to Jesus.

Nevertheless, the question remains: Can a Christology be "Christian" if it is open to the possibility that Rev. and Mrs. Moon might be the Second Coming of Christ?

IS UNIFICATION CHRISTOLOGY CHRISTIAN?

Before attempting to answer this question, I would like to establish two points, both of which presuppose that Christian orthodoxy is defined by scripture and the ecumenical creeds:

1. Unification Christology falls within the bounds of Christian orthodoxy in its description of the person and work of Jesus Christ.

2. Christian orthodoxy does not exclude or proscribe the Unification claim that the work of salvation is to be completed by a new incarnation.

On the first point, the Definition of Chalcedon states that Jesus Christ in his divine nature is "homoousion" with the Father, while in his human nature he is "like us in all respects, sin only excepted."[28] The two natures are hypostatically (meaning substantially and not just morally or extrinsically) united, unconfused but inseparable.

It seems to me that *Divine Principle* clearly considers the divine nature of Jesus Christ to be fully divine. The Word which confronts us in Jesus Christ is not a subordinate demi-god (as in Arianism), but the same God who created the universe. When *Divine Principle* cautions that Jesus "can by no means be God Himself," just as "the body can by no means be the mind itself," it is merely taking care not to confuse the human and divine natures.[29] When *Divine Principle* "does not deny the attitude of faith held by many Christians that Jesus is God," it is not implying that Jesus' divine nature is divine in name only, but is acknowledging the validity of the *communicatio idiomatum* which has played such an important role in Christian piety and liturgy.[30]

As for the human nature of Christ, *Divine Principle* echoes Chalcedon when it describes the human Jesus as "no different from us except for the fact that he was without original sin."[31] Furthermore, in *Divine Principle* the Logos does not take the place of Jesus' soul, so Unification Christology is not Apollinarian.

Since the four-position foundation is the basis of Unification ontology, it seems to me that *Divine Principle* affirms the ontological equivalent of a hypostatic union between the divine and human natures of Christ, and avoids falling into the Nestorian error of positing a merely moral union. (It would be unreasonable to suppose that Christian orthodoxy requires us to affirm the Hellenistic metaphysics underlying the creeds.) Furthermore, since "we can never sever the relationship formed when God and perfected man become one body," Unification Christology affirms that the divine and human natures of Jesus Christ are inseparable.[32]

The objection might be raised that *Divine Principle* holds an adoptionistic view of Christ, since Jesus had to go through a growth period before reaching perfection. However, *Divine Principle* does not claim (as the adoptionist heretics did) that Jesus was merely an exceptional man, adopted from the mass of fallen humanity on the basis of his merits. Instead, Jesus was born sinless and was predestined from birth to be the Messiah. If it should be further objected that much of the Christian tradition has held that the hypostatic union was complete from the moment of Jesus' conception, I would answer that this is only one possible interpretation. It is not necessitated by logic or the creeds, since two "hypostases" can become one "hypostasis" through an appropriate process of uniting with each other (cf. the passages in *Divine Principle* describing how two beings "become one body"[33]).

As for biblical affirmations, *Divine Principle* agrees that Jesus will always be the unique "first fruits" (I Corinthians 15:23).[34] Furthermore, Jesus laid the only "foundation" for the Second Coming (I Corinthians 3:10–11).[35] And the prophecy that "this Jesus... will come in the same way" (Acts 1:11) is fulfilled by the account (mentioned above) of Jesus' appearance to Rev. Moon in 1936.

Scripture and the ecumenical creeds are comparatively reticent about the work of Jesus Christ, hence the variety of atonement theories in the Christian tradition (no single one of which can be considered normative for "Christian-ness"). Jesus came "for us and for our salvation," and his work can variously be described as "ransom," "sacrifice," "redemption," etc. This much is clearly affirmed by *Divine Principle*, and beyond this Christian orthodoxy does not require us to go. The Christian tradition has always affirmed the Second Coming as (in some sense, at least) the completion of the work of Christ.

On the second point, although God was incarnated in Jesus Christ He cannot be limited to Jesus Christ. God is infinite, eternal and omnipresent, while the human nature of Jesus is temporally and spatially finite. The distinction is orthodox, and the tradition has generally recognized that there is infinitely more to God than can be manifested in one human nature. Thus, for Thomas Aquinas the Logos is capable of assuming more than one human nature; and human nature includes body, soul, intellect, will, etc., i.e., all that we moderns generally mean by "human being."[36] The distinction between the infinite divine nature and the finite human nature surfaced prominently in the Reformation disputes over the so-called *extra Calvinisticum*, when the Lutherans attempted to go against the tradition by denying the *Logos extra carnem*.[37] Therefore, it seems clear that Chalcedon does not exclude the possibility that more than one human nature can be hypostatically united with God, and thus that Unification Christology is not unorthodox in its openness to further incarnations.

Given the reticence of normative claims for the work of Christ, and the ambiguities inherent in the variety of Christian eschatologies, it seems to me that nothing in scripture or the ecumenical creeds excludes the possibility that the completion of the work of Christ will involve further incarnation(s). In fact, several passages in Revelation (2:17, 3:12, and 19:12) strongly suggest that Christ will bear a "new name" at his Second Coming.

CONCLUSION

Based on the two points above, I conclude that Unification Christology affirms, in essence, what scripture and the ecumenical creeds affirm, and refrains from asserting what they proscribe. Therefore, Unification Christology cannot easily be dismissed as heretical, much less as "un-Christian."

Nevertheless, it seems clear that *Divine Principle* goes significantly beyond the Christian tradition in many of its claims. Unification Christology is not merely a restatement of traditional Christian doctrines, and cannot simply be deduced from them or reduced to them. However, I conclude that Unification Christology is continuous with traditional Christian orthodoxy, in the sense that it is not inconsistent with any claims which are essential to orthodoxy. In other words, a faithful Christian does not need to abandon the essential elements of the traditional revelation in order to become a faithful Unificationist. The transition from being a traditional Christian to being a Unificationist is undoubtedly a conversion of sorts; but I am convinced that it is a conversion which embraces and enlarges the traditional view rather than abandons it.

NOTES

1. Jaroslav Pelikan, "The Emergence of the Catholic Tradition," in *The Christian Tradition* (Chicago: University of Chicago Press, 1971), Vol. I, p. 226.

2. I have dealt with some of the trinitarian issues elsewhere, in "Some Remarks on Trinity and Christology in Unificationism," August, 1981 (unpublished).

3. I am indebted to Pelikan (*op. cit.*, pp. 174–175) for this formulation of the distinction between trinitarian and Christological issues.

4. *Divine Principle* (New York: Holy Spirit Association for the Unification of World Christianity, 1973), pp. 41–42.

5. *Ibid.*, pp. 45, 55, 77, 82, 97.

6. *Ibid.*, pp. 24–25.

7. *Ibid.*, pp. 43, 140–141.

8. *Ibid.*, pp. 28–39,141, 209.

9. *Ibid.*, p.206.

10. *Ibid.*, pp.43–44, 101–102.

11. *Ibid.*, pp. 41–45, 100–102.

12. *Ibid.*, pp. 74–75, 83–84, 88.

13. *Ibid.*, pp. 208–209.

14. *Ibid.*, p. 206.

15. *Ibid.*, pp. 210–211.

16. *Ibid.*, pp. 213–218.

17. *Ibid,*, pp. 110, 147, 228.

18. *Ibid.*, pp.367–368.

19. *Ibid.*, pp. 140, 212, 214.

20. *Ibid.*, pp. 209–211.

21. *Ibid.*, p. 140.

22. *Ibid.*, pp. 140–147.

23. *Ibid.*, pp. 151–152.

24. *Ibid.*, pp. 183, 359–361.

25. *Ibid.*, pp. 165–171, 212, 360–362.

26. *Ibid.*, pp. 147–149, 364.

27. *Ibid.*, p. 16.

28. John H. Leith, ed., *Creeds of the Churches*, Revised Edition (Atlanta: John Knox Press, 1973), pp. 30–36.

29. *Divine Principle*, pp. 210–211.

30. *Ibid.*, pp. 209–210.

31. *Ibid.*, p. 212.

32. *Ibid.*, p. 206.

33. *Ibid.*, pp. 31–46.

34. *Ibid.*, p. 213.

35. *Ibid.*, pp. 362–370.

36. St. Thomas Aquinas, *Summa Theologiae*, III, 3, 7.

37. See E. David Willis, *Calvin's Catholic Christology* (Leiden: E.J. Brill, 1966), pp. 2, 9–10, 74–75, 109–110. Also, Karl Barth, *Church Dogmatics* (Edinburgh: T.&T. Clark, 1978), Vol. 1, pp. 169–171; and Vol. 4, pp. 52, 181.

Lloyd Eby

The Kingdom of Heaven

The concept of the Kingdom of God on earth as a grounding for a social theology and practice goes back at least as far as Walter Rauschenbusch, and probably to Augustine and beyond. As Rauschenbusch wrote in *Christianizing the Social Order*:

> ...Christ's conception of the Kingdom of God came to me as a new revelation...I found that this new conception of the purpose of Christianity was strangely satisfying. It responded to all the old and all the new elements of my religious life. The saving of the lost, the teaching of the young, the pastoral care of the poor and frail, the quickening of starved intellects, the study of the Bible, church union, political reform, the reorganization of the industrial system, international peace—it was all covered by the one aim of the Reign of God on earth. (p. 93)

This insight or motif dominated and inspired all of Rauschenbusch's subsequent writing, teaching, and work.

Within the past two decades another similar appropriation of the Kingdom of God motif has been made by the so-called liberation theologians of Latin America. The liberation theologians are, of course, a diverse group, and it may be a mistake to treat them collectively without differentiation, but I believe we can safely and accurately say that they have many things in common, and that we can give a general description of liberation theology that applies more-or-less accurately to the liberation theology movement as a whole.

In Part I of this paper I will present a paradigmatic development of liberation theology, relying primarily on the work of Gustavo Gutierrez. In Part II, I will present a reply to liberation theology based on Unificationism, and I will try to show that Unificationism is a theology of liberation *par excellence*.

PART I

Probably the most thorough, reflective, and well-known liberation theologian is the Peruvian Catholic, Gustavo Gutierrez. In his *A Theology of Liberation* he identifies or emphasizes three levels of meaning of the process of liberation: (a) *liberation* as opposed to *development*; the aspiration of oppressed peoples and economic and social groups to escape the oppression of the wealthy nations and oppressive classes; (b) *liberation* as an understanding of history in which man assumes conscious responsibility for his own destiny, leading to "the creation of a new man and a qualitatively different society;" and (c) *liberation* as the transformation of man through the encounter with Jesus Christ: "Christ the savior liberates man from sin, which is the ultimate root of all disruption of friendship and of all injustice and oppression. Christ makes man truly free, that is to say, he enables man to live in communion with him; and this is the basis for all human brotherhood." (pp. 36, 37)

For Gutierrez and liberation theologians in general, there is a close link between salvation and justice. The growing Kingdom of God is the arena in which justice and liberation occurs. Liberation is simultaneously personal, historical and soteriological, but the historical moment or movement is the important precondition of the others. Liberation theology replaces the traditional Catholic "natural law" ethic with the dynamic of "liberation," operating in history.

Gutierrez, and Latin American liberation theologians in general to some degree or other, employ three weapons of implementing their program. These three are Marxism, socialism, and utopianism. From Marxism these liberation theologies take the notions of class struggle and class oppression, coupled with alienation, and a notion of history as energized and moved forward by a struggle between the oppressors and the oppressed. God and Christ are seen as identifying with the oppressed.

The solution to the economic difficulties of Latin America, and the Third World and other economically disadvantaged (poor) people in general, is seen in socialism. An economic revolution that destroys the bonds of capitalism of the landowners, and of the powerful nations and corporations of the North (especially the United States and the multinational corporations) is seen as necessary, and socialism, especially a socialism indigenous to a particular country or region, is taken to be the desired alternative to the status quo. Without this break with the economic (and attendant political and religious) status quo, there is no liberation (and hence no salvation).

Utopianism interpreted positively provides a vision for radical change. Utopia "leads to an authentic and scientific knowledge of reality and to a praxis that transforms what exists." Three elements characterize the notion of utopia as Gutierrez develops it: its relation to historical reality, its verification in praxis, and its rational nature. In terms of history there is a denunciation of the existing order and an annunciation of what is not yet. The stage between denunciation and annunciation is the time for building, which can be achieved only in the praxis. Finally, utopia belongs in the rational order; it is neither opposed to nor outside of science (pp. 232–239).

When he speaks of sin, Gutierrez says that it is not only an impediment to salvation in the afterlife, but:

> ... a historical reality, it is a breach of the communion of men with each other, it is a turning in of man on himself which manifests itself in a multifaceted withdrawal from others. And because sin is a personal and social intrahistorical reality, a part of the daily events of human life, it is also, and above all, an obstacle to life's reaching the fullness we call salvation (p. 152).

One emphasis of Gutierrez is universal salvation. This leads to the question of the presence of the Lord, and to the religious significance of man's acts in history. One is turned to consideration of this world, and sees the afterlife as the transformation and fulfillment of the present life, and not the "true life," as it was often seen to be in previous notions of salvation.

Gutierrez says that the Bible establishes a close link between creation and salvation, and states that "the link is based on the historical and liberating experience of the Exodus" (p. 153). He says that the Bible deals with creation not to satisfy philosophic concerns about the origin of the world, but as part of the salvific process; not as a stage previous to salvation, but as creation with an end in mind. Creation and salvation are thus the initiation point and continuation of history, of the human struggle, and of the work of God (Yahweh). Political liberation, of the people of Israel, and, by extension, of the oppressed of today, is the active self-creation of man. The liberation of Israel from Egypt in the Exodus was a political event, and the Exodus experience is paradigmatic, remaining vital and contemporary due to similar historical experiences which the People of God undergo.

A second important Biblical theme leading to the same conclusion, according to Gutierrez, is eschatological promise. This theme appears throughout the Bible; the proclamation of the Kingdom of God is the annunciatory theme of both the Old Testament prophets as well as of John the Baptist, Jesus, and the writers of the New Testament. What is characteristic of this message is that what is to come "cannot be understood as the continuation of what went before" (Gutierrez quotes Von Rad). The New Testament, however, changed the interpretation of the Old Testament texts by spiritualizing them, raising the promises from the "temporal," "earthly" or "carnal" level to a "spiritual" one. But Gutierrez resists that spiritualizing. He says, "If by 'present life' one understands only 'present *spiritual* life,' one does not have an accurate understanding of eschatology." The prophets announce peace, but peace requires justice, and peace, justice and love are not private or only internal, they are "social realities, implying a historical liberation" (p.167). But we must not be misled: although the eschatological promises are being fulfilled through history, they cannot be completely identified with any one or another social reality; they go beyond and open up new and unsuspected possibilities. "The complete encounter with the Lord will mark an end to history, but it will take place in history" (p. 168).

Gutierrez is probably the most thorough of the liberation theologians, but most of the others would subscribe (with varying degrees of emphasis) to what Gutierrez has been represented above as saying. There has been an expansion of liberation themes in North America as Latin American liberation theology has encountered, fertilized, and joined forces with Black theology and feminist theology. Latin American liberation theology seems generally, however, to be more closely allied with Marxism and with political revolution than has been Black and feminist theology (with various exceptions).

PART II

In one of his speeches Rev. Moon proclaimed:

Our goal is to liberate the human heart from under Satan and liberate our Heavenly Father, God, who has been suffering so long. That is our goal. (Vol. II, p. 36, #9)[1]

On many occasions he has said similar things. For example:

You will liberate our God by yourselves. Restoration will be completed when these sons and daughters restore this condition and liberate our God. (II, 38, #17)

And on another occasion:

We are the ones who can assure God His happiness, His joy, His peace. We are going to liberate the heart of God and His anguish and sorrow. By doing so, we are liberating all mankind and its burden and sorrow. Finally we can push the entire Satanic world out of this world. (II, 39, #21)

At Madison Square Garden in 1974 he stated:

Before we cry out for our salvation, let us cry out for the fulfillment of God's will. We must liberate God from His sorrow, His grief. When we have solved God's problem, man's problem will be solved automatically. (II, 44, #41)

But lest anyone think that Unificationism holds that God can be liberated without solving human sin, Rev. Moon said in 1976:

Our goal is to forge ahead to win the salvation of the world. We are proclaiming the liberation of God. We will liberate God from His sorrow. That is our goal. No matter how many years it takes, humanity is destined to accomplish this goal. It is not just by our choice. It is our destiny. There is no other way. Unless humanity is liberated from sin, then God cannot be liberated. (II, 48, #56,57)

The liberation of God and of mankind and the world are inextricably linked. Neither can be accomplished without the other.

> We join together for the liberation of the world and the liberation of
> mankind, but that's not all. We are gathered together to liberate the heart of
> Jesus and of God himself. (II, 48, #58)

The liberation theme is central to Unificationism. Unificationism, however, has a much more complex understanding of liberation than does
any liberation theology. In the Unification view, liberation is not confined to any specific class or color of people; all of humankind and most
of all God needs liberation.

From the Unification perspective, Gutierrez was quite correct in noting that the Bible begins with creation, and that creation is connected
with salvation. In the Unification view, however, the intervening parts of
the Old Testament, namely the Fall, and all the course of Divine providential history leading up to and beyond the Exodus are paradigmatic. The
Fall was an historic event; its occurrence makes salvation necessary. Unless we understand the origin of sin, its precise etiology, and the precise
Divine providence or prescription for its elimination and solution, we
cannot work knowingly toward bringing about the Kingdom of Heaven.

Unification theology has three major divisions: the Principle of Creation, the Fall, and the Principle of Restoration. According to the Unification view, creation would naturally and more-or-less effortlessly have
resulted in the Kingdom of Heaven (or Kingdom of God—the terms are
interchangeable) had the Fall not occurred. The Principle of Restoration
(or Salvation or Liberation—again the terms, as used in Unification
theology, have nearly identical meanings) was the Principle instituted by
God after the Fall to re-create humankind, liberate them from sin, and
restore them to God, to one another, and to their true humanity.

The fundamental relationship between God and humankind is the
Father-son, or parent-child relation; the first man and woman, Adam and
Eve were the son and daughter of God, and should have grown to
maturity, when they would have produced offspring that would in turn
have also been sons and daughters of God. The growth to maturity of
Adam and Eve—and the process of restoration of human beings to the
Kingdom of Heaven—has three movements, corresponding to what
Unificationism calls the Three Great Blessings: the first is perfection of
individuality, the second is perfection of the family (husband and wife,
giving birth to children), and the third is the perfection of human
interaction with all things of creation (the material and spiritual worlds).

Perfection does not mean lack of error, but maturity and completion of love. Individual perfection means maturity of love between the individual and God. Family perfection means that love between husband and wife becomes inviolable, patterned on and centered on the Divine love. This love results in children, and since children are born with the characteristics of their parents, the children of such a family would be born into the divine lineage, having the ability and propensity to grow to perfection themselves. Since all of mankind should be as one extended family, in such circumstances the love and harmony of the divine family would extend to all of humankind, and from all of humankind to all of creation.

All this failed to occur. Unificationism takes the Biblical account of the Fall to be an historical event, involving the original man and woman, who are taken to be historical individuals, and the archangel Lucifer, who became Satan. God is understood as having created for love and in order to have a recipient and sharer of His love. In the Fall, Adam and Eve united in love centered not on God, but on Satan: Satan usurped the position of God and became the father, as it were, of the human race. Both God and mankind were thus thrust into bondage; God because He lost His children, and mankind because it lost God, lost the grounding and source of love and its ability to give and receive love, and lost its true humanity because it took on the characteristics of its false father Satan— the characteristics of lust, greed, selfishness, violence and hatred—in the interchange. All of mankind since the Fall has existed under these shadows. The task of liberation, then, is the task of freeing both God and mankind from the devastation of the Fall. This means that mankind needs rebirth into the Divine lineage, and this rebirth can be accomplished only by True Parents, i.e. a couple sent by God as True Man and True Woman to replace the sinful Adam and Eve, and through whom all mankind can be reborn.

The task of restoration/salvation/liberation is a historical task, and began with Adam's family. Again, in Unificationism, the central characters of the Old Testament—Adam, Cain, Abel, Noah, Ham, Abraham, Isaac, Jacob, Esau, their wives and children, and so on—are understood as being genuine historical persons, as well as paradigmatic characters.

Sin disrupted all relationships—the vertical relationships with God as well as relationships between husband and wife, sister and brother, family and family, class and class, nation and nation, and so on. Human beings were partly responsible in the beginning for their perfection— their historical development, if you please—and they remain partly responsible in the Providence of Restoration. It is God's task to send the Messiah, but people must exercise their responsibility in completing certain historical conditions so that salvation/liberation can be brought about. The two paradigmatic movements in liberation are the development of faith and the restoration of unity through harmonization. Faith restores the relation of love with God. Harmonization restores relationship with others—spouse, sisters, brothers, opposing tribes or nations, opposing classes, and so on. Unificationism speaks of this harmonization as restoration of the Cain-Abel relationship.

Restoration of the so-called Cain-Abel relationship needs to take place before liberation can be achieved, but it is the key to liberation. Whenever two human entities achieve unification centered on love and the Divine ideal, liberation is accomplished. To speak of liberation in terms of class conflict, as Marxists and liberationists do, seriously misrepresents liberation. Class conflict is the opposite of liberation but harmonization and unification of different classes is an example of true liberation.

Liberation must be achieved on every level. I quoted above several instances in which Rev. Moon spoke of liberating God—I know of no so-called liberation theologian who recognizes or speaks of God's bondage, but in Unificationism the bondage of God is the most serious bondage of all. In addition, there must be personal or individual liberation, family liberation, liberation from racism and racial hatred and intolerance, liberation of tribes, liberation of social and economic affairs, liberation of nations, and finally liberation of the whole world and God. Even Satan must finally be saved or restored so that he can be free of sin and give and receive love in a Divine manner and according to the Divine provision.

Unification praxis attends to liberation within its developing historical and eschatological unfolding. The key to family restoration is in Divine Marriage, effected through the True Parents. In this marriage, the love relationship between husband and wife is effected, centered on God through the True Parents. Since the Original Sin was a relationship of love between man and woman centered on Satan and Satanic desires, and since the fundamental desire of God in creating was having the Divine family, the institution of Divine marriage (called 'the Blessing' in popular Unification terminology) is the key to the solution of Original Sin, and the necessary precondition of all other liberation. The key to racial liberation is also found here—through Divine marriages between persons of different races.

Liberation in the social arena—classes, nations, and world liberation—comes in practice through Cain-Abel harmonization. This liberation does not come through violence but through sacrificial love. Violence is of Satan and whoever tries to achieve liberation through violence is taking the course of evil. Concerning wealth and poverty, Rev. Moon has said:

> You should love the world in such a way that you would want to have God bless a prosperous country all the more, and you would pray to God that He bless the nation to such an extent that this nation would be the leading nation of the world: "I want to see You being joyful over this prosperous country, after having poured out all the blessings You have concentrated on this nation." On the other hand, if you see a miserable people, an underprivileged and underdeveloped nation, then you should feel the zeal swelling up in your heart to make that nation see the sunshine some day. You should want to help elevate the standard of living in that nation, because you hate to see Father in anguish over that nation... (I, 270, #13)

Unificationism is not insensitive to or unknowing of or uncaring about economic and political degradation and evil. It does not, however, accept the Marxist analysis of the origin of these evils, or its prescription for them. One of the most innovative and intriguing proposals recently made by Reverend Moon is for building a global highway, starting in Asia and connecting mainland China through North Korea and South Korea and then by bridge or underwater tunnel to Japan. The western leg of the highway would traverse Asia and connect with Europe and Africa. By extending the highway northward from Asia it could connect North America through Alaska (again by bridge or tunnel) and move south from North America into South America, finally linking all the major continents of the globe. The highway, as proposed, would be a mile-wide free-trade and free-flow zone, within which would be built hotels, shops, airports and so on. Travel and trade would be unrestricted.

This proposal may seem bizarre or naive at first glance, but on reflection it is much less bizarre and naive than proposals for violent revolution, as intended solutions to economic and political oppression. Violence leads only to further violence and resentment, and the skills needed for successful violent revolution are practically useless in subsequent nation and society-building. But a global free-trade and free-movement system would allow a great migration and intermingling of peoples and cultures and economies. Furthermore the skills of harmonization and construction that would be necessary in planning, financing, and constructing such a global system are precisely the skills needed for global harmony, well-being, and social and economic advancement. If a cadre of young and enthusiastic people forms around this project, and if more and more people from more and more countries come to support it and work for it, then indeed a global harmonization heretofore unseen and unforeseen could begin.

It should be apparent by now, that while it profoundly agrees with liberation theology on many particulars, Unification theology is generally profoundly opposed to the received liberation theologies. This opposition is not because Unificationism favors the status quo—either racially, politically, or economically—but because it is opposed to the materialism, the violence, the class hatred, the selfishness, and the narrowness of liberation theology. Liberation theology has been criticized many times in the past, and some of its most thoughtful proponents, such as Jose Miguez Bonino in his *Doing Theology in a Revolutionary Situation*, have themselves addressed its internal contradictions: I do not think it necessary, therefore, to address those here. Only a theology of sacrificial love and service will break the chain of violence (both institutional and overt), repression, hatred, conflict, and selfishness that has enslaved all the peoples, societies, institutions, and nations of the world.

Although God does indeed identify with the miserable and oppressed and poor of the world, it is a fact of the Fall that all people, regardless of political or economic status, are oppressed by sin. Economic and political oppression are one additional example of and expression of sin. No person is truly human without being reborn through the True Parents, and attempts at salvation through political and economic revolution fail to understand and deal with these deeper expressions of sin.

Unificationism, like received liberation theologies, is an historical, eschatological, and hopeful theology. The Kingdom of God must arrive on earth, in history, as the culmination of sinful history and the beginning of a new order. This is the hope of both God and mankind, and the present age is understood in Unificationism to be the beginning of the new age. Thus, rather than 'Utopia,' which has overtones of the impossible, Unificationism is a theology of present and future realized hope.

As I began this section with quotes from Reverend Moon concerning liberation, I will end it with some things he has said concerning the Kingdom of Heaven:

God's goal of creation is to have man and the world of happiness, that is, the Kingdom of Heaven, reflecting the love and creativity of God, which relate to mind and matter respectively. We know this is true from the fact that man's ideal is actually to seek after such a man and world. (I, 311, #2)

In a 1973 speech on the Kingdom of Heaven, he said:

The Kingdom of Heaven is a place where there is happiness, peace and the ideal. That's not a place where people fight with one another. It's a place where there is no jealousy, no arrogance; it is filled with righteousness, goodness and justice. That must be a place filled with God's grace and ideal. You must know that you are destined to go there and it's a serious matter... There are no such things as jealousy, complaint and other ugly feelings in the Kingdom of God. (I, 313, #6,7)

Concerning racial harmony:

We have to love men of the north, south, east, west and all directions, and also, white people, yellow people, black people, and all people, then we can go to the highest heaven. From that place the Kingdom can be started. (I, 313, #10)

The Kingdom of God is not something ready-made:

The Kingdom of God on earth, the ideal kingdom, is not a ready-made thing which we can go and get—but we are making it, establishing it, with our hands. (I, 313, #12)

Concerning discrimination:

There is no discrimination in the Kingdom of Heaven. (I, 314, #17)

On humanity and nature:

What is the Kingdom of God? The Kingdom of God is the place where we live together with God, nature, and men in harmony and peace. The Kingdom of God is the place where we love each other, we love God, we love nature, we love man. (I, 319, #40)

And finally, speaking of the role of the Messianic Couple (True Parents) in bringing about the Kingdom of Heaven, Reverend Moon declared:

> If you and your ancestors and your children become one in love and harmony centering on the True Parents, then the world will easily become the Kingdom of Heaven centering on Divine love. The five races will be united into one... If you carry the will of God and True Parents then even if you die right now you will bring the Kingdom of Heaven. (I, 259, #92)

In this paper I have attempted to present a summary-overview of Latin American liberation theology. I have tried to present that theology as accurately and comprehensively as possible in a short space. Following that, I have presented Unificationism as an alternative liberation program. I have attempted to show the ways in which Unificationism agrees with liberation theology, as well as its profound disagreements. My stance toward Unificationism has been acceptive and presentational, rather than critical. It is my view that Unificationism does represent the historical, eschatological, hopeful, and even scientific[2] Divine prescription for the liberation of God and mankind today.

NOTES

1. There is, up to the present time, no generally available edition of Reverend Moon's speeches. Some have been collected in a volume called *New Hope*, and others have been published singly. All the quotations in this paper come from a two-volume edition of excerpts entitled *The Way of Tradition* (New York: Holy Spirit Association for the Unification of World Christianity, 1980). Citations here are by volume number, page number and excerpt number from that work.

2. This aspect was not treated above, and is only beginning to be explored in the literature.

BIBLIOGRAPHY

Bonino, Jose Miguez. *Doing Theology in a Revolutionary Situation*. Philadelphia: Fortress Press, Confrontation Books, 1975.

Gutierrez, Gustavo. *A Theology of Liberation*. Maryknoll, NY: Orbis Books, 1973.

Moon, Sun Myung. *The Way of Tradition*. NY: Holy Spirit Association for the Unification of World Christianity, 1980. 2 vols.

John Andrew Sonneborn

God, Suffering and Hope: A Unification View

Unification theology depicts God as the immutable Creator Who, wholly loving and responsive, suffers as a consequence of human recalcitrance yet is potent and ultimately victorious, fully worthy of worship. The theological interfacing of immutable sovereignty with suffering is importantly paradigmatic for the response to suffering of Unification believers in their personal and evangelical life.

In this essay the Divine response to suffering (given the existence of unnecessary evil and human suffering) is elaborated theologically as rational and just, and is brought to bear on selected crucial topics of traditional Christianity (e.g., justification, transcendence and immanence, freedom, love, omnipotence, desire and need), a philosophy of suffering is developed, and various theories of Divine and/or human suffering are reported and reflected upon.

There is an over-all flow of thought in the essay. It may be simply stated. God is the Creator. There is evil in the creation. What will God do? How will God do it? What does it mean for God? What would God have us do?

In the essay's four parts are presented, essentially: 1. the Creator's *immutabilities* remaining in the face of evil; 2. the *nature* of the suffering Creator's appropriate outward response toward a world with sin and evil, of God's potent remedial action; 3. that the Redeemer God is the transcendent and immanent Creator enables the *effectiveness* of his remedial action, the content of the redemptive way of love being specified; 4. that God (successfully depending upon human cooperation) will succeed in the permanent abolition of personal suffering. Thus, we will present God as the basis of hope, having created in love and working in love to end suffering, and will indicate the nature of the effectiveness of God's working, of the sureness of God's total triumph, and the responsibility of humans having faith in God.

The presentation is in accordance with an understanding of the basic insights of the Unification Movement which was initiated by the Reverend Sun Myung Moon. Its standard philosophical analysis of God-in-Himself[1] is probably most clearly stated in Sang-Hun Lee's essay, "God in the Unification View" in S. A. Matczak (ed.), God in Contemporary Thought. *We will at this point preliminarily set forth in condensed formula some aspects of our concepts regarding God-in-relationship.*

We view God as with a fundamental relational impulse, Who became Creator of all else that is, Who has remained in loving relationship to His creation, and Whose dynamic is for the continuing development of creation and extension of relationships through incorporation of unions as foundations in greater unions according to a determined scenario. The universal patterns of interaction, union and development are explained in Dr. Lee's essay[2]. Man is viewed as in this image of God, with the same fundamental impulse and relationality while being a creature participant, in himself and with others, in the foundational scenaric development. The whole creation is so formed that new or greater entities are formed through interactions of paired entities mediating God's creative action and drawing power into the combined entity formed.

God's being logically precedes His purpose for acting which precedes His design of creation. "After"creation and through time the essence of God remains the same. This is the God of love which is the source of life, acting as love and for development of value in the beloved. God's purpose of creation is itself wholly insubstantial and His Word and force exist originally in a dimension beyond the cosmos. For substantial creation, God's love must be mediated through the creative "thinking and practice" of an entity in creation.

A series of responding interactions in creation begins inwardly with the stimulation of man's original mind. God's love has been *received* when a human acts with love towards interaction and sharing with another. However, God is the Creator of the substantial cosmos, and *full* response requires interaction of two substantial beings with a result of value for God's further creating, actualizing God's love. Thus a full response of God is cooperative and includes the openness to further loving.

(Often, in the essay a thinker is cited or represented; unless otherwise evident,

representation of his or her views is concluded in the sentence containing the citational footnote.)

I. GOD'S IMMUTABILITIES

A. Perspective of God as Creator

God is understood as the Creator. There is disunity in the creation. Before we consider the Creator's response to the disunity we consider the perspective of the Creator, His motivation, eternity and joy.

1. God of heart: desire of heart, creation, desire. According to the Unification Principle, the essential feature of God is heart, the impulse which seeks joy and desires to give love to an object.[3] God with this desire then has the self-experience of the desire. Then from the self-experience of the desire to give love to an object and find joy arises the desire to create the object.

In Aristotle's view,[4] the perfection of God lies partly in His not being One needing friends. We simply state that God *desires* to create an object for relationship. We can think of the Creator God as prior to creation but not as a creator who will not create. God desires relationships. What appears presently at stake is that if desire is not of the essence of God, then man in God's image is essentially reactive.

God, seeking joy, has created responding objects. He has, in fact, created living objects, including man who fully shares His creativity.[5]

These concepts of God are also appropriate inference from an account of creation in which creaturely development is characterized by increasing continuity of special relationships. This is true of individual development and of development in history. Taking responsibility for juniors and offspring became characteristic of the more developed species. Man generally feels and seeks unending special relationships.

God, to joy fully in the response of His object, must create the object in His direct image and therefore His object also must love and receive joy before God's joy is full. Further, the object in the image of God the Creator must fully exercise its creativity for God's joy.

God cannot duplicate Himself as His own object. God is unique and omnipresent. He created beings distinct in space. The mutual relating of these beings requires periods of time. Then when God gives love and seeks a response of relating within the creation as well as to Himself, that response may conclude only in the future. There will be the process of stimulation, period of inner response, and outward response. (This two-staged responding is given philosophical form in *Unification Thought*, pp. 17–26 which is summarized in Lee's essay, p.747.)

God Who is the Creator seeks joy and desires to give love to His creatures and find receptive and active response.

2. God of heart: desire, purpose, plan, power, action. God may not cause his own extinction nor alter His essential nature. Then we may say that God's desire to give love and find response is ineradicable.

Many peoples with "primitive" views of God(s) were concerned that their God might cease from desire for the loving relationship. This was a concern of the people of the Bible even to the times of Hosea and Deutero-Isaiah.[6] Nevertheless, the perdurable human love of those in relationship is a basis of the religion of the Jews. According to Jewish tradition, Cain could not kill his relationship with Abel, Noah was impelled to attempt the salvation of those who mocked him, Abraham went to the rescue of Lot who had left him, Jacob made great gifts to the hostile Esau, and Joseph experienced redemptive love for his brothers who had sent him towards death.[7]

In the stories of Abraham, Jacob and Joseph, man is shown as not a mere animal, but as created in the direct image of God with ineradicable love. Yet, Christians believe, Jesus found it necessary to preach extensively on God's perduring love,[8] with the absolute proof being given through crucifixion, resurrection and salvation.[9] (A relevant clarification of perdurable love demonstrated in the climactic event of Jesus' life is given in Y.W. Kim, *Divine Principle Study Guide*.[10])

God's primary will is to fulfill his desire. His activity is purposeful toward the fulfillment.

This activity cannot be wholly random (else "Creator" and "God" would be inappropriately applied to Him). Then we consider God's Logos or Word. God has a plan for accomplishing His purpose. According to Genesis, God, conceiving an ideal in which His loving would find response, expressed a scenario in which humans should become mature, multiply, and come to govern other creatures.[11] Jewish and Christian philosophical theologians since Hellenistic times have generally considered this scenario a segment of a scenario of creation from its inception to its full realization. In the usual Judeo-Christian view, God will in no wise alter his Word.[12]

God will not withdraw His plan: it is for the fulfillment of His desire. Further, God must not be a mere designer of creatures and their development but must be an exerciser of power towards the realization of His plan (else, again, He could not be called "Creator" and "God").

That God has ineradicable desire and irrevocable will to accomplish the

*purpose of fulfilling the desire according to unalterable scenario of lasting media-
tional relationships and that He has created beings according to His Word and
should continue to act towards realization of the scenario, is appropriate to the
Unification view of the God of heart.*

3. God of vision. God, having created, being the author of the cosmos,
"knows" (through self-knowledge) its constitution. He "sees" exact
opportunities for action. He knows His purposes and the ends He seeks.
In every human situation He knows the interactions which can fulfill a
step in the desired foundational sequence of development. He knows the
conditions in the scenario to be accomplished, definitive increases in the
scope of union. God always sees His correct action towards His desired
result.

Also, God sees that only action initiated by Him will achieve change
towards the desired result, else there will be an increase of disunity.

God knew in principle the dynamics of action and result. Acting into
the cosmos, he experienced the actual result of actions. He created the
non-human creatures and the innocent humans, all of whom responded
fully to His action and returned joy. Then, He experienced, sinful humans failed of sought response (certain interactions between created
beings). However, God sees that even if His action be directly largely
fruitless it is ultimately effective towards His goal, and that in the future
He will give to greater reception, will give more life.

The Bible records that after humans first had violated God's commandment, He was near them, called to them simply, spoke with them simply,
and acted to give them clothes of animal skin.[13] When the Kingdom of
God is established on earth He will take full and increasingly powerful
actions enabling complex interactions.

*God sees the way to His goal; He visions the significant levels of unification
and the mode of action for foundational unification, and understands the combinations of actions for realization of His scenario.*

4. God of sureness. God is sure that there is opportunity for change
resulting from right action. (This is true despite the disunity in the
cosmos.) We state, although we have not shown it as logically required,
that God knows that His power will always be sufficient that opportunities for truly developmental change in the cosmos will continue to occur.

God desires to act, knows the desired activity, sees that there will be
opportunity for action with some response and that the result of the

response will be a foundation in a sequence of desired changes. God is sure of total victory, the definite realization of His primary will, the accomplishment of His whole purpose. This latter statement is our assumption; it will be important later in the essay to validate it.

God's indestructible sureness is that right action is always foundational towards His ideal to be realized.

5. God of just loving. Having sight and assurance, God always acts with justice, that is, He gives love appropriately, offering both maintenance and maximum advance towards the fulfillment of all. God acts with rightly purposed love and respecting the inner responsiveness of his objects. God acts and awaits the response.

   With inorganic or non-human organic beings, God awaits response, but the beings are bound by the principle of creation to respond. With man, God's action of rightly purposed love is an offer. God desires man's totally free response because he wills fully contributory creativity.

God always wills the development of unity. But with man, God's actions may find resistance. In the inner responding of a human subject or object may occur the temporary rejection of part of God's offer. The resistance may stem from false valuation. It may stem from addiction to alternative response.

Even a temporary rejection of God's offer causes separation of man from God, that is, man does not then function as one with God, passing on all the love received and returning joy to God. This separation causes God to suffer.

God creates through just love offering development of unity. The offer can be and has been disdained, partly, only by distracted man.

6. God of just loving: His suffering. When man rejects God's offer of love, a foundation is not laid, joy is not returned to God, He is not presented with the opportunity for greater giving of love. Instead, there is disunity of God and man. Interhuman relations of love face dissipation and distortion. Also, on rejecting God's spiritual guidance, man is prone to cause disorganization of the physical. Thus, when God offers love to man, He faces the possibility of suffering.

   Brunner conceives that in eternity God, "in Himself," the Father, has "no Word, no light, no life."[14] Without relating to creation as it is, God is considering only His ideal. Then, it is in relating to creation as it is that

God does have life, Word and light, and the creation may depart from them and bring suffering to God's heart. Thus God in engendering the Logos opens the possibility of suffering.

God's Word is unchanging through time, but is communicated progressively in time. God's ideal and His purpose to realize it also remain throughout time. Von Hügel notes that man seeks the timeless and unchanging.[15] These are found in God. Yet the ideal is realized, the purpose accomplished only through a process in time, and the ideal will then be expanded through temporal process.

Schopenhauer reasons that the capacity to feel the greatest pain is held by man of all creatures.[16] The more far-ranging the creative love, the greater the possible pain. Therefore, God has the capacity for the greatest suffering.

In the sinful world, the rejection of love *de facto* occurs to some extent; (Sölle, 163: "love does not 'require' the cross, but *de facto* it ends up on the cross.") The extent is variable and it has not been proven that such circumstance is permanent; however, God's love is declined by the unjust. The increase of God's flow of love is then precluded.

God's vision and sureness reach beyond sin. Spurned, how will God act? A general answer must be: continuingly with power and love.

When God's love is not fully mediated for actualization, He cannot continue a development of unity. Man is functionally separated from Him and in further fragmented circumstances. When God perceives this, He finds not joy but great suffering. God's ideal and purpose are changeless and His sight and sureness are transcendent, but his just love has been thwarted.

7. God, Satan. If God is the source of love only properly directed for unification and increase and of the reception of that love, then there is some other cause of the contrariety that is found. We say that Satan, not God, caused contrarient disunification—isolation and arrogatory maintenance. Such disunity tends toward more disunity.

(Some of the dynamics of disunification will be set forth at various points in this essay: at the end, an account of the origination of Satan. The concern here is the Divine perspective.)

In the normal process of developing unification, where a complex of parts is functioning as a whole, the *development* may call for separation of some parts externally; but since the development of the whole will not be interrupted there is no significant loss of value. However, development may be halted not only by lack of opportunity for whole action but by severe disunity involving parts. This is separation contrarient to the purpose of the whole. The parts are not responsive to the center of development.

When creation is responding to God, unity is developing. When the work of Satan interferes, parts of the creation are disassembled and a development cannot directly be resumed.

Not all events are fully the will of God. God initiates all activity, and does so for good. But Satan's work is the perversion of God's love and the formation of conditions of unity apart from God's over-all fabric of unification.

God's will for creation is not the cause of suffering. Suffering was not caused by God as a challenge to man. Also, for man, being created through and born by our parents is not the cause of our suffering; it is the cause of our existence as a desiring being. In the face of our desire to give love, conditions of disunity cause suffering.

Satan is the one who caused evil separation and the blocking of development; the unresponsiveness causes suffering. Thus God is continuingly intent to create according to His original plan. God, true desire, and true development do not necessitate nor cause suffering.

8. God's frustration. Satan's partial domination of circumstances makes impossible the acceptance of the fullness of God's love. Man imagines scarcity and is addicted to illusory or shortlived security. In the creation, the mediation of love is hampered by lack of communication, sharing and cooperation.

In Satan's realm, man's faithlessness, addiction, and isolation must resist God's offer.

9. God contravened. Satan tempts circumscribed man and in the event that man succumbs man accuses God and man and newly rejects God. Satan and his human agents stimulate lack of faith in future abundance, offer evil advice of immediate consumption, despair and grasping, and practice seduction. The pattern of sin is repeated, culminating in misappropriation. Cliques are formed to seek power according to other than the highest standard of love available. Lavell writes, "every bad will pursue isolated ends which, sacrificing the whole to the part, always contaminate the integrity of the whole."[17]

Through Satan's tempting and man's succumbing there is further rejection of love, and sin and misappropriation develop.

Review and prospectus. Thus far we have seen (i) the Unification view of God as Creator Who, *seeking ever-increasing joy*, ineradicably desires to give love in relationship with an object and find mediational response, *acts* according to a permanent *scenario* for the establishment of His Kingdom on Earth, visions the levels of significant unification towards and sees opportunity for right action ultimately effective towards realization of His ideal, and is sure that there will always be opportunity for truly foundational change.[18] God is love respecting the nature of and the inner response of the object. His action of love is an *offer* to man for response in full freedom. (ii) Man can temporarily reject part of the offer, breaking functional unity. This *separation* and the halting of creation (*lack of foundation*) must bring suffering, not joy, to God. Thus it was offering love in time according to Word that *opened the possibility of suffering* for the eternal unchanging Creator. (iii) God and creative desire *did not cause disharmonious disassemblement*; the scenario is not proven inappropriate. Suffering is caused when created beings enter into conditions of unity which prevent their functioning for God's purpose of the whole. The unities are founded on falsity and they frustrate God's desire for development in creation. Man yields to temptation of false valuation, responds pervertedly to God and forms non-participating unions. *Thus God the Creator is confronted with distortions in the creation; the Creator experienced suffering.*

We should find if the view of God with these features, this motivation, and these immutabilities is tenable in the light of continuing rejection, distortion and suffering. Can we understand a *response* of God (with these characteristics) to suffering, one that is consistent with His nature and the nature of the creation, according to revelation and experience, and such that God remains worthy of worship? Through considering alternative conceivable responses to suffering, and their significance, we should further validate our view of God and more deeply understand God and suffering.

To fulfill this, we should show that our view of God affords hope in that God is presented as *motivated* to sustain distorted creation and to remedy suffering and as *justified* in doing so, and in that He is immutably capable of ending suffering; that God with the capacity of being Creator has the capacity of being *Redeemer*.

B. Perspective of the Creator as Redeemer.
God's internal response to the fact of distortion.

1. God unaltered: desire. God's suffering follows from the broken relationship between God and His creation. God feels love and can express love but the love cannot wholly be actualized. This is externally caused suffering; there is no return from without to stimulate God's heart. (Of course, there is some response, at least deep within man. Adam, sinful, according to Genesis 3:8, was not ignorant of God's presence. There is some joy from any response. But there is God's great suffering. In light of this suffering, which nothing in this essay is intended to construe as total, we will not always refer to the joy.) God could not develop His cosmos, it was shattered. Then, why does not God ignore the circumstances? Why does not God abandon creating (and creation), show indifference?

We have said that whether or not we think of God as *needing* friends, the Creator *desired* a responding object and created to fulfill that desire, and that the desire is of God's heart, His essential feature. Then, God would not be perfect if the rejection by His object caused Him to alter desire. God must also be less than a perfect creator if he created beings who rejected Him permanently. (But it may be that the best creating was to create the object who might reject Him temporarily, that God so creating can still be seen as perfect. Then the actual fulfillment of the possibility would not alter the fact of His perfection.) God must desire the return of the separated object. Again, this is not "necessity" of God but desire of God Whose essential feature is to seek joy and to give love. When we say that God "must" do something, it is to say that He must do it if He is to achieve His desire of love.

If fundamental desire were to be killed, there would be no pain. If God were to "stop," there would be no suffering. But we must also say that when man thinks of his own "stopping," there emerges from his depths a scream and this is of the greatest suffering, the scream of the suicidal. Since essential desire is unalterable, then mental withdrawal from deep desire is a separation *within* the desirer, an inner disunity causing suffering. If we have a God who abandons creation or simply waits with no desire, then He has no frustration and no rage. But the consequence for man is that desire is not of the depth of *man*, and man could also kill desire (or existentially choose to be only sub-human, merely animal, with limited desire), then suicide or narcosis would be a remedy for any suffering.

God's desire is unalterable. God is the source of man's desire and loving, He is the cause of our continuing existence and desiring, and when our deep desire is frustrated we suffer. Also, God is the source of the love which is distorted in Satanic action which causes the conditions which cause the frustration. Thus, there would be no human suffering if there were no God who continues loving. Sölle[19] concludes that God is justified in loving only if He is suffering, sharing man's suffering; He is also not justified (does not have just love) if He watches suffering now and acts only later to lift it. If God is omnipotent and fully loving but not devoting all adequate force for change, rather waiting until a later time to remedy circumstances causing pain, then we either now cannot contribute to the remediation or else may so contribute only wholly apart from this God (and possibly with some other God). Man seeks a God of victory to end fragmentation. If God's remedial action is to occur only later, it is difficult for man to *believe* in any forthcoming victory; what evidence would we have? Only intuition? "revelation"? If so, how could we know the revelation as a *true* revelation? Even a past victorious act of God, even the resurrection of Jesus, for instance, does not prove the ultimate victory of God if He is not acting now towards that end. Meanwhile injustice continues. If God appears inactive now, man may be tempted to seek a "more just" deliverer.

If God is not creating and acting for the removal of obstacles to creation, He is either a God of the past only, or a God bound up in the cycles of nature, or a God apparently disconnected from nature; such a God is not a supernatural God.

One might conceive of a God (and humans) not indifferent to separation and simply *bearing* separation with great calmness. But the testimony of experience indicates that this is not the reality; none has testified to such a God.

It may also be asked why God does not annihilate the divided creation and commence creating anew. If He were to, He would then have *no* response to His loving. (A true parent will never wish the annihilation of his most beloved child, no matter how great the recalcitrance.) Whatever receptive condition of unity exists is an objectification of God Himself and a foundation for God's development of unity, of reunification towards resumption of development of creation. God the Creator will never seek the sure lessening of His foundation in His creation.

God's desire is frustrated by man's rejection. The desire of the perfect God remains unaltered and is to be fulfilled ultimately, through man's return, although its absence would end all suffering. To fulfill His desire, God is to continue loving, sharing man's suffering and willing to devote all adequate force towards its remedy. Supernatural, God is not to destroy, but should act demonstrably in the cosmos toward the end of fragmentation.[20]

2. God unaltered: supernatural understanding. God knows that His purpose to establish the Kingdom of Heaven on Earth and continue its establishment in expanded form will continue unchanged, as will His force. Thus God's imagination goes beyond the limits imposed by suffering as experienced and foreseen by humans.

God loves life, and since, as mentioned, only God may initiate change towards the result desired by Him, God is not passive. Nor does he simply wait for *others* to remedy the conditions (which, admittedly, God did not cause), for there would be a conflict within God, a disunity and inner suffering were He to withhold loving help which He has the power to offer.

The way of non-life and that of annihilation being alien to God, He actively seeks change of His creation from death to life. The supernatural understanding of suffering stimulates action for change.

God seeing that although not all His love is received there is opportunity for reception (and hence loving His creation), and knowing of the infinite continuity of His purpose and force, comprehends beyond the limits from suffering to the full reception of love. Perfect vision affords supernatural understanding of suffering which stimulates activity: God loves life, is without passivity, and is unified as solely and unreservedly creative.

3. God unaltered: justice and sureness. "God Who says 'Behold, I make all things new' (Rev. 21:5), cannot himself exist now without suffering over what is old."[21] The question then must be, how is God to seek change? For God there are no interactions in which He is beggar; a weak God is not God. Also inappropriate for God, especially in light of His ideal, is any unjust action: coercion (relational action in disrespect of inner process) to achieve more unity, or possession (frustration of inner process) to prevent the worsening of circumstances.

The living future-oriented God must purpose true value. God can value the equivalent rewards of future moments equally with those of the present for He knows now of His presence in future moments. Therefore, God can have a calmness with suffering and this calmness is one with His freedom to act lovingly now and act with more powerful love in the future.

Noro says that God's blessedness consists of His love, perfect without any object.[22] We say that God's blessedness, His perfect love, indeed precedes the relationship with the object, in fact created the object, and remains blessed *in* relationship: the perfect love does not require any remoteness. (In our piety, we call God "Father" and consider that He must be in relationship. A father should be blessed before begetting a child; he might thereafter be blessed in himself, considered apart from the child; but the parent's heart does not ever forget the child.) In contradistinction to Noro who considers that God's suffering would indicate a disturbance of His blessedness,[23] we say that God remains blessed while suffering.

In the Near Eastern culture, in contradistinction to major civilizations of the Far East, blessing always indicates readiness to create. This blessedness of the unselfish loving creator is not necessarily blessedness free from frustration from the spurning of love. This blessedness is also not the Hinduistic calmness of the selfless "bearing" of suffering. A sufferer, even if remaining blessed, is yet unfulfilled.

To conceive of the continuing blessedness of the God of love is, as Noro points out (on pp. 4, 316), important to our worship, that we else find no possibility of our blessedness, of any tranquility.

As God is sure of victory despite present oppositions, there is for Him no fall into rebellion against the order He has set up, neither is there any despair.

Thus God is wholly free to continue his just loving. Then, where shall He focus His loving? As the cosmos has been created it is only through mankind that all things will come together in unity under God. Therefore, since God does not destroy the creation, He must act for and through man for restoration.[24]

God, to end suffering, will not beg for change nor act unjustly. Living and eternal, and calm in seeking true value as possible, the suffering Creator is free to act with just love at all times, sure of more potent future action; ultimate victory being assured according to the order as created. God, blessed with perfect love, remains blessed in any relationship, perfect love being indestructible, remaining creative even if spurned. God acts for and through man to bring about the unity of all beings under God.

4. God of action with continuing suffering. God continues in correct loving action in circumstances inclusive of separation and He offers according to the circumstances for the increase of unity and love. But Satan prevents full development. So Satan is the cause of God's *continuing* to suffer. God "permits" this suffering.

Does this "permission" indicate any passivity of God? Scotus offered a proposition that God is not passive, saying that to be passive means that something more interior is active, whereas God is the first principle.[25]

Divine Principle points out that activity is always linked with receptivity. No subject exists in a void; activity implies relationship. But relationship is sustained by give and take.[26] Once a human is created, with God assuming permanent responsibility for him, God and the human can be considered as in a whole, of which God is interior and the human is exterior. It is urged by Von Hügel that logically God does not have emotions because He has no body.[27] But by no greater anthropomorphism, the Church is considered the body of Christ, and, in line with Jesus' statements in *John* of God dwelling in individual humans, *Divine Principle* considers the individual also to be the body of God. In line with Brunner's theology,[28] at least in time "God for man" has emotion. Then, with Barth, God in Himself is identical with God for man. As do the mental faculties from the body, God, directing man, should be receiving information of condition and activity from man. God is the first but not the only actor. Thus there should be a reciprocal relationship between God and man. (To posit of God "an emotional life" necessarily of joy only, as is characteristic of Thomas and Von Hügel, is to speak only of a state of bliss, not referent to a usage of emotion as linked with sensitivity and to inter-responsiveness with a body.) If God were passive in the sense used by Scotus, there might be a cessation of communication from the requisite more interior or "higher" God. Then there would be diminution of receptivity for "our God" and a consequent diminution of His activity. But since "our God" *is* the first principle, all His receiving is from those inferior.

That God has no superior seems to be at the heart of the concern for God's aseity. Noro,[29] in a discussion based upon Barth's *Die Kirchliche Dogmatik 2, 1.*, suggests that the perfection of God is His aseity; His agape love comes from his aseity; His aseity is required for His freedom. In the Unification view we must show that God always can offer more love and meet any challenge, for He has more love to give, not needing to receive to have it; thus He has perpetual freedom. This is the most interior freedom, the freedom of desire and for giving (Von Hügel: God is not exhausted by creation, incarnation, redemption.[30]) A full meaning of freedom of loving should embrace receptive opportunity. But with the total inner freedom of original love, God is unchanging in His readiness to give any love. This is the standard sought by Noro and Barth.

There is no restraint from any superior (Satan, who caused suffering, is a creature of God), and, from the inferior, no man can add nor subtract from God's purpose and ideal nor add nor subtract from His force. Although he may find the spurning of His love, God is not essentially changed by suffering. Thus God can be and is fully receptive and fully active. God is not "passive" but He does suffer.

Being God, the suffering Creator cannot annihilate Himself; rather, He continues giving love for increase of unity and love. Activity is always linked with receptivity. As God offers love according to the circumstances and Satan continues to prevent full development he becomes the cause of God's continuing suffering. God is initially active toward all from whom He receives, being in no way passive; God's ideal, purpose and force are not dependent. God is fully active and fully receptive: God has inexhaustible potency for loving and is eternally ready to give more love; He has totally and perpetually the most interior freedom, of original love. He "permits" His suffering and continues essentially unchanged.

5. God of affirmative love. Does God's receptivity and suffering affect the quality of His love? God is not "blind"; He neither thinks nor pretends not to suffer. God loves life so much that He affirms it even if inclusive of suffering. This is to say that God's love for life is not dependent upon conditions. God's love is immutable. Thus God accepts the fact of suffering. This acceptance does not end it as suffering.

God accepts suffering *because* he is determined upon change and the realization of His ideal. He affirms the abnormally painful life only as temporary. With no affirmation of life, God's love would be inward love only. Then God's Kingdom would be only in a "heaven" wholly apart from any creation. However, heaven is also for humankind. Heaven is not *for* God Himself but from and with God. God affirms life inclusive of suffering so that God can act creatively.

Loving life unconditionally and unqualifiedly, God perpetually affirms it. God accepts the fact of his real suffering because His love is not only inward and He is determined upon the end of all suffering and the realization of His ideal, the Kingdom of Heaven for God and humanity.

6. God of rationally applied love: His endurance. God's love is directed firmly towards the goal. God has the capacity to endure suffering without alteration of His ultimate purpose or of His giving of love. Sölle writes[31] that if one has a greater goal of unlimited helping of *all*, one can have that capacity for suffering which, Nietzsche noted, excludes antipathy, division and resistance. With this firm goal, God's justice is immutable.

God is *for* humanity. In God is perfect oneness of heart, love, force and ideal. Thus God can endure the limitation of the effectiveness of His forceful offer of love. God's outer freedom is limited; His energy of love is somewhat imprisoned: There is discrepancy between the extent of spiritual and physical power in creation and the opportunity for increase of unity, because the power is fragmented; full opportunity is lacking for the actualization of love. Yet, for God, there is no inner rebellion against this; and there is no inner imprisonment in God: no lapse into any sense of futility, no unwillingness to express His love. God loves Himself and that self is love, and love moves also always outward. God never dies, but God continues without inner limitation to offer true help to all. Thus there is with God no vacillation of the expression of love. God knows the Satanic from the Godly. There is never uncertainty for God, and no self-criticism of His thoughts and actions. There is never, in God, internally caused suffering.

With immutable justice God loves Himself Who is love, being also always for man. There is for God no internally caused suffering: in oneness of heart, love, force and ideal, God distinguishes the Satanic from the Godly, and holding the goal of unlimitedly helping all and committed to the original scenario as the only way of realization of the ideal, God is continuing, willingly and with self-validation, in ceaseless helpful activity.

7. God's will. Weatherhead writes of God's "intentional will."[32] This is God's will for direct increase of unification. If God's intentional will had always been followed there would have been no suffering. In the fallen circumstances when God's intentional will is followed God achieves a goal of increased unification without increase of suffering, a diminishment of suffering results. Weatherhead also speaks of God's "circumstantial will." This is God's will where evil conditions have led to resistance of His intentional will.[33] In this one sense God wills His suffering to be now: His "circumstantial will" is for actions of love to result in suffering in order to end suffering soonest (it, also, is towards realization of His ultimate will to establish a world of full give and take of love, hence of increase).

8. God's circumstantial will. Because God is firm in His purpose towards His goal, and because He knows what is reaped from sowing, God can exercise creativity under the circumstances of delay and He frames a new strategy with new tactics to achieve the same eventual result. The over-all plan remains unaltered. To accomplish the tactics is God's circumstantial will.

God's circumstantial will, His "new planning," seems to indicate change in God. Many Christian theologians have been among those insisting on the immutability of God. In support of this, Noro[34] quotes

James 1:17 as saying that God is "the Father of lights, with whom is no variableness, neither shadow or turning." However, an examination of the original wording in context shows that what is really being said is that there is no alloy at the side of God. We have posited God changeless in heart, desire, ideal, purpose, vision, sureness and justice. Barth has emphasized that God is always loving; this is a necessary quality of the Person in whose fellowship man is embraced and loves.[35] God must always be presenting Himself for participation in fellowship, offering opportunities for loving. The changelessness of God here is essentially His unlimited loving. If God had not this constancy man's love would be limited and would be no love.

Thus God has the same lovingness, the same purpose, the same project offered for man's participation. God has the same over-all plan. Yet in each planning for founding the same successive stages of unification and extension of love the specific detail would accord with the actualities of the relationship in which the love is being offered.

God's desire has always been to act with and through man towards His goal. Hence, when man does not respond God suffers and *so* knows man's suffering. God's knowledge is not abstract and not magical. God then knows that He must suffer *with* man.

According to God's circumstantial will, God is to give love, working in such foundational conditions of unity as exist yet among circumstances with the dynamic of increase of disunity. His will is to replace the conditions tending towards disunity with conditions of unity in which God can work, foundations for God's greater work.

Lewis[36] wrote that God does not prevent evil but actively opposes it and seeks to destroy it. In the Unification perspective, we speak of a good condition as one conducive to God's further magnification. Identically, in Genesis 1, whenever God has proclaimed a condition to be good, further action for development can occur. An evil condition, then, is one preclusive of development, one in which God cannot work. To destroy an evil is to disorganize the evil condition for re-organization of the parts as a good condition. God's motivation is not any revulsion at the evil, but He seeks restoration in order to have his rejected love received.

Suffering experienced by God consequent to His expression of love according to His circumstantial will is God's "voluntary suffering." It is received during the course of a series of actions restoring conditions as foundations for God's work. God does not wait for suffering to vanish (for the estranged to return to unity with Him); rather, He acts according to opportunity and at all times for salvation. Since the accomplishment of God's circumstantial will depends on the free will of man, any instance of God's willing may be refused. Then the deeper suffering is prolonged.

But suffering will in any case not be ended until there is the unity of all. God is sure that some human will sometime someplace cooperate with His circumstantial willing for the establishment of a foundation and that His intentional will for establishing the next greater scope of unity will likewise be accomplished, and that there will thus be successive preparations and developments with the whole unity ultimately attained. Thus any suffering coming to God in the process of circumstantial volition, whether from accomplishment of His will or from disobedience of it, is to be endured in light of the dream for the whole. God will establish a cosmos in which evil can never occur. This cosmos will be governed by God and humans who are freely bonded in mutually satisfying developmental reciprocal relationships centered on God. This "new" cosmos will be constructed from the present reality. It is nowhere else to be fabricated.

With constancy God presents Himself and His embracing fellowship for participation and opportune loving. God's project continues the same. The detail of his planning accords with the actualities of the relationships in which His love is to be offered. God's circumstantial will is to accomplish new tactics in His new strategy to realize the original scenario. God actively seeks restoration in order to have His rejected love received; God relates and gives love to and works in and through only conditions of unity offered to him as foundations for increase. God's circumstantial will, involving God's suffering with man, is for action as a means of disorganizing the evil conditions of unity, preclusive of development, and reorganizing the parts in good conditions of unity, conducive to God's further magnification. In order to achieve His whole purpose, God willingly suffers for the sake of restoration; where His will for restoration is denied the suffering is increased and prolonged.

Review. Based on the Unification view of the nature of the Creator God, we have seen His internal response to the fact of distortion in creation. (i) The perfect God of fundamental love seeks to end suffering through return of the separated object to union with Him, continuing to suffer (as both loving and just) rather than to avoid suffering by desertion or annihilation. He *affirms* the created order. (ii) God is *unified* as solely and unreservedly creative. He is *objectified* in His creation, always finding some response and joy.[37] His initiative and only his initiative can and must result in remediation of the dysfunctional separation and the suffering of God and man. The Creator and source of love is justified as a supernatural, omnipotent, loving God because He responds by *devoting* all adequate force for immediate remediation. God acts for and through man for restoration. (iii) We have shown that God so viewed *can act* for salvation. The blessedness of perfect love and lovingness is not impaired by suffering due to rejection of love. The *receptivity* of God *enables* His actions of love which must accord with the actualities of relationships, so that, although He continues to suffer due to the power of Satan (His creature), *He is not passive*. In circumstances where power in the creation is fragmented, God's power cannot fully work; but, we have stated, God has powerfulness sufficient for remediation and He is unhesitantly willing to use power unsparingly for that purpose. He does not will continuing suffering but affirms life inclusive of suffering in order to restore and develop His creation for man to be with Him, to end suffering the soonest. Thus we have shown, against certain challenges, that the suffering God of unchanging and unified motivation, love, purpose, Word and power retains unimpaired blessedness, *aseity* and might, and is fully receptive and variously active, with perpetual inner freedom, although temporarily externally limited.

God as presented thus far is worthy of hopeful worship, for He is wholly, continuingly, fully loving, suffering with man, unchanged, and with no limitation of powerfulness. This is the immutable, suffering Creator.

II. GOD'S CONTROLLING, RESTORATIONAL, INITIATIVE RESPECTING MAN'S FREEDOM

[God, wholly loving, sovereign and dynamically capable, inspires our hope; but God has not fully won man back to Him, ending suffering. We here indicate an outward response of God to suffering, a just potent remedial initiative fully respectful of human freedom, yet sovereign. Further definition of good and evil is offered in subsection 8.]

A. Tactics of Restorational Love.

The suffering Creator's remedial yet respective initiative.

1. Locus of restoration. Satan has not changed any laws. There are no natural laws which caused separation from God and human conflict. Separation and conflict did not originate (as have been suggested by some) because sexual reproduction has death as a necessitated antithesis. They did not originate because man's plasticity gives him freedom. Satan freely seduced man and man freely chose to love illusory fantasy and inertia, and exclusion and possessiveness. Man wavers; first individually, then in groups wavering because of wavering individuals. Once an exclusive or possessive group is formed it has inertia distinct from that of its members.

Man lives with inadequate standards for loving and limited freedom. The life of a group may be transformed through exposure to a new standard, but any new elevation of standard must come about through an individual human. The change must begin *in* the individual human.

Many physically mature humans have gained well-developed physical and emotional power and mature desire, yet abnormally limited standards of loving enable formation only of unions so limited in range and endurance as not to bring deep satisfaction. In growth according to God's norm, the standard of conscience would develop along with emotional and physical development. Fallen man, suffering, needs elevation of standard.

2. Disuniting forces. Satan works through man when man seeks a lower unification than God desires, one relatively narrow in time and space. This occurs upon disinclination to follow high standards or in ignorance of how to use power, resulting at best in the search for simple repetition. Progress is stopped, God suffers, others are affected; disunity is increased, descendents are harmed. When man is disinclined to follow the highest standard known and forms a union, Satan claims the union.

3. Forces of stasis. Man born with original sin is not receiving God's love fully.[38] He cannot receive God's love fully. Also, it is our corrupted nature, unable to center fully on God, to be attracted to Satan, to center on Satan, our false "father."

Man centered on Satan is attached to that which is relatively external, determining to maintain relationships without willingness to seek or enter greater relationships. His attachment is based on the false word: the word is of limitation, finitude and self-reliance. The word is based upon supposed scarcity. This attachment becomes anchored in a religion of limitation and finitude. Man's responsiveness is limited; this is the internal condition of the limitation.

If man receives God's love he will act to give love. Yet, in the world centered on Satan, others are prone to reject him. In giving love for a wider relationship, the present relationships have been disorganized but there is some hope for their reorganization in a larger structure of relationships. When, receiving God and giving love, man, being reject-ed, finds no embracing structure of organization, he remains with the disruption from giving (which normally is compensated). Then he expe-riences pain from without. So each man fears the consequence of loving and the fears of the other justify the fears of the one. Then, if man is acted on by God, receiving, he envisions coming to pain. For this reason, being acted on and experiencing pain are both called, in English, "suffering."

Tauler and Eckhart[39] presented this analysis. There is "a self-centered possession of things, among which can be reckoned one's own achievements," even one's relationship with God. These have all been finite. The possession of them is for oneself who is therefore possessed by them. Then if these are lost as is inevitable (according to laws governing the finite), one suffers passively. The problem is that the *refusal* to experience pain from separation from that affording relatively external value causes unwillingness to be receptive to God.

When man is unready to expand his giving, he cannot receive greater love from God. To receive may be to suffer. Therefore the refusal of God is the refusal to suffer. Due to original sin and to addiction we refuse to experience normal separation for growth and, under the Satanic circumstances, to experience abnormal pain in the cause of uncertain development. The refusal frustrates man's deeper desire and causes him suffering. This refuser is the man who resists suffering; as a result, God directly suffers.

God always calls for separation, offering eventual reintegration in larger unities of greater value. Satan offers his word: a vision of scarcity, opposing faith with limitation; a standard for maintenance, opposing justice with finitude; a predication of doubt, opposing hope with self-reliance. Man fears that activity in response to God's call for unification will result in open-ended suffering. Congenitally attached to the finite and addicted to values and modes of replenishment, fearing God's voice, man refuses God. The result of inactivity is suffering.

4. God's work. Identifying Satan and Satan's objectification in conditions as the cause of suffering, of blocking the development of love, God must seek elimination of the causal conditions.

God may not just eliminate (or reform) Satan at the outset if He wants man to develop in full responsibility; it was man who allowed himself to be drawn to Satan and fell into the alienated condition. God rather seeks, by the elimination of alienating conditions, within man and socially, to free man so that man can grow in love.

How does God act for changing man's condition from that of being blocked and resistant to God's love to that desired by God? Man's deepest desire is always to love. Therefore, God stimulates the desire for increase of loving. This God always does, whether with totally free man or as

God's fundamental action in the course of restoration.

As man resists his desire for more far-reaching values, being otherwise attracted, God shows or would persuade man not to continue in the present course of life. In the course of restoration, this is a call for repentance.

God presents standards. These are of the truth needed for wider expression and actualization of love, for action in accordance with desire. This God also will always do for free man or as a man becomes free.

God also will set up a situation in which man can have give and take action, establish a structure of unity, actualize love, and establish union. The situation encourages action in accordance with desire. God would always do this, but in the fallen world to establish the structure requires a chain of repentance.

To attract man to free himself from Satan's orbit so as to express love more widely, God stimulates desire for joy, calls man to turn from the way of failure, and presents the higher standard and the opportunity for more fruitful interactions and union.

5. Deprivation through laws. God's laws operate to show man that his limited way will not succeed in the maintenance of valued union but will lead to added suffering. God then stimulates thoughts of repentance.

Behind the disasters caused to man in accordance with God's laws, God has no sense of hostility or "revenge." Rather, these laws work for man's reclamation. God's prophets warn of suffering as "punishment" but only if there is no change of behavior. So God is *responsive* to human response.[40]

God works through laws to warn of impending suffering. He seeks man's repentance to end suffering.

6. Law, suffering and repentance. God, through his laws, endorses suffering from loss of inflexible or partial relationships and of illusions of full satisfaction. This, God's legal punishment, is a demonstration. In the affliction is the demonstration that man cannot defy nor long misappropriate the laws of God. Man must see his weakness and his bondage to God's natural law and spiritual law; so man's hubris is to end.

God does not become greater through man's humiliation, but God's greatness can be perceived, that God's Word is greater than man's word.

Man perceives that God *is* greater than himself.

When, through the laws of God, man is deprived of the values he earnestly sought to fix, he becomes open to the experience of dissatisfaction and desire and he may know of his desire for greater value. The frustration of the deeper desire is causing man (and God) the greater suffering.

While God's laws operate autonomously and inexorably, God can only proffer to man the call for repentance. Man may reject the call. He may choose merely to redouble his efforts to regain and gain relatively trivial unification. Laws in themselves only through attraction serve the unification of complementary commonly purposed elements and, through lack of attraction, cause separation in any other case. Only God's initiative of love can lead to the change of internal conditon in man preparative to external action for greater change.

This is the purpose of God's legal action against man, that if man *accepts* suffering from external loss he may find liberation of the desire for greater unity, he may repent of his limiting ways. Also, he may become aware that he is suffering due to his ignorance, his not knowing to change, to overcome frustrating conditions; thus he may discover his need for God's new Word and for power to change conditions.

7. Deprivation by volition. Although God wills unification and happiness, not disunification and suffering, in the circumstances of the fallen world His circumstantial will must be for separation from undue attachment to old values and thus for suffering. This is suffering from lack of fulfillment of false desires (desires whose fulfillment will obstruct fulfillment of desires for more inclusive value). God wills man's detachment from certain relatively external relationships and the detachment causes suffering since it has been through these relationships or in dependence on them that man's love has been expressed.

For a period of time, man must be stripped of these relationships. If he strips himself in seeking freedom, the period is a sacrificial period. The dissolution and suffering will happen sooner or later, one way or another, voluntarily or through inexorable laws (for the relationships are untenable without being part of a larger structure which is being disdained). If man holds to overly external values beyond a certain time opportune for repentance and sacrifice (often specified by God's Word according to His circumstantial will), the suffering to be experienced will be greater. So God only speeds inevitable suffering, seeks to minimize suffering, and urges its *use*.

God urges and requires the suffering of detachment as a means of education: as a reminder of deeper desire and the deeper suffering which man is, in fact experiencing, and as a reinforcer of knowledge that only through greater unity can present values be maintained indefinitely. God's urging of sacrificial suffering would be of no great effect and His laws valueless if He did not persist in the more fundamental activity of stimulating man's deep desire for greater value. The overall hope in detachment is the liberation of man for action towards the ending of deeper suffering. In cases where God's physical and spiritual laws have already forced detachment and newly exposed deep desire, God urges voluntary sacrificial suffering then, as a bulwark against temptation to re-attach. Sacrifice, bringing immediate suffering, is to compensate for earlier attachment. God has given man his marvelous brain and nervous system and the ability to use symbols and perform rituals. Thus man often can establish new conditions of relating[41] by merely symbolic sacrifice, and the suffering will be much less. In any case, after a sufficient period of successful sacrifice, man is to relate again to objects such as that sacrificed, but without the attachment.

The period of sacrificial frustration is also a period of training; a benefit of suffering resulting from detachment from pursuit of lesser values is the practice of endurance of such suffering and of the particular organization required during it, so that flexibility is gained enabling greater offering of love. Thus the detachment is actually for reparation of relationship with God, to restore the ability to function with God.

Man may resist God's circumstantial will for sacrificial suffering, thinking peace and happiness to be jeopardized. But this is based on unawareness of deeper desire and sufferings.

Apathy is an illusion: some suicides *seem* to feel nothing (a case of total consciousness of apathy is beautifully portrayed in Moore),[42] but inside there is a scream; in the catatonic, the rage is turned inward, but inwardly there is the raging from the frustration of God-given desire—one cannot extinguish it.

Sölle[43] wrote: "The God who is the lover of life does not desire suffering of people, not even as a pedagogical device, but instead their happiness." Yet, God must urge the hastening of inevitable suffering so that desire may be liberated for greater happiness and eventual fulfillment through realization of greater values from conditions of unity in circumstances also inclusive of conditions affording all true lesser values. Love is an "ardent attachment," writes Mastrantonis.[44] Disunity from detachment is real and the suffering from the disunity is real; there is real deprivation and loss of vitality until the love is re-directed for greater value *and* finds response. Humans of vitality mediate God's and in man's suffering God suffers. Thus, as noted, God's circumstantial will is for suffering to end suffering.

8. Love and suffering. God's way in His circumstantial will is the way of unconditional love for the object with whatever foundation He finds, and He will endure suffering, as man suffers, for the sake of later values.

God's foundation in human society is human desire, awareness of it, determination and vitality, and relationships and conditions of unity objectifying the desire and vitality without preventing objectification of greater desire. In its own level of scope and durability, any condition of unity is inherently good with a suppositive potential for serving as foundation. God's prime force of attraction works to sustain any condition of unity. At the same time, His will is to unite all conditions of unity, ending disunity. In His plan for the greater foundation and His desire for the greater union He works normally for re-organization of lesser conditions of unity, and, in the case of resistance His circumstantial will is for abnormal or wasteful division of the lesser condition of unity, although His force is working also for its unity. Obstructive of a greater condition of unity, a lesser condition of unity, inherently a good condition, may be considered an evil condition.[45]

God's center of attention is upon the conditions of unity which can be foundations for the unity of the *whole*, and specifically it is upon the foundation with the greatest potential for serving as the unifying center. Even these foundations are often established through compromise and partial rejection of God's intentional will for greater union. Yet God must value these central foundations especially, regardless of their history, and he must dedicate them for the future of the whole.

Although there is insufficient foundation for the reception of all of God's love, He seeks to establish conditions for greater fulfillment. So God is wholly *open* to suffering: in relating to insufficient foundations He is open to suffering; in urging separation from abnormal attachment He is open to suffering; in urging human love which will be rejected He is open to suffering. God abandons himself to suffering. He never holds back love nor seeks retaining of value because of the threat of suffering. He never degrades love: he never retreats, coerces nor possesses.

This unconditional love is God's parental love of which human parental love is the most "visible" paradigm. It is unconditional love for specific humans and for all reality including God's own desire, laws, purpose; love regardless of immediate fulfillment but expressed as offer enabling immediate change. God's capacity for suffering enables him to use suffering. According to Sölle,[46] "true acceptance of suffering" is acceptance in relation to a promised better future, of "a restoration of elemental goodness" and the abolition of anguish (and of any evil power involved). Without present fulfillment God loves.

Parental love is love for the object as it is; love not dependent on conditions to be satisfied before the lover yields to the beloved. Parental love for the unresponsive requires accepting of continuing or possibly increased suffering. God affirms present reality. He thus also affirms His desire to end real suffering. This is also God's love for Himself, His own future, as it were, for all possible reality states. Hence, unconditional love does not negate the desire to change reality: specified conditions are not the basis of love, but conditions for fulfillment are sought *by* love. Love exists first, and it is truly expressed to conditions which are foundational for fulfillment.

God with unconditional love for each creation relates to responding desire or any other unity foundational towards His Kingdom. His normal work is for re-organization with reintegration in greater combinations. Where His intentional will was resisted, His laws bring abnormal division or wasteful destruction of some units obstructive of greater unification. Then, He must rely on human response to his circumstantial will that humans, through greater attraction to His hopeful Word, might establish new conditions for relationship, putting behind temptation so as to override bonding forces which themselves manifest God's primary force of attraction.[47] In God's love for the whole, He never withholds any love nor would retain any value because of suffering to come. God is wholly open to suffering: where there are foundations insufficient to receive the fullness of His love, when he urges separation from abnormal attachment, when He urges emulating human loving. This is parental love, love regardless of condition, love precedent to response and unchanging even if rejection brings suffering. This is God's transcendent parental love. His transcendent self-love is manifest in His affirmation of present reality and His determination for restoration and development.

9. God rejected. God's love is expressed as an offer: it may be rejected; then there is no manifest result but suffering. God with love spurned is as dead. However, this is not the end of God. (There is no power outside of God that can grasp Him or that can drain His force.) Although the rejection of God's offer and resulting suffering of God and man may appear to signal the death of God's activity, God perpetually lives and acts because He has objectified Himself, His glory is in creation, and He is relating to His creation. So, surrounded by darkness, there is the reappearance of His activity.

10. God continuant. When God stimulates and man resists, God without alternative continues offering. God has positive intentions and He speaks. (Man would wish God to stop stimulating his desire with an offer causing suffering, for he does not wholly believe in resurrection, but the Creator does not stop, that man might be free.) Hence, in the circumstances, God, man and the whole creation are suffering.

> "Man's separation from God brought spiritual death to man and has caused all the sorrow, misery, tragedy and evil within himself and in the world." "Looking at fallen man, God sees His wounded and broken creature, still bearing the divine spark, the seed of protection, but unable to respond to Him freely." "His manifestation is limited by the degree of human response and capacity... Throughout thousands of years of history, God's love has never been requited..." "Ever since man's fall God has been seeking His lost family." "On the other hand, mankind has been suffering from hunger and thirst in spirit, separated from the love of God."[48]

With God's unkillable desire fulfilled only through free response (and with man's desire for give-and-take) God alone cannot end suffering. Human love for God can, but from and with God only. Man alone cannot end suffering. The end of suffering will not stem from the external causes of social progress, neither just from individual or capitalistic concern nor just from societal or socialistic concerns. God, speaking to man, continues with determination for the higher standard of love requisite for his goal. Practice of such a standard may entail suffering for man and God but God has neither fear (for He has "drunk" fully of His suffering) nor possessiveness of the present, to waste His energies, nor is His mind thrown into the confusion of some blind anger or blind aggressiveness or hatred. The Creator is not bitter but continues suffering in seeking betterment according to His original Logos. God's response to His suffering is never one to communicate with Satan (slowing the cause of unification) but always in furtherance of God's full ideal according to His original scenario. God's *Word* is unalterable.

God, suffering, acts for realization of His full ideal; according to His original and unalterable Logos, true development is possible only through human practice of increasing standards of love. The Creator continues speaking a higher standard. He desires and requires man's freedom and free response. Both God's love and man's exercise of God's love are required for the termination of suffering. God has fully endured rejection and the apparent death of His activity, and hesitates not. Man doubting resurrection, would protest God's offering causing suffering.

B. Approach of Redemptive Love

The parental Redeemer's love, controlling yet respectful.

1. God's offer. God cannot abolish suffering by a fiat of God, and He thus "allows" it; but this does not mean that He finds it good (He did not create it). God never "learns to tolerate it" but uses the fullness of His force, with knowledge, to end it. Buber said: the real exile in Egypt "was that they had learned to endure it."[49] God is not dead nor absent: *man* hides.

God's only way is to give love, abandoning the immediate outcome to man, committed to the total outcome. There are no alternatives. If it is true that God is sure of final victory, this is no act of blind faith on His part but derives from His sight, His vision. God does not shrink from action in the face of suffering. To "avoid" suffering is to avoid relationship. But God has passion for life, seeking intense joy, and He created *for* relationship. Therefore, it may be asserted that God empties Himself in loving creations. The fate of God is dependent upon human response.

God acts totally for that moment in historical time and that location in created space and for the being He is loving, to maintain contact and to stimulate healing of its past and change for its immediate future; yet inertia may oppose him. So God often appears as a slave to inertia and entropy, doing again what He had before. It is simultaneously because God is sure of final victory that He as God can commit Himself fully to action of variable direct outcome, and because as actor He does so commit Himself that the final victory is sure.

But of these, the latter is, after all, logically prior. When all has been said about the "mental" aspect of the suffering Creator, about Word, strategy and tactics, about perspective, it is the living heart of the Creator moving outwards towards what created life exists that is primary and original data (the remainder is more or less explanatory).

Ferré wrote[50] that God who lives forever blessed in Himself suffers "temporarily" for the sake of fuller sharing of his fellowship of love; the suffering does not continue forever but is terminated by victory, resurrection.

God, passionate for relationship and life and joy, suffering and hating suffering, committed to the ultimate outcome of whole unity, can offer only love, the direct outcome abandoned to man, His fate placed in human hands. The Creator's commitment to full and minutely specified action for His beloved creature enables His sureness of final victory and his sureness enables His committed action.

2. Offering, loss and resurrection. God is open to any possible loss. This is the relationship of omnipotence to fundamental love: Because fundamental desire is fulfilled only through love God accepts limitation on the effect of specific force. God, having replenishable force, would save nothing of His might if He let a moment in historical time pass without offering all in love. He would lose exactly that moment of opportunity during which disunity would tend to increase in creation, *diminishing* God's foundation and the opportunity for effectiveness of force. Even if it were possible that His loving effort were *totally* rejected the outcome could be no worse than if He failed to give in full abandonment. God is, in fact, sure of some change, if only in the deepest recess of a human. He has no doubts; the action is valid.

Even with great loss, God gains. For instance, in Jesus God had on earth a human of response to the great love of God. Well might God have desired other humans to adopt this standard of love. This desire was prevented; those who had the opportunity to objectify Jesus all deserted him, could not embody the standard. Jesus was crucified. The result was loss for God of His great joy through Jesus' actions as an individual man on earth. Yet, consequent on that loss and God's continuing love, *a little* of Jesus' new standard was sown in some, the beginning of a standard of unification above those previously held, and many came to this in time. Thus God did widen His foundation. Upon the loss of Jesus' physical life and leadership came the loss of the milieu of Judah (Judea) where one could live in the highest ethical standard known, and this caused further and great suffering for God. Yet, *after* some persons adopted the new and higher standard and exchanged their love with the potential of embracing *all*, God was suffering less than He had before He *sent* Jesus to His people. God exalted Jesus to be with Him as immediate foundation and Jesus is spiritually in the fellowship of the disciples on earth, even though there is yet no home for God and His children. However, there was less fruit than if Jesus' willingness to suffer, his sacrifice of relationships, had been accepted and he remained on earth to objectify God and deliver his nation for the world.

The Unification view here is in accord with Weatherhead's question and responses. "Was it God's intention from the beginning that Jesus should go to the Cross? I think the answer to that question must be No. I don't think Jesus thought that at the beginning of his ministry. He came with the *intention* that men should follow him, not kill him." "God's will in the circumstances which men's evil provided, was that Jesus should accept death, but accept it in such a positive and creative way as to lead to... the redemption of man, winning back to God, not in spite of the Cross, but using the Cross, born of man's sin..." "It was not the intentional will of God, surely, that Jesus should be crucified, but that he should be followed. If the nation had understood and received his message, repented of its sins, and realized his kingdom, the history of the world would have been very different. Those who say that the Crucifixion was the will of God should remember *that it was the will of evil men...*"[51]

Weatherhead also affirms[52] that people *"might* have known," in Jesus' lifetime, the things belonging to peace, and *might* have followed him then.

God always knew the principle of resurrection, so He can always go the sacrificial-way-of-the-cross, sure of laying a foundation. So God's circumstantial will entailing suffering is not masochism. God's love is for the reality for which he has unconditional love. God's love is given in the world for effect beyond any individual, pair-relationship, group-relationship (or any sub-unity of reality), and thus is "supernatural." Since God, even if blocked, never has cessation of creativity, effort and love, He never loses ultimate control of the over-all situation.

Lewis[53] wrote that foreknowledge is not a necessary attribute of God, since "there is in God the power to be equal to any occasion, in so far as His purpose calls for the occasion to be met;" God's ultimate control then lies in this power. But this view is insufficiently assuring. In the Unification view, God has control because He foreknows the steps of the *scenario* (the sequence of the magnification of love and the establishment of foundational unions), because He is to act continually towards realization of the steps, and because His power is receivable. Then it is not necessary for God to foreknow the particular events which will, in fact, realize the scenario, whether or not, as Barth holds,[54] all *possibilities* are known by God. Quick[55] said that God became "externally" passible through creating, but that "God is never acted on by anything which... he does not himself always control by his over-ruling power." But, in our view, what is important to God's control is that He *is* involved and responsive to man and *hence* can act with the offer appropriate to the actual events. Thus we find uncompelling the argument of Noro[56] that since "the certainty of our salvation" depends upon God's "unfailing power to achieve His ultimate purpose" we cannot be "sure about our final salvation when God is influenced by the contingencies of the time-process."

God has the control and God chooses to *share* the control with man, establishing man, as it were, as co-pilot. The Unification view, especially as set forth in *Divine Principle*, Chapter One, accords fully with Barth's view that God is the absolutely superior partner of man.[57]

If God's control lies in exercise of omnipotence not expressed through love, with just love's insistence on freedom, then man only submits. In this case, man would not be strengthened. There would be no partnership, oneness in heart with God. Man then is a servant but not a child of God who shares heart, Word and power. God then merely delegates some powers. In this is no justice.

So it is directly for the sake of man that God continues and chooses love with attendant suffering, and indirectly for His own sake, the sake of his heart's joy. In this loving He maintains contact with man, pursuing him to the end. It is only in the sense of God's calling that will ultimately (either directly or mediately) attract each human that we can speak of God's *over-ruling* power as regards free beings. It is precisely for the sake of man's freedom that God shares his suffering. With this freedom *man* is called to remedy God's loss and end God's suffering.

Randlers[58] made the point that if God suffers because we do, then *we* must suffer deeply on account of Him, the greatest sufferer. He notes that this must spoil our otherwise purely blissful worship. In our view, these remarks are very true. However, Randlers means to object to a suffering God. He suggests that if God therefore has to suffer perhaps we should choose *not* to be saved. In our view, that would be to reject God's grace from which He will anyway have His reward. We do not approve that an ill child should kill himself to remove the burden on a long-suffering parent. Randlers further notes that the concept of the suffering God stops us from exulting at His all-sufficiency and transcendence of evil. We can view this as meaningful and suggest that the time for exultation should be carefully chosen. We should be aware of, grateful for and praising of God's obligation. Our understanding of this obligation accords with Anselm's classic form. Since God freely obligated Himself in the act of creating, the obligation does not attenuate God's freedom.

Noro persists with the point (p. 92ff.) that if God *needs* creation, then His grace is not "free"; our being created must be free, not a necessity for God. In our view, God, as parental, *desires* children and desires that they be free. Thus His creating is His original grace, which was granted for fulfillment of all desire and which would have continued to flow freely had creation maintained its *full* freedom for fulfilling the created desires by fully mediating God's gracious love. Once the creation left God, *then* it became needed, its return needed as a *preparation* for the fulfillment of all desire, God's and creation's. Thus God's grace, flowing from His freedom, has had the characteristic of "long-suffering grace," saving grace. God's chosen obligation may be further understood: if He *gives* freedom and responsibility He can no more *keep* it. As God did not err in the giving, the freedom and responsibility are permanently to be shared. God's wish is that man speedily *assume* our designated portion of responsibility and attain our full freedom for love. God's self-limitation preceded the fall of man and existence of Satan. In Christ, Christians have met, to our shock, not the desired, expected unlimiting God (to do all things to us) but exactly the self-limiting God which is love.

Anselm further said that God is victorious because He can pay the price. Those who would view God as solely transcendent of evil are often those also looking solely past the existence of physical life and expecting no return of Christ to earth for the establishing of full freedom and love (referred to in *Divine Principle* as the Second Advent of the Lord).

To say that God's way of suffering has been part of His way of love is one thing. But, as Hedinger pointed out,[59] saying with the mystics that God suffers is not saying enough; suffering must be fought and we need to *show* that (and how) God will *end* suffering, else God is not truly omnipotent. It would be nobler to love God even if we did not know of His final victory (worshipping a God not necessarily omnipotent), than to settle for a retreat from desire (worshipping a God of faltering heart); but we are in sympathy with Noro[60] that "faith longs for the victor over the evils of human life, the victor through and through. Only on Him can we rely absolutely." It is important, however, that the search for victory be a search for victory through love only, since suffering is the blockage of love. Thus, in any case we may not find God among the non-loving. Sölle's emphasis is appropriate, on the supernatural love ready to suffer to produce change.[61]

This supernatural love must be found *in* history, among and within "natural loves" as well as beyond.

With radical love and inexhaustible force God accepts limitation of the effectiveness of specific force. According to the principle of resurrection God's internal foundation in creation always continues and God always brings about some development of His foundation in the cosmos. To hasten the end of suffering God is open to any loss of external foundation, and consequent increase of suffering, where the internal foundation is developed: where God's Word is implanted its substantiation is sure to follow. Thus God can always go the sacrificial-way-of-the-cross. God seeks to restore the whole of creation as foundation for its infinite development; His love is supernatural. Thus the ever-loving Creator God capable of sacrificial action has ultimate control of reality, having incessant Creativity, effort and love, and foreknowing the levels of foundational unification to be successively realized and being eternally present in His creation.

God exercises His control through His involvement with and responsiveness to His creation: He expresses His omnipotence through love, making offer always appropriate to conditioned reality, choosing to share His control with man for the sake of justice and joy. In seeking man's exercise of responsibility, God chooses love and to share man's suffering. God's creation is His original grace flowing from His free desire for children of freedom, granted for fulfillment of all. Due to Satan's work, God needs His creation's restoration as a foundation for that fulfillment and His freely chosen grace is salvific and preliminarily for fulfillment.

God's immutability is grounded in His principles.[62] God's determination, self-limiting, to be eternally Creator, Father, love, logically preceded creation.

For man to be convinced of God's omnipotence in creation and gain confidence to fight suffering he must comprehend how God will bring final victory. For this he must, first of all, find supernatural love in history, among and within "natural love."

3. God and man. Because of concentration on heart of desire for increase (He has by no means cut desire) God pours forth His love for investment, for a human's detachment from misgained values so that he might have more unity within himself in readiness to be more greatly foundational in God's work of the development of the scope of substantiated love. When the opportunity is created God will then elect him for greater loving. For the establishment of foundations towards His whole goal, for future joy, God's love often has been invested in humans who have been receiving little of external value and despairing of that. God got great glory on earth in Adam and Eve, but the fullness of that glory cannot now shine.

God's glory is lowered into exile in the world. This is the Kabbalistic tradition reported by Buber. Sölle (pp. 245–6) summarizes Buber's reporting. God in His exiled glory shares the suffering of creation. God did not forsake the suffering world needing redemption, but God's glory descended into the world into exile, dwelling with the unclean. In this God shares the suffering of people in exile, prison, martyrdom, taking on pain. Only man can redeem God's pain.

God, not masochistic, not seeking suffering, demands much, not little, from man.

"By the fall of man, God lost his beloved children who were created in his image as his substantial bodies. When God saw that man fell, He could not bear it. His heart was broken and he felt the greatest sorrow. God created man to be such a loving being, and God poured out everything he had, His heart, love and energy to make men His children, the masterpieces of all His creation. Man was created as such a valuable being that without man, God's ideal could not be realized. However God lost his children by the fall.

Also, God lost all the creation, because the lords of creation, men, were taken by Satan. God's purpose and ideal of creating man and the universe was to receive joy and happiness by having perfect give and take action with them. God lost everything, and because of this, God came to have no object which fully reflects His own Sung-Sang and Hyung-Sang to perform give and take action with. Thus, God could not realize His purpose of creating man and the universe.

Instead God saw the most hateful relationships develop between fallen people and Satan. The men who were created to be God's children became Satan's children. The men who were created to be the lords of all creation became the servants of servants. However, fallen men do not know of their miserable state, and are content with it. Fallen men deny the existence of God, and do all kinds of evil against God, realizing the world of tragedy. So, God lost not only His children, but God's children came to stand against Him as His enemies. God repented that He created man, and said that it grieved Him to His heart (Gen. 6:6).

God stands in a paradoxical position; He cannot hate fallen men because they were created as His children originally by Him, and He cannot fully love them, because they became children of Satan. He cannot destroy them, but must work to save them from the fallen state to the original state of creation.

When God sends His representatives and even His beloved Son, fallen man just opposes them, stoning and killing them. Therefore, the purpose of God's creation was never accomplished, but on the contrary, the opposite results came about, increasing God's sorrow. Isaiah 1:3: 'The ox knows its owner, and the ass its master's crib; but Israel does not know, my people does not understand.'

God's expectation for man was so great when He started His work of creation that the disappointment and sorrow and anguish which God felt when man fell were very great. We cannot find any man or being more grievous than God. Whenever God sees His fallen children and creation, it reminds Him of the fall of man and makes God sorrowful. God desperately wants to have His children restored and wants to love them. For this He is doing salvation providence.

Therefore, we must ease his suffering and comfort Him, and return joy to God by restoring our original position as His children."[63]

4. Faithful sacrifice. This is the realism of God, that He cannot rely on that which is peripheral. God's only resource for saving man and receiving joy is love from the heart. God brings about the future kingdom through suffering believers. Believers in God (according to whatever form they may cognize Him) sacrifice, willing to suffer; but all human sacrifice is, in fact, a response to God's suffering, it is motivated by love and God is the source of love, God's restorative love the source of man's. The blockage of love seeking relationship causes suffering. Suffering, which inspires sacrifice, remains until the whole in which a human may relate is interresponsive to love, therefore each desires to perceive this unified whole environment and suffers until it is established; so the sufferings of all humans are, at base, common and the source is God's suffering.

God relies on love from heart invested for the liberation of man. The future kingdom will be brought by God through sacrifice. Sacrifice is motivated by love; it is inspired by God's original suffering and man's suffering when love seeking relationship has been blocked: believers in God are willing to sacrifice for God's relief. God and man suffer until the whole environment is interresponsive to love. Therefore, God invests his heart's love to end the suffering of man and God.[64]

5. God's example. God needs humans with Him. He needs humans to serve through attracting others. God's love despite suffering and abandoned to freedom of response, should be exemplary for man.

But how is God's example to be perceived by humans? Either through abstracting from our own experience the experience of God the causer or through direct revelation, any of us might find out God's example. Yet, since the forces of inertia and temptation are so strong, God did not develop a community in substantiation of His example through His direct communication of His example to a multiplicity of individuals. Rather, God has to rely on pioneer humans establishing examples in the mode of God, that other humans might see in them God's exemplary loving and suffering.

Since neither is there the end to God's suffering by initiatives from without Him nor can He, by Himself, end the suffering. He must expose His pain and seek a solidarity of suffering. God's suffering can be inspirational and can lead to liberation of power in man and hence of God's power. God's aim is to have an object ready to serve in the cause of ending suffering. He seeks a human ready to accept suffering in the cause, so that even where his loving is presently externally futile, resulting in the suffering of defeat (or loss), he will have become stronger, closer to God. Then the result of that human's loving will be more developed power for God. God is willing to suffer to get such a deserving human.[65]

To reconstruct His creation, God needs pioneer humans to set example mediating God's exemplary loving and suffering. God reveals Himself as wider love and seeks humans to recognize Him and attract others to join in substantiating this standard. God's direct aim is to have with Him a pioneer open to further suffering from loss or defeat in the process towards the ending of suffering. God is willing to suffer to find that human and He vocalizes His pain to inspire humans and for their liberation of power and for solidarity with God.

6. Satan's victory. God sends the pioneer human, who is responsive and with Him, often to his further suffering. God does not enjoy the full value presently possible. Satan may taunt when God makes this sacrifice, but there is no alternative for God.

God experiences the pain from unconditional love in contradictory circumstances, from sacrificing true value for the sake of unity with the undeserving. Since those rebellious are needed for the establishment of God's perfect kingdom and desired by God for their sakes and for the sake of His joy, God would have more pain if holding back his ready pioneer than in sending him even to considerable loss: God must seek to extend the scope of action. Koyama writes that God seems inefficient in acting only with love, traveling with the exiled, etc.; he speaks of a "supreme sacrifice of God" which was implemented by an inefficient process.[66]

The pioneer sent to suffering might be a "saved Christian." Christians have professed imperturbation over their own suffering on earth, but Ferré argues[67] that if *God* suffers *this* disturbs the bliss of saved men in Heaven. It is indeed clear that in the Unification view so long as God suffers saved persons must also continue to suffer. Suffering is frustration of heart's desire. Then is there any reason to suppose that physical death (cessation of life of the physical body) would bring an end to suffering since the spirit still lives? No matter how "moral" life has been or how faithfully a physical death is accepted, heart's desire unfulfilled remains. According to *Luke* 23:43, Jesus said that he and a thief would be in paradise, the day of their physical deaths. It is hoped and believed that many other humans are also "in paradise." Have those saints no longer responsibility? Are they inactive? If they are living this cannot be so. We say that the thief died without fulfillment of his heart's desire. Then there must be at some time and place in some way an opportunity for him to be active and loving; else, his Creator's desire for him is also frustrated eternally. The view that physical life, with its goals, is but a trial which if weathered leads to an a-natural bliss, we reject as a gnostic narcotic (which, we suspect, found a home in Christianity when analogy was made between individual physical life on earth and the beloved nation of Israel which was killed, its efforts seemingly wasted and then atrociously misunderstood as a trial for humanity or a moral lesson in failure and of no intrinsic value, humanity in Christ now seen as having passed on to the tranquil spiritual life apart from the frustrations of the national seeking of social change or economic welfare).

For the Unification understanding of the activity of the saints after physical death, the reader is referred to Part I, Chapter 5 of *Divine Principle*. Here, we may attend specifically to the question of *Jesus'* activity since his crucifixion. Whether considered to be "in paradise" or "at the right hand of God" (*Acts* 7:55), Jesus is, according to nearly all Christian tradition, the "head of the Church" which is his "body." This body is known to be ill, malfunctioning, suffering. Then Jesus, as head, cannot be living without suffering the frustration from rejected or distorted directives.[68] It may be said that Jesus, at least, reached a fulfillment. Unification theology agrees with Christian tradition that Jesus is irrevocably one with God the Father, and this unity is indeed a desire of heart. Yet this unity is not the whole fulfillment of a human according to any biblical or biological scenario. The resurrection of Jesus after the crucifixion was not just a "resurrection of God" (i.e., a renewal or elevation of God's activity), but a resurrection of the human Jesus. It is for this reason that the Church has emphasized that Jesus, after the crucifixion, still or again has his human body. The nature of this body is in dispute but the significance is that Jesus can still act, can communicate with others, can respond.[69] We must think that others departing "this life" also continue to love those of earth, thus living and seeking fulfillment of the human spirit through human activity.[70]

There is further response required by Ferré's argument. Since God is internally unchanged by the experience of suffering, then when the kingdom of heaven is established on earth, *then* neither God nor the saints on earth will suffer and all who have been living, whether on the earth still or only in the spiritual realm, will find opportunity for fulfilling activity. The bliss is yet to come, and the "communion of saints" awaits it also. Save for the perfect, Christ, all humans have continued doing Satan's will in part, because of false valuation and conflicting desire; and even Jesus has not realized his full inheritance of the unified world. Our desire for Heaven, the home, is not fulfilled. Christians are at best adopted children or spiritual sons and daughters of God (Romans 8:14–24).

In affirming that the opportunity to become true children of God is at hand and that heaven will become a reality, we accord with Mascall that "if suffering were strictly or formally contained within God" then if we unite with Him we suffer eternally.[71] In contradistinction to Kitamori's view of God's suffering, we find that suffering is not "native" to God. With Christian tradition we believe that Jesus' victory "overcame death" and the power of the devil; yet, Satan still has power, through our sins, and taunts God.

Christian theologians have responded to what appears to be accusation against God. It has long been recognized among Christian writers that suffering resulting from sacrificing relationships and suffering from the rejection of a pioneer's offerings for the establishment of relationships of more encompassing love are sufferings consequent upon initiatives according the will of God. Augustine then suggested that *all* suffering has been willed and foreknown by God and that believing this then obviates our thinking that God is disturbed as a consequence of any earthly event.[72] Also, Calvin suggested that since the actions resulting in suffering are planned by God for our benefit, we should not think that God suffers in this suffering.[73]

In the view being presented, however, suffering does not lie in disturbance nor surprise (although disturbance can lead to suffering). *Suffering results from prevention of creation.* Even if God be undisturbed by the first suffering as by later sufferings, He would not have willed the original frustration of His loving. Also, even if God were to foresee the suffering of one purifying himself or pioneering in hardship and to know that the suffering, although resulting from external loss, benefitted the individual and, in fact, served God's providence of restoring the whole creation back to union with Himself, yet the immediate suffering of God is, as we have shown, real in His loss during the period of devitalization of the purifier (which was necessary owing to prior sin), or in the pioneer's loss (which occurred owing to prior sin).

God must send the responsive pioneer, often to further suffering, sacrificing the full value presently possible. Satan, having exercised his power through man's sin, taunts. Suffering, caused through sin, may be consequent upon actions in accordance with God's will to hasten the end of suffering through reclaiming all the rebellious, but it is nonetheless suffering. Although imperturbable during any loss, God Himself suffers nonetheless. Even righteous persons presently suffer before and after the cessation of the life of their physical body.[74] According to Divine Principle *their Creator's desire for them and their heart's desire would remain unfulfilled did God not bring about in some manner further opportunity for active and successful responsibility, for fulfillment of potential for giving love to reception and for receiving joy. The human Jesus, resurrected and active and responsive in love for all on earth, is a model for other saints also seeking total human fulfillment. Even Jesus, directly one with God the Father, has not received his full inheritance.[75] Heaven on earth will be realized, providing unlimited opportunity for fulfilling activity: then all will stand finally as true children of God joyfully exercising their full capacity of love. Suffering is neither strictly nor formally contained in God and He would never originate suffering, therefore when the Kingdom is established all can be eternally and actively blessed.*

Review and prospectus. In Section II we saw the *tactics* of love and God's *approach* of love to fallen man, His tactical initiative to bring about restoration, and showed the basis of the effectiveness of unchanging loving. (i) The suffering Creator seeking restoration through call and offer is wholly present to partly blinded man, appearing according to man's condition and situation, and thus is in position for effectiveness. In His restoring and creating, He is dependent on free human response which alone can fulfill His purpose of creation: for love God has given a share of control to man, so that the effectiveness of His tactics is not necessarily proportionate to His might. Intrinsically unlimited, God appears in the form of limitation. (ii) Whether or not God foreknows all possible responses, He retains ultimate control because of His steadfastness, His respectfulness of and perpetual affirmation of created natures, His undisturbed freedom and creativity, His receivable power and His foreknowledge of the states of the scenario to be fulfilled, and precisely *because* the unchanging God exercises His control through His presence, responsiveness and immanent loving activity. (iii) The Creator's sole motivation is for the joy of God with and through joy and harmony in all creation. Since the sole purpose of the suffering Creator is restoration, God always wholly gives Himself and all that is in union with Him. He is open to any diminishment of His substantial foundation in the creation, and consequent suffering and his action always results, at least, in development of His spiritual foundation in the creation. (iv) God wholly giving appears dead when rejected, and at all times to be victimized and grieving, yet He is worthy of worship as vibrant and calm and promising perpetual life with eternal bliss. God is justified in calling for suffering: He only hastens inevitable suffering, limits suffering and will end it the soonest. Sharing suffering, he exercises full responsibility. Although righteous persons can, with God, have inner peace, their potential for loving is now unfulfilled and, with God, they suffer; however, since suffering is not native to God, nor essential to creation, it can be ended for all. Physical life ends, even in martyrdom, but even as God never dies so is there no extinction of the spiritual man; rather is there resurrection. As the creation becomes whole, the righteous, whether living on earth or only in the spiritual realm, will find fulfillment through creative, loving activity. (v) God's just tactics include the unchangingness of His laws. In His gracious approach He steadily attracts man from Satan's domain, stimulating hope in the highest standard of love yet revealed and calling for repentance from limited ways to hope. God calls for sacrifice inspired by His suffering and motivated by love. Man's responsibility is to reunite with God according to his Word, willing to suffer in mediating God's example inspirationally to others. When humans unite around the standard revealed, God will reveal the higher standard which alone makes possible greater true unification and the further relief of suffering.

Thus based upon God's motivation, His immutabilities and His responsible and responsive relationship with the creation, we have shown the basis of the *nature* of the effectiveness of God's tactics of restoration.

Having seen God's approach, we should explicate the quality and content of the interaction of God and fallen man, of God's *actions* and of human response and of God's appreciation of the response, also considering God's freedom and limitation in history. Through the consideration of God's relationship with His creation we should further validate and justify the tactics of restorative love as *effective* towards and giving basis of hope for not only immediate and partial remediation but for whole fulfillment.

III. HOW GOD CAN DEPEND ON MAN FOR COOPERATION TOWARDS THE RELIEF OF SUFFERING

[We here suggest that God can depend on human response and cooperation toward the ending of sinfulness through redemptive suffering with God, considering the intimate communication to man of the transcendent God, the nature of man as God's creature and the perspective of the Creator regarding history.]

A. Suffering and Hope: the immanent inspiration of the transcendent Redeemer.

The discussion moves towards the functional unity of God and man in the effective transmission of mercy, forgiveness and grace.

1. Suffering Creator transcendent of history. God knows the principle of resurrection; there is no death that has any hold on God, He is free to invest all foundations, (even though separation may temporarily increase), in order to gain future value. When a foundation is laid, the transcendent Creator always has power to build upon it.

The Creator God has freedom to invest and power to build upon any foundation.

2. The unity, in history, of transcendence and immanence of the suffering Creator. One of the aspects of human suffering is that we suffer from reluctance and we experience indecision regarding whether to give or not to give love in the face of possible rejection. (Actually, the suffering in this case is due to the resistance of a function of man external to desire, with the result of separation within man.) Augustine considered that suffering is confusion of mind,[76] Confusion and indecision result in suffering because during indecision desire cannot be fully expressed. Once the decision to give is made, there is not that internally caused inner suffering; on the other hand, God, enduring all loss and separation and affirming the principle of loving according to circumstances, does not suffer after this manner of humans.

God has always had some joy and with unconditional love He has related to His creatures as they have responded. But God has never related to created beings for His sake exclusively, rather, always for the sake of the other (and *through* that end to His consequent joy). Hence, He can freely stimulate others to mission entailing possible separation and suffering. In this way, as mystics have taught, God is calm and fully energized, remote and fully present, poor and rich, free and involved. God values both the security and the creativity of each and is qualified to send each human out in love despite indeterminate immediate fate. This is God's transcendent freedom amidst connectedness. For fallen man, this comes only after a painful process; in God it is abiding unity of polarity.

3. Powerfulness in history of the transcendent/immanent suffering Creator. When His object is responsive God can act with and through the object, to spread His standard of unification towards establishing the whole world of unity. Since God endures any suffering, His power not being determined by others, His freedom and justice transcend the world. God can always be just; the power of the causer of suffering does not affect God's force. This inner freedom of God is the foundation for His pure action. God's suffering affects Him only as giving Him information from the world. The non-actualization of God's love brings suffering to God's heart which is used as knowledge for the expression of love then appropriate, but the disunity and suffering do not affect the fact of God's loving. There is no sin of or in God, in Him is no need for forgiveness preparatory to justness. God's actions are always one with His heart and purpose.

God's responding aim for any being causing his suffering is to free it to return to Him. Ultimately He will liberate even Lucifer from his guise (role) as Satan and restore relationship with him. God has that freedom for unlimited helping. Ferré writes, "the solution to moral evil existentially means... will those dear to me be saved: If all that lives is dear to me... the question becomes, will all be saved?"[77]

Many have suggested that God suffers in sympathy.[78] We understand that this view arose because the information received by God which causes Him suffering then causes Him to act for our liberation (preliminary to resuming His development). As Bell writes,[79] in God there is a transmission of pain into a thing creatively used. In our view, then, any sympathy felt by God must not be something distant but a genuine feeling with that in creation which is still in unity with Him, that there is a direct line of feeling and not just an observation and comprehension of the feelings of another followed by a discrete "mental" response.

God is God for a bigger possible unity than any unity which may be destroyed. Ultimately, there will be the unity of all time and space, the coordination of all change, therefore all value feeds ultimately into God's kingdom. God's action of love, even if partly rejected and returning suffering, is not vain. God Himself is the harvester. Also, God never suffers alienation for He is exerting full optimum action for restoration and all will be restored, there will be full and ongoing creation; God is in all instances restoring and creating. Thus God's love is borrowed from Him but not stolen, just as a teacher's efforts are not stolen from him if a pupil is only slow to learn and/or commits remedied errors.

The concepts of sympathy and forgiveness are linked, and both bear further scrutiny so as, in turn, to throw more light on the Divine response to suffering and evil. The scrutiny is important also in order to point to functional unities of God and man, and to the relationship of hope and suffering. Then, what is the nature of identifying something as evil and/or as causing suffering? Clutton-Brock wrote, in 1921, that

"The very definition of evil... concerns, not only the nature of evil, but our relation to it."[80] Our viewpoint is first of all that this relation is not that of a sympathetic appreciation which itself causes no suffering. A book by Jacques Sarano, a physician, is insightful here. A central thesis of the book is that to call a thing "evil" is to see it in history and view it with passion, not being indifferent to it.[81] A condition exists and it gives us pain, but, says Sarano, for us to name it as pain and call it evil is to express an impulse for change.[82] From this observation, Sarano develops an account of the "*unity* of empirical knowledge and of eschatological knowledge... of knowledge and of hope—the unity of hope and experience."[83] *Hope* is the mediator between the underlying passion and the impulse for change in the face of evil, the revolt against objective evil. Then, Sarano says, I cannot revolt against objective evil unless I see it as objectively evil by awareness of its effect on myself, relevant to *my* concerns for the future.[84]

We can place Sarano's analysis in the context of our discussion. In this context we see pain as information received by a subject that an object, i.e. an entity with which he is in relationship, is altered in a manner indicative of its disturbance or suffering. The subject conceptualizes the existence of an evil condition, that is, a condition in existing circumstances which is disappointing and calling for re-direction and/or re-application of the subject's efforts. If the object is found to be corrupted the subject is aesthetically displeased or if the object is found to be imprisoned the subject is sympathetic (and if the subject finds himself to be the cause of the object's misery he perceives in himself a prior evil condition and may be repentant); however, in all these instances the precedent condition for the subject's findings and conceptualization is his own personal concerns which are affected, and the findings imply a personal negative judgment. That this information may be highly useful in no way alters the judgment of the disappointing condition as a blight. So the subject perceiving "evil" is *affected*, he desires to give love to and through the loved object, but is unable to complete a fruitful circuit of give and take action. To what extent he may avoid *perturbance* depends upon the degree and quality of his hope, approaching to the Divine or eminent virtue of assurance.

Presently, we are discussing continuing suffering. In continuing suffering a subject has been affected by a disappointing condition of alteration of his object and has not departed from the relationship (nor has the disappointing condition been wholly remedied). Continuing suffering implies a *dynamic* of the subject meeting resistance, along with a determination to change circumstances. Can this suffering suggest, of the subject, the emotional distance of "sympathy" which that term often connotes? Max Scheler, in *The Nature of Sympathy* writes that, characteristically, sympathy is always reactive, where love is spontaneous and free from this limitation.[85] The fundamental dynamic of God, as Subject, is creative love; this preceded any appreciation; appreciation is external to it. The Divine appreciation is *with* love and the love is dynamic and creative. The dynamic of the heart of man, God's beloved object, His child, is also creative love. Clutton-Brock wrote that "if there were no life evil could not be."[86] Creative love is interior to life. According to J.Y. Lee "sympathy is an emotional identification through a process of imagination" and is not in itself creative.[87] We conclude, then, that the Divine appreciation of evil finds the dynamic of the Creator's love blocked by the disappointing condition which indicates the blocking of the true desire of man (causing human suffering); thus God's suffering is functionally one with man's. For this reason, God and man together face and combat evil. This observation undergirds that of the relationship between God's will and evil. Wyon's often-read comment may be rehearsed: That Jesus confronted evil daily and on Calvary shows us that evil is not the will of God but that the fact that we are brought into contact with it *is* His will.[88]

One can logically conceive that God might appreciate the cosmos in which man suffers as wholly good, wholly according to plan; however it is difficult to find in this concept any guidance for man who faces evident contradictions in himself and in the world. In the light of the above, a God who recognizes evil and is, as held by virtually all Western theology, working for its reduction and/or extinction must be said to suffer in some manner. This process of judgment and combative action is not, as Mascall points out, well comprehended by the term "sympathy".[89]

In view of our considerations of Divine appreciation and suffering, we turn our attention to consideration of forgiveness. Could any meaningful forgiveness be motivated by a remotely serene decision to countenance the offender? This is to put the question in an extreme form as a limiting point; there are several levels of possible motivations for meaningful forgiveness ranging perhaps from that of disinterest to that indicated by the passionate exclamation of the Messiah on Calvary during the very process of martyrdom.[90] Thus, in the first place, God conceivably might be forgiving because not really caring. Archbishop Temple, based on his interpretation of St. Paul's letters, denied this position. He states that when God forgave, people thought Him either unrighteous or indifferent, but that the sacrifice of Jesus which *cost* God showed His hatred of sin: "There are two ways of expressing antagonism to sin; one is to inflict suffering upon the sinner, the other is to endure suffering"; neither course shows indifference.[91]

A consciously pioneering analysis of the dynamics of forgiveness is contained in an essay by Moule written in 1971.[92] The heart of Moule's analysis, which is compatible with the Unification view, is as follows: "Real forgiveness is undoubtedly costly to the forgiver." The cost, of course, may not be to the extent of a crucifixion, and it may have been secretly borne (as in the case of the father in Jesus' parable of the prodigal). As in shared suffering, then, shared reconciliation supposes mutual and deeply personal involvement. "The wronged party will be less than his full self as a person if he is...not willing to pay for his gift of forgiveness" and "the offender will be less than his full self if he does not wish to compensate." "Although forgiveness is a costly gift," the offender "cannot purchase it for anything, but neither can he receive it as a gift

without giving everything of himself." Also, the true repentance preceding reception of meaningful forgiveness means that "the offender
conceives a burning desire to make reparation and to share the burdens of
the one who forgave him." Moule is aware that love is not weighted.
Payment is not an aspect of the *relationship*, but "cost does enter into the
description of the *process*": there turns out to be a sacrificial output for
both sides. "The generosity of forgiveness... wakes... an echo from the
recipient, and he too gives out all that he has in response."

   In accordance with this view we find that in the actualizing of forgiveness as well as in the experience of suffering which required the forgiveness, God and man are functionally united; then the forgiveness reveals
reconciliation and is a further clearing of the way for the true functional
unity of Creator and creature, the functional unity in love and creative
activity. God, in forgiving man, in having won man's forgiveness, may be
serene but not remote. God, acts in the world and all-spendingly.

   God responds to the beings causing him suffering. God directly suffers with
man.[93] Evil affects man and God alike. Thus there is functional unity of God and
man in suffering, in the combat of evil, in the actualization of forgiveness and in
the loving activity of God and reconciled man. God is the initial investor,
sacrificer, forgiver and developer; and God will harvest all value.

4. Limitation of the immanent suffering Creator. God cannot compel the restoration of unity which He requires nor will God alone create
the conditions for uniting. God would have sent the Messiah to Adam
and Eve at the beginning of fallen history if He would elevate without
prior change in man. We know from experience that God does not work
that way. God acted to limit the degradation of man[94] and will always
provide opportunity for and stimulation towards purification. He will
offer a standard of love for sharing and cooperation towards a given scope
of unity. When humans have fully responded God will reveal wider love.

   God, Who is always restoring and creating, works His providence of external
opportunity and stimulation for purification. God needs man's free participation
in establishing a structure affording greater uniting.

5. Dependence of the immanent suffering Creator. God must depend
on offering and then offering again on the basis of whatever foundation is
established through response to His offering. Even if God might work
something miraculous He is dependent, for its effect toward re-unification,
upon man's perception of it and interpretation of it, that man might see in
it God's Word for sacrificial actions. Insofar as God's offer is rejected the

manifestation of His Word in time and space is retarded.

To a person or group externally powerful God delivers a Word of love and truth which is also a Word of judgement, for either the recipients will harken and make free power for God's work, or, in rejection will "harden their hearts," setting their thoughts against new hope, and become brittle and decadent so that they will not be an external obstacle to unification being developed by God with some other person or persons which should eventually benefit them along with all other persons.

God is dependent on human readiness to receive the guidance and leadership that He is ready to provide. In love He urges sacrificial action.

6. Defeats of the immanent suffering Creator. When man's efforts are blocked he may become confused; God's Word of suffering may cause man intellectual indecision resulting in psychologically caused suffering. Also, when man embarks on mission for God (offering to share love and truth and all their fruits), Satan may claim the first attempt. When man is rejected the result is more separation.[95] The elect may be mocked because vulnerable. There may be social degradation, even assaults unto death. If man then rebels against God, God is locally helpless.

7. Immanent powerful expression of the transcendently suffering Creator. God who is free, can act within the limitation of His creation by stimulating the inner man through expressing heart, love and truth according to man's freedom to receive.

God expresses His heart-longing for greater unification, expresses the distance between the love and joy now possible in fallen circumstances and the ideal of love (in a sense, this expresses dialogue in God, His "prayer"). God expresses His desire to give and His truth that victory over evil comes through sacrifice. This is God's expression of love and truth in the process we call restoration through indemnity.[96]

In this expression God focuses His full spiritual power. God gives full attention to His ideal and the distance to it, to action towards its realization, originally the kingdom which is coming. God's attention is focused on the problem posed by disunity. Then with this attending, from His purposeful desire springs re-creative ability. So God specifically expresses His Logos: a part of the original scenario of creation still to be effected God expresses, in the circumstances, as a Word of sacrifice, a commandment. God fully expresses Fatherhood and in doing so articulates the suffering of all creation. And through one man God expresses Himself more visibly to others.

8. Grace of the immanent/transcendent suffering Creator. Kitamori[97] writes that in our pain we witness to God's pain, but only believers understand this value. When one is willing to sacrifice deserved true love and unity for the joy of one rejecting him, ready to embrace him, his suffering shows the pain from unconditional love. From the fact that Jesus was willing to suffer such great loss to give us opportunity for freedom from slavery we consider that God was all along willing to suffer for the sake of our freedom. All pain witnesses to God's; if we *know* that, we can build on any foundation.

> "The God we know is a suffering God, a heart-broken God ... we must understand His heart so that we can take His burden upon our shoulders. That is the only way we can comfort God. We must stand in God's position where He was persecuted for many thousands of years. No one has suffered more throughout history than God."[98]

God is expressing the aggrievement of the innocent party and all His history of aggrievement and the full concentration of pent-up energy towards change.

> One might argue that it is when God succeeds in further creation that there must be a lasting change in the mind of God (as He then has a new object and is to prepare for new creation), but that when completion of a creative act is delayed there is precisely no significant change. Yet we must articulate the desire of God blocked of fulfillment, the impulse of heart unstimulated by receptive opportunity and joy. So with the Bible we speak of the resentment or "grudge" of God or God's heart filled with grief or sadness, and that this grief is not one of withdrawal or inactivity. Despite the wound of heart the impulse exists, the purpose is unaltered, activity continues.

Through God's expression we may know God is fully *present* in His response to the fact of suffering. This supposes that there must always be some human capable of receiving and sharing God's heart at some level of love. The original mind (or "intrinsic heart") of every human is also aggrieved by historical iniquity.

Christians hope for the *eschaton*. According to Christian scripture, the *eschaton* will come when all hear the Gospel; also, it will come after much tribulation. We find a relationship between these conditions: in preparation for the *eschaton* God is to be more deeply understood and in the *eschaton* God will be newly manifest; then, if God is a suffering God we may well consider that He will be understood (and the Gospel believed) only through tribulations, which point through suffering to His suffering. These tribulations could occur in the course of witness to the Gospel, or, if witness falters the tribulations could result from God's laws dissolving present unities in order to arouse again the desperate longing for world unity. In *The Politics of God*, Joseph Washington writes that cognizance of suffering is a reminder that the Kingdom of God has not yet come, and it is essential for participation in efforts to bring in the kingdom.[99]

Christians holding that God suffers usually stipulate, as we have, a doctrine of unconditional love, along with a doctrine of special election. To those saying that God suffers, Noro[100] then challenges with the question: Is fallen man inside of God's embrace or outside of it? And he further asks, if man's sin and rebellion lie outside of God's omnipotence, omniscience and omnipresence, how can He bring about His victory? General answers to these are implicit in Brown's statement: In reference to the forgiveness through the cross he said that the Son's great agony was also the Father's great agony; in it the Father "was laying hold on the lost world with the arm of His all-suffering all-conquering love and drawing it righteously to Himself."[101]

As we understand it, God is connected to each man's heart and offers a little more of what he desires. God does not withdraw but through the responding heart of man and greater foundations developed in extension of heart God confronts the separation in the world and urges restorative love. This judges. According to Kitamori, the love of God wins because the sinner cannot leave its embrace, even while rebelling, and because it judges.[102] Thus Kitamori sees the sinner as wholly embraced. In our view, God *loves* all creatures, and readily *embraces* that which is brought to Him, offered to Him for participation in His creative endeavor. Then what of that not offered to God? We have said that a distinctive function of *agape* love is to create lovable value in others. In the sinless world there is no unlovable, and creation of new lovable value is unimpeded. For the fallen world God has, as Von Hügel says, "a love which loves...in order to render lovable in the future what at present repels love."[103] (Such redemptive love must indicate that the Redeemer already loves those who are "unlovable," that is, those who repel His love.) We say that God's redemption is brought about through that which is devoted to Him. One more richly manifesting God witnesses to Him, attracting and drawing out that of God already present in his brother and further enabling the overcoming of that inner falsity which is the cause of all outward separation. Thus God does not embrace addiction, falsity or illness, but embraces the heart in the miserable. That which is healthy and yearning in sinful man exists in the unstable unity which is the sinner. God chooses the good part and offers power for liberation. This is God's pre-venient grace. Again, this act of grace is no compulsion, the attraction is both through the expression of suffering and the presentation of opportunities for love; with this two-fold action hope is aroused.

Noro asks, Is God said to be suffering to bring man back *to* relationship or to raise him higher *in* relationship?[104] We may answer this. It is a distortion of love that is involved in addiction; therefore, God's preliminary aim is for purification of man and further restoration of relationship, and then God offers His love for manifestation by man, man thus coming the more into the embrace of God's fellowship and participating in greater scope in God's project.

God's long-suffering grace is to dispel man's accusation against God. This accusation is inspired by Satan (and his human agents). The original accusation against God is not that He does not love or desire creaturely welfare but that He will not or cannot help, that He does not have creative love sufficient for fulfillment of creaturely desire; from this accusation stems the temptation to seek fulfillment elsewise. The sinner knows of God's love at some level and in some fashion but accuses God and separates functionally from Him. In the sacrifice and forgivingness of God's elect, a sacrifice entailing God's suffering as well, God shows His all-out effort to help, and in inspiration, and in blessings given after sacrifice He shows His power to help. It is only through such grace of exemplary supernatural love in history that the self-centered sinner can turn and accept suffering for the sake of union with those whom he has presently not even encountered. We can say then, with Barth, that God, who is love, rejects the existing social order and comes amidst it to build something new out of it.[105]

Barth often reminded of the possibility of dropping from God's grace, holding that the choice to do so occurred through man's finite freedom.[106] He also believed that the essence of creaturehood is the possibility of the disastrous choice. We affirm the truth in the Biblical story that God was fully available to first-created man and fulfilled all His promises and also taught man a commandment for life, yet man departed from God. We hold (with Noro) that man can become perfect in love through unity with God. If fallibility is the essence of creaturehood then either the Creator must countermand an essential nature of that which He created or else there will always be the possibility of falling, rather than an eternally assured Heaven. According to our understanding, the essence of man's creaturehood is his free love for God. In the Kingdom of God there can be no fall of man; if this be due to the overwhelming grace of God that would be an overwhelming love offered precisely in respect of creaturely essence.

Since the appeal to hope is crucial in God's work of redemption, it is important to determine the nature of hope, that is, for what may we hope. Noro[107] has hope for man's perfection in love and that man will attain the unchanging blessedness of God. For Bushnell the hope was clear. He wrote that man will never have omnipotence but will be *morally* immutable like God, free forever of temptations. According to Bushnell, the immutable man "must have found his bearings in *principles* that do not change, in God." Man "so far has gotten the sure presentiment and germ of a perfectly unchanging change finally to be consummated." This is because the Kingdom of God is not yet established on Earth.[108]

In the Kingdom of Heaven God's grace will be fully humanly mediated. It is not only that mature humans will be perfect but that the Kingdom will be perfect. There will be care so that any immature yielding to a temptation would not infect, and full reintegration would quickly follow. There could be neither cause nor possibility of another fall from God.

Since God acts with pure offer, willing to suffer until we respond, we may well hope and expect that we shall be called upon to do our part in the transformation of ourselves and our world to become God's home and our home. And we may hope again for God's free, gracious and decisive action to afford us the opportunity to fulfill our responsibility.

God expresses Himself to and through human beings. The effectiveness of God's action depends on man's interpretation of God's action for apprehension of God's expression, and upon man's according action. Through one man God expresses Himself more visibly to others. God expresses suffering and Fatherhood: He expresses longing to realize the ideal of love, and His desire to give; He expresses the long-suffering aggrievement of the innocent party and the truth that victory over evil comes through sacrifice only; and God expresses, as commandment, a Word of sacrifice for further realization of His original scenario of creation.

The "intrinsic heart" or original mind of man is aggrieved by historical iniquity. Embracing in unity, amidst disorder, the heart of the miserable, God confronts the separation in the world and urges restorative love. God must arouse again the desperate longing for world unity revealed in the Gospel, the awareness of suffering essential for man's participation in establishing the Kingdom of Heaven on Earth. Then God will bring the eschaton. *God arouses hope through expression of suffering and presentation of opportunities for love. Man should understand God's heart and take up the burden of God. The suffering, sacrifice and forgivingness of God's elect and invitational love witness to God and belie the original accusation against God.[109] Since the essence of man's creaturehood is his free love for God, each can be attracted from the word of Satan and to overcome inner falsity. Man, fulfilling responsibility, is to adopt God's unchanging principles, becoming morally immutable and establishing God's kingdom of love and care where God's grace is fully humanly mediated so that there be no fall from God.[110] It is reasonable to hope that God will act decisively to afford opportunity to separate completely from Satan, to be devoted to and embraced by God for participation in transformation of self and world to be God's home.*

9. Freedom of the immanent suffering Creator. God stimulates man for the purpose of the welfare of all including God Himself, thus God's actions are *dedicated* and express dedication. God is the One giving; dedicating, not seizing; nor is the expressive action seized from Him, *He* dedicates.

This also is the model for man representing God. Bell writes: "sorrow, if we understand it and dedicate it, can release a vast dynamic which alone can build values, build them not merely in the sufferer himself but in the whole world of humanity." We must offer our sufferings to God, freeing the self and becoming co-creators with God. In this process we go beyond a present level of felt sorrow to seek remedy in a higher level of unification.[111] This greater unification has innately long been sought by us.

Review. In Section A we gave an explication of the *quality* and *content* of God's action in history directly to the human heart and through human external activity. (i) according to the *motivation and unity of God*: the transcendent God is *free* to invest His foundation; the transcendent and immanent God is *just* in doing so; the immanent and transcendent God aims to free *every* being and *will* do so for their and His sakes, He will harvest all values. This is the restorational transcendence and immanence of the God Who is the Creator with just love, sight and sureness. The transcendent freedom in immanence of God is a model for man who should dedicate his sufferings to God. (ii) there is a *functional unity of God and man* in suffering, in action to remedy suffering, in the actualization of forgiveness (reconciliation), as well as in love and creative activity. Functional unity of God and man is grounded on the communion of God and man's heart and points also to the *unity in the manifestations of God*. God's motivation to end suffering includes His eternal Personal desire for continuation of creation and increase of joy; this is the unity of motivation of God manifest as Creator and Redeemer.[112] The same manifest God, Who created and creates, restores; the same God Who is manifestly unlimited by time and space manifests Himself in limited form and in the changing form of His creatures. (iii) With fallen man, God is the initiator. In His initiative He expresses truth and His aggrieved heart, revealing *His* love. Throughout history God has waited for the responder, revealing Himself the more greatly to the more prepared. He has depended on interpretation of His initiative. He has depended on the hope and endurance of those who have heard and responded. It is man's essential nature, as creature, to respond to God's grace, and each human will become and remain perfect in a perfect developing world eternally free of disorder. In His restorative initiative, God embraces, amidst disorder, the heart of the sufferer and all activated by that heart. God fulfills His responsibility. Man is also responsible for ending all suffering, to bring comfort and joy to God and to the whole creation, expanding the unity of desire, hope, appreciation and determination reflecting the unity of God and, in responding initiative, vitiating accusation in revealing to each other, and to all, God's love and God's love in man's love.[113]

Thus God's action is effective in restoration and the magnitude of its effect is determined by the internal responding and external activity of man. God is developing His world within the fragmented world, establishing the successive scopes of unity that would have been established in creation so easily had man not fallen from God but now are established at great cost, and against accusation, in restoration and re-creation. The development, through a limited number of stages of unification and marked by decisive action of God, occurs according to a time-process not wholly evident to fallen man.[114]

B. God and The Elect in the Process of Universal Reconciliation

In this brief subsection we show the relief of suffering through sacrificial restorative activity of man.

1. Way of suffering. In the course of restoration, for substantiated action towards ending suffering there must be with God the human also able to bear further suffering in the mode of God. There is a tendency for humans to retreat, in the face of frustration and suffering, towards comforts within smaller unities. Fallen humans should learn, from parental example, tradition, and a structure of family reciprocity, to absorb certain suffering. If the parental models are presently not available on earth then the tradition must be received from God (and/or learned from history).

If a human is to serve God he must first be attracted by and to God and desire to be not dependent on lower values available, in order to relate for greater value. As Messner states, love wants to expiate every injury against God, by sacrifice.[115] A preparative condition of separation from Satanic enticement is established on completion of a sufficient period of voluntary detachment. The sacrificer will have experienced the depths of uncertainty and the temptation to despair is overcome. This way the pioneer becomes one with God, ready always to receive power, inherit it for spreading of unification.

For fallen man the only way to God lies through suffering and endurance. God Himself is not just a dreamer and observer. "Suffering, not just believing is the way to God—first one must endure hell."[116] When there is knowledge of readiness to suffer, one is not blocked by threat of suffering, much less by imagination of impending threat. Then one might expand the readiness for suffering from the individual level to the family level, national, and world levels. In doing this he is taking responsibility for suffering, and the greater responsibility overcomes resentment at that level of relationship.

The man who is ready to receive power for substantiated action towards ending suffering has been attracted by and to God, separated from dependence on available values after experiencing deep uncertainty, and gained confidence in readiness to suffer in order to form relationships of greater value. Ready to emulate God, he becomes one with God for the expansion in scope of the tradition of readiness to suffer. In taking responsibility for suffering man has overcome resentment at that level of relationship.

2. Way of Blessedness. God's grudge is satisfied at that level because man has turned from the temptation to seek satisfaction only from former values. Satan has not defeated God and man but is overcome at that level. Man is not so impeded. Although the whole creation is still shattered and God cannot pursue whole development so that He still has the great suffering, the blocking of God's developing of the individual, which also caused Him suffering, is lifted by a degree.[117]

Man's suffering and the suffering of God (Who stimulated man's desire for the missing unity) have not been vain, for after sacrifice man has and knows he has the desire and now is free to act on the impulse towards greater unification. In the pioneer who has dedicated his outwardness for the sake of greater unities God has a developed foundation for His work of reunification. The internal foundation will remain so long as the pioneer or one influenced by him remains dedicated.

The moment of decision is for mission. God's elect has come to a new way, for greater loving. To the extent that he now participates in God's fellowship and project the justified one has diminished self-caused suffering; but it is not only our own sins that cause us suffering. According to Koyama, in contrast to Buddhism Christianity does not call for the elimination of self but the re-direction of will.[118] The internally liberated pioneer has the desire for sharing the way, he desires unity with others, made possible through sharing, for the establishment of optimum conditions for children to learn and practice the way; and he also recognizes as necessity that others join in or at least respect the way. Cognizant of his own desire and suffering, he recognizes that others are suffering, also seeking unity, and could be liberated to join. Furthermore, where he had sought simply to maintain values he had been that far isolated, resentful and ready to be resentful of others; if he is now both forgiving and desiring unity he will seek unification, willing to wait further for greater joy.[119]

The mission is through suffering and after having suffered and through receiving the power for action from God. God has already shown suffering and that He has the power for mission entailing suffering.

The elect opens himself to God. This is "receptiveness to God"[120] (Who is receptive to His own will). It is "to experience God," "to be attuned to the action of God;" "The spirit can assimilate God and become one with Him."[121]

While God's love flows more freely now, through the justified, it is not fruitful for a substantial foundation for restoration until the love is shared and there is cooperation with others on earth; the elect may yet be engulfed. There is this give and take between God and his justified elect: God says, I can bear your sacrificing in mission; and man says, I can bear sacrifice at this level and am willing to seek the desired greater unity.

Having become externally vulnerable man becomes internally strong; man becomes parental. Archbishop Temple wrote in *Christus Veritas*[122] of the moral progress of Jesus Christ, saying that his will was "always one with, because expressive of, the Will of God."

The increase of freedom of the sacrificer to act responsibly marks a defeat of Satan and a relief of suffering. The sacrificer, who has forgiven, opens to God and receives power towards the cancellation of the consequences of many sins and the accomplishment of God's will. The ready elect chooses mission, desiring and needing greater unity, determined upon unification at whatever immediate external cost. In the dedicated and dedicating pioneer is a developed durable foundation for God.

3. Way of suffering blessed. In the process of liberation God is now organizing (rather than speaking only to the individual). The process of liberating may entail further suffering as God's power is sent with lasting effect in the world, towards substantial change.

This is the renewal of the life of God the Creator. Realization of His plan was interrupted and He cannot now resume it, yet he is working successfully for re-creation through the active pioneer. (God has created a resilient species.) But, in a sense, God bears the scars of any former disunity healed. Sinful, man always may slip back, and each human may be tempted at all levels if not receiving perfect nurture in a family in a whole society. As it is, even the fully committed may be tempted by the rebellious. So the scars will exist until the Kingdom of Heaven comes down to Earth.

As God's pioneer embarks to mediate God's unifying power, the Creator's life is renewed. Re-creation begins. Since in the careless fallen world each human may be tempted at all levels and might succumb, God will bear 'scars' until His kingdom covers the earth.

4. Way of justification. Man can count on as fact that God will endure suffering at any level (He having proved to endure any suffering at all). A human who is justified at any given level is one committed to endure suffering with and for God at that level.

Only through grace stimulating desire did the pioneer repent of the temptation to consume values at hand, then grace enabled him to remedy the internal circumstances of vulnerability to the temptation. He can expect grace in his sacrificial outward mission. Grace received while suffering is more valuable than physical healing.

The level of justification is the level of commitment to endure suffering as, with and for God. Grace preceded justification and grace will be available in mission.

5. Way of redemption. God and a justified man are in a secure relationship of trust. A justified human is to act with and for God to build up a group of humans at his level of loving, a community substantiating God's exemplary giving. Such a group is to broaden its scope so that it is ready to receive God's new Word for a higher level of loving.

God's commission, based on mutual trust, is towards communal substantiation of God's exemplary suffering at a certain level of loving, and further in preparation towards reception of a higher level of loving.

6. Way of redemptive suffering. In the process of group-building, God may send the newly justified human out from his home. (He may be rejected at home for his advanced standard.) In any case, he may find more frustration and suffering. He seeks to share and may find opportunity but be weak relative to objective hostility. But the justified one will not in this experience be separated from God.

(Even if he rebels against God when rebuffed by man, he ventured only because having learned to trust God; he knew of God's action and must hope that God will act again, so even if he cries out to God in despair at one moment he may yet easily reunite with God the next after only slight suffering from confusion and re-commitment. Preferably, he will know from God's victory in him that, even though Satan taunts, something of a pure offer is always received into a unity with foundational value.)

If God were not to send His chosen one to the world, God would get joy in him only and at that level of growth only. Yet if the one is sent, he separates from friends at home who might receive him (albeit with limited possibility for the spread of the standard), so he forfeits that joy and vitality, and if he then is not received in the world he is further deprived, suffering, and through him God suffers deprivation.

One who lived a high standard, having chosen suffering as discipline, was among friends and now is gone into the world; if scorned he suffers the alienation of his efforts; he may be imprisoned, become enslaved. So God sends him out only because not resigned to the suffering of others, but suffers, and because of the need to demonstrate the standard of loving to the ready, sacrificing, if necessary, to demonstrate, going God's sacrificial way. Such human suffering has worth as extension of God's suffering.

God has not given His justified only a new standard of purpose but a tradition. He has liberated the desire for an ideal world and given opportunity for participation in God's saving action. In this participation man gains happiness; but not yet true joy.

Sacrificial giving to offer freedom to another through a sharing of love and friendship, entails suffering; but once the unity is won, that level of suffering is over in victory, resurrection. With life in community structured for loving at some level there appears some joy. However, each human still suffers because the actualization of yet greater loving is blocked by attachments and/or the lack of receptivity in the world. For God and man the whole of restoration history is a circumstantially necessitated history sustained by desire for and hope for whole fulfillment and joy.

IV. THE PROPONENCE THAT GOD WILL SUCCEED IN ENDING ALL SUFFERING IN HISTORY

[Here we present the basis for the hope and conviction, in the Unification view, that God, who fully respects and promotes human freedom and has greatly been grieved by man, will bring about the permanent end of the suffering of God and man. In the context of the Unification perspective, that end will require the elimination of forces disrupting harmonious development. The hope for this fulfillment is linked to the Unification understanding of the origin and focus of these contrarient forces.

The limitations of this closing Section afford only a brief account and discussion, virtually an outline of the following: the origin of evil; the nature of God's scenario; the idea that progress is developmental, not just temporary; the belief that God will bring total victory over evil, not just progress towards that end.

The Unification view holds that the end of suffering cannot come without salvation requiring God's special, unique and decisive action. Lest eschatological action appear tardy, it is appropriate to discuss also man's role and responsibility in history, thus far and now, in the light of God's action.]

Origin

Our Unification account of the origin of evil tells of the innocence in Eden[123] of the ancestors of all present humanity. They were immature,[124] together in a wholly opportune environment, and growing according to a tradition imparted by God, of spontaneous and full communication-sharing-and-cooperation in a common project centered on God: so their love for God and each other developed.[125] In the events of the Fall of Man, however, their love became perverted, misdirected to illusory self-attainment. They fell both spiritually and physically (through spiritual relationship and substantial relationship) leaving themselves and their descendants internally and externally divided; loving wrongly (divided in purpose of love) and actualizing love wrongly (forming substantial conditions of unity apart from God's developmental creating). In the process of the series of interactions, the angel, Lucifer (created as a good angel for service to God and man but becoming jealous, then unbelieving of God's love for him, then seeking substitute love from man and finally seeking to monopolize human love for himself), fell and became Satan as first one human was spiritually seduced by him and then the one seduced the other in a disastrous substantiated interaction of loves. In this, the humans vainly sought instant fullness of love, eternity, apart from God and genuine care for each other;[126] the same was true of the angel except that he sought the eternity of replenishment of love.[127]

At heart, man seeks to leave Satan and return to God; but man had come to believe Satan's word of false love. Far from God and alienated from each other, they underwent degradation of sensitivity and capacity and saw the degradation of their physical environment. Murder and war occurred. Man's conscious hoping came to have the most narrow focus.

God still acts for the completion of His original scenario of creation, but, due to the Fall, at every step He must overcome man's fallen nature of envy and self-centeredness. He also must save man from the most drastic effect of the Fall—original sin derived from the illicit love relationship of the first parents centered on Satan, bringing confusion of identity and purpose and resulting in the grasping of unities which should be devoted to God.[128]

Several alternative accounts of the origination of evil are contradicted by this Unification view. One modification that has been suggested to us is that external misadventure in the course of exploration was ultimately responsible for the originating disunification. However, the children, growing in responsibility, must have known from experience that greater love and satisfaction comes through the way of cooperation according to God. Therefore, they should have maintained faith despite any apparently untoward circumstances. So, whatever the external occasion, the origination of all evil and suffering must have been a distortion of love, a seduction whose contemplation might have been avoided. It must have been a distortion of the greatest love possible since it blocked development to ideal maturity, and was not remediable by those falling. The Unification position is further supported in that children of fallen man experience deep conflict: the source of the problem should be found, in the parental relationship. The history of suffering begins with a false parental relationship—each parent not responding to God, and the parents forming a very narrow union covered over with cross-purposes regarding greater value.

Outline of Restoration

How will God correct this deviance from the potential He gave His children? In the Unification view, God's scenario calls for a specified number of stages to be achieved in finite history, centered on the relationship of man and God. Where human interactions are concerned, these are stages of the expansion of social unity culminating in the unity of a globally unified human society with its spiritual and physical environment. The expansion of social unity, involving both mutuality of love and understanding and shared substantial activity, is based on the development of sensitivity and capacity and the trust that God works through the perceived natures of others and of self. Spiritual growth is interior to social unification, and this is interior to humanity's development of the physical environment. Thus, spiritual growth is interior to the development or complexification of civilization.[129]

The means by which God induces humans to love and trust Him and each other (and to act towards fulfillment of His strategy) have already been indicated in this essay. But it is important to clarify that there are specified stages in the development of love, capacity and trusting action. Each stage of spiritual growth enables comprehension and application of a standard for foundational unification based on a certain depth of intimacy and affording a certain scope of union. The application of such a standard characterizes an age of restoration history.[130]

There are only four ages of the restorational development of human society,[131] which may be demarked, therefore, by an initiating point, a culmination point and three intermediate points. In the fallen world, every relational sequence culminating in actualization and the readiness for new initiative follows this pattern of four time-periods demarked by five points. (In the ideal world, the initiating point and the first intermediate point coincide, so that what would have been a time-period in the sequence is wholly spiritual and timeless; the initiative of God immediately is accepted by His creature.) According to this interpretation of Unification Theory, at the *first* intermediate point in any sequence of developing social unification an *example* is established, an exemplification of love, love capable of a certain scope of unification. At the *second* intermediate point, a *tradition of relationship* embodying the standard of that scope of love is firmly established. This tradition leads to the accomplishment of the *third* intermediate point where a social *structure in a society* embodies the standard and relationships and affords easy propagation of truth and nurture of heirs. Progress from example to group tradition is tenuous; but a true tradition, being spiritual, indestructible and motivating, is bound to become manifest in a concrete, loving community.[132] The conditions denoted by these intermediate points are difficult to establish (for fallen man), but once (at the third intermediate point) a structure, a home base is established in purity, has gained spatial security and is dedicated to God, the culmination point will be easily reached and the society will then give birth to—and be the initial host for—an exemplar of greater love, so that a new history commences.[133] Thus, in the over-all history, once God (at the second intermediate point) established among humans a firm tradition of His world-embracing love and commitment to His ideal, this must lead to the worldwide society substantiating God's love in social interaction (at the third intermediate point). This is a society filled with understanding of God's purpose and with rationally supported hope. From this point the final providential age of governing the environment can move swiftly to the concluding point. This ends fallen history and marks the beginning of the completed Kingdom of Heaven on Earth and in Heaven.[134]

As indicated above, progress *per se*, even under God, cannot bring the total unity of God and man, for man must be purged of the original sin. In fact, the capacity for spiritual development, upon which depends all foundational progress, is limited by original sin. The commencement of the third age in providential history, for instance, could not occur until the spiritual fall of man had been indemnified. Jesus Christ was uniquely conceived, without original sin; he came to effect the full salvation of humanity and establish throughout the earth God's Kingdom, ending the ages of restoration history. He was rejected by other humans and executed, but God resurrected him and exalted him. Then he commenced the work of spiritual rebirth into a living hope, indemnifying the spiritual fall of man, and offering spiritual salvation to all who believed in him and Him who sent him. Rebirth is given through the interacting loves of God the Father, the resurrected Jesus (the Son of God, the Word incarnate) and the Holy Spirit.[135] Thus, God the Father is in Jesus the Son, and Jesus the Son is in the human being to whom he is giving rebirth.[136] The Holy Spirit also dwells in those given rebirth.[137] So Jesus and the Holy Spirit stand in the position of spiritual parents to Christians who are their children of rebirth.[138]

Temple wrote, of Jesus Christ:

> "He inaugurates a new system of influence; and as this corresponds to God's Will for mankind its appeal is to the true nature of men. So He is a Second Adam;...it was the inauguration of a new system of influence destined to become...universally dominant...by the spiritual process of mutual influence and love that calls forth love...by a spiritual transformation, wrought out...through the process of time and the course of history."[139]

Now, many religions and ideologies dream of and hope for the whole unity of mankind, and some labor for it. But in their actions they war on each other. Thus it is evident that there is still confusion of purpose and action. Furthermore, while the great religious and ideological traditions are skillfully propagated, they are often rejected by the beloved children of the propagators. In the past, then it has been clear that the final stage of human history has not commenced, the point of the true structure of love not having been attained, and the effects of the physical fall of man still being present.

Man still bears original sin substantially and suffers because of its consequences. He is unable to act wholeheartedly or unhesitantly and in true concert. In order to cross the threshold into the final age of man, a second Messianic coming is required on the foundation of the advent of Jesus 2,000 years ago. This time man must be saved spiritually and physically. Since the condition at the third point in a sequence is established on the basis of the condition for the second point, "in the third instance the providence will not fail to be realized."[140]

The Messiah comes when preparatory internal and external conditions are established. He comes when man has, at God's direction, established a foundation to receive the Messiah; this is the requisite internal condition. Had the children of the first ancestors established the proper foundation, God would have sent the Messiah in their original lifetimes, to lead the way of dedication and growth and to give rebirth at the appropriate point.[141] As previously indicated, fallen man lacks faith in God and holds to that which is old; thus virtually every moment calls for repentance, fresh faith in the Word of the age, and sacrifice. The Messiah comes for the start of an age, for a new expression of God's Word. Then, how is his home base secured? The Messiah's initial base is established in the previous age. It involves conditions of unity. Historically, it has become secure and foundational by the reconciliation of foremost rivals in a society.[142] This offering and level of love substantiated the standard of the age and is characterized by the people's uniting with parental figures in honoring that standard. This means that those preparing to receive the Messiah and with a foundation of faith in God's Word must accomplish a certain restorative act successfully, in the way of redemption previously indicated, so that a foundation of substance (that is, substantial foundation) may be formed. This then becomes a foundation to receive the Messiah.[143] Clear examples in the Bible include those of Jacob and Esau and of Joseph and his brothers, who established foundations of substance to receive a new foundation in God's historical providence. Such foundations can also be laid between representatives of tribes or other social units, through the unity of the followers with their representatives as observed, for instance, throughout the Book of Numbers. In regard to the Second Advent it is consistent with this understanding, which has been explicated in detail in Unification theology, that in order for the now coming Messiah to stand on the requisite base, a worldwide substantial foundation is required.

God sends His Messiah only when his foundational base is of sufficient scope and potency, vis-a-vis other social realities, for the external circumstances to be opportune for the success of his mission; this is the external condition.[144] The Messiah comes to liberate human love and actions to receive God's power for greater unification, that those who receive him may join in overcoming with love those with whom they have been in conflict and thus establish new unification. Conflict in history has spread from that within the individual human to conflict of brothers, tribes, nations, empires and cultures. At the worldwide level of conflict we expect to find on the one side representatives of religion seeking a unified world under God, and on the other, representatives of ideologies seeking a unified world centered on man. Some representatives are tempted to attack with violence. However, God's representatives must win only through love and truth. The coming foundation to receive the Messiah will be established with the sufficient unity of those committed to act in common sacrifice to realize God's ideal on earth centered on Jesus' standard of love. This must be a cross-cultural unity. Some have come to believe that now is also redemptive history, although not everything in it, and that in the Bible we are given the norm by which we can discern the divine economy present. We are then called to integrate ourselves into it and thus respond to the divine challenge.[145]

Culmination

The coming Messiah must perform the work of unifying at the highest level. He must appear as the fulfillment of all religions, expanding the foundation of Christianity. Then he must embrace and absorb all the materialist ideologies by also fulfilling their hopes in concert.[146] He must cause all to live as in one family.[147] Furthermore, he must expand the standard of Jesus to embrace all the actualities of living so that all desirable unities, be they political, social or economic, become possible.[148]

The Messiah comes in order to complete the redemption of man from the effects of the Fall of Man, spiritually and physically. Through this he is to make possible the substantial unities desired. For this, the Messiah must be born as a human, as at the first Messianic advent.[149] Because of the Unification view's particular understanding of the relation of God and man (His image) as reviewed earlier, there is no reason to suppose that God's powers of incarnation are limited to incarnation as one white male and to one time in history. In fact, a proper understanding of this relationship affirms the reverse: God should freely be able to incarnate, and every human should come to manifest in substantial form God's Logos specifically. Jesus, uniquely conceived, became the first perfect human, where Adam and Eve had failed; he was the first-fruits offered to God the Father. At the Messianic coming, not only the Lord of the Second Coming will stand as perfect but his bride will stand with him as perfect. In their perfect oneness, they will stand in the position of parents representing God on earth and forming a substantial trinity with God. Their relationship, as well as their individual lives, will be the standard for the unities to come; being visibly manifest and substantial it will well serve this purpose. Then all humans will ultimately form substantial trinities as families of blessedness, and every human relationship can take this form. Thus there will come to us God's incarnation and visible manifestation as a true husband and father and also His initial incarnation and manifestation as true wife and mother. They come for the establishment of Heaven, the Home, on Earth. They come in the context of the hopes and aspirations of all men and women of whatever race or identity, poverty or might, and of the aspirations of all creation.

Recognizing the world as present to be unified, a gift from God, benefitting from the understanding and traditions of the past and fulfilling his own responsibility to develop love and penetrate the truth and articulate it, the Messiah will comprehend and be able to clarify for others all the essential patterns of history, including the nature of Satan's original crime, the common origin of sufferings and the sequence of the Fall of Man. He will speak God's truth without parable, including the truth of suffering. Recognizing heartistic nature, the Messianic couple is to focus on an all-transcending purpose. With devotion to this purpose, man will see his dream of the future become the actual future, the spiritual and the physical become one. With this goal, and in hope, members of families participating in the social effort of the new society will be conditionally as in an Eden, grafted to the Messiah and able not only to know God's will but to do God's will freely.

Man's Responsibility

We can locate our responsibility towards realization of the ideal if we can understand God's action and the nature of creation and its development. If we understand the original deviation and how it came about consequent to man's free choosing, we can understand the remediation and man's role in it through a chosen course. Yet we find that man cannot complete the remedy. Fallen man cannot find the freedom for perfect choosing and cannot create that which was originally lacking. Therefore, since God neither supplied originally that lacking nor instantly liberated fallen man, we conclude that God must initiate salvation and bring it about through man, and that God must supply the lack but do it with necessary cooperation from man.

As elements of full security lacking at the species initiation, and which will be present when all potential is fulfilled we find: 1) parental guidance of the immature; 2) the condition that the loving guiding parents also be loving masters, under God, of the entire habitat, (finding mastering of the environment, as in most species, a condition for ideal parental care). This finding supports the revelation of the nature of the original deviation. Mankind has found from experience, and established in tradition, that in the environment given we need, in order to survive, not only expansion of relationships in individual life but the expansion and maturation of mankind as a species, for man must multiply throughout the planet in order to transcend local changes in external conditions and this future alone can insure healthy conditions for each and every individual. This purpose is stated in Genesis as given by God. But to multiply and fill the earth lastingly requires exactly that parenthood that can nurture children of cooperation (which is not instinctively programmed). A tradition of learned teamwork, familihood, should be a hallmark of human history. Man did not fully cooperate in his first habitat, therefore, else the spread throughout the earth would have been cooperative. Therefore we conclude that the foundational humans did not fully learn, will, and practice perfectly foundational teamwork but came to be functionally largely separate from each other and from the God of foundational and orderly development, uniting sufficiently to produce offspring, but not so as to be able to completely exemplify, teach or offer teamwork to their children.

Combining these observations and also existential observations we find also that man would not have fallen had they been aware of their full purpose of creation, had God's purposeful love been fully incarnate in them. From the foregoing, we conclude that man is now to respond to God's grace, exercise remaining freedom to separate from Satan and form conditions of purity for God's decisive salvific action to be established and received, and that in this event God must send to mankind

True Parents who will fulfill the original responsibility to God and man. They will become loving masters of the angelic world and of the earthly "garden." In uniting and humbly serving as parents under God in the new creation, they will embody the true canon of normal growth and communicate it in an earthly home. Fully humanly mediating God's gracious love, as might have but did not come to pass at first, they, along with all other humans as their children, will end God's historical suffering for the end of all suffering.

The period of the possibility for suffering was precisely that period of initial human growth through which God sought to establish at the beginning His full incarnation in creation, that God the Creator be fully represented as God the Parent. Through the human fall that period was prolonged with great suffering. God gave the world to first created man, exchanging it for a spot in man's heart. Man broke the world and took it from God. But God did not count His loss as total—He has that spot in man's heart. There has been restoration and there has been gradual reconstruction. There has been a drawing closer to God. As restoration develops, more of the nature of God's ideal has been known, more of His suffering, more of His power and victory, more of His scenario of widening love. God's mode for change has been visible in created structures and was clarified in Jesus Christ, the Son of God. But God's poverty as regards the world has never changed, the betrayal of His original trust never completely indemnified, His original suffering never finally solaced. God has longed for the day when He could reveal His full love substantially through the truly parental couple who would transmit to true-born children the standard for whole unity. Only when such a family lives in the restored habitat can God finally see His creations fully in His image: exercising full freedom and responsibility, fruitful creativity and receiving the fullness of God's love that He had purposed to give. God is sure to see this Day on earth. This is the Unification view.[150] The very fact that these steps towards God's fulfillment can be thought of and characterized within man's responsibility is itself an indication that the responsibility will be assumed.[151]

Sun Myung Moon has said, "Our heart of love, centered on God's love, must be enlarged and elaborated to reach out to the whole world." "God sets His hope in us, and we also have our own hopes, flickering like fires within us. But we have to multiply that fire and multiply our love to destroy the world of evil. We may now have only a flickering candlelight, but we want to shed light into the whole world. The light will be multiplied, and the whole world will be illuminated by it in God's love." He also said, "If you shed tears, sweat and blood for the sake of the whole world, you will find that God has been shedding tears, sweat and blood for you."[152] This is the Unification view of God, suffering, and hope.

NOTES

Please see the bibliography following the notes for full references.

1. The use of the pronoun is not intended to imply gender of God (see *Unification Thought* p. 9n.). The essay also uses "man" and "he" only as species-representative.

2. S.H. Lee, in Matczak, pp. 737–46.

3. *Ibid.*, p. 732.

4. Cf. Sölle, p. 42.

5. *Unification Thought*, pp. 16, 162–63.

6. So God, through Hosea, reassured the people, (Cf. Hosea 11:1–11, 12:9, 13:4–14:4), and again through the later prophets, (e.g., Isaiah 42:18–43:4).

7. Genesis 4:8–11; Hebrews 11:7, 2 Peter 2:5, 1 Peter 18:20; Genesis 13:14; Genesis 27:41, 32:1–33:20; Genesis 42:7, 14–24, 45:1–15.

8. Cf. Luke 15:1–32.

9. Acts 2.

10. Y.W. Kim, pp. 140–141.

11. Genesis 1:26–31.

12. E.g., Isaiah 46:8–10.

13. Genesis 3:8–21.

14. Brunner, p. 367–68.

15. See Noro, p. 217, on Von Hügel.

16. Schopenhauer, p. 400 (Vol. I, Book 4, Chap. 59).

17. Lavell, p. 41.

18. A scenario outlines a sequence of value realizations; it need not specify fully how the values are to be achieved.

19. Sölle, p. 149.

20. Mastrantonis wrote that "for the normal development of love the fundamental condition is that there shall be joy in the object to which it is directed" and that "sorrow is in reality a search and longing for a lost joy." G. Mastrantonis, *Christian Love*, p. 4.

    Koyama wrote that it is *because* God is God that He is determined to create even if with suffering. (p. 149).

21. Sölle, p. 102.

22. Noro, p. 305.

23. *Ibid.*, p. 316.

24. K. Koyama, *op. cit.*: God who is love is prepared to act in history (p. 66).

25. See discussion in Mozley, pp. 117–19.

26. *Divine Principle,* pp. 20–21, 28–30.

27. Von Hügel, *The Reality of God...*, pp. 131ff.

28. Brunner, *op. cit.*

29. Noro, pp. 299ff.

30. Von Hügel, "Morals and Religion," in *Essays and Addresses on the Philosophy of Religion,* p. 206.

31. Sölle, p. 162.

32. Weatherhead, p. 37.

33. *Ibid.*, pp. 12–13.

34. Barth, p. 5.

35. *Die Kirchliche Dogmatik,* 1,1, pp. 310, 320.

36. Lewis, *A Manual of Christian Beliefs,* p. 59.

37. On the objectification of God, see Bonhoeffer, p. 34.

38. Cf. Christine Pleuser, *Die Benennungen und der Begriff des Leiden bei Johannes Tauler,* pp. 73–94.

39. See discussion in Sölle, pp. 97–98.

40. Of course, God's laws also have brought disasters to those who are conscientious and/or more or less continuously repenting. Judeo-Christian tradition preponderantly claims that these disasters would not have occurred had humankind taken the opportunity given by God to fulfill its potential. In any case, they will cease to occur when the potential is fulfilled, when humanity comes to full cooperation, collectively governing the cosmos with and for God in accordance with His spiritual and physical laws. This will become opportune only when man has become reclaimed from reliance on the illusion that present standards can afford full satisfaction.

41. On grace, symbolic sacrifice and the dynamics of indemnification of attachment, see John Andrew Sonneborn, "The Motivation and Dynamics of Restoration-through-Indemnification," in *The Unification Thought Quarterly,* forthcoming, 1984.

42. Moore, *Chocolates Before Breakfast.*

43. Sölle, p. 108.

44. Mastrantonis, p. 3.

45. Ferré developed a perspective on evil similarly, and seeks to correct a Whiteheadian position that every separation is an overall evil; pp. 25–27.

46. Sölle, p. 102.

47. Alves: Suffering, when it engenders the negation of that which is, is the mother of hope (p. 120).

48. Young Oon Kim, pp. 38–39.

49. Buber, p. 315.

50. Ferré, p. 83.

51. Weatherhead, pp. 12, 37–38, 23.

52. *Ibid.*, p. 20.

53. Lewis, *A Christian Manifesto*, p. 156.

54. Barth, *Die Kirchliche Dogmatik*, 2, 1, p. 622.

55. Quick, pp. 184–85.

56. Noro, p. 321.

57. Barth, *The Humanity of God*, p. 44.

58. Randlers, p. 175.

59. Heidinger, p. 149.

60. Noro, p. 97.

61. Sölle, p. 100.

62. H. Bushnell, *Moral Uses of Dark Things*, pp. 330–31. He argues that immutability should not be grounded in omniscience or omnipotence which are quantities.

63. Young Whi Kim, pp. 30–31.

64. According to Savage, God is our parents with both the father's heart and the mother's heart, and suffers with the hurt children. God offers parental succor (pp. 212–13). It is not clear that Savage has thought of the implications for parental suffering when the child is bent on rejecting the succor.

65. Paton has a vivid account of the value of suffering in apparent defeat, and concludes, "one does not seek suffering, one seeks judgement." Alan Paton, in *Creative Suffering*, pp. 20–21.

66. Koyama, p. 66.

67. Ferré, p. 84.

68. For a Japanese view on Jesus' continuing suffering, see interview with Mokichi Okada, in *The Christ Weekly*, 1 May 1954.

69. This is also the view of Richard R. Niebuhr (p. 153).

70. The Roman Catholic theologian, Ladislaus Boros, in *Pain and Providence*, pp. 46–47, states that after physical life ends the soul does not become "a-cosmic": not wholly disconnected from material events, "it takes part in shaping and determining the events in the universe."

71. Mascall, p. 143.

72. Augustine, xiv, 27.

73. Cf. Hunter, pp. 126–27.

74. "The greatest suffering is not of the body but of the spirit. This is why it cannot be *seen*." Voluntary bodily suffering is evidence that spirit exists. Richardson, in *Creative Suffering*, pp. 119–20.

75. Boros, *op. cit.*, p. 47, states the "the risen body needs the transformed, glorified cosmos as its sphere of being;" that the full resolution of "resurrection-corporality" will be experienced "only when the world has entered into the state of glory."

76. Augustine, viii, 17.

77. Ferré, p. 31.

78. Some have then said that God will not always have sympathy for the recalcitrant.

79. Bell, pp. 10–11.

80. Clutton-Brock, p. 148.

81. Sarano, see especially Part II, chaps. 1 & 4, and Part III.

82. *Ibid.*, pp. 107ff.

83. *Ibid.*, p. 113. The theory is developed in pp. 194–204.

84. *Ibid.*, p. 113.

85. Scheler, p. 142.

86. Clutton-Brock, p. 148.

87. J.Y. Lee, p. 11.

88. Wyon, p. 52.

89. Mascall, p. 142.

90. Luke 23:34.

91. Temple, *Christus Veritas*, pp. 260–61.

92. Moule.

93. Bryden wrote that a love that is remote and objective to the other's hurts would be no love at all. God's love involves Him as our Creator so that He shares our suffering and joy. pp. 111–12.

94. See Gen. 4:9–17.

95. As distinct from suffering caused by uncertainty of conscience or defiance of conscience, suffering here resultant is caused by frustration of the conscientious attempt to give love. Paton, p. 18, suggests that these are two different kinds of suffering. We can agree only if first stipulating that both denote thwarted love.

96. See *Divine Principle*, pp. 222–27.

97. Kitamori, pp. 70–80.

98. S.M. Moon, *The Dignity of God and Man*, p. 8.

99. Washington, p. 169.

100. Noro, pp. 35ff.

101. Brown, p. 39.

102. See discussion in Noro, p. 53.

103. Von Hügel, *Essays and Addresses*, p. 160.

104. Noro, p. 35f.

105. Barth, *Der Römerbrief*, pp. 476–77.

106. Barth, *Die Kirchliche Dogmatik*, 2, 1, p. 566.

107. Noro, p. 305.

108. Bushnell, pp. 330–31.

109. In this manner, God and Christ established, on Calvary, the redeeming condition for spiritual salvation, for the resurrection of Jesus and that all wholly uniting with him might receive new spiritual life.

110. It is true that only in loving God and all that God loves can man avoid wavering; however it is man's given nature, long corrupted, to grow with God to feel God's heart and understand God's purpose. Perfected man will commit himself to another: then the triple bond between God and the couple can never be sundered. *Divine Principle*, pp. 82–83.

111. Bell, p. 11.

112. God limited Himself in Creation and had unlimited fulfillment of His desire. This is the self-limitation of the loving, giving Father. After man's fall, God accepted limitation of the fulfillment of His desire, continuing to

suffer for the sake of future unlimited fulfillment of His desire. This is the accepted limitation of the sovereign as servant.

113. On God's love manifest in human love, see *Unification Thought*, chap. 4, "Ethics."

114. The patterns, factors, progress, and setbacks of restoration history are the subject of *Divine Principle*, Part II. A philosophy of history is initiated in *Unification Thought*, chap. 5.

115. Messner, p. 63.

116. T. Müntzer in Sölle, pp. 22–23.

117. Kitamori: "after the painful sacrifice God has forgiven and forgotten, and His love can flow more freely." (p. 246).

118. Koyama, p. 149.

119. Ferré wrote: "God never forgives, therefore, unless we also forgive all who owe us," because His forgiveness would otherwise be ineffective; "when there is full forgiveness all around, consequences of guilt are also eventually cancelled in nature." (p. 14).

120. Meister Eckhart, quoted in Sölle, p. 98.

121. *Ibid.*

122. William Temple, *Christ the Truth*, p. 179.

123. The account is an interpretation of events reported in Genesis 1:26–3:22. Cf. *Divine Principle*, chap. 2, and Y.O. Kim, *op. cit.*, chap. 2.

124. St. Irenaeus wrote: "God also was indeed able himself to bestow on man perfection from the beginning, but man was incapable of receiving it: for he was a babe." (*Adv. Haer.*, xxxix). Lewis also held that the tradition of Adam as mature and falling is impossible since if mature he would have learned to deal with moral problems. (*The Creator and the Adversary*, p. 220).

125. Pp. 1–27 in Ladislaus Boros' *Providence and Pain* are recommended as delineating a position closely approaching that of Unification theology in these matters, and beautifully elaborating elements of that position.

126. This despite the fact that God had given them a commandment, saying that the premature attempt to consummate the fullness of love is death. This was a commandment for orderly growth in community, to protect them until they reached maturity and could relate perfectly with God and with each other.

127. For a fuller explication of this account of the course of the Fall of Man with the angel, commencing with the angel's motivation, see Y.W. Kim, *op. cit.* pp. 82–84.

128. On fallen nature and original sin, cf. *Divine Principle*, pp. 65, 88–91; *Divine*

Principle Study Guide, pp. 92–94; Y.O. Kim, 64ff.

Rubem Alves wrote that God, through His suffering, "declares the inhumanity and falsity of the powers that dominate the present." Alves refers to all spiritual and practical powers; in our terminology the reference is to Satan and to all entities and forces manifesting him. Alves, *op. cit.*, 120.

Bowker, in his extremely valuable book, *Problems of Suffering in the Religions of the World*, records that in Christianity are "two different ways of understanding the nature of human deficiency . . . it is to be seen as a consequence either of an original capacity for goodness which has not yet been realized; or as an original sin which has had its effect on all subsequent individuals, almost like a disease passed from one to another" (p. 82). To the Unification understanding, these are not exclusive alternatives: in addition to relative incapacity, there is congenital attachment to Satan; failure to wholly employ our capacity for life is evident.

129. Cf. S.H. Lee, *Communism: A Critique and Counterproposal*, pp. 193–213.

130. For explication, with sociological analysis, see J.A. Sonneborn, "The Providential History of Re-creation."

131. Cf. *Divine Principle*, Chapter 5, Section II (1973 Edition) 173–175; these ages are referred to as (1) Providential Age for Foundation of Resurrection; (2) Formation Age, or Age of Justification by Deeds (e.g. according to the law of the Old Testament); (3) Growth Age, or Age of Justification by Faith (e.g. belief in the Gospel of Jesus Christ); (4) Perfection Age, or Age of Justification by Attendance (serving the Lord in person at His Second Advent).

  Cf. Also *Divine Principle*, Part II, Section III, Nos. 1–6, (pp. 232–237). To that presentation may be added that the ages are characterized, respectively, by physical intimacy, that and external mental intimacy, those and spiritual (internal mental) intimacy, and those and intimacy of heart.

132. These points can be seen in the developing unification within each providential historical age. For example, in the first or preparatory age, for the establishment of a foundational *family* according to God's scenario of development, the initiating point was manifest in God's clothing the first ancestors with the skins of animals (Gen. 3:21), the foundational *exemplification of love* enabling a foundational family is reported in the Biblical story of Abel's faithful and loving husbandry of animals (Gen. 4:3–4), the *tradition of relationship* based upon faith in God's valuation of the laws of the natures of physical substances and upon corresponding human respect, fidelity and responsibility, is reported in the stories of Noah (Gen. 6:9, 19, & 12–17, 8:1, 11–22, 9:5–11, 20), and a purified *home* was finally established, as reported in the story of Jacob and Rachel (with Joseph) at Bethel in the land of promise, having buried divisive idols (Gen. 35:1–10). Then they found full unity, security and dedication in Egypt with Joseph. Similarly, in the next age for unification as a foundational *nation*, the central revelatory stories focus on Joseph (Gen. 37:5–17, 39:6–10, 41:36–57, 45:4–15, and especially

50:21 and 24–6), Moses' mother and Moses (Ex. 2:1–12), Moses (later Joshua) and the Levitical tribes and the other tribes of Israel (and the tribes of Canaan), and, after a failure in Solomon's time (paralleling that of Abraham in the previous age), the establishment of the purified Second Temple in Judea (a multi-tribal home base, later re-established by John the Baptist even as Joseph later re-established the base of Jacob's family in the previous age). Cf. Sonneborn, *op. cit.*

133. For example, Jesus came to be conceived in Mary's pure person and was to live and benefit also from Mary's purified family and John the Baptist's purified society. He was born in Judea and there his work commenced.

134. Since the patterns of individual growth, and even of the sequence of repentance, sacrifice, evangelism and establishment of assemblage, and especially those of restorational development within each age and in overall history are congruent (that is to say that there is a similar pattern of stages within the stages of a whole), historical development is best graphed as a spiral (and a multi-dimensional one at that). Cf. *Unification Thought*, pp. 99–101.

135. I John 5:4–5, I Peter 1:23, John 3:3–6.

136. John 14:20–23.

137. Acts 2:4.

138. Cf. Y.W. Kim, pp. 197–98, entire.

139. Temple, *op. cit.*, pp. 182–183.

140. *Divine Principle*, p. 365.

141. In that case, the development of full human maturity would have preceded the expansion of social scope to the national, world and cosmic levels; in Eden, full maturity should have preceded the blessing of marriage and establishment of family life. The most rudimentary standard of love enabled the foundational family of Jacob's family. When family life is in the perfection stage of individuality and the capacity for perfect cosmic life is achieved the fullness of personality will be invested and originate in the family unity.

142. *Divine Principle* explicates this relationship in relation to the Cain-Abel archetype (e.g., Biblical revelation illustrates God's unceasing effort to restore the model of relationships true to His original principle of creation.) As God's work proceeds through history towards its ultimate goal of full restoration, the unity of the symbolic Cain and Abel initiates a new level of success in God's restorational task. Examples of this restoration process in relation to history and scriptural accounts are typified by the story of Jacob and Esau (1973 Edition, p. 278), Joshua and the Israelites (1973 Edition, early relationship, pp. 321–322, later relationship, pp. 332–333), the resurrected Jesus and his disciples (1973 Edition, p. 361.)

143. The process of establishing foundations of faith and substance in order to have a foundation to receive the Messiah is depicted in detail in *Divine Principle*. Cf. especially Part II, Introduction, Section I, and also chapters 1 and 2.

144. For examples of external circumstances evaluated as having been not opportune even though the internal foundation was laid, and for examples of external circumstances said to have been opportune although no internal foundation was established, see *Divine Principle*, pp. 280, 339; 423–424, 429, 453–454.

145. O. Cullman, *Salvation History*.

146. Cf. Y.W. Kim, *Divine Principle Study Guide*, pp. 5–6.

147. *Ibid.*, p. 21.

148. Cf. *Divine Principle*, pp. 127–133.

149. On the coming of the Messiah with a new name, see Rev. 19:12, also Rev. 3:12. On the Messianic coming in humanity, see *Divine Principle*, pp. 510–512, 363–364.

150. In this essay, suffering has been linked to creativity, not as necessary to creation but as thwarting it. Satan is presented as one who could have continued supporting creation but instead became the interrupter of growth and creation. Therefore, the state envisioned as consequent upon God's victory in ending suffering must be a creative state, in which man finds not just contemplation of God and immortality in God but unity with God in creative activity.

151. See Sun Myung Moon, *Past and Future Generations* (esp. p. 8).

152. Sun Myung Moon, "God's Grief" in *New Hope*, pp. 103, 99, 102.

BIBLIOGRAPHY

Alves, Rubem. *A Theology of Human Hope*. St. Meinrad: Abbey Press, 1972.

Augustine. *The City of God*.

Barth, Karl, *The Humanity of God*. Richmond: John Knox Press, 1960.

———, *Die Kirchliche Dogmatik*, 1, 1, 6th ed. 1952. 2, 1, 3rd ed. 1948. Zollikon-Zürich: Evangelischer Verlag A.G.

———, *Der Römerbrief.* Zurich: Evangelischer Verlag, 1947.

Bell, Bernard Iddings. *Why Suffering?* West Park, NY: Holy Cross Press, 1946.

Bonhoeffer, Dietrich. *Creation and Fall*. Translated by John C. Fletcher. London: SCM Press, Ltd., 1959.

Boros, Ladislaus, *Pain and Providence*. Translated by Edward Quinn. London: Burns & Oates, 1966.

Bowker, John. *Problems of Suffering in Religions of the World*. Cambridge: Cambridge University Press, 1970.

Brown, James Baldwin. *The Doctrine of the Divine Fatherhood in Relation to the Atonement*. London: Ward & Co., 1860.

Brunner, Emil. *Die christliche Lehre (Dogmatik, Band 1)*. Zürich: Zwingli Verlag, 1946.

Bryden, James Davenport. *Letters to Mark on God's Relation to Human Suffering*. NY: Harper, 1953.

Buber, Martin. *Tales of the Hasidim*. Translated by Olga Marx. NY: Schocken Books, Vol. 2, 1948.

Bushnell, Horace. *Moral Uses of Dark Things*. NY: Charles Scribner's Sons, 1868.

Clutton-Brock, A. *Essays on Religion*. NY: E.P. Dutton & Co., 1926.

Cullman, Oscar. *Salvation in History*. Translated by Sidney G. Bowers. NY: Dodd & Mead, 1958

Ferré, Nels F.S. *Evil and the Christian Faith*. NY: Harper & Brothers, 1946.

Hedinger, Ulrich. *Wider die Versöhnung Gottes mit dem Elend: Eine Kritik des christliches Theismus und Atheismus*. Zürich: Theologischer Verlag, 1972.

Hick, John. *Evil and the God of Love*. NY: Harper & Row, 1966.

Holy Spirit Association for the Unification of World Christianity. *Divine Principle*. Washington: Holy Spirit Association for the Unification of World Christianity, 1973.

Hunter, A. Mitchell. *The Teaching of Calvin*. London: James Clarke & Co., 1950.

Irenaeus. *Adversus Haeresis*.

Kim, Young Oon. *Unification Theology and Christian Thought*. Revised ed. NY: Golden Gate Publishing Co., 1976.

Kim, Young Whi. *Divine Principle Study Guide*. Holy Spirit Association for the Unification of World Christianity.

Kitamori, Kazoh. *The Character of the Gospel*. Kyoto: Nishimura-shoten, 1948.

Koyama, Kosuke. *Waterbuffalo Theology*. London: SCM Press, 1974.

Lavelle, Louis. *Evil and Suffering*. Translated by Bernard Murchland. NY: The MacMillan Co., 1963.

Lee, Jung Young. *God Suffers For Us*. The Hague: Martinus Nijhoff, 1974.

Lee, Sang Hun, *Communism: A Critique and Counterproposal*. Washington: Freedom Leadership Foundation, 1973.

———. "The Unification View of God," in *God in Contemporary Thought*. Edited by Sebastian A. Matczak. Louvain: Nauwelaerts, 1977.

Lewis, Edwin. *A Christian Manifesto*. NY: The Abingdon Press, 1934.

———. *The Creator and the Adversary*. NY: Abingdon-Cokesbury Press, 1948.

———. *A Manual of Christian Beliefs*. Edinburgh: T&T Clark, 1927.

Mascall, E.L. *Existence and Analogy*. London: Longmans, Green and Co., 1939.

Mastrantonis, George. *Christian Love*. St. Louis: Ologos, n.d.

Matczak, Sebastian A. *Unificationism: A New Philosophy and Worldview*. Louvain: Nauwelaerts, 1982.

Messner, J. *Man's Suffering and God's Love*. Translated by Sheila Wheatley. NY: P.J. Kenedy & Sons, 1941.

Moon, Sun Myung. *The Dignity of God and Man*. NY: Sun-Up Press, Holy Spirit Association for the Unification of World Christianity, 1977.

———. *New Hope*. Washington: Holy Spirit Association for the Unification of World Christianity, 1973.

———. *Past and Future Generations*. NY: Sun-Up Press, Holy Spirit Association for the Unification of World Christianity, 1977.

Moore, Pamela. *Chocolates Before Breakfast*. NY: Rhinehart, 1956.

Moule, C.F.D. "The Theology of Forgiveness," in *From Fear to Faith*. Edited by Norman Autton. London: S.P.C.K., 1971.

Mozley, J.K. *The Impassibility of God*. Cambridge: The University Press, 1926.

Müntzer, Thomas. *Die Fürstenpredigt: Theologisch-politische Schriften*. Stuttgart: Reclam, 1967.

Niebuhr, Richard R. *Resurrection and Historical Reason*. NY: Scribner's, 1957.

Noro, Yoshio. *Impassibilitas Dei*. NY: Union Theological Seminary, 1955.

Outler, Albert C. *Who Trusts in God*. NY: Oxford University Press, 1968.

Paton, Alan. "Why Suffering?" In *Creative Suffering: The Ripple of Hope*. Boston: Pilgrim Press, 1970.

Quick, Oliver C. *Doctrines of the Creed*. London: Charles Scribner's Sons, 1951.

Randlers, Marshall. *The Blessed God, Impassibility*. London: Charles H. Kelly, 1900.

Richardson, Herbert W. "Varieties of Suffering." In *Creative Suffering: The Ripple of Hope*. Boston Pilgrim Press, 1970.

Sarano, Jacques. *The Hidden Face of Pain*. Translated by Dennis Pardee. Valley Forge, Pennsylvania: Judson Press, 1970.

Savage, Minot J. *Life's Dark Problems*. NY: G.P. Putnam's Sons, 1905.

Scheler, Max. *The Nature of Sympathy*. Translated by Peter Heath. New Haven: Yale University Press, 1954.

Schopenhauer, Arthur. *The World as Will and Idea*. Vol. I. Translated by R.B. Haldane and J. Kemp. London: K. Paul, Trench, Trubner and Co., Ltd., 1906.

Sölle, Dorothee. *Suffering*. Translated by Everett R. Kalin. Philadelphia: Fortress Press, 1975.

Sonneborn, John Andrew. "The Providential History of Re-Creation." In *The Unification Thought Quarterly*, 2 (March 1982).

Sontag, Frederick. *The God of Evil: An Argument from the Existence of the Devil*. NY: Harper and Row, 1970.

Steimle, Edmund A. "Preaching and the Biblical Story of Good and Evil", in *Union Seminary Quarterly Review*, 31, 3 (Spring, 1976).

Temple, William. *Christus Veritas*. London: Macmillan, 1949.

Unification Thought Institute. *Unification Thought*. NY: Unification Thought Institute, 1973.

Von Hügel, Baron Friedrich. *The Reality of God & Religion and Agnosticism*. London: J.M. Dent and Sons, Ltd., 1931.

———. *Essays and Addresses on the Philosophy of Religion*. 2nd Series. London: J.M. Dent and Sons, 1926.

Washington, Joseph. *The Politics of God*. Boston: Beacon Press, 1969.

Weatherhead, Leslie D. *The Will of God*. NY: Abingdon Press, 1976.

Wyon, Olive, *The School of Prayer*. Philadelphia: The Westminster Press, 1944.

Therese Stewart

Unification and the Middle Years

Gail Sheehy's bestseller, *Passages: Predictable Crises of Adult Life*, appeared on the bookstands about six years ago and almost overnight placed the hitherto undifferentiated middle years of the adult life cycle in the limelight. Levinson's *Season's of a Man's Life* followed along soon after. Ericson's *Identity and the Life Cycles* and the works of Kohlberg, Fowler, Wilcox and others on faith and moral development, while not popularized to as great an extent, reflect a growing interest in stages of life. They are also raising the consciousness of our society to those stages and to the changes within them. Many recent books focus on the Christian family and recognize the problems and potential of middle aged parents.[1]

My husband and I appreciate the opportunity to share our thoughts on "Unification and the Middle Years" provided by this conference. We would first like to provide a frame of reference from the literature on this life stage which is a growing interest in society today. Then we want to share some background for our arrival on the threshold of the "new middle years," concluding with remarks about how being with the Unification Church affects the middle years and how middle years members contribute to the movement. Preparation for this conference led us to a less well known publication which we have found informative and interesting, *Issues and Crises in Middlescence* by Joanne Stevenson.

Defining the Middle Years

Stevenson provides some historical background and other insights relevant to both family living and middle age. She points out that for centuries only two phases of life were recognized: infancy and adulthood. Other stages of life are only studied and written about when a large number of persons in a certain age range become in some way problematic or troublesome to the larger society. The middle aged have defined the problematic groups: adolescence as a life stage needing study in the 1930s, the elderly as a group with special problems in the 1940s, and the youth of America as a problem group in the 1960s. In the 1970s, the middle aged began looking at themselves.

In 1900 the average age expectancy was 50 years. By 1975 it had increased to 72 years, an increase of 22 years. (A life expectancy of 120 years is projected for people born nearer the twenty-first century!) Stevenson comments, "It is an error to visualize the additional years of life as tacked onto the end. Rather, we should think of them as slipped into the middle."[2] She also speaks of the years between roughly age 30 and 50 as the core years of Middlescence-I and refers to the "new middle years," ages 50 to 75, as Middlescence-II.

Tasks of the Middle Years

Our society has certain expectations of those in each life stage. In Middlescence I people are expected to be responsible not only for their own personal growth but also for that of organizational enterprises, for the major institutions in the society: business and industry, government, religion, education, charitable organizations, health care, marriage and family.

> The issue here is not whether they do it well or poorly. The point is, they do it. Society expects them to do it. The very young expect them to do it perfectly. The very old expect them to do it better than their own generation did.[3]

These persons are also expected to provide help to younger and older generations without, however, trying to control them.

The developmental tasks of these years include:

1. Developing socioeconomic consolidation.

2. Evaluating one's occupation or career in light of a personal value system.

3. Helping younger persons to become integrated human beings.

4. Enhancing or redeveloping intimacy with spouse or most significant other.

5. Developing a few deep friendships.

6. Helping aging persons progress through the later years of life.

7. Assuming responsible positions in occupational, social and civic activities, organizations and communities.

8. Maintaining and improving the home or other forms of property.

9. Using leisure time in satisfying and creative ways.

10. Adjusting to biological or personal system changes that occur.[4]

Members of this core middle age group fill many of the leadership positions in society. They also own, control or govern over 90% of the real estate and other forms of property. Stevenson points out that within the norms of our culture, those in middle adulthood are expected to be their own person—to know how to guide their own lives. However, often they have not learned the skills or gained the confidence to do that and crises then develop.

New Middle Years

The author sees as the major objectives of the new middle years (the 50–75 year range) the assuming of primary responsibility for the continued survival and enhancement of the nation at its many levels. The highest positions of responsibility are given to these people—the presidency, cabinet positions, congressional seats and comparable positions in state or local governments, business enterprises, organized religion, social and civic organizations and the military.

Developmental tasks of the new middle years include:

1. Maintaining flexible views and openness to emerging trends, yet taking responsibility to slow down too rapid acceleration and providing wisdom and restraint.

2. Keeping current on relevant scientific, political and cultural changes.

3. Developing mutually supportive relationships with members of younger generations.

4. Preparing for retirement and planning another career when feasible.

5. Adapting self and behavior to signs of the aging process.

In addition, the developmental tasks include a continuation of many of those begun during Middlescence-I:

6. Reevaluating and enhancing one's relationships with a spouse or

most significant other.
  7. Helping aged parents and relatives through the last stages of life.
  8. Deriving satisfaction from increased availability of leisure time.[5]

Growth and Development in Middle Years

Stevenson points out that as children, North Americans are taught to believe that being grown up is one long static plateau. Because the education process has not changed this concept, these false assumptions continue, even among the middle aged and elders themselves. But adulthood can no longer be viewed as one big hunk of life, a plateau reached in the early twenties and maintained until old age or death. Many scientists have found that there are unique features, problems and processes with each decade of adult life. Perhaps these are more culturally than biologically determined but they are the genuine experiences of many persons. There are transitional crises as one passes from one decade to another followed by calmer periods in the middle of the decade. Both the crises and the calmer periods can be growth producing.

Among the *transitions* identified in middle adult life is the "catch 40" or midlife transition between about 39 and 42, which tends to be a time of discomfort, of coming to terms with reality about the implications of earlier choices, education and experiences. Then, in the mid-forties there is often a troubled period reminiscent of the adolescent years from age 13 to 15. Restabilization usually occurs between 48 and 50. "In contrast to 40-year-olds who focus on what they must hurry up and accomplish in order to fulfill their personal goals, 50-year-olds focus on what they have learned and how they evolved during the half century of their existence."[6] Female menopause begins late in this phase and may put stress on the family system or the marriage partners in particular. Separation, divorce and remarriage are relatively frequent in the middle years. Less is known about the ministages and transitions from 45 to 70.

Stresses during the later years may be related to retirement, changes in living arrangements, dealing with aging and the final phases of the climacteric. Illness and death are again crises of this stages of life. Retirement may make people unstable for a time. Moving to a retirement village often creates stress.

Work is important to people in their middle years. As mentioned earlier, persons in this stage carry responsibility for much of the work of an entire nation. Work may occupy the central focus of the middlescent's life. It usually is not just of economic significance—it also provides structure and continuity to daily living, links individuals to the society and community, provides a means of self expression and has to do with feelings of self worth.

Theoretically, some of the business of young adulthood fades with middlescence and then middle aged adults have more time to spend in *leisure*. For some there will be little distinction between work and leisure, for others a great deal.

Family changes are almost inevitable. By their mid-forties, most American couples find themselves without any small children underfoot. Some develop a closer relationship, others grow apart. Some search for new relationships. Alcoholism, drug dependence, obesity may signal maladaptation in the middle years. There may be stresses from teenage and young adult offspring.

Middle aged persons often accept greater *community responsibility* than younger or older adults. For some such activity is leisure; for others it becomes a second career

Values Shift. Value reorientation is common in the middle years. There is often a change in attitudes, feelings and behaviors from the mastery orientation of the thirties and forties. By the age of fifty, both men and women report a mellowing of their emotions, feelings and relationships.[7] They become more patient and tolerant in their relationships. They tend to live in the present. What one author calls "increased interiority" characterizes the thought life of people in their fifties, reflecting back on their lives.[8] To Sheehy's comment that the motivating phrase in the twenties is "I should," in the thirties, "I want," in the forties "I must," Stevenson adds that the phrase that best sums up the fifties is "I am."[9]

Stevenson, adapting the variations in value orientation chart from Kluckholn and Strodtbeck,[10] works from three basic type models: "Don Quixote," "Live and Let Live," and "Great American Dream."

This paradigm, in simplified terms, outlines three distinct world views, based on defining human nature, the relationship between man and nature, time frames, activity and valued relationships. Stevenson concludes, working from the research data of Gould and Neugarten,[11] that the shift in value orientation from young adulthood to the new middle years for most adults goes from the more idealistic, futuristic, "Great American Dream" to the more accepting, here-and-now, "live and let live" view. Says Stevenson, the majority of adults are engaged in working

VALUE ORIENTATIONS

DIMENSIONS	DON QUIXOTE		LIVE AND LET LIVE		"GREAT AMERICAN DREAM"
Human nature	Evil	Neutral	Mixture of good and evil		Good
	Mutable Immutable	Mutable Immutable	Mutable Immutable		Mutable Immutable
Man-nature-supernature	Subjugation		Harmony		Mastery over
Time	Past		Present		Future
Activity	Being		Being-in-becoming		Doing
Relational	Lineality		Collaterality		Individualism

VALUE ORIENTATION SHIFT DURING ADULT LIFE

Adult Phases	Young Adulthood	Core of the Middle Years	The New Middle Years	Late Adulthood
Value Orientations	"The Great American Dream"		"Live and Let Live"	
Human nature	Good➡		Neutral or mixture of good and evil	
Man-nature-supernature	Mastery over➡		Harmony with	
Time	Future➡		Present	
Activity	Doing➡		Being-in-becoming	
Relational	Individualism➡		Collaterality	

on the integrating process of the "live and let live" orientation most of their middle years. She has summarized this in a table.[12]

Unification and Middle Age

There is often a dramatic contrast in the world view and values orientation between general mid-life adult population and those in middlescence who are open to the Unification Church. One distinction of middle-aged Unificationists is their optimistic hope for life and continued efforts to better the world. The value shift from individual orientation ("Great American Dream") to the greater valuing of others seems universal in mid-life, although those who are likely to become involved with the Church sometimes must temporarily sacrifice time with their own loved ones for the sake of working on a community, national or worldwide level.

Being a Unificationist at this point in history clearly affects one's lifestyle regardless of age. Depending on the degree of one's understanding of and commitment to the Church's teaching, active participation will differ. For some in their middle years whose children are grown or who have no children, involvement has often meant full time, unsalaried volunteer work and community life in a Church center.

Because the Church has been comprised primarily of unmarried young adults, emphasis in centers is on outreach, service, fundraising and on personal and community renewal. There are some hearty middle agers who have taken on all of the challenges of younger members—long days, short nights, limited living quarters and such activities as fundraising and street witnessing. Some participate in Church activities on a part time basis, serving as housemother or assuming special responsibilities. One of the areas of stress that develops for some older members is rejection by or estrangement from former friends or from family because of the controversial nature of the Church and the media's negative impact upon the public.

For some middle agers involved with the Church, peer companionship is provided through jobs or previous interests and commitments. Some may experience age discrimination and be considered too old to take on a foreign mission at 40 or 45 or being ineligible for graduate school at 35. However, the stereotypes about the meaning of middle and older age and about what is appropriate and possible for older people probably exist in the Church to a lesser extent than in the larger society.

The middle-aged members who do live in centers will probably be a minority there. According to 1976 statistics, the percentage of Unification Church members aged 40 and older was 1.9 percent. Persons 29 to 39 years was measured at 20 percent at that time and the younger group, between 22–29, was a predominant 66 percent, and below age 22, 13 percent. There has been some increase in the proportion of older adults participating since the advent of the Home Church ministry and increased community involvement. These middle aged continue to live in their homes, are involved with selected Church activities and serve as a constructive influence in the neighborhoods and organizations to which they belong. Before the alternative of Home Church mission, many adults were limited in their Church activities by the demands of full or part time center life because of dependents or established responsibilities.

What do they contribute?

Middle aged persons tend to bring a certain stability to Church centers or other Unification work. There are many opportunities to use their knowledge, skills and life experience which they have acquired over the years. One important contribution mature members can make is in the area of relationships between generations as a "mentor" to younger Church "brothers and sisters."

Since the period of provisional adulthood, according to Stevenson, is one of drawing away from the family of origin and lessened dependence on peer support, the 22 to 29 year old is searching for role model adults for counseling and examples.[13] Sheehy stresses the value of just such a mentor to the young adult man and woman. The middle-aged adult, who is seen as more proficient and learned than the youth, can teach in an informal manner, help the youth overcome conflicts with their own parents and aid with contacts and experiences that will be useful. Since Unification movement leaders and members are often under thirty, middle-aged members can offer the wisdom and maturity of their years and broaden the intergenerational experience with the Unification family.

The parental role within the center or home church group often falls to the senior member regardless of the time spent within the movement. Since much of Unification philosophy teaches respect and value for parent-teachers, mid-life members quite naturally serve as advisors and resource persons in the personal life of the religious community as well as public and professional relations with the larger community. The older member offers the qualities of patience, confidence and practical experience as substantial contributions to a youthful movement. In exchange, middle-age members receive inspiration and stimulation from young adult members full of physical energy, pure hope and childlike innocence.

What do they find?

One of the greatest challenges for those in the middle years participating in the Church has been to find "spiritual" parental models themselves and to find guides for behavior that is appropriate to both their physical and spiritual age.

Why do middle-aged adults join the Unification movement and what are they looking for in life that they haven't found anywhere else? There may be one clue in the reasons why younger adults join the Church, if it is true that potential members of whatever age abound in idealism. Here Hulme is speaking to ministry professionals and parents when he writes that:

> We need to be integrated around a purpose bigger than ourselves—bigger than our families. Youths are especially sensitive to this need. In their natural idealism they desire to devote their lives to something more than to the accumulation of our society's status symbols. This is one reason why they are drawn to the religious cults that have been the notorious Pied Pipers of recent times. The tune they play draws our children because it calls them to a higher cause.[14]

There seem to be three situations which attract older adults to a religious movement such as Unificationism in their middle years. First of all are the mid-life individuals, single, separated, or divorced, who are personally searching for meaning and commitment. Either through individual witnessing, professional contacts or media coverage, they learn of the Unification movement and respond by becoming part-time or full-time members.

Richard met the Church in 1979 at the Denver Public Library when he was 37 years old. For the previous ten years he had lived in California, working a variety of construction and repair jobs. In 1975 he was divorced but he continued to share in the care and support of his one son. At the time he met and joined the Church, Richard was considering joining a brotherhood of the Episcopalian Church, intending to attend a seminary in the near future.

Instead, he was attracted to the Divine Principle because it shed great light upon the Bible for him. Richard was also drawn to the Church by the word "family;" he thought that family might be just an old fashioned idea in the modern world but he wanted for it to work. He was grateful to restore his faith in families when he saw successful models in the movement, and in July, 1982, Richard married a wonderful Japanese sister, Kazuyo. For three years in the Church, Richard worked in businesses in Colorado and New York. He currently attends Unification Theological Seminary.

Secondly, there are parents of members who, through their sons and daughters, recognize value in their young adult child's involvement. Through time and study these mid-life adults become involved themselves:

Ann (name changed) is a member of the Unification Church in her early fifties. Her ex-husband is an executive in a large corporation. She is a college graduate and the mother of four children. Her son introduced her to the Unification Church. She later obtained a divorce from her husband (they had been more or less separated for some time). She converted her home into a "mother-child" Church center and became a lecturer in one of the Church's workshop centers. Ann entrusted her 10-year-old and teenage daughter to their father. Not being able to care for them herself was a sacrifice that required Ann's deep faith, for both children faced many problems during their teenage years. Ann is now on the administrative staff of the Seminary and is taking courses part time and preparing to fulfill a long time desire to be an evangelist. In 1978 she also brought her mother into the Unification movement, and later she brought her younger son. Ann is engaged to be married.

Many parent-members have made a valuable contribution to Unificationism by working to establish parent organizations and conferences for other parents of members, in addition to valuable mission work.

The third type of older adult to join the Church seems primarily drawn by their connection to their adult offspring, who is a Unificationist; this drawing power seems to be increased by more than one child in the movement or the marriage of their son or daughter and the arrival of grandchildren. It is as if parents in their later years realize that their future rests with their lineage and over the years overcome their personal objections to the lifestyle or teachings of the Church.

Dan and Mary, in their late fifties, inquired about the Unification Church when their second son joined the movement, their first son having joined earlier. The parents' inquiry led them to join also. This was about six years ago. For several years they continued to live in Tarrytown and to participate in some Church activities as home members. Three years ago they sold their home and moved into the World Mission Center in New York City and took on responsibilities as full-time members. Dan manages an office for one of the Church's foundations while Mary counsels, sometimes cooks, and assists new mothers with care of their newborn.

Personal Testimony

My husband and I, like the friends we have mentioned, have undergone many of the same transitions that other persons go through in their young and middle adult years. The differences in our experiences are reminders that developmental tasks are not rigidly applicable to everyone and that specific individuals may not fit neatly into the stages.

My young adult life was spent in a religious community of teachers, nurses and social workers. The local religious community, of which I was a member, functioned as a family in many ways. Along with several other members of the group, I also participated in various local and state professional and community organizations. These years culminated in a transition period somewhere in my early thirties during which I experienced internal conflict and a sense that something was amiss in my life. Nevertheless, during this period I was involved in one of the community's education and service institutions for several years.

In 1965 my community asked me to begin graduate study; the overall experience proved valuable and challenging. I learned a great deal about education and also about myself, in part through a death in my family and subsequent counseling. In late 1967 I met the Unification Church and again experienced new life, a deeper sense of fulfillment and a vision for the future. Six months later I left the religious order to become fully involved in the Unification movement, aware that this was the next step in my life of faith. I lived and worked in Washington, D.C. for four years and then in New York for two years. In 1975, my husband and I were married in the 1800 Couples Blessing in Seoul, Korea. This represented another major transition and became a time of much personal growth. For the past eight years I have been involved in the opening and development of the Seminary.

My husband, Ernie, retired from the Army in 1969 after twenty years of military service. During that period he served in the United States and in Germany, Japan, Korea and Viet Nam. In Japan, he met and married a

Japanese woman in 1953. From 1956 he was very active in the Baptist Church. In 1963, Ernie met the Unification Church in San Francisco and soon became a member. A year later he was sent to Korea where he met Rev. and Mrs. Moon and many of the early members of the Church. Although his wife was initially open to the Church, she later opposed his involvement. They gradually drifted apart and were divorced in 1971. He did pioneer missionary work for the Church and participated in the Day of Hope rallies in the early 1970s. After our marriage in 1975, my husband continued his mission at Belvedere in Tarrytown, New York and in 1977 joined me at the Seminary, also in administration.

In his words:

> My early experience in life was narrow and my relationships with others extremely limited, mostly to my own family. Through my first marriage my horizons were broadened tremendously, both socially and in a spiritual way, as I sought more answers to the problems of life and relationships with people I was encountering. I had a relatively successful marriage, a comfortable apartment, and friends, but I felt the need for something more deeply satisfying. This desire led me to a strong religious commitment with the Baptist Church but I continued searching. In 1963, I was introduced to the Unification Church and there found answers to many of my questions. I could see many of the mistakes I had made in my marriage and relationships and also was deeply moved by the rich spiritual experience and love which again expanded my horizons from a personal/family orientation to a more cosmic vision.

Like many other middle aged couples, we have through the years participated in community service, helped take care of aging parents and experienced death in our families. My husband has experienced a divorce and retirement and both of us have second careers. We have redirected our lives, oriented our value systems and experienced growth in personal and professional competence. There has been social growth and a deepening of friendships for Ernie and myself, as well. We have been, and to some extent still are, counselors and teachers to younger persons. There are opportunities to guide and help them—to support them in many ways including their maintaining or improving relationships with their own parents.

My husband and I and other couples we know find living among younger persons stimulating. We believe that it has kept us younger, more hopeful and positive in our thinking.

To me it seems that the overall experience of middle age is enhanced by involvement in Unificationism, depending on the initiative and creativity of the person involved. In one sense, age does not seem to matter. Much seems to depend upon an individual's self concept and one's own attitudes about age.

The real benefits, challenges and opportunities far surpass any negative or limiting aspects of experiencing middle age in the Church. Perhaps the greatest of these is the genuine rebirth experience, the deepening of one's life of faith and the vision for a better world. Divine Principle teaches that now is the time to build the Kingdom of Heaven on earth, that we can now restore the world of God's dominion, lost at the time of the Fall. Building the Kingdom is seen not simply as something in the hearts of people but something in the building of which, persons, families and nations are transformed through a step-by-step process of restoration. As I experience and see others experience a quickening of life and growth of character, the coming of the Kingdom of Heaven becomes more real. Many insights in Unification teaching and many requirements in its lifestyle encourage growth, and push one toward the fullest development of one's potential and toward taking responsibility for the larger purpose. Building the Kingdom of Heaven on earth is seen not only as possible but as one's responsibility for the sake of God and of humankind.

I am more and more convinced that young, middle-aged and older persons can together, through mutual love and dedicated effort, transform this world of reality into a shining ideal where every one will share and partake of its light.

NOTES

Part of this paper was originally presented at a conference on "The Family and Theology" at the Unification Theological Seminary in Barrytown, N.Y. on May 30, 1981.

1. See Dolores Curran, *Family: A Church Challenge for the 80s* (Minneapolis: Winston Press, 1980); Gloria Durka and Joanmarie Smith, eds., *Family Ministry* (Minneapolis; Winston Press, 1980); William Pinson, Jr., *Families with a Purpose*, (Nashville: Broadman Press, 1978); Charles Sell, *Family Ministry: The Enrichment of Family Life through the Church* (Grand Rapids: Zondervan Publishing House, 1981).

2. Joanne Stevenson, *Issues and Crises During Middlescence* (NY: Appleton-Century-Crofts, 1977), p. 14.

3. *Ibid.*, p. 19.

4. *Ibid.*, p. 18.

5. *Ibid.*, p. 25.

6. *Ibid.*, p. 184.

7. *Ibid.*, p. 185.

8. *Ibid.*, p. 190.

9. *Ibid.*, p. 190.

10. Kluckhohn and Strodtbeck, *Variations in Value Orientations* (Row, Peterson, 1961), adapted for Stevenson, *op. cit.*, reprinted by permission.

11. Stevenson, *op. cit.*, pp. 11–14.

12. *Ibid.*, pp. 185–186. Reprinted by permission.

13. *Ibid.*, p. 137.

14. William E. Hulme, *Mid-Life Crises* (Philadelphia: Westminster Press, 1980), p. 104.

BIBLIOGRAPHY AND FUTURE READING

Ericson, Eric. *Identity and the Life Cycle*. NY: International Universities Press, 1959.

———. *The Life Cycle Completed: A Review*. NY: W.W. Norton, 1982.

Hulme, William E. *Mid-Life Crises*. Philadelphia: Westminster Press, 1980.

Kluckhohn and Strodtbeck. *Variations in Value Orientations*. Row, Peterson, 1961.

Levin-Landheer, Pam. "The Cycle of Development," *Transactional Analysis Journal* 12, No. 2 (Ap '82) 129–139.

———. *Cycles of Power: A Guidebook for the Seven Stages of Life*; 1981.

Levinson, Daniel, et al. *Season's of a Man's Life*; NY: Ballantine Books, Inc. 1979.

Noyce, Gaylord. "The Seasons of a Cleric's Life," *The Christian Century* 100, No. 4.(2–9 Feb '83), 90–93.

Rubin, Lillian B. *Women of a Certain Age*; NY: Harper and Row, 1979.

Sheehy, Gail. *Passages: Predictable Crises of Adult Life*; NY: Bantam Books, Inc., 1977.

Stevenson, Joanne. *Issues and Crises in Middlescence*; NY: Appleton-Century-Crofts, 1977.

David S.C. Kim

Marxism and the Unification Alternative

One of the most controversial, but least understood, aspects of the Unification Church movement is its opposition to communism. Currently, interplay between the movement and the varied reports from the media and others about its activities, have given this active opposition to communism many confusing faces. Therefore, the issue of the Unification Church and Marxism is extremely important to clarify. Further, it is an issue involving many fundamental aspects of man and his ideological relationship to the world. Therefore, it is useful to present a brief explanation of the Unification counterproposal to Marxism, in a way understandable to the Christian clergyman, layman, or student. In the following paper I will review this topic from three points of view:

1. The precise character of the Unification movement's religious perspective concerning Marxist communism.

2. The nature of the Unification movement's own particular world view.

3. The historical context in which the Unification counterproposal to Marxism emerges as a new ideological alternative for man.

The Unification view hopes to both subsume and surpass the breadth of Marxist comprehension about reality and bring to bear Marxism's ideological strengths by relating them to a concept not of atheism, but of God. Because of the breadth of the issues, an elucidation of the particular view of the Unification movement in relation to Marxism serves generally to clarify many fundamental issues which concern mankind, both communist and religious alike.

Development of the character and work of the Unification movement has been a historical process. In Asian countries, where the movement has long been active, Unification theology and Unification thought have been elucidated in some detail. In Asian nations there has developed a substantial communication between the Unification view and the particular cultural and religious perspectives of others. In the western countries, however, where the Unification movement has only recently become widely established, articulation of the intellectual and ideological position of the Unification view in relation to particular modes of thought, social structure, and ways of understanding, has only begun.

In Europe and America particularly, press and media have reacted to the work of the movement with confusing ambivalence. Although their views vary, they are generally dominated by a characteristic eclecticism which, coupled with commercial interests, make the sensationalist approach most common. As a result, some of the media have given the impression that the work and point of view of the movement in relation to communism is simplistic, reactionary, ill-informed, or fanatical. Similar misrepresentations concerning other areas of the movement's work or thought have tended to disappear quickly with the availability of accurate information and the growing sympathy and participation of scholars, clergy, and others who are socially concerned in the movement's varied work. However, in this trend toward more actual comprehension of the real character and goals of the Unification movement, the clarification of the position concerning communism has been less easily approached. This has seemed to stem from two factors, which are themselves particularly interesting in relation to the subject of western religions and the communist phenomenon:

1. There is a lack of understanding within Christianity of the precise ideological nature of Marxism, and the points on which it is uncompromising. Further, there is little comprehension of the need for Christianity to develop a comprehensive ideology and corresponding ministry of works representing its own ideal, vision and direction.

2. Within the still-remaining western democracies, and especially in the media, recent years have witnessed the growth of a generally naive tendency for extreme self-criticism. This self-criticism has been characterized by deep cynicism concerning the failures and weaknesses of the West. Though such criticism often has good social reason, it lacks a worldwide perspective. Obviously, other forms of government, not just democracies, have basic corruptions and problems. But this self-accusative tendency, often pursued by some of the most knowledgeable and well-

meaning, has been counterproductive in numerous areas of politics and culture. In many ways it has cleared the way for gains by world forces opposing the fundamental characteristics of democracy and religion.

Thus, the articulation of the particular view of the worldwide Unification movement in relation to this global ideological situation is not only useful as information for people concerned about the movement itself, but also serves to emphasize one of the movement's major goals. The movement wants to suggest a more balanced and whole perspective concerning democracy, with a clear approach to its inherent value, but still allowing constructive critical analysis of its strengths and weaknesses. Most especially, the Unification view is concerned with the future-of democratic governments and human rights in their religious setting. It seeks to emphasize the dangers which confront this future, from within and without. The Unification view suggests that only with a renewed kind of wisdom and worldwide perspective can the peoples who have democratic and religious roots attain an ideal for man and become the harbingers of new hope for a fully humane future for mankind.

I. THE NATURE OF THE UNIFICATION POSITION CONCERNING MARXISM

The position of the Unification movement concerning Marxism stems from the global and holistic nature of the movement's views of the world and religion. This position can be characterized as a completely God-centered view. It states clearly that the world was intentioned by God to be His "Kingdom of Heaven on Earth," that is, the visible expression in time and space of God's own perfect nature, expressing and fulfilling in image all the qualities of God: love, harmony, and eternity.

Clearly, the world is not this way. Hence, history is itself God's process of achieving this intended ideal for man. Therefore, if in such a situation an ideology like communism exists, backed by economic, cultural, political, and military powers and is (despite its own purported intention of good and humanistic work) dedicated to the ideas that 1) God does not exist, and 2) morality is not accountable to a higher reality or being, but only to men, power, and competition, such a system represents a dangerous imbalance and error. This mistaken view represents the position of atheistic communism.

The liberation of mankind is actually the function and mission of religions. But in this role they have historically floundered. There has been little testimony to the truth of God carried out in men's living of religion. This failing of religion notwithstanding, it is still the weaknesses of the atheistic position, its 'unreality' in relation to God, that is the fundamental tenet of the Unification position against it. Further, it is exactly the restoration of the original path and position of religion as the vehicle for God's attaining his ideal for man that is the Unification movement's intended mission on earth.

Specifically, the character of dialectical materialism as an ontology, typifies a religious system in itself. On the basis of this ontology, it gives clear definition to all the issues with which religion concerns itself. Since the conclusion of its ideology is that of atheism, it is an anti-religion by nature. The dialectics of Marx do, in fact, understand and comprehend basic aspects of mechanics and relationships in reality, but these are used not to make statements about the nature or reality of God, but to prove that God does not exist. Hence, it is the conclusion of the Unification view that though elements of Marxist philosophy and insight are correct, the basic atheistic premises, and more importantly, the flow of logic which concludes with atheism, are fundamentally wrong. The Unification view, on the other hand, which is a comprehensive system embracing both spiritual and material elements, is not limited to either issue.

The historical pattern of communism has been that of accusing religion for failing to solve the problems of the world. Though this argument has a basis in fact, it must not be used to frustrate religion and deflect it as the major path toward the fulfillment of God's ideal for earth. Thus, the position of the Unification movement is twofold:

1. Religion itself must be turned around; it must begin to heal and repair the failure of its history, entering upon a restoration of its original and true mission to serve mankind's future ideal.

2. Opposition to communism is not based on simple historically or politically based antagonisms, but on a clear understanding of the position of materialist atheism in God's world, and comprehension of the critical importance of a fully integrated counterproposal which can fulfill materialist and religionist alike.

A. The Religious Nature of the Counterproposal

The basis of the counterproposal to Marxism is expressed in the theological, philosophical, ideological, scientific, and cultural approaches of the Unification movement, which have been articulated by the Rev.

Sun Myung Moon. Fundamental aspects of this viewpoint have been recorded in the book *Divine Principle*,[1] and in Rev. Moon's public and private speeches. Also, beginning recently in Europe and America, these views have begun to be exegeted in commentaries concerning their implications for theology, philosophy, and science.[2] Though firmly grounded in existing work both written and oral, the process of more precise definition and elucidation of all areas of theory and application has only begun.[3] This is consistent with the history of any comprehensive religious vision as it begins to interface with culture. Christianity, Judaism, and other historical mainstreams of God's work, as well as humanistic philosophies and ideologies, have followed a pattern of the gradual interweaving of their ideological and abstract constructs with the practical applications necessary to culture and society.

B. The Historical View of Religious and Humanistic Approaches: Hebraism and Hellenism

The Unification view recognizes a particular pattern in the historical path of religion on the one hand, and the more humanistic or atheistic approaches on the other. To understand the present character of ideologies on the planet in relation to a concept of God and His coming Kingdom, it is of interest to review this concept. First considered will be religion. Historically, religion's approach has often been characterized by otherworldliness, an emphasis usually resulting in a retreat from responsibility to the physical world. Atheistic and humanistic ideologies or philosophies, to the contrary, have been typified by more scientific, world-related structures and organizational patterns. Communism, for instance, has so completely interfaced its ideology with culture that it is often understood by the more ill-informed simply as a socio-economic structure. However, this naive outlook neglects the fact that the entire structure is actually firm in ideology and rooted in certain uncompromising positions, one of which is atheism. The attractiveness of the humanistic work of Marxism has been such that even religious persons have joined the Marxist ranks for the sake of the short term goal of tangible change in the world's social condition. Unfortunately, because of the ideological problem, they have either been misled or are openly willing to leave aside the more basic issue about the worldwide power group for which they inadvertently operate as a peripheral agent. Such a position would not be so dangerous if it were not for the fact that at the base of these groups' support are political and military regimes supplying the finances and direction. This situation only reinforces the need for religions to fill this social gap. It is perhaps fortunate that the lack of accountability to any higher ideal leaves the communist world divided and less effective than it might otherwise be.

The Unification view has articulated the relative strengths and weaknesses of the two basic mainstreams of man's attempts to save himself, the religious and atheistic, and has called these trends 'Hebraism' and 'Hellenism,' respectively. One orientation has historically been toward a concept of God but characterized by failure to respond to the needs of the world; the other has usually been atheistic or agnostic, but dedicated to earthly progress and development. The spirit of one has been vertical and abstract, the other more tangible and concrete. It is the marriage of these two traditions into one God-centered view that will produce the world-serving ideology which can lead to the culmination of human history.

The Unification view is, then, a subsuming vision, encompassing the fulfillment of both of these tendencies and historical mainstreams. Thus the ideological content of the Unification view includes some of the characteristics of dialectical philosophy, but uses this same world view as a statement about the nature of God and His creation. The character, goals, and direction of the Unification view imply the fulfillment of both the horizontal and vertical ideals, resulting in the Kingdom of Heaven on Earth. Thus, it is not surprising that the dimensions of Unification thinking (theology, philosophy, ideology, science, technology, economics, culture, etc.) include many of the structural insights of Hegelian metaphysics on which Marxism was based. But, contrary to the Marxist view, the Unification ideology culminates instead in a God-centered view of creation and an acknowledgment of the democratic and human rights of such religious men under God. Thus, Unification theology as an ideology (the applied aspect of theology or philosophy) has the potential to become a basis for culture into which all areas of endeavor can be integrated, unified upon one God-centered viewpoint. Marxism is the only other such comprehensive view existing in the world. Its present gains worldwide attest to the world's need for such a comprehensive sociological solution for man.[4]

As an ideology, the Unification view's particular construction of an idea of being or existence (ontology) has been characterized, not as 'dialectical,' but as a concept of 'polarity,'[5] 'relative aspects,'[6] or 'complementarity.'[7] It can be expected to undergo a long period of development and exegesis in relation to particular areas of insight:

1. Theology ('Unification Theology,' since the particular view must be applied to the idea of God, scripture, history, and the sociology of religion).

2. Philosophy ('Unification Thought,' since there is particular relevance of the insights to the major areas of philosophy).

3. Science (general commentary, since the structures and models in the Unification ideology are fully applicable to similar operations in scientific philosophy and foundations concepts).

4. The Specific Nature of the Counterproposal to Marxism ("The Theory of Victory Over Communism").[8]

C. The Historical Context of the Unification Counterproposal

1. Marxism's Historical Expansion:

Marxist ideologies rely on the present condition of religion as one key to their eventual success. Historically, their writers have pointed to the closed vision and complacency of Christianity, in contrast to their own revolutionary activities. Further, they use this same accusation as a basis for completely undermining public confidence in the social power of religion. Their claim of Christian failure in the West hopes to discredit the Church and allow the work of communist groups to go unopposed, to cast Marxism in the position of representing good against the evils of capitalism. Further, they characterize Christianity as a major contributor to the world's social ills. The behavior of the Western powers, especially in colonial times is an argument Marxists have used again and again against Christianity.

Christianity seems unable to recognize either the threat these characterizations contain, or even more surprisingly, the elements in Judeo-Christianity which could initiate a religiously-oriented social position effective enough to counter the Marxist social revolution. Such a reply, through a completely religious ideology coupled with serving works and action, has not been forthcoming. However, such a theological and social reaction by religions of the West could restore the social and moral force of religion, bolster the remaining Western democracies with citizenry responsible and enlightened enough to maintain these unique constitutional governments, and give future credence to options for mankind characterized by liberty, the morals of religions, and human and civil rights.

2. Marxism's Criticism of Religion

Two thousand years have passed since the death of Jesus, whom Christians acknowledge as the Christ. War, tension, chaos, poverty and disease are still abundantly manifest, even within nations with large Christian populations. The life of the Church and life in society have been dichotomized into 'religious' and 'secular.' Economic, social, political, and scientific concerns have been relegated to the 'secular' category and the Church fails to deal effectively with these. This *status quo* has even been supported by scripture, alluding only to 'meekness,' 'humility,' 'turning the other cheek,' and 'looking to Heaven' as man's station in life, and for a spiritual reward in a life beyond this earth.[9]

From Marx forward, communists have been all too ready to point out Christianity's failures and use these to discredit the Church and its mission. Such accusations are replete in the works of Marx and Engels, marking the ineffectiveness of religion in relation to massive human ills and problems. The Church is criticized for promoting, under the guise of sanctity, poverty and misery for the lower classes, and of supporting the bourgeoisie in their repression of workers for personal gain.[10]

In ridding the world of religion, especially Christianity, communism recommends itself as a newer religion, answering "the religious questions of the human soul,"[11] and giving meaning to life. Communism is a religion of the state. Marx's ideal was "not religious freedom of conscience but the freedom of conscience from religious superstition."[12] Engels, colleague, lifelong personal companion, and translator of Marx, was equally eloquent in deprecating the spiritual life as any answer to the realities of human existence: "A person who makes his whole being, his whole life, a preparation for heaven cannot have the interest in earthly affairs which the state demands of its citizens..."[13] Engels' caricature of a religious man was of one who has striven to achieve the highest goal and failed, settling then for ardent faith instead of accomplishment. The Christian is a weakling, relying on some improbable unseen Supreme Being on whom he can depend as a substitute for the realities of existence. Along with Engels, Nicholai Lenin joined the deprecative attacks begun by the founding father of his philosophy. He deplored the way religion was used to exploit the masses, saying "Religion is one aspect of the spiritual oppression which falls everywhere upon the masses who are condemned to eternal labor for others by their need and their loneliness.... Religion is a sort of spiritual brandy in which the slaves of capital drown their image of humanity and their demand for some sort of worthy life."[14]

The history of communism from the time of its foundation has been controversial in relation to how truly violent its adherents were against religion. Some confusion has resulted from verbal service oft-times paid to religion in public statements and propaganda seeking to influence people of religious nations. Communist delegates have participated in such bodies as the World Council of Churches, and recently with the communist takeover of Vietnam, the government itself has assumed the power of the ordination of priests as one route toward control and weakening of its foundation. However, it is the historical pattern of removal of religious persons and institutions, sustained through massive persecution and even murder behind the borders of communist lands, which has provided contradictory evidence. Obviously, Marxism will take a definite stand against religion once communist rule is attained.[15]

In theory, communism proposes to answer the problems of society, economics, politics, and science which Christianity has usually left outside the realm of its responsibility. Therefore, communism as a materialistic and revolutionary philosophy continues to initiate conflict and aggression throughout the world. It has become increasingly obvious to those Christians, who analyze the modern world in a faithful and sensitive way, that Christianity can no longer be comfortable in this situation. Rather, it must act from God's side to solve the problems of the earth. However, to accomplish this in a complex modern world, religion must have a philosophical counterproposal which can logically defeat the well-entrenched communist ideology by providing answers for man from religious teachings, especially those of the serving person of Christ. Jesus prayed for the Kingdom of God on earth, and it is the Christian mission to actualize this potential through an expansion of Jesus' kind of teaching to all areas of life, including those called the 'secular.'

3. Christianity's Historical Alternatives (the Social Gospel, Liberation Theology, Christian Radicalism of the 1960s, Black Theology, and the Christian-Marxist Dialogue):

Within Christianity particularly, history has witnessed constant awakenings to the materialist's challenge concerning the role of serving mankind. It is within the context and particular histories of these movements that the work and vision of the Unification movement should be understood. These social awakenings within Christianity have been characterized by Christians' efforts to develop the social reality attested to by their faith. It is impossible to review all of these, but the following are of interest because they represent distinct aspects of this effort which has continued to occur within Christianity: the Social Gospel, Liberation theology, Christian radicalism of the 1960s, Black theology, and the Christian-Marxist dialogue. They can be characterized briefly in relation to their role as precursors to a view of worldwide religious restoration.

Advocating the interdependence or all aspects of society, the Social Gospel movement maintained that humanity, rich and poor, rose and fell together. It was a holistic view of the application of religion. Richard T. Ely, in his doctrine of "social solidarity" advocated full religious responsibility to social reform through the influencing of social legislation and supplying of moral energy and example through the churches. Walter Rauschenbusch, in his *Theology of the Social Gospel*, articulated the new meaning of socially conscious Christianity in the already familiar texts of Biblical scripture. The movement, with the outspoken support of such literary geniuses as Matthew Arnold, became the major source of humanitarian concern during the process of Western industrialization. But the movement was relatively short-lived, weakened by lack of a concise statement of ideology or organization, and by an over-reliance on the belief that moral energy itself was enough to effect lasting social change.[16]

Influences of the Social Gospel movement remained apparent throughout the early twentieth century, but it was not until new social confrontations challenged the stability of Western nations that new movements, centered on the social implications of Jesus' teachings, appeared and defined still new directions in this restorative trend.

Out of the relation of sensitive Christians to the poor and disenfranchised of class-ridden Latin American countries came the movement of Liberation theology. Strongly influenced by the Marxian ideals of collectivism and mutual help, it reacted as a vector of change for the oppressed masses.[17] Its leaders, primarily Catholic, developed a mystical and practical blend of faith hoping to forge a new society in which "the worker is not subordinated to the owner as a means of production *but* in which the assumption of social responsibility for political affairs will include social responsibility for real liberty and will lead to the emergence of a new social consciousness."[18]

North of the Latin American dilemma came the confrontation in the United States concerning the civil rights of minorities and the morality of undeclared war. The Church again came to the forefront, though in an ambivalent posture. Sensitivity to the element of Marxism was evident.

Fr. David Kirk, in his best-selling *Quotations from Chairman Jesus* re-emphasized the proper spokesman for the oppressed and the people of hope. The movements which became controversially known as the "Underground Church" reacted against the authority of Church institutions to repress their desire for social action.[19] These movements, again, tended to disappear as the issues they confronted passed from the public mind, but the issue which did remain was the problem of civil rights. This time it was the Protestants in the persons of the Baptists and African Methodists who provided the leadership for the movement that led to political enfranchisement, at least in law, for American minorities. Martin Luther King became the leader of a host of new American public figures, and from another section of world religions, the Black Muslim movement rose from the jails and streets to set another new standard of hope and constructive contribution for the oppressed. The action of these movements on the society was generally a favorable one. The religious influence of the church gave the moderating tone and influence to an otherwise dangerously violent potential. Theologians of the new groups echoed the standards of Jesus, of forgiveness, of repentance, and of reconciliation.[20]

It is on the stage of this history of active movement toward a full religious life in western societies that the Unification movement has emerged. It has its own roots in a history of oppression in Asia, and its membership is made up of people bridging gaps created by hatred and war. Anchored firmly in the Christianity that was exported to the East by Christian evangelicalism, it returns with a modern revelation of the character of the world and the future of world religions.

II. THE CRITIQUE AND COUNTERPROPOSAL TO MARXISM

A. The Nature of Marxist Ontology

The dialectics of Marxist communism deal with the same issues as religion, but claim to use a methodology compatible with modern science. From the religious viewpoint it is of critical interest whether the ontology itself is defective, and hence prevents Marxism from claiming a methodology that is genuinely scientific.

As is widely known, the communist philosophy treats all things as objective and made of matter alone. It also asserts that all things contain contradictory elements. All things change, move, and develop not through the interrelating of complementarity or relative aspects, but through the struggle of contradictory elements against each other. The fundamental contradiction is characterized as mutual needing, on the one hand, and mutual repulsion on the other. Need determines the quality of unity; repulsion characterizes the struggle. Societies are overthrown and replaced by new ones through conflict and struggle because the relationship between the fundamental element in things is most basically struggle, not mutual assistance or interdependence.

According to this Marxist ontology, entities are not a union of relative aspects in harmony, or of paired relations in a mutual interdependence of love and freedom, but acquire internal or external unity only temporarily through the process of negation, the winning of one side over the other. This particular dialectical outlook had its origin in Hegel's philosophy. In his *Logic* (variously published; this paper references 1892, *loc. cit.*), Hegel developed a theory of essence stating contradiction not simply as opposition, but as sharp opposition involving complete denial or repulsion of one of the aspects. He implied complete denial and repulsion, not a common purpose or common interdependence.[21] It is in Hegel's notion of thorough negation, that the Marxists find the basis for their negative statement about the nature of process.

Hegel's concepts were used first by the mechanistic materialists and later by the dialectical materialists to develop a logic in which the problem of first cause, the problem of the existence of a God, could be ruled out *a priori*. Not only could God be ruled out *a priori,* but He must be. Only this liberating denial of God, a first cause, could allow a logic based on the supremacy of matter alone. Engels, in his book *Dialectics of Nature* (1846) cited many natural phenomena in mathematics, astronomy, physics, biology, and dynamics as examples of how the universe is characterized by material and processes based on the principle of contradiction. In all cases, Engels invokes the perception of repelling or negative relations to explain his observations, rather than a view of affirmation, coordination, or mutual harmony. Though it is true that the sophistication of these arguments has changed with time, the general lack of an affirmative tone has not.[22]

To the Christian, who is used to a concept of sin as the reason for man's earthly dereliction, it may seem strange that the dialectical materialists never considered the possibility they were unnecessarily extending to the whole universe the type of contradiction and internal confusion they observed in man. The negative values, implicit in the ontological view given by the Marxists, were developed in the materialist system to describe the relationships between people, determine the value of the individual, legitimize conforming to the state, relate economic and social evolution, and, even more recently, create a repressive psychiatry.[23] The moral bias of the negative tone is great, and it is here that the element of negation characteristic of Marxism has affected society the most. The path of Marxist governments toward totalitarian dictatorship, characteristically without regard for human and individual rights, has been the usual social result of nearly all Marxist acquisitions of power.[24]

Regarding the possible existence of a spiritual reality, the conclusions of Marx, Engels, and their colleagues, are indicated by their denial of religion. According to Marxism there is neither God nor soul. There is spirit, but this spirit is an emergent quality coming from man's speculative ability and consciousness, which exist only as they emanate from the physical brain. To the Marxist, the emergent quality mistaken by the religious as eternal soul is not even a product of the brain; then it could exist independently. Rather, it is an expression of function, an artifact of man's observation. Matter is the subjective component here. Students of the history of the development of Marxism, through Hegel, Feuerbach, Marx, Engels, Lenin, and Stalin, are familiar with the efforts to which dialectical materialism has gone to exclude any possibility of God as a first cause.[25] Allowing the spiritual to be seen simply as an artifact of man's observation of the function of brain tissue is to the Marxist one of the most liberating insights—it frees him from an oppressive allegiance to a higher authority.

Dialectical materialism takes on its full development in relation to the consideration of how matter participates in motility and historicity. Hence, much of Marxism deals with dynamics in material, and the processes it delineates as man's experience of history. Originally, the precursors to the dialectical materialists, the mechanistic materialists, distinguished between movement and matter. They regarded matter as static until it was affected by some outside force. But inherent to mechanistic materialism, as with idealism, was the problem of first cause, the problem of the existence of God. It was the dialectical materialists who perfected the developed dialectical theory that movement was not only just an attribute of matter, but its very mode of existence. The solution of the Marxists was: there cannot be matter without movement, or vice-versa. Thus, for the dialectical materialist, the way to solve the problem of first cause was to attribute movement to matter. Otherwise, it must originate somewhere. If it originates somewhere, there might be first cause, and this first cause is what man has experienced as "God." Dialectical materialism had to deny mechanistic materialism precisely on this point, because unless one reverses the logic, completely allowing matter to be the subjective quality of existence, one admits, *de facto*, that God might exist. Instead, movement is the changing process within matter itself. It has self-causation. The origin of this movement is the unity and struggle of the contradictory elements of the dialectic. All matter, then, has the dialectical interaction of two contradictory elements, continuously accepting and rejecting each other. It has no origin; rather, it relates to process through this relation of opposites, "thesis" and "antithesis," which resolve themselves through negation and struggle to some synthesis.

For Marxism, this insight becomes the classic model of what the Unification view would consider a partial Quadruple, the "Thesis, Antithesis, Synthesis" (Figure 1). Because Marxism is not concerned with cause, it has not considered its model as Four Position in nature. A Four Position model centers the relation of the "thesis" and "antithesis" on something. It is only an embrace of *cause*, centering the relative components on an origin or purpose, that makes an actual Quadruple, or what in Unification terminology is often called a "Four Position Foundation." In the actual Quadruple, or Four Position Foundation, the uniting of the components (negatively called by Marxism "thesis" and "antithesis," by Unificationism "relative aspects" or "polarities"), takes place because their activity is centered on a mutually harmonious purpose (Figure 2).

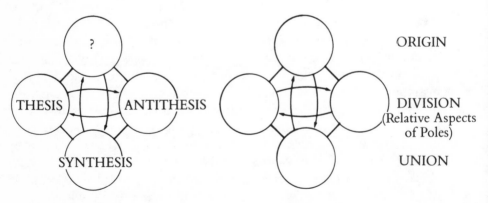

Figure 1   Figure 2

The problems which have developed in Marxism because of this lack of purpose or ideal upon which they can center the "thesis" and "anti-thesis," which they instead see as struggling in antagonism for some synthesis through competition, negation, and exclusion, have been tremendous. These cannot be explained here in detail, because they have been developed through a long historical process in Marxian logic. But, a crucial moral problem develops from their logic which can be reviewed as follows:

All matter exists in time and space. Hence, each entity participates both in "practice" (pursuing what it does) and in "recognition" (being acknowledged by others). To the Marxists, because of the negative logic, and the concept of motion as the nature of matter, *practice* (e.g. work), not recognition (e.g. rights), is what justifies an individual. This becomes coupled with their idea that the value of the individual is not primary, but secondary in relation to its participation in the whole. Of course, the state and ruling party determine what the value or standard of the whole is. This philosophy was perhaps an honest effort to resolve the conflict between the needs of individuals and the purpose of the whole. But, the imprisonment of the opponents of Marxist regimes, the labelling of the religious and other dissidents as psychologically ill, and the restriction of freedom of expression in the arts and letters, have been outgrowths of the ideology as it is applied. Engels, in his *Socialism: Utopian and Scientific*, expresses what is probably typical of the search for a balance between individuals and the whole. Written at a time when the world was nearly everywhere oppressive, Engels uses his observations as an accusation against the metaphysicians and the religious:

> the metaphysical mode of thought...in the contemplation of individual things, forgets the connection between them.[26]

This was not inaccurate. However, it creates vicious consequences in a system that places the prime importance on the role of the individual in *practice* as defined by the whole (the state). It also considers the human being to be matter that has been conditioned by the environment. This view of "conditioning" results from the particular evolutionary viewpoint of the Marxists. Animals have evolved from lowest to highest; if instinct in animals is the result of programming to the environment by adaptation (through mutation and natural selection) and if the instinct in animals corresponds to the spirit in man, man must take on his spirit in relation to his conditioning. Hence, not only is man simply the result of conditioning, he must be properly conditioned. Further, he must be conditioned by the atheistic Marxist society, not by the religious notion that he has some inherent freedom in himself.

It is this view of practice that becomes the theory of action, labor, and production characteristic of modern Marxism. Man takes on his role as the architect and conscience of matter, and only with the proper ideology can he program himself in the proper way. Man has evolved through a long progression to discover this proper way of conditioning himself; man is to find his destiny in this discovery through the attainment of the materialistic dialectical vision. At this point, utilizing the proper ideology to program himself, man can enter a utopian era. By revolution he can establish himself with a culture truly recognizing human nature and humanity's place in reality.

In Marxist theory, history develops through the repetition of three stages—thesis, antithesis, and synthesis—and is finally resolved through the process of negation and struggle. The world is not unfolding based on purpose or Divine Providence. This is only true in the Unification version of the dialectic.

B. Counterproposal to the Atheistic Dialectic: the Concept of Polarity in Religious Thought

Among contemporary theologians, Paul Tillich has articulated the Trinity in dialectical form in his *Systematic Theology* (1966). For him, the doctrine of the Trinity is neither irrational nor paradoxical. Rather, it is dialectical. The trinitarian symbols are dialectical, reflecting the dialectics of life, namely, the movement of separation and reunion. If this dialectical concept of the Trinity is meant as a description of a real process, it is to Tillich a precise description of all life processes. Obviously, this is a basis for a view of God compatible with nature, unifying those things which were formerly divided into the "spiritual" and "natural".[27]

According to Tillich, trinity is the innate answer to man's situation. He based his belief on the notion of three natural needs of mankind mirrored in the developments of revelation history. First, there is the tension between the concrete elements in man's life and those in which he experiences the Absolute. Second, man is inevitably relating his life to a "divine ground" of being. Third, man experiences religious reality as creative power, salvific love, and transforming ecstasy. Man and his God develop their relation (finally, union) under the condition of their existential separation. It is this independence of being which makes love possible, as has been recognized in the traditional notion of trinity. This is especially true in the connotations surrounding the term "hypostasis." For Tillich, the three concepts of God as "Father," "Son," and "Holy Spirit" are essentially derived from the three basic ontological characteristics of man. The first two persons of the Trinity, God the "Father" and God the "Son," correspond to what Tillich calls an inner, intangible "ground" and an external substantiating "form," respectively. This means that there has to be a vertical dialectic of (1) a nature and character *outside* space and time ("Father") relating to (2) a form of *image* of the character *within* the dimensions of space and time ("Son"). Finite man and his relationship to God can be compared to the idea of God Immanent and God Transcendent, e.g. we know God by His manifestation or substantiation on earth, Jesus the Christ.[28] The third Person of the Trinity is established after the concrete development of the relationship between "Father" and "Son." As Jesus said, "If I do not go away [to the Father], the Counselor [the Holy Spirit] cannot come to you" (John 16:7, RSV). We can understand, then, God the "Father" (Transcendent) and God the "Son" (Immanent) as two necessary aspects of the Triune God. This can be cast as a complementary dialectical relationship between two relative aspects and a third—their unity. In this light, we can understand more clearly a similar impression of St. Paul, in Ephesians, where he speaks of the persons of God as a unity bound together in the perfect love of the Holy Spirit.

This model can be transferred to the relationships within the world which should reflect God as His image. For example, as a man and a woman (husband and wife) form a bond of love, their union produces a child. Most interestingly, this aspect of their unity reflects God's image in creativity; in English it is called "procreation," indicating the relationship. The child becomes the most personal object of the love shared by the parents. The "procreation" of the third person of the family expands the dimension of the family unit and reflects the dual natures of husband and wife in one entity. Through this three-dimensional relationship, three types of love are given to the child, that of Father, Mother, and Parents. St. Paul says "... let each one of you love his wife as himself and let the wife see that she respects her husband" (Eph. 5:33 RSV) and "Children, obey your parents in the Lord, for it is right. "Honor your father and mother . . ." (Eph. 6:1–2 RSV). At the center of this relationship in the Christian concept of marriage is God, whose image people reflect. Through the marital relationship, man and woman, as co-equal parents, form the complete image of God (Gen. 1:27) with God as their center. The child, as the image of God and image of the Parents, completes the unit (Figure 3). Similarly, when the Christian, through the inspiration of the Holy Spirit accepts Jesus as Savior, he also becomes the mystical or "spiritual" child of Jesus and the Holy Spirit, thus forming the mystical family of God (Figure 4). With such a succinct insight available into the nature of God and man, using the dialectical understanding and the Quadruple model, it is hard to imagine what value these paramount aspects of life can have to the atheist, when there is no center or direction on which they are purposed. A unique contribution of the Unification ideology is its unifying of these concepts within a precise understanding of how all of reality is structured. The religious person understands, then, in a way compatible with all experiences of life, the meaning of these most intimate and personal things.

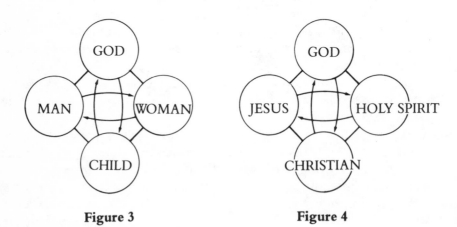

Figure 3   **Figure 4**

C. The Specific Critique and Counterproposal to Marxism in the Unification View

Central topics in the dialectical materialist's idea of being include theories of interrelationship, the existence of contradiction, the process of negation and the dynamics of development. These can serve as a basis for a fundamental critique and counterproposal from the Unification view. To give more of an idea of the nature of these Marxist concepts and their potential restatement from a religious point of view, one that includes the existence of God, I will review these theories below. Further, since it is helpful to use examples in clarifying many of these ideas I will consistently use the analogy, already introduced, of the relationships within the human family.

1. The Theory of Interrelationships

Without exception, things in the material world do not exist in isolation. Rather, they participate in complex webs of mutual interconnections and relationships. This is corroborated by modern scientific knowledge. Recognizing this, the Marxist dialectic makes the existence of mutual relationships and interconnections in nature a fundamental statement. But because the dialectic is exclusively materialist and thus atheistic, it cannot deal with the problem of an original cause, it says nothing about *why* such relationships exist or toward what ideal or state they may be striving. In fact, because of the nature of the ideology, the dialectical materialist cannot even make this his concern. Since matter is placed as the inherent subjective cause in all things, the materialist can only explain matter centering on his logic which maintains a concept of process without the problem of first cause. In the dialectic, the problem of motive, reason, and cause in and beneath the existence of things and their processes is closed. Without the concept of original cause, these concepts of being and existence treat only results and resultant processes. Interest in pursuing the basic source is closed. This aspect of dialectical materialism is one critical point of error. After all, it is more scientific to assume God *may* or may *not* exist than to assume that He does not. When constructing a world view, the margin of error between the extremes is quite great!

A God-centered point of view considers *why* mutual relationships exist and come into existence. To develop this insight, we begin with the assertion that the universe is an organic whole, unified and directed by purpose. From this insight, religion perceives mutuality of relationships, harmony, development, ideal, direction, and purpose. Religion claims that without a purposeful principle inherently operative throughout the universe and recognized by man as the center of his own being, man cannot have a concept of true value, morality, or love.

In the Unification Principle we consider this issue of mutuality from the point of view of how mutual relationships between all things involve the "give" and "take" interaction of "subject" and "object." According to our argument, fundamentally equal but complementary and mutually coactive subject and object parts attain a unity and completed identity and purpose through their participation in the motion of harmony and mutual care. Thus, from the smallest relations of protons and electrons in atoms to the complex structures and cycles of the celestial bodies, everything exists in magnitudes of these relationships of give and take in subject and object pairs. This universe is thus a gigantic organism composed of myriad relationships sharing give and take action vertically and horizontally. It is one universal body of life directed with a common purpose. This common purpose originates from the reality of God. Every creature participates as part of a common goal and ideal, with its ultimate ideal being the expression of God's own image. This image of harmony, mutuality, and all that is affirmative, is expressed first in symbol (in fundamental relations inherently functioning in this principle), but ultimately it is expressed in man, where God's unique characteristics of freedom, creativity, and love are incarnated. The material things of the universe have mutual interrelationships, harmony, order, and principle because they exist as the base to fulfill God's ultimate purpose: His incarnation in men and women.

2. The Theory of Contradiction and Negation (Thesis-Antithesis-Synthesis)

In the Marxist dialectic, process is accomplished through the complementary struggle between elements that are in contradiction. All things and their modes of development are necessarily composed of two contradictory aspects; one is affirmative, the other, negative. For a time, the two contradictory elements develop, participating in two relative dynamics, unity and struggle, attraction and repulsion. They continue to develop until they reach a critical stage when culmination of the process forces a synthesis (called the "negation of the negation"). This makes an end to the struggle for that period of development. The synthesis is neither affirmative, nor negating; rather, it is an entirely new thing. In it, however, the characteristics of affirmation and negation remain intact. This synthesis, the new thing resulting from the negation of the negation, the resolution of struggle between attraction and repulsion, includes within itself a new resultant opposing element. This element then begins to negate the synthesis. The new thing, thus, has its own element in opposition to the synthesis and because of this, new conflict and struggle is initiated. This is again consummated by a new, but higher level, negation of the negation. Therefore, without end, the two opposing, contradictory elements continually repeat this process of conflict and struggle toward unity and the pathway of this process continues forever.

a. The Concept of Contradiction: As stated before, in the Marxist understanding of the dialectic the two fundamentally opposing elements need each other on the one hand, and are repulsive to each other on the other. Their relationship of mutual need is their "union;" their relation of mutual repulsion is "struggle." All things have within themselves these two contradictory elements, seeking unity yet opposing each other. Thus, through unity and struggle all process occurs. The dialectical examples for this idea of being include such things as plus and minus in mathematics, action and reaction in mechanics, positive and negative charges in physics, combination and separation in chemistry, and class struggle in sociology. With the exception of the last item, these examples come from the natural sciences and are relatively simple and observable concepts. Also, in all cases but the last, it is just as easy to suggest that a unity exists between the elements through their inherent complementarity and harmony, rather than a struggle. But this option is not entertained by the Marxists. Although there is an ideal of oneness, it is at the same time identical with the process of antagonism and struggle. The Marxist makes this erroneous identification because he has not rightly underscored the metaphysical aspects of matter from some original static or dynamic point. Rather, since he sees everything in relation to a faulty view of change and development—a mechanical and materialist one—he always sees conflict and struggle in the two uniting things.

From the Unification view one can agree that the concept of contradiction applies to much of the process of social change. Social development has nearly always been characterized by struggle. But the other relations are not as easily assumed to represent the dialectical position, *except* as they might follow from our observation of struggle in human nature. For example, the birth of a child can hardly be seen as a struggle between the fetus and the mother; rather, after a regular period of maturation, the stability of tissues in the mother's womb discontinues in response to certain hormonal action. The hormonal action is itself initiated as response to indicators released by the process of maturation. The mother's tissues then respond, allowing the birth of the child. The tissues of the mother expelled at birth cannot be viewed as tissues that have been overcome, but tissues that have fulfilled their purpose and no longer have a meaningful existence. In an even more simple example, in natural science, we would be hard pressed to see struggle in the neutralization of electrical charges or the relation of proton and electron in the atom.

According to the Unification view, development in nature does not take place through struggle, but through a unity achieved by mutuality and complementarity of relationships. These are typified by harmony, correspondence, and cooperation. Struggle is secondary. The Unification view treats the problem of man as a very unique problem, as should be expected since as a religious view it entertains the notion of the significance of man's spiritual life. Man's history is his history with God, a history which represents man's inability to achieve the ideal of harmony and unity. For God, man (invested with the very potentials that allow his deviance) was and is to be the culminating illustration of God's own nature. The struggle of man is not one in a blind universe typified by fundamental elements of contradiction and antagonism. Instead, it is a long journey back to an understanding of how mutuality and unity are achieved, an understanding of how man can use his freedom and creativity to share his life with God and be a co-creator with Him.

b. The Concept of Negation: Marxists believe that any transformation from one level to another involves opposing action. Hence, the synthesis or resolution of any struggle contains its own opposing element. Negation in the dialectic is the concept used to explain the process of development in all things: through negation the previous state is sublated, with its positive aspect preserved and embraced in the negation. Thus, negation takes place only in form, while content is actually preserved. Hence, concerning the tissue of the womb in the mother and the position of the child, the fetus maintains unity for a time with the antagonistic element of the mother's womb, but later is negated by the child and attains the synthesis of birth. The child, which is the negation of the fetus, does not in this case abandon the fetus; rather, it is only a further development of the fetus. Thus, there is neither reconciliation nor abandonment, but a developmental negation leading to preservation through sublation. Negation is an idea that is much like the idea of contradiction: the process of negation takes place through the struggle of conflicting things. The culmination of the struggle does not imply lasting peace or harmony.

The Unification view considers the matter from another point of view. The things in God's world are basically complementary in nature, and they develop through the mutual and motion-initiating relationship of subject and object. The action of give and take between subject and object ceaselessly and necessarily operates. It is called the "Law of Give and Take." Through the action of give and take, all existence, multiplication, and action is initiated and sustained. It is not an action of opposition and conflict but one of harmony, cooperation, and correspondence. Thus, unity in development is continuous. Through development, things change, but within a basic context of harmonious give and take.

Within the problem of sin and its origin, man would also have developed completely in this way. Man's deviant state came about because he, as the element in the position of the object, did not define his identity in relation to co-responsiveness and mutuality with the subject, God. Instead he sought to establish this relationship with himself. Mistaking the nature of his freedom and creativity, he has foolishly tried to occupy the subject position and, hence, the relationship of give and take has become one of conflict and struggle. Atheism tries to perpetuate this error. Consequently, history has been a process of struggle between the original principle of subject and object inherent in man, but which is only accessible through the proper use of free will, and the element of contradiction that man himself introduced through his failure to correctly understand his covenantal position with God and with other men. Hence, even history reflects this contradiction of inherent and introduced standards; there are times of peace, prosperity, and harmony, and times of war and conflict. Therefore, the concept of good and evil enters the Unification view. Evil is the tendency toward disorder in relation to the original principle or harmony (called in Christianity the "diabolical" tendency); good is the tendency toward the ideal of the original principle of harmony, mutuality and cooperation. History can be viewed as the long struggle of man from contradiction to the ideal, not simply, as in the Marxist view, one of class struggle, the succession of power groups, and the culmination of production cycles. Patterns in history exist, but it will be demonstrated in the following sections that they are not described by the Marxists adequately.

3. The Theory of Progress

In the dialectic, all process is the result of contradiction. In the contradiction there is struggle, conflict and opposition. Where these occur, process and development occur. It is not a development characterized by unity and harmony; rather, it is one in which quantitative increase is interrupted by abrupt qualitative change acheived through a clash, after which a higher state begins. In this fashion progress through negation is able to move from the lower to the higher.

a. Quantitative and Qualitative Change: Gradual development does not go on continuously, but is interrupted by sudden changes through which a new level is achieved. Again, the example of the birth of a child might serve as an illustration. This phenomenon is called the "Transition from Quantitative to Qualitative Change." Qualitative change takes place on the base of quantitative change. The nature of the qualitative change is the one of negation, that is, one element or group overcomes the other. For instance, in Marxism this is often seen as the relationship of the ruler and the ruled. In the dialectic, one of the contradictory, opposing elements is considered to be superior; the other, inferior. Hence, process involves one party subordinating itself to the other, one gaining power over the other. At some point in time, however, these relationships characteristically go through a reversal. For instance, the child will eventually dominate his aging parents. Thus, in Marxism, new contradictions are always developing as the characteristic of process and progress. The child of one day will move on to fulfill its own relations of negation through having his own child. The qualitative change is characterized by this kind of reversal.

Obviously, it is possible to see this same content in another way. Certainly there is a relation between qualitative and quantitative change. Nearly all process expressing abrupt change: boiling of water, freezing of water, eruption of volcanoes, initiation of avalanches, etc., also show gradual change. Other natural processes are characterized completely by gradual transition—seasons, growth, the piling of objects, and so on. But more importantly, the entire structure of this concept can be re-examined in the light of the Unification view.

For the Unification view, all process and change result from the give and take action of a subject and object. A basic problem in Marxism is that it is unable to grasp a fundamental complementary relationship between quantitative and qualitative change. It is limited to having one lead to the other. A deeper concept of progress also admits the case in which there is a simultaneity and mutuality of qualitative and quantitative change. The basis for this insight is inherent in the Unification Principle's concept of Sung Sang ("Internal Character") and Hyung Sang ("External Form"). The Hyung Sang of things refers to their material properties: shape, structure, size, and the like. Sung Sang refers to the quality, character, or function of things. During development, Hyung Sang does not change to Sung Sang, or vice versa, although they can affect each other. Both of these are relative aspects for a complementary relationship. They exist simultaneously. They co-facilitate progress. Thus, the birth of a child also involves the simultaneous fulfillment of the purpose of the tissues of the womb. Also the attainment of the form of the child (quantitative) and the character of "child" (qualitative) occur together. Also, the purpose of the mother in having a child and the purpose of the child in living his life can be fulfilled simultaneously. These are relative aspects of one thing, existing in a dialectic of polarity.

Both cause and effect in the physical world (the world of effect) exist as manifested effects of prototypes which exist simultaneously in the complementary world of cause. The complementary world of cause is the larger Sung Sang, the invisible dimension called in the Unification view of God the "Inner Sung Sang and Hyung Sang" of God. The Sung Sang and Hyung Sang that exist in all the physical processes are called in the Unification view the "Outer Sung Sang and Hyung Sang." In the Unification understanding of God there is a dynamic concept of interrelated levels of Sung Sang and Hyung Sang. The Inner Sung Sang and Hyung Sang existed before the outer Sung Sang and Hyung Sang, but they now exist simultaneously with them and they all affect one another. In the general relationship of Sung Sang and Hyung Sang, the Sung Sang and Hyung Sang of the invisible world of God can also be said to be prior to the Sung Sang and Hyung Sang of the physical world in the complementary sense that it is the subjective position by nature of its being eternal. Sung Sang and Hyung Sang entirely of the physical world is transitory. Thus, Sung Sang and Hyung Sang coexist simultaneously and Sung Sang is revealed through Hyung Sang. Therefore, for something to exist in reality, the simultaneous action of Sung Sang and Hyung Sang are required.[29]

In summary, this marriage of cause and effect in such a universal cosmic model as the Unification view allows for a more complete insight about the nature of process in the physical world. It is called in Unification thought "the Law of the Change of Sung Sang and Hyung Sang." There is not a question of dominance in this concept as in the inferior and superior, or the ruler and the ruled, only the concept of process through complementarity. This is the relationship of subject and object, and their give and take action in the motion of harmony, co-equality, co-creation, and co-potentiality. There cannot be dominance in this model because both the Sung Sang and Hyung Sang are relative aspects of one thing centered on purpose. Since the relation of Sung Sang and Hyung Sang, that is, subject and object, is one of mutuality, progress takes place by the give and take, which involves exchange or position—circular motion. Since this continual exchange of position in the relationship is the unity of harmony, and this is the source of development, one cannot conclude that qualitative change comes about through the type of sudden reversal or abrupt change purported by the Marxists. The changes in development are primarily harmonious, gradual, and peaceful in quantity and quality although they produce distinguishable stages of development along the way. They do not inherently harbor contradiction, struggle, negation, suddenness, and destruction. Rather, these attributes are the result of the already existing or created disorder caused by the deviance man has introduced into this life through his conduct.

b. The Forward Tendency of Progress: According to the dialectical materialist, contradiction is inherent in process, and this necessarily initiates movement in certain directions. This movement is viewed as forward movement, in other words, progress. For instance, the child grows from a fertilized egg through the various cleavage stages, the stages of embryonic development, and finally becomes a fully mature newborn child. Also, the dialectic recognizes non-directed movement and random or repetitive movement. Originally, Hegel, a mechanical idealist, stated that movement was not inherent in things, but that spirit or a consciousness operates in the universe giving the natural movements their direction. But, as mentioned before, dialectical materialism went farther and concluded that spirit is simply a product of material, and not an independent one at that. Hence, the dialectical materialists hold that there must be a difference between forward and repetitious movement. For instance, in some developmental pathways, when the essential cause of quantitative change is within the process itself and consistent, movement will obviously be of the progressive or forward kind. But, oppositely, another kind of direction, repetitious movement, is caused when the force initiating the change is only an external one. From the example, the development from embryo to fetus and child would represent an internally directed movement, which is called progress. The unnatural external inducement of birth by drugs, however, illustrates a repetitious movement, with direction being only a repeatable reaction of the womb tissues to the effect of the drugs themselves.

This dichotomy concerning kinds of movement seems plausible, but historically has caused difficulty. It is unable to deal with how forward and directional movement can occur when the essential cause of quantitative change exists within the changing process itself. For instance, it is not entirely accurate to say that the drug-induced birth only follows from the action of the drug itself. Rather, it results from a series of pathways of response within the chemistry of the mother after the initial reaction to the drug. Without the inherent internal pathway, facilitated by the nature of the chemistry of the mother, the drug would have only a small and isolated effect. Further, the natural birth is actually the reaction to a constellation of stimuli, some within, some without, and some inherently built into the organism through thousands of years of environmental and genetic development.

How, then, is this problem more clearly resolved through the more comprehensive Unification view? Simply, it is enlightened by the relation of Sung Sang and Hyung Sang. The cosmic model of Sung Sang and Hyung Sang, the invisible dimension of God and the "spiritual" in direct and simultaneous complement with the physical and finite dimension of man and creation, allows a complete understanding of directional process in the physical world. Admittedly, the concept of Sung Sang and Hyung Sang is not a simple one to grasp, but it is a crucial concept in the Unification view. To simplify the concept for Unification teaching purposes, often the term "life force" or "universal prime force" has been adopted to indicate the resultant directive force from the successive levels of Sung Sang and Hyung Sang which proceed from God Himself. But it must be remembered that this "life force"[31] or "universal prime force"[32] is not an existent entity in itself as is implied by similar uses of the term in other philosophies.[33] In the Unification view it is not a separate entity invoked as a cause. Rather, it is one of the resultant components of the Origin-Division-Union resolution (the Unification view's God-centered alternative to the thesis-antithesis-synthesis of Marxism) in the relations of successive Sung Sang and Hyung Sang from God's initiating point. As stated earlier in the brief discussion of the Four Position

Foundation and the three-stage process of its achievement through Origin, Division, and Union, prime force is the union of the complementary aspects centering on purpose. The concept of resultant "prime force" is related to the Unification view's concept of *Logos*.[34] Thus, the Unification view would not subscribe to the materialist idea that the force of direction in things is inherent in material. Instead, it exists as a part of the relationship of Sung Sang and Hyung Sang. Concerning the example of an embryo, the Unification view would not look to the material of the embryo to find the directive force apparent in its life. The directive force is seen within the cosmic view, including the position of the initiating reality of God. This is why the Unification view is able to speak of "creation" though not exactly with the same meaning that "creationism" has often had—a simplistic idea of some kind of magic performed by an outside omnipotent being. Rather, the Unification view would see "creation" within the model of Sung Sang and Hyung Sang as has been here expressed.

c. The Spiral Concept of History: The Marxist idea of progress in the dialectic also includes the concept of the negation of the negation. It is said that any given thing which during development is doubly negated has attained synthesis and a higher state of existence. Importantly, this synthesis, attained through double negation, also completes a cycle. This is how the oft-seen cycles in nature are explained. For instance, negation of a fetus is a new-born child, this child grows up and produces a fetus, and this is a cycle.

From this view of cycles, the communists recognize stages of society which they claim must be repeated. These predict the coming of the worldwide communist state. Society began with the primitive communal form, and has progressed through slave-holding societies, feudalism and capitalism, which will be followed by socialism. Each of these stages except the first is a repetition of an earlier stage at a higher level. The cycles of history are spiral in nature. They are characterized by repetition of stages at higher levels of comprehensiveness and development. Thus the original primitive communal society is thought to predict the eventual utopian communist state: the class societies that negated the original classless society, will be negated in turn by the coming classless society.

Like the Unification view, communism affirms the reality of the circular movement resulting from the interaction of complementary or dialectical elements and their resolution through the Origin-Division-

Union. But why such movement occurs, or how it is significant in the sense of direction or purpose is not a question that can be approached using communist philosophy. In other words, the materialists cannot clarify why the negation of the negation necessarily takes a circular pattern.

Because of its comprehension of the relation of cause and effect in the cosmic model of Sung Sang and Hyung Sang, the Unification view has a more comprehensive idea of circular movement (called "the Law of Circular Movement"). According to the Unification view all things are created by the law of resemblance; they are created in the polarity of object and subject and resemble the polarity and perpetuity of God. To have perpetuity, all things must circulate through give and take relationships because this is the pattern of sustenance and eternity. Briefly, though the concept is much more complex, God's perpetuity itself is maintained by Himself being centered in circulating polarity upon his own absolute nature called "heart" in Unification theology.[35] Thus, if this is the nature of the Sung Sang of God and the Sung Sang and Hyung Sang relations within this Sung Sang, all corresponding things in the Hyung Sang world of the physical creation (and their Sung Sang and Hyung Sang relations) revolve not only in space but in time. Hence creation illustrates cyclic patterns of generations, periodicity, parallelism, and so on. As the things of creation move through time, they are created to exhibit higher levels of completeness. Such development can be comprehended without any reference to the negation of the negation. Rather this can be understood as from the action of give and take. The shifting and growing is one of progress towards the ideal.

It is because of the problem of sin that man's progress has not fallen within the natural movements inherent to the patterns God created. Instead, man's misuse of his freedom and creativity, his "fallen" nature, have led him to deviate from the actual principle of creation. History has been a long arduous path of restoration through successive stages based upon God's continual sacrifice and love for man. In this history, God has been assisted by the work of those men who, comprehending Him, have aided His own course of historical re-creation of the original ideal for mankind. Hence, the Unification view regards historical cycles as a "Providence of Restoration" restoring the original ideal and possibility lost through man's misuse and misunderstanding of himself and God.

D. Summary of the Critique of Dialectical Materialism and the Argument for the Unification Counterproposal

It is useful, especially since the implications of ideology are most graphically expressed at the levels of personal experience and application, to review the very general results of atheism and religion as they apply to human life. These can be summarized in a number of points which plainly express the differences between dialectical materialism and a comprehensive religious view as it would be lived out by man.

1. Dialectical materialism contends that material is the source of all things. The Unification view looks to God as the ultimate first cause. There is a spiritual and physical complement to existence, an invisible world of God and spiritual reality outside space and time, and a physical creation complementing it as its finite image. Spirit and matter exist in mutual complementary and simultaneous oneness through give and take action.

2. According to communism there is no life after death because spirit cannot exist independently from matter. The Unification view acknowledges life after death. Man's life continues in the spiritual world through eternity, since this is the nature of that dimension. Spiritual and physical life are interconnected by the give and take action of their respective positions of subject and object, but the former remains forever.

3. Dialectical materialism focuses on social classes which struggle in antagonism through successive stages of domination and submission. The Unification view accepts that such conflicts and class antagonisms exist but does not assert that they reflect fundamental life processes. Rather they reflect a state that is "fallen" away from an original ideal that is as yet unfulfilled. The Marxist confuses the "fallen" state (tension and struggle in society) with the real and ideal principle of God in which life is an expression of the oneness of love and the ideal of organic unity. Marxists, who assert in their metaphysics that contradiction is essential to life itself, have never achieved harmony and unity within their party, society, or nation.

4. Communism contends that history requires it to force its ideology upon others, as part of the universal pattern of struggle. Therefore, it does not regard human rights as primary. The Unification view, being a religious view, gives ultimate universal value to the uniqueness of personhood. Progress comes through service and love, not through dominance and force.

5. For the materialist, the ideal for man will be the communist utopian state where man is properly conditioned to his nature. For religion, since the ideal is mutual harmony and unity of diversity, the future of man is very different. The contradiction of sin will be eradicated and man, a liberated spiritual and physical being united with God's spirit, will achieve the completed image of God: the Kingdom of Heaven on earth and in the spiritual world. (Figure 5).

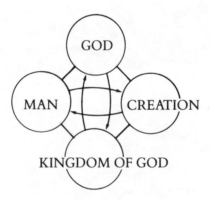

Figure 5

III. THE SUBSTANTIAL COUNTERPROPOSAL TO MARXISM: THE MINISTRY OF WORKS

There is one final aspect of the counterproposal to Marxism. It is the substantial counterproposal in the ministry of service and love. Sun Myung Moon has said:

Go to the most miserable place and volunteer. For whom were you born? For yourself, or for the sake of others? For the world, for God? God actually made us not to serve our own purpose but to serve others...

Why should an eye be made the way it is? An eye is made to perceive for the sake of the body. Your senses are all made to perceive others and to relate to others

The definition of a "saint" is very simple from this point of view. A saint is the one who sees not for himself but for the sake of the world, for the sake of God. His point of reference is not himself and he finds no joy in selfish living.

History has seen many great religions and great teachings, but all those doctrines put together point to one simple truth.

If our members must sacrifice themselves to save the people then the first one to suffer is me. People of the world are dying and desperately suffering. If they are your brothers and sisters, then you have to reach them and cry out for them.

At one time America was trying to serve the world. America is in a position to lead. If America's 220 million people were united together to give themselves for the sake of the world, how great America would be. Americans need to do just that.

You and I are here to tackle the major headaches of God. The will of God is the liberation of the world. We are gathered to participate in the historic mission in which Jesus and God will take delight. We certainly have the answer to communism.[36]

The substantial answer to communism is the substantial living out of religion or religious ideology in the ministry of works. In the Unification ideology, words and action form a polarity. One is in the position of Sung Sang, the other Hyung Sang. One has to do with the "Foundation of Faith" in God, the other with the "Foundation of Substance," the substantiation of these words and faith in life and action. Neither has any meaning without being bound together and united through give and take action centered on purpose. Thus, the Hyung Sang, or substantiation of the counterproposal to Marxism is the substantial ministry of serving works.

It is the task of religion to initiate a return of its devotees to this path of service, but not simply one with small goals. The movement must be massive, a complete challenge to those who believe to live their faith in a way that will lead to the real physical salvation of the world. God has had infinite capacity to sustain His sacrifice for others. In like manner, when God chose Jacob to lead a path of restoration and reconciliation to his brother Esau, Jacob left his usual ways, and under the persecution of scorn and accusation labored many years in Haran. Then, after he had amassed wealth of which others might be envious, he gave it all away. Christianity, and the richly blessed economic powers of the world are in this role of Jacob. The time has come for this kind of revolution within Christianity. Networks of groups and organizations must be formed to mobilize the churches to actual service. This has been the historical task left unfinished by religion. This has been the point of accusation and victory for the Marxist materialists.

Communism has succeeded where it has put its ideology into practice. It has not and cannot succeed ultimately because of its ideological weaknesses, but it has tried to impress the world with its willingness to work and sacrifice for its concrete goals. Christianity, though marked for its saints and its outbursts of sacrificial ideal, has had neither a universal ideology nor a unified and organized channel through which to serve. It has not been able to meet the requirements of its faith.

When Mao Tse-tung sent his troops into the villages of China, he said:

> They (meaning the Nationalists) only come to collect the taxes. Go meet the village leader. Give the people your food, teach the people how to read.[37]

Mao's actions convinced the people that he was a man to follow, and he had nothing to offer them but the weaknesses of atheism, and a philosophy that has resulted in an untimely death for millions of Chinese.

IV. CONCLUSION

Jesus spoke of the realization of brotherhood when he said, "By this all men will know that you are my disciples, if you love one another" (John 13:35, RSV). It has been this absence of true love for one another which has led theologians like Karl Heim to indict this lack as the cause of the rise of secularism.[38] The appearance of secular and atheistic dominions of power has become commonplace in our contemporary world. These realities have largely replaced any substantial hope in the coming on earth of "the Kingdom." Dietrich Bonhoeffer, the Lutheran theologian who returned to Germany to resist and be executed by Adolf Hitler, asserted that history involved the relationship of struggle between a community of meaning (Faith), and a community of purpose (Substance). He bemoaned the fact that man's communities have never achieved an ideal of the latter.[39] Truly, this ideal has never been achieved by Christian *or* communist. Relativism has plagued the Christian community; it has too often settled for standards far below those taught by Jesus, standards thought of as too abstract or too idealistic to be achieved. Yet, Niebuhr asserts that

Christianity must offer tangible, reachable goals[40] and Moltmann says that Christianity is called to save the world, not to leave it.[41] Berdyaev states that true Christianity must be coupled with a tangible idea of history and progress.[42] Tillich insists that the Church should be at its highest standard at any given moment.[43] Nothing less than the actualization of the standard of Christ is central in the thinking of Christianity. However, the relative standards which vary from church to church throughout the hundreds of denominations in the Body of Christ have left it with a lack of effective ability to stand and carry out the role of Christianity: the realistic establishment of God's Kingdom on earth.

On the communist side we can readily observe an effective program for the actualization of social power. Similar power, from unity of purpose and solid vision and direction is not evident in Christianity. It stands as ineffective against a strong Marxist program, putting its theoretical ideology into organized practice throughout the world, standing as a potential pseudo-Kingdom of God on earth. The communist *Logos*, the actualization of the atheistic state stands clearly in opposition to the fundamental concepts of the Christian counterproposal. It stands on the difference between contradiction and harmony. It is here that it can be successfully attacked by Christianity. Christianity can take the dialectics of Marx and make them into a strong expression of God and Creation. In doing so, it can create a religious world view compatible with science and form the base for the religious holistic fulfillment of man. The dialectics of Marx have opened a powerful base of truth, only to be twisted by the exclusion of God. It must be obvious to Christianity that this challenge is the central one. Religiously evaluated, the elements of dialectics are elements for understanding God, His Image, and His Creation. They are also the base for religious unity with science and technology. The emergence of Christianity as an ideology effective as the God-centered counterproposal to Marxism in word and in action can lead to the fulfillment of religion's historical responsibility on earth. This is the goal toward which all history and God's own work has been leading—the establishment of the Kingdom of Heaven on earth as well as in the spiritual world.

NOTES

1. "Divine Principle" is the name for both the general view of the Unification Church movement and the title of a book including explanations of some of those concepts. These usages should not be confused. The book *Divine Principle* is cited in the bibliography.

2. Useful commentaries include (with the book titles cited in the bibliography):

Theology: *Unification Theology and Christian Thought*, by Young Oon Kim; *Divine Principle and Its Application*, by Young Oon Kim; "The Unification View of God," by Sang Hun Lee in *God in Contemporary Thought*, Sebastian Matczak, ed.; "A Dialectical Concept of the Trinity and Its Implications," by Peter M. Borgo, in *Journal of the Society for Common Insights* (hereafter J. Soc. Com. Ins.) 1 (1): 73–103; "Christianity as a Constructive Revolutionary Ideology, the Scientific and Social Aspects," by Kurt Johnson in the *Proceedings of the First National Conference on the Church and Social Problems* (hereafter Proc. Nat. Conf. Church Soc. Prob.), Vol. 2, 69–90; "Restored Christianity as a Counterproposal to Expanding Marxism," by David S.C. Kim, in Proc. Nat. Conf. Church Soc. Prob., Vol. 2, 91–111; "The Implications of Foundations Concepts on Theology and Ideology," by Kurt Johnson, in the *Proceedings of the International Symposium on Foundations Research and New World Models* (hereafter Proc. Int. Symp. Found. Res. New World Models) (in press); "The Character of Unification Theology as a Modern Christian Statement," by Thomas Boslooper, available from Interfaith Affairs Committee, Unification Church; "A Look at Unification Theology," by Herbert Richardson, available from Interfaith Affairs Committee, Unification Church.

Philosophy: *Unification Thought*, by the Unification Thought Institute; "The Unification View of God," by Sang Hun Lee, *loc. cit.*; "Founder's Address," by Sun Myung Moon, in *Proceedings of the Fourth International Conference on the Unity of the Sciences*, I:9.

Science: "Founder's Address" by Sun Myung Moon, *loc. cit.*; "The Evolution/Creation Problem vis-a-vis the Ontological Nature of Paired Relationships," by Daniel A. Yatkola, in *J. Soc. Com. Ins.* 1 (1): 33–71; "The Need for a Theology Based on the Nature of Relationships if Science is to Comment on Moral Values," by M. Craig Johnson, in *J. Soc. Com. Ins.* 1 (1): 17–31; "Christianity as a Constructive Revolutionary Ideology, the Scientific and Social Aspects," by Kurt Johnson, *loc, cit.*; "The Four-Position Paradigm in Biodynamics," by Kurt Johnson and M. Craig Johnson, in *Proc. Int. Symp. Found. Res. New World Models*, (in press); "A New Structure for the Concept of Life and Culture in Medicine," by M. Craig Johnson, in *Proc. Int. Symp. Found. Res. New World Models* (in press); "The Hyperbolic Spiral Model," by Brian S.C. Corcoran, in *Proc. Int. Symp. Found. Res. New World Models* (in press); "The Hyperbolic Spiral Model: Commentary," by Olaf Alexanderson and Klas Lundberg, in *Proc. Int. Symp. Found. Res. New World Models*, (in press).

Counterproposal to Marxism: *Communism, A Critique and Counterproposal*, by Sang Hun Lee; *Victory Over Communism, the Role of Religion*, by David S.C. Kim; "Restored Christianity as a Counterproposal to Expanding Marxism," by David S.C. Kim, *loc. cit.*; "The Implications of Foundations Research on a Counterproposal to Dialectical Materialism" by David S.C. Kim, *Proc. Int. Symp. Found. Res. New World Models*, (in press).

3. The Unification Thought Institute has had translated into English several papers concerning the potential relation of the ideology to man. These

include: The role of Unification Thought in establishing a unified world (*Unified World* 2: 53–64), Progressive movement and growth of man (*Unified World* 3: 53–60), and a philosophy of history, past and current (*Unified World* 4: 53–64). The New World Forum has presented an analysis of the theory of value in Unification thought (A systematic theory of value, *Unified World* 9: 37–49), and an analysis of interdependence in societal structures (Tyman, Kathleen; A philosophy of interdependence, *Unified World* 7: 47–52), Jacob van Rossum (*Unified World* 5: 53–60; 6: 59–68) has commented on the ideological counterproposal in relation to the policy of east-west detente.

4. Alvin M. Johnson, in a paper (*J. Soc. Com. Ins.* 1 (1):3–16) has examined some of the problems of actually dealing with a concept of a possible religiously oriented social solution on a global level. Although some of his views differ from the Unification view, many of the observations are applicable.

5. Young Oon Kim has used the term "polarity."

6. Sang Hun Lee has preferred the terms "relative aspects."

7. Western commentaries have used the more scientific concept "complementarity." *Divine Principle* often uses the term "duality" but this has often been misunderstood as classical dualism.

8. The "Institute for Victory over Communism" has been established to pursue this ideological development.

   Obviously, the breadth of a counterproposal to Marxism must include a historical perspective on the development of the Marxist context. It must develop comprehensive counterproposals to Marxist ontology. A further analysis would be needed for at least these aspects of dialectical materialism: the Labor Theory of Value, the Theory of Surplus Value, the Laws of Economic Movement, the development of Mechanistic Materialism, the history of Feuerbach's materialism, the view of matter and spirit, the view of motility and historicity, the view of man, the interpretation of the dialectical nature of matter, the Theory of Qualitative Change, the Theory of Progress, the sociological application of the dialectic (especially of Stalin), and so on. Further, the philosophical base must be critiqued along with the applied base: social development, production relations, problems of assumption in application, revolution, family, psychology, psychiatry, and so on. Further, there must be a critical realization of the lack of any major comprehension of these concepts or their possible counterproposal in modern religion.

9. Though a complex issue, the history of this fatalistic attitude toward Christianity's role on earth and potential fulfillment appears in Christian classics like St. Augustine's *City of God*, where he writes (Book XIX, Chapter 15) concerning the position of slave and worker in society. As late as 1931, the papacy (Pope Pius X, *Quadragesimo anno*, encyclical) repeats the same neglect of the position of the working class.

10. Heimann, in *Reason and Faith in Modern Society*, indicts Christianity directly as the wedge between worker and employers. Marxism on the other hand is credited with the characteristics of self-rule, collectivism, autonomy of human rights, rationalism, and self-realization. Berdyaev, in *The Origin of Russian Communism*, explains in detail the militance of communism in its anti-Christian propaganda.

11. Berdyaev, *loc. cit.*

12. *Ibid.*, p. 159.

13. In Marx and Engels, *Selected Works*, vol. 2, p. 363.

14. In Berdyaev, *loc. cit.*, p. 161.

15. Documentation of this kind is overwhelming, especially in the literature following the historical progress of communism in Tibet, North Korea, Vietnam, Cambodia, Laos, the Soviet Union (especially in relation to Judaism) and China. Kim Il Sung, dictator of North Korea has boasted: "Today there are no churches in North Korea." (in *Juche*, 1972). Numerous commentaries can be found in the popular literature (e.g., publication of R. Wurmbrand's *Jesus to the Communist World*) and in the scholarly literature (e.g., E. Snow, *Red China Today; Stalin Must Have Peace*). The oppression of religion has not been evident, however, in the activities of South American and Western European communists, though no communist government has long remained in power in these areas.

16. Richard T. Ely's *Social Aspects of Christianity*, and Matthew Arnold's *The Social Law of Service* are classic compilations of this period.

17. See, for instance Gutierrez and Geffe, *Liberation, Theology and Proclamation*. Also Bonino, *Doing Theology in a Revolutionary Situation*.

18. Gutierrez and Geffe, *loc. cit.*, p. 61.

19. See Boyd, *The Underground Church*, and Gray, *Divine Disobedience*.

20. Two leaders of the Black theological movement represent the poles of Christian searching for the Godly equity, yet the entrenchment of the Church in the values of forgiveness, love, and reconciliation. In *Black Theology and Black Power* (1969) James H. Cone decried the enslavement of the black man to this day by the white population. He especially indicts the white Christian. He calls the Church to repent for establishing itself as a racist institution, to change its attitude toward the essence of Christ's teachings (brotherly love) and to identify and act to overcome the oppression of the black race (p. 81). J. Deotis Roberts, in *Liberation and Reconciliation: A Black Theology* (1969) calls blacks and white together for the Christian act of reconciliation as a further step toward the Christlike life. Liberation of the black race can only occur through its acceptance as co-equal with the white race. Part of this liberation is looking at the Messiah through the eyes of black people from the context of the black religious experience. Simply

stated, "the *black Messiah* liberates the black man. The universal Christ *reconciles* the black man with the rest of mankind" (p. 140).

21. Although the view of Hegel differs markedly from that of Aristotle, it nevertheless reflects a difficulty in most western ontological views, a difficulty that goes back at least to Aristotle. In his *Metaphysics* Aristotle states that contraries are not affected by one another (Book XII 1075 A 30). Since presumably matter and spirit, or the material cause and the formal cause, are contraries, then neither can give rise to the other.

22. For example, Engels says (p. 66) that after one cuts a magnet or an earthworm in half, the same opposition or contradiction is maintained. One must consider if this is accurate. On the contrary, do not the positive and negative poles in a magnet exist for unity, not repulsion or exclusivity? Certainly in an earthworm, the mouth and anus cooperate in maintaining life: taking in nutrition and excreting metabolic waste. Engels says (p. 78) that analysis and synthesis in chemistry have the same relationship of opposition. Implying this, chemistry cannot exist without a contradiction. But, analysis and synthesis are as easily understood as relative methods used together to acquire scientific knowledge. Why invoke the repelling or negative relation rather than the coordinated and affirmative one?

23. Professor S. Bloch, of the London School of Economics, has analyzed these recent developments in detail (*Psychiatric Terror*).

24. Sir Karl Popper, in *Open Society*, has openly critiqued the political development of Marxist regimes; Conrad Zircle, in *Evolution, Marxian Biology and the Social Scene*, has analyzed the problems of the dialectic in the development of Marxist science; Alexander Solzhenitsyn (*Cancer Ward, The First Circle, Gulag Archipelago*) has provided first hand accounts of the repression of Marxist social application in the repression of political dissidents.

25. The reader is referred to any of the substantive literature on the development of the materialist's break with idealism, and the later division between mechanical and dialectical materialism. For analyses closest to the communists' own experience, see the "Philosophical Notebooks," "Materialism and Empirical Criticism," in N. Lenin, *Selected Works*.

26. Engels, *loc. cit.*, p. 412.

27. Tillich, *loc. cit.*, pp. 284–285.

28. *Ibid.*, p. 288. Unification theology makes clear that this relationship illustrated by Jesus was originally, and will be, the relation of all men to God (as Jesus himself indicated in John 10:31f.).

29. Actually, the levels of Sung Sang and Hyung Sang are much more complex than is apparent from their presentation here. Man stands between God and the physical world and has a four-part nature: a spiritual mind and spiritual body and a physical mind and physical body. Man's spiritual nature is to his physical nature as God's nature is to the nature of the created world. A fuller

explanation of this concept is given in *Unification Thought* (cited in the bibliography). It is not known whether an evaluation of the Unification *Divine Principle* released by the Faith and Order Commission of the National Council of Churches in 1977, and used widely in the media to discredit the movement, was a deliberate distortion or not. However, the lack of comprehension of this basic paradigm rendered much of their analysis inaccurate.

30. It must be pointed out, in order not to oversimplify this view, that the relation of Inner Sung Sang and Hyung Sang, and Outer Sung Sang and Hyung Sang relates to the Unification view's idea of *Logos*. Dr. Sang Hun Lee has detailed the relationship of this concept to the Four Position Foundation in his "Unification View of God," *loc. cit.*

31. Sang Hun Lee has preferred the term "life force."

32. The *Study Guide* to Divine Principle published by the Unification Church in America has preferred the term "universal prime force."

33. "Prime force" has been used in vitalism (see esp. the works of Cuvier in the philosophy of science) as an outside force invoked to explain energy and dynamism in nature. The similarity of the usage is unfortunate, since the use in the Unification ideology does not imply this meaning.

34. See Sang Hun Lee, "The Unification View of God," *loc. cit.*

35. See *Ibid.*

36. Taken from the speeches of Rev. Sun Myung Moon to members of the Unification Church movement, 1976–1978.

37. Dunayevskaya, "Mao's China and the 'Proletarian Cultural Revolution' " in *Marxism and Freedom*, appendix.

38. See Heim, "Christian faith and the growing power of secularism," in *Religion and Culture*, edited by A. Leibrecht.

39. Bonhoeffer, *Sanctorum Communio*.

40. Niebuhr, *Human Nature and Destiny*, p. vii.

41. Moltmann, *Religion, Revolution and the Future*, p. 139.

42. Berdyaev, *The Meaning of History*, pp. 161ff.

43. Tillich, *Political Expectation*, p. 172.

BIBLIOGRAPHY

Arnold, M. *The Social Law of Service*. Oxford: Oxford Univ. Press, 1898.

Augustine, (Saint) Bishop of Hippo. 1963. *The City of God*. Washington, D.C.: Catholic Univ. Press, 1963.

Berdyaev, N. *The Origin of Russian Communism*. Cleveland: Meridian Books, 1961.

————. *The Meaning of History. Cleveland: Meridan Books, 1962.*

Bible. *The Holy Bible*. Revised Standard Version. NY: American Bible Society.

Bloch, S. *Psychiatric Terror*. London: Basic Books, 1977.

Bonhoeffer, D. *Sanctorum Communio*. London: Collins, 1963.

Bonino, M. *Doing Theology in a Revolutionary Situation*. Philadelphia: Fortress Press, 1975.

Boyd, M. *The Underground Church*. NY: Sheed and Ward, 1969.

Cone, J.H. *Black Theology and Black Power*. NY: Seabury Press, 1969.

Dunayevskaya, R. *Marxism and Freedom*. Detroit: News and Letters Committees, The Materialistic Friends of the Hegelian Dialectic, 1957.

Ely, R. *The Social Aspects of Christianity*. NY: T.Y. Crowell, 1889

Engels, F. *Dialectics of Nature*. NY: International Publishers, 1946.

————. *Socialism: Utopian and Scientific*. in Marx, K. and F. Engels, *Selected Works*. Moscow: International Publishers, 1968.

————. *Frederick Engels on Capitalism*. 2nd Edition. NY: International Publishers, 1960.

Feuerbach, L.A. *1804–1972: The Fiery Brook-Selected Writings of Ludwig Feuerbach* Garden City, NJ: Anchor Books, 1972.

————. Opposition of the materialist and idealist outlooks. I. in *The German Philosophers*. London: Lawrence and Wishart, 1973.

Gray. *For Divine Disobedience*. NY: Alfred A. Knopf, 1969.

Gutierrez, G. and Gaffe, C. *Liberation, Theology and Proclamation*. NY: Herder and Herder, 1974.

Hegel, G.W.F. 1892. *Logic*. Oxford: The University Press, 1892.

————. *Hegel's Philosophy of Nature*. Oxford: A.V. Miller, 1896.

Heimann, E. *Reason and Faith in Modern Society*. NY: International Publishers, 1961.

Holy Spirit Association for the Unification of World Christianity. *Divine Principle*. NY: Holy Spirit Association for the Unification of World Christianity, 1974.

————. *Study Guide for the Divine Principle*. NY: Holy Spirit Association for the Unification of World Christianity, 1974.

International Cultural Foundation. *Proceedings of the Fourth International Conference on the Unity of the Sciences. 2 volumes. NY: International Cultural Foundation, 1975.

Kim, D.S.C. *Victory Over Communism, the Role of Religion*. NY: Vantage Press, 1971.

Kim, Y.O. *Divine Principle and Its Application*. NY: Holy Spirit Association for the Unification of World Christianity, 1960.

———. *Unification Theology and Christian Thought*. NY: Golden Gate Publ. Co., 1975.

Kirk, D., ed. *Quotations from Chairman Jesus*. NY: Bantam Books, 1969.

Lee, S.H. *Unification Thought*. NY: Unification Thought Institute, 1973.

———. *Communism: A Critique and Counterproposal*. Washington, D.C.: Freedom Leadership Foundation, 1973.

———. "The Unification View of God." in *God in Contemporary Thought*, edited by S. Matczak. NY: Learned Press, 1977.

Leibrecht, A., ed. *Religion and Culture*. Freeport, NY: Books for the Library Press, 1959.

Lenin, N. *Selected Works*. Moscow: International Publishers, 1966.

Marx, K. *The Essential Marx*. NY: Herder and Herder, 1966.

Marx, K. and F. Engels. *Selected Works*. Moscow: Progress Publishers, 1966.

Matczak, S., ed. *God in Contemporary Thought*. NY: Learned Press, 1977.

Moon, S.M. "Founder's Address." *Proceedings of the Fourth International Conference on the Unity of Science*, Vol. 1. NY: International Cultural Foundation, 1975.

———. "Reverend Sun Myung Moon Speaks On . . . " (collection of speeches of the Rev. S.M. Moon, 1976-1978). NY: Holy Spirit Association for the Unification of World Christianity, 1976–1978.

Moltmann, J. *Religion, Revolution, and the Future*. NY: Charles Scribners Sons, 1969.

National Council of Churches. *Report of the Faith and Order Commission* (concerning the Divine Principle of the Unification Church). NY: National Council of Churches, 1977.

New World Forum. Unified World, Volumes 1–9. NY: New World Forum, 1972–1978.

Niebuhr, R. *Human Nature and Destiny*. NY: Charles Scribners Sons, 1964.

Popper, K. *Open Society*. Princeton, NJ: Princeton University Press, 1966.

Roberts, J.D. *Liberation and Reconciliation: A Black Theology*. Philadelphia: Westminister Press, 1969.

Snow, E. *Red China Today (The Other Side of the River)* NY: Random House, 1961.

Society for Common Insights. *Proceedings of the First National Conference on the Church and Social Problems.* 2 volumes. NY: Society for Common Insights, 1977.

————. *Proceedings of the International Symposium on Foundations Research and New World Models.* 2 volumes. NY: Society for Common Insights, 1978.

————. *Journal of the Society for Common Insights.* Volumes 1–3. NY: Society for Common Insights, 1976–1978.

Solzhenitzyn, A. *The First Circle.* NY: Harper & Row, 1968.

————. *Cancer Ward.* NY: Dial Press, 1968.

————. *Gulag Archipelago.* (Arkhipelag Gulag, 1918–1956) Paris: YMCA Press, 1973.

Stalin, J. "Dialectical Materialism and Historical Materialism," in *The Selected Works.* Davis, Calif.: Cardinal, 1971.

————. "Marxism in Philosophy," in *The Selected Works.* Davis, Calif.: Cardinal, 1971.

Sung, K.I. *Juche! The speeches and writings of Kim Il Sung.* NY: Grossman, 1972.

Tillich, P. *Systematic Theology.* Chicago: Univ. of Chicago Press, 1966.

————. *Political Expectation.* NY: Harper & Row, 1971.

Zirkle, C. *Evolution, Marxian Biology and the Social Scene.* Philadelphia: Univ. of Pennsylvania Press, 1959.

Thomas Boslooper

Unificationism and Biblical Studies

The question of Unificationism and Biblical Studies should be prefaced by a brief consideration of the question of the relationship of Unificationism to the Bible and to *Divine Principle*. This may be described in several ways.

The Reverend Sun Myung Moon personally has told members of the faculty of the Unification Theological Seminary that the Divine Principle is a revelation that came to him from God as a result of his own personal intense study of the Bible over a period of nine years. Since *Divine Principle* spans not only the period of biblical history but also the history of western culture up to modern times, *Divine Principle* may be looked upon as Rev. Moon's interpretation of the Bible and subsequent history in the light of God's revelation to him.

At the same time it is known from the many leaders of the Unification Church that Rev. Moon did not write the black book entitled *Divine Principle*. The black book, the 1974 edition of *Divine Principle*, is the seventh or eighth attempt on the part of various of Rev. Moon's followers to put his revelation into written form. It is also apparent that some of the sections of *Divine Principle,* such as the ones covering the history of the Papacy and the Reformation, were not revelations from God to Rev. Moon put into writing but were applications of Rev. Moon's basic ideas to these periods of history with which the follower of Rev. Moon who wrote these sections was acquainted. The material was not within the span of Rev. Moon's personal knowledge.

What has also become apparent is that *Divine Principle* in whatever version it may appear is viewed in various ways by even the closest followers of the Rev. Moon. This writer has heard Colonel Bo Hi Pak, one of Rev. Moon's closest assistants, speak of *Divine Principle* as the "Third Testament." There is the Old Testament, the New Testament, and the Third Testament. As the New fulfills the Old, so the Third fulfills both the Old and the New. This writer has also heard Dr. Young Oon Kim, the chief theologian for the Movement, the first missionary to the U.S.A. for Unificationism, the Professor of Theology at the Unification Theological Seminary, and the author of several books on Unification theology, speak of *Divine Principle* as being in a relationship to the Bible on a level similar to that of John Calvin's *Institutes of the Christian Religion*.

At the dedication of the Unification Theological Seminary in September of 1975, Mr. David S.C. Kim, President of the Seminary, cut a ribbon surrounding a large Bible, read from the opening words of the first chapter of Genesis and from the closing words of Revelation and proclaimed that the Bible and Jesus Christ were central to Unificationism and to the vision of the Seminary.

There is no denying the importance of the Hebrew-Christian scriptures to Unificationism. There is also no denying the importance the written *Divine Principle* holds for Unificationists in their religious experience. One of them, in answering queries concerning a hypothetical 'Guyana,' stated unequivocally, "In such a situation we would desert Rev. Moon and follow The Principle."

My observations concerning Unificationism and Biblical Studies are based upon my own reading of *Divine Principle* and a number of manuals that purport to expand upon it, discussions with prominent leaders of the Unification Movement, and my involvement with more than 400 students at the Unification Theological Seminary over a period of seven years. Each of these students has taken at least one course with me: Introduction to Biblical Studies or Introduction to the New Testament. More than half of them have taken two or three additional elective courses in either New Testament or Old Testament: The Writings, the Life and Teaching of Jesus, The Life and Letters of Paul, The Primitive Church (Acts and Hebrews), the Johannine Literature, and Romans. All of them have studied the Bible with me from the historical-critical point of view as well as from my own Christian-Protestant-Calvinistic perspective.

Striking to me has been how Unificationism stands in relationship to the history of hermeneutics; the contemporaneity of Unificationism, the

Unificationists' view of Scripture; Unificationism's understanding of Jesus and his mission; and Unificationism's eschatological perspective.

Unificationism is a biblically oriented new religion. It may be looked at from the standpoint of how it assumes a posture within the discipline of Biblical Studies. Even though during the entire life of the Church since its inception in Korea in 1954 the Movement has not gotten into its membership a single biblical scholar, at the time of this writing two of the graduates of the Unification Seminary are enrolled as doctoral candidates at Harvard majoring in Biblical Studies. Another is engaged in similar studies at Yale.

All of these factors make what can be said about Unificationism and Biblical Studies complex as well as difficult. What can be said results not from what is apparent but rather from an underlying potential. What can be said results not from taking *Divine Principle* and Unificationism at their worst, as a document and theology and religious system noted for appalling naivete, historical errors, and statements that defy explanation, but from taking them at their best, as the summary of and statement of a new theology which makes a bold attempt to give meaning to the Bible, history, and the universe.

I believe that when and if the Unification Movement produces biblical scholars they will help develop Unification theology and relate it to modern religious concerns along the lines suggested in what follows.

I. ITS PLACE IN THE HISTORY OF HERMENEUTICS

Unificationism thought of in relationship to Biblical Studies must be viewed with reference to its place in the history of interpretation of the Bible. It must be understood against the backdrop of what may be called the historical conflict between supernaturalistic and naturalistic interpretations of the Bible. Unificationism has the potential for bringing about a synthesis between the two.

Up to the time of the Protestant Reformation all interpretation of the Bible was "supernaturalistic." The Bible in its origin and development as well as in its nature and essence was considered to be the work of God. Scripture therefore was to be interpreted literally, although ironically it was during this period that spiritualizing and allegorizing flourished.

Beginning with Sebastian Franck, a contemporary of Martin Luther, this view of Scripture was criticized. With the publication in 1539 of his *Das mit sieben Siegeln verbutschierte Buch* he challenged the literal interpretation of scripture because of what he described as discrepancies and contradictions.

The critique continued. Early in the seventeenth century, the "natural science period of the Renaissance," Francis Bacon's *Advancement of Learning* (1605) and *Novum Organum* (1620), René Descartes' *Discourse on the Method of Rightly Conducting the Reason and Seeking the Truth in the Sciences* (1637), and Thomas Hobbes' *Leviathan* (1651) decisively, although unintentionally, deepened the roots of resistance to biblical authority. The methods were intended to be applied only to philosophy, but the successors to Bacon, Descartes, and Hobbes applied their scientific methodology to all religious questions as well.

Bacon was able to accept the view of the orthodox Anglican Church and maintain at the same time his scientific methodology, since he held the realm of revelation on which faith was based to be outside the concern of philosophy. Descartes' revolt against tradition was in philosophy. His principle, "Cognito ergo sum," the consequence of which was the establishment of reason as the focal point of authority, was intended by him to be applied chiefly to matters pertaining to philosophical inquiry.

Thomas Hobbes' *Leviathan* showed that for him, as well as for Descartes, religion was outside the realm of philosophy and should be understood on the basis of theology and accepted on the authority of the state. Hobbes accepted miracles as a form of God's direct revelation. He did make an important distinction, however. He did distinguish between miracles in the biblical record and miracles in the lives of the saints and traditions of the Church, and he insisted that the private man is always at liberty to believe or not to believe those acts which are described as miracles. For Hobbes, nevertheless, "when it comes to confession of that faith, the Private Reason must submit to the Publique."

It was not long, however, before Scripture itself came under attack from philosophical circles. Whereas Bacon, Descartes, and Hobbes placed revelation and miracle in a special precinct to which the principles of their philosophy were not directly applicable, David Hume (1711-1776) and others such as John Toland, Thomas Chubb, and Voltaire turned the full force of naturalistic philosophy upon religion. Instead of conceiving philosophy and religion to exist in separate spheres, according to Hume's notion, religion as such and not just the abuses of religion must be subject to the scrutiny of reason.

No longer would words like those of the philosopher John Locke (1632-1704) be heard in philosophical circles: (speaking of the Scriptures)

"Therein are contained the words of eternal life. It has God for its author, salvation for its end, and truth without any mixture of error for its matter."

Hume set the world of nature over against the world of religion. A miracle had come for him to be "a transgression of a law of nature by a particular volition of the Deity, or by the interposition of some invisible agent." Philosophically, he could not deny that no event could take place in violation of these laws, but he was convinced that experience demonstrates that man can depend much more upon the uniformity of natural events than upon the accuracy of human testimony. Hume's understanding of the nature of the universe was patterned after the monistic philosophies of Spinoza (1632-1677) and Leibniz (1646-1716). His theory on the nature of the universe and its relation to God excludes the concept of a particular providence and its counterpart miracles. In Hume, philosophy and religion no longer were to reign supreme in separate spheres. Now religion was to be held accountable to philosophy.

The most influential mark in applying naturalistic philosophy in an analysis of the biblical record was made by Herman Samuel Reimarus (1694-1768) and Gotthold Ephraim Lessing (1729-1781). Lessing was the philosopher who brought before the world the philosophical criticism of Scripture developed by Reimarus. For Reimarus miracles belong to the unessential elements of faith. Although for him the miracles of the New Testament were neither as outrageous nor as disgusting as the miracles of the Old Testament, in both Testaments the miraculous is a sign of lack of authenticity. For him miraculous meant unhistorical.

As the primacy of reason became even more firmly established by Kant (1724-1804) and Hegel (1770-1831) there was an accompanying shift of emphasis. For Kant and Hegel the crux of interpretation of a biblical passage became the moral significance and the religious meaning of the narrative rather than the determination of its historical or scientific value. They focused attention on the meaning of the narratives and refused to judge a biblical idea solely on the basis of its scientific credibility.

With Kant's emphasis on the "seat of religion in the moral consciousness" and Hegel's concept of the "double meaning" of a narrative the way was paved for Johann Gottfried Herder (1744-1803) and Johann Jacob Hess (1741-1829) who encouraged readers to pay little attention to the outward details of biblical stories and to seek instead the truth of their "inner realities." For them the meaning of a miracle should be sought in its ethical teaching.

Like Kant and Hegel, Schleiermacher (1768-1834) had developed a strong distaste for both the naturalistic rationalism and the supernatural- ism of his day. The error of both parties with which he was so dissatisfied was their common notion that Christian faith consists of a number of doctrines that stand in contradiction to rational thought and in need of defense by orthodox theologians. The Christian faith, Schleiermacher claimed, does not consist primarily in any number of doctrinal proposi- tions that can be made either by philosophers or theologians, but in a condition of devout feeling, in a fact of inward experience based on personal self-consciousness.

In his *Life of Jesus* (lectures in 1832, published in 1864) Schleiermacher looked for meaning in stories that involved the miraculous by trying to analyze the author's poetic imagination. For him an estimation of Jesus' nature does not depend on the historical credibility of the narratives which describe him but on his nature and superior self-consciousness of God. Similarly Ritschl in *The Christian Doctrine of Justification and Reconcil- iation* (1870-1874) emphasized Jesus' moral superiority.

The publication of David Strauss' *Das Leben Jesu* in 1835 inaugurated another major development in the question of the consideration of the historical nature of biblical tradition. Being convinced of the numerous difficulties and inconsistencies that either supernaturalistic allegorism or rationalistic euphemerism produced, Strauss turned to another method which heretofore had been applied only to the Old Testament.

Johann Eichhorn (1754-1827) in his studies during the last decade of the 18th century and during the first quarter of the 19th century ap- proached the Old Testament with the presupposition that much of the material in it was mythic in nature.

Whereas George Lorenz Bauer (1755-1806) had proposed in 1802 that single myths could be discovered in the New Testament such as in the birth stories, even though "eine Total mythische Geschichte" is not to be sought in the New Testament, Strauss set about to apply the mythical principle to the entire New Testament. He brought his analytical powers to bear most forcibly on the record in the Gospels. For him the applica- tion of the mythical principle would provide the synthesis for the thesis and anti-thesis created by supernaturalistic literal interpretation and nat- uralistic rationalistic interpretation.

In the introduction to the third edition of his *Life of Jesus* (1838) his own theory of myth and how it should be applied to the life of Jesus is clearly stated: myth, when it is applied to the Gospel narratives, is "evangelical mythus," a narrative that relates directly or indirectly to Jesus. An "evangelical mythus" is not to be considered as the expression of a fact. It is to be thought of as an idea of Jesus' earliest followers. The "evangelical mythus" was classified by Strauss into two main categories: what Strauss called "pure mythus" which constitutes the substance of the narrative and "historical mythus" which is an accidental adjunct to the actual history. The former has two different sources out of which the mythus arises: one, the Messianic ideas and expectation that existed in several forms in the Jewish mind before the time of Jesus and independently of him; two, in the particular impression that was left by Jesus' character, action, and fate, as it served to modify the Messianic idea in the minds of Jesus' contemporaries.

Strauss also used the term "legendary" to describe those parts of the evangelical history which are characterized by indefiniteness, lack of connection, misconstruction, strange combinations, and confusion, which for him were the natural results of the long course of oral transmission, and by highly colored and pictorial representations.

These three categories—historical mythus, evangelical mythus, and legend—designated for Strauss the boundaries of the unhistorical element in the Gospels. He insisted, however, that these classifications do not involve the renunciation of the "historical" which these narratives themselves may contain. He did, however, insist that myth is not history, but fiction.

The element of myth in a narrative for Strauss could be determined when aspects of the narrative are irreconcilable with the known universal laws that govern the course of events and when an account reveals inconsistencies within itself and points of contradiction appear when considered in relationship with other parallel accounts.

Strauss conceded that the most difficult question in historical criticism is the determination of the boundary line between the historical and the unhistorical when two accounts of the same event contradict, and he believed that the boundary line between the historical and the unhistorical in such accounts will forever be unsusceptible to accurate delineation.

Bruno Bauer (1809-1882) picked up where Strauss left off. Writing in 1877 in *Christus und die Casaren* he attempted to elucidate and refine Strauss' concept of myth. He felt that Strauss' concept of myth was too vague to explain adequately the transformation of the personality of Jesus. The "experience" of the church, he suggested, is the real cause of the portrait in the Gospel history, the starting point of the Gospel narrative being the belief in the sacrificial death and resurrection of Jesus. To Bauer the formation of the church and the development of the idea that Jesus is the Messiah are one and the same thing. For him Christianity was a new religion, the spirit of which was Roman and the outward frame of which was furnished by Judaism.

Since he received severe criticism of his views throughout his professional life, Bauer was driven by an almost insane desire to ruin the theological systems of his adversaries. This motivation behind his rational-mythical method propelled him to interpret every point in the early Christian tradition with increasing skepticism until he denied the historicity of Jesus and the genuineness of all the epistles of Paul.

The ideas of Strauss and B. Bauer combined with efforts of the proponents of the *religionsgeschichtliche Schule*, which had its beginning toward the close of the 18th century and which tried to relate Christian ideas and concepts to those in other religions, produced an even more radical understanding of biblical history.

Jesus Christ himself had become a myth. Drews, Kalthoff, Robertson, Mead, Jensen, M. Paul-Louis Couchoud, and Smith became familiar names on the roster of scholars advocating not only the mythical character of the traditions but also the mythical character of Jesus himself. This Christ-Myth theory was especially popular at the beginning of the 20th century.

One of the most startling developments out of this school of interpretation was the spin-off of "psychological lives" of Jesus. In this type of attempt to understand history the historicity of Jesus is not denied, but the whole portrait of him is considerably altered. The seed for "psychological lives" was planted by Strauss' suggestion that Jesus' conception of an immediate future kingdom ushered in with a blaze of supernatural glory, qualified him as a fanatic.

From there on the imaginations of such writers as P. de Régla, E. Bosc, C. Binet-Sangle, G. Bergeur, G. Lomer, W. Hirsh, E. Rasmussen, and G. Stanley Hall ran wild in their attempts to understand Jesus from the standpoint of psychology and psychoanalysis. The question was: from what emotional or mental disorder did Jesus suffer?

One of the most healthy developments came by way of critiques made of the Christ-Myth School. In replying to Drews and his colleagues, Johannes Weiss, Frederich Loofs, Shirley Jackson Case, Arnold Mayer, Fred C. Conybeare, Johannes Leipoldt, Maurice Goguel, and Martin Dibelius spelled out the fallacies of the denials of the historicity of Jesus with such clarity and scientific acumen that it has been impossible since that time to make any kind of an intelligent denial of Jesus' actual existence.

The most positive reaction to the radical position of the Christ-Myth School and the weaknesses of Strauss' approach to the Bible came in the form of the beginnings of what has come to be called "tendency criticism" and "source criticism."

An example of the former was the work of Ferdinand C. Baur (1792–1860) who accepted from Strauss that the mythical approach to Scripture destroys the historical truth of much of the biblical record; however, he felt that the critic must go on from there and try to discover the whole connection of circumstances out of which not only individual ideas but also the writing itself arose. Adopting a Hegelian scheme of thesis and antithesis, for him much of the New Testament witnesses to various reactions to and attempts to create a synthesis between conflicting aspects of Judaism and Paulinism. Similar approaches were also taken by Adolf Hilgenfeld (1823–1907), who pointed out the Jewish "tendency" in the Gospels, and by Otto Pfleiderer (1839–1908), who showed how Christian ideas developed not only against Jewish backgrounds but also against such rivalries as the early Christian community carried on with the disciples of John the Baptist.

During the same period and as part of this same movement Gustav Volkmar (1809–1893) made the Gospel of Mark the sole source for his life of Jesus. Volkmar did not believe that the historical Jesus had put forth any Messianic claims, and he looked at ideas developed in the Gospels as attempts to reconcile opposing Petrine and Pauline factions in the early Christian community.

Volkmar functioned as a bridge between tendency critics and source critics. Volkmar had support for his use of Mark for within literary criticism what has come to be called "the Marcan hypothesis" was being developed by Karl Lachmann (1835), Christian H. Weisse (1838), and Christian G. Wilke (1838).

From this point on more familiar names and figures emerge: Albert Schweitzer, Martin Dibelius, Rudolf Bultmann, Oscar Cullmann, along with Eichrodt, Vriezen, von Rad, Conzelmann, Bornkamm, Dodd, and Jeremias. All of them along with a host of biblical scholars on all continents continued to struggle with the conflicts between religion and science, between the supernatural and the natural, between the spiritual and the rational, as well as between myth and history.

At the same time that the historical-critical approach to the interpretation of the Bible has been developing since the Protestant Reformation it is obvious that the exclusively supernaturalistic approach so characteristic of Christianity before the Reformation has continued in various forms in both Roman Catholic and Protestant Christianity from the days of the Reformation until now.

The older supernaturalistic type of interpretation of Scripture has been maintained especially in Protestant evangelical circles where in recent years Missouri Synod Lutherans and Southern Baptists have been embattled in a struggle to maintain such terms as "inerrancy" and "literal" in their vocabularies pertaining to the Bible. Harold Lindsel, the former editor of *Christianity Today*, evangelical Christianity's number one magazine, tried to take Christianity back to pre-Reformation days with his arguments and appeals for the relevance and the necessity of a view of the Bible that includes "inerrancy."

Unificationism may function as a possible synthesis of what may be referred to as the thesis of supernaturalistic interpretation of the bible and the antithesis of naturalistic interpretation of the Word of God. I have noticed that Unificationists who use the biblical critical approach even in some of its most radical forms are not threatened spiritually, nor does the scientific approach to scripture for them depreciate for them its religious value in any way.

For a Unificationist, ideas and narratives in the Bible may be viewed as either mythic or historical or as both mythic and historical with no consequent depreciation in moral or spiritual value. Since for them history may be written in mythic forms, myth itself has an historical quality, and since for them myth is thought of primarily as a form in which to express universal truths, a myth may be of more value than an account given in strictly literal historical terms.

For a Unificationist who has studied the Bible from the standpoint of historical biblical criticism the symbolic and the literal merge into a single unit. Any given idea or narrative in the Bible may be viewed at any time as symbolic or literal, but in either case real. Any given idea or narrative in the Bible may be viewed at any time as having both a literal and a symbolic character, since every idea and every incident is a part of a universal process or unified field in which beginning and end, origin and goal, ideal and ultimate are the same.

A pertinent example of this is the fact that Rev. Sun Myung Moon interprets Genesis 1-3 literally; whereas Dr. Young Oon Kim interprets the same section of the Bible symbolically. A comparable range of diversity may be found throughout the membership of the Unification Church.

Any of the data in Scripture for the Unificationist—narrative, poetry, myth—all may be illuminating, inspiring, and authenticating.

II. ITS CONTEMPORANEITY

The nature of Unificationism is such that it also produces characteristics of contemporaneity for Biblical Studies. In addition to coming at the right moment in the history of Biblical Studies, when a bridge is needed to span the gap between supernaturalists and naturalists in all their multifarious forms, it provides a special quality for arising out of the needs of the modern world and responding to the aspirations of young adults of today. It possesses a broad-based and far reaching ecumenism related to a profound idealism. Rather than being censorious of diverse traditions it seeks that they become complementary to each other and to Unificationism.

As Unificationists engage in Biblical Studies, the possibility presents itself for resolving the conflict that arises between those who would "get back to the Bible" and recreate today the community of faith that existed in the first century, and the existentialist whose primary demand is to respond to twentieth century situations. The contemporaneity of Unificationism is different from the contemporaneity of either Pentecostals or Bultmannians. It casts aside neither the cultural developments of the modern world nor the richness of experience and tradition of the ancient world. It reaches out to the modern world without severing its ties with the ancient world. It analyzes and examines the traditions of the ancient world being fully aware of the magnificent scientific developments of the modern world.

When theologizing on biblical materials, Unificationists are fully aware of the contributions made to our understanding of scripture by Ignatius and Justin Martyr, Irenaeus and Tertullian, Clement of Alexandria and Origen, Arius and Athanasius, Jerome and Augustine, Abelard and Thomas Aquinas, Luther and Calvin, Wesley and Swedenborg, Wellhausen and Gunkel, Strauss and Schweitzer, C.H. Dodd and Vincent Taylor, Barth and Brunner, Bultmann and Bornkamm, Tillich and Niebuhr, Conzelmann and von Rad. But Unificationists carry on their discipline with an awareness of these traditions without being locked in by any of them.

In addition, they have great respect for councils and decrees and dogmas and confessions but view them as events around which biblical ideas have been summarized at a given time in history, and as reservoirs and resources for future and further developments of faith, rather than as great balls of twine for binding the wrists of those who would put their hands to the study of the Bible in any other way.

Another even more significant aspect of Unificationism's contemporaneity is that it makes of Biblical Studies a truly religious enterprise. That is, it makes it "religious" in the most profound and meaningful sense of the word. Religion by definition and in essence is intended to give meaning and wholeness and unity to all of life. Unificationists try to make Biblical Studies a discipline that produces a sense of meaning for all of existence, and an awareness of the wholeness and unity between all members of the family of humankind.

The study of the Bible, for Unificationists, is always within the context of the true function of religion—the unifying of the diverse and complex areas of life. This they seek to do in at least seven crucial areas.

a. The religious life—combining revelation with experience, inspiration and effort, the individual and community, meditation and action, piety and politics, the psychic and the scientific.

b. Science and religion—receiving with appreciation the results of scientific investigation in every area of life; using the results of scientific study to meet human needs and to give meaning to life; and considering scientific inquiry in itself to be a religious enterprise.

c. World Religions and Christianity—viewing all the religions of the world not as competitors but as contributors to man's quest for meaning and truth; looking at Christianity in its relationship to the others not as exclusive but as inclusive. This is of importance in Biblical Studies in considering the relationship between Christians and Jews and in evangelism for considering the relationship between Christians and followers of all other religions of the world. The scriptures are searched not for walls but for bridges.

d. The Church and the churches—seeking to discover a basis for unity not only between the church of Protestantism but also between the four major branches of the Christian Church itself: the Eastern Orthodox, the Roman Catholic, The Protestant Churches, and the Anglican Church. Unificationists encourage the student of the Bible to search the scriptures looking more for the force than the form of the Church, since like New Testament Christians, members of the Unification Church know that Christianity is, first of all, not a form but a force.

e. Male and female—relating the sexes to each other in such a way as to insure the wholeness of each; looking to the ideals established in the Bible for the proper relationship between the sexes, and seeking to make them patterns for life, rather than taking from the Bible sinful and fallen experiences between the sexes and making them guidelines for male-female relationships. Unificationists expound the liberation of both sexes and assist the student of the Bible in maintaining this freedom by examining biblical materials with a realistic approach.

f. The races—showing how every human being is a child of God, not only dealing with every individual human being as a soteriological prospect, but also as equally qualified as any other to understand God's will and to do God's work. Equal respect for the thought forms and life patterns of Orientals and Occidentals makes possible a bridge between these traditionally opposite and opposing worlds, geographically and spiritually. Openness and acceptance of all national, racial, and ethnic groups helps to produce results in Biblical Studies that truly relate to all manner of men. Exegesis is made meaningful to Indians and Africans, Chinese and Indonesians, Japanese and Koreans, Germans and French, Scandinavians and English, Russians and Americans.

g. Politics and sociology—considering the importance of each of these areas of life and their relevance for religion and relating them mutually to each other. Unificationists insist that religion be relevant to the political and social situations and issues of the day. As a result their focus is on the world's foremost enemy of religion, Communism, and seeks to establish and provide a rationale which will effectively combat it and defeat it. At the same time Unificationists insist that positive social patterns and programs must accompany political idealism. They also hold that political expediency should in no way limit social urgency. Redemption is not only from antagonistic spiritual powers but also from political and social systems that are opposed to faith. Christianity is strengthened by pitting itself against the forces which oppose it. Unificationists try to prevent the church from being weakened because of its failure to recognize or correctly identify its opposition, and they assist the student of the Bible at all times in making his work relevant.

These are some of the characteristics of an idealism that give Unificationism its unique contemporaneity and which in turn become an idealistic contextualization for Biblical Studies.

III. ITS VIEW OF SCRIPTURE

Unificationism's view of Scripture is tied in closely with its place in the history of hermeneutics and its contemporaneity. Since a focal point in history is the development of the Judeo-Christian tradition, and since in its view an enlightened interpretation of this tradition can encompass and embrace all religions, philosophies and world-systems, the Old and the New Testaments take on unique and dynamic characters.

Unificationists refuse to take sides in the traditional dilemma which has been a divisive force in Christianity: whether the Bible *is* the Word of God or whether the Bible *contains* the Word of God. Unificationism suggests that the Bible cannot be identified with the Word of God, since the Bible itself describes the Word of God as something other than a written document or collection of documents. The "word" with which Elijah sealed the heavens, the "word" that is like a hammer that breaks rocks into pieces, the "word" that is sharper than a two-edged sword, the "word" that became flesh and dwelt among us, is a term that cannot be identified with written documents in the form of the question: is the Bible the Word of God? From the Bible's own description of the "word" it is also obvious that the Bible does not necessarily contain the word of God. Where is the sealer, the hammer, the sword, the flesh? For Unificationists to say that the Bible contains the word of God is to imply that some of the material in Scripture is not the word of God, and this Unificationists are not willing to say.

For Unificationists the Bible is the chief literary expression of the "word." "Word" is one of the principles of the universe which has expressed itself in many forms including the Old and the New Testaments, in what has come to be called extra-canonical Judeo-Christian literature, and in the scriptures of other religions. The Old Testament and the New Testament, however, because of the character of God which they describe and the history of restoration which they unfold, and the revelation of Jesus which they set forth provide a norm for the interpretations of all other religious literary traditions.

Thus, in Unificationism there is the highest regard for scriptures of all religions of the world. At the same time the authority and normative value of the Old and New Testaments are held in greatest esteem. In the Judeo-Christian Bible the sovereignty of God, the providence of God, the nature and destiny of man, judgment and restoration are seen most clearly. In the Hebrew-Christian scriptures the script is given for the drama of salvation.

Although Unificationists regard the Bible with eternal and ultimate value, it is never looked upon as the object of idolatry, and Christians are warned not to deal with the Bible as the Jews dealt with the Torah. The Bible must be prevented from becoming for us what scripture had become for the people of Jesus' day, a fixed tradition that depended on experts for interpretation.

Unificationists also demand that the Old and New Testaments be understood in the light of what transpired during the early Christian Church. Unificationists face the fact that the Bible as we know it is a product of the experience of nearly four centuries of the early Christian community. Since there were Christians who did not know, or did not regard as authoritative, some of the Catholic Epistles, the Book of Revelation, some of the Epistles or Paul, one or more of the Gospels, then what was the shape and substance of their faith? Was it less than ours, who have a broader and more inclusive canon?

Similar questions arise with respect to text. From textual criticism much can be learned about the diversity of texts in the ancient church. Is our Bible, a conflation of texts, superior to older texts which represent different and diverse records of the ancient testimonies?

Although a Unificationist's faith may depend a great deal upon the Bible, it is not necessarily shaped or shrunken by what one may think about any book of the Bible or about any part of any book of the Bible.

Thus, a Unificationist may love the Bible as deeply and dearly as the most devout Fundamentalist and analyze the Bible with an acumen as sharp as a radical biblical critic.

In Unificationism, heart and mind approach the Bible with faith and love. This is possible since faith is not dependent exclusively on Scripture. It is dependent primarily on a personal relationship to God in Christ.

With respect to its view of Scripture, Unificationists are also appreciative of what some scholars have been saying and writing recently concerning what is considered to be the major theme or concept of the Old Testament or the New Testament or the entire Bible. Gerhard Hasel of the Adventist Seminary at Andrews University in Berrien Springs, Michigan recently wrote: "The central concern of the whole Bible is not reconciliation and redemption, but the Kingdom of God." For Hasel the Kingdom of God is to be found in both testaments and forms the most natural bridge between the two.

Hasel also notes the importance of a revival of an older type of methodology in relating the Testaments, that is, the use of typology. Used by both Eichrodt and von Rad, typology is a designation for a peculiar way of looking at history, the types being persons, institutions, and events of the Old Testament which are regarded as divinely established models or prerepresentations of corresponding realities in the New Testament salvation history.

Unificationists posit the Kingdom of God and God's creative and redemptive power as part of a unified scheme, the major theme of the whole Bible, and the primary concern of contemporary society. They also consider typology as one of the principle motifs for the interpretation not only of the Bible but of subsequent human history.

Cain and Abel, Jacob and Esau, Moses and Joshua and many other biblical characters become for Unificationists not only dramatic historic biblical figures but also the bases for the dynamics of life throughout all history. For them numerology also takes on a typological character. For example, 3, 7, 21, 40 and 100 become for them not only the number of times a biblical hero did something or the number of years of a king's reign or the number of days or years someone spent somewhere but also the number of days they should spend in workshops studying the Divine Principle, or numbers for days or years in sequences of what they call providential history.

Obviously related to Unificationism's view of Scripture is its view of history. This may be described as structures on a series of parallels, periods of pre-Christian history comparable to periods of Christian history. Although these structures as outlined in Unification literature are artificial and noteworthy for certain conspicuous historical errors, they do provide Unificationists with a means of relating scripture to history.

At the same time, in the Unificationist's view, history moves towards a definite point, determined by the relationship which man keeps with God. Consequently it was not a problem for Unificationists that the Kingdom of God did not come on earth in 1981 as Rev. Moon had promised that it would. Now the time is projected to the end of this millennium. But again, the coming of the kingdom will be dependent upon humanity's response to the will of God.

Also, Unificationists may use the Hegelian principle of thesis, antithesis, and synthesis and the Darwinian principle of evolution, even when applied to social processes, to illuminate biblical themes. Thus, Unificationism takes several major patterns of historical thinking from both the pre-scientific and the scientific worlds and allows each to cast its own light on historical processes.

In Unificationism, then, history is a unified continuum, in which all processes of the universe participate in rhythm and in order, affecting each other with diversity and change, and moving from an original perfection to an ultimate ideal. In trying to understand the historical nature of the literature, such a view produces profound effects upon Biblical Studies.

Unificationists call for a confrontation with the totality of the biblical record in Biblical Studies. Unificationists encourage and respond to biblical criticism. They view it as a way of "testing the spirits to see whether they are of God." They are interested in interpretations and methodologies and theologies that are rooted in reality and reflect and produce faith in God.

IV. ITS CHRISTOLOGY AND THE MISSION OF JESUS

Unificationism has come under considerable criticism particularly for one aspect of its faith; namely, its Christology. Since it does not affirm the Trinitarian formula of conservative and orthodox Christianity and refuses to equate Jesus with God, it has been labelled un-Christian or non-Christian. Many critics have labeled it heretical and associated it with movements in early Christianity. It has even been referred to as a modern form of one of the early heresies or as a new form of Gnosticism. Oddly, however, the Unificationists' Christology is the opposite of the Gnostic and is more closely identifiable with the Ebionite, placing emphasis on the humanity of Jesus. (See Wells' essay in this volume for a Unificationist's view.)

The Unificationists' view of Jesus is that his birth was from a human mother and a human father and that his resurrection is to be thought of as fundamentally spiritual rather than primarily physical. According to their interpretation of I Corinthians 15, Paul is describing both the resurrection of Jesus and the resurrection of believers as spiritual in nature in contrast to the physical and material, and from their readings of the birth narratives in Matthew 1-2 and in Luke 1-2 they do not hesitate to think of Jesus as having had a human father.

At the same time Unificationists ascribe to the Christology stated by the author of the Fourth Gospel in John 1:1ff, by Paul in Colossians 1:1ff and by the author of Hebrews in 1:1ff. For them Jesus is truly the Son of

God. They possess what is known as a functional Christology as over against an ontological Christology, and understand the term "Son of God" primarily in an ethical sense (Hebraic) rather than in a metaphysical sense (Greek).

Similar views on each of these issues is held by Christian scholars and clerics in Germany, Great Britain, and in the United States. Generally their views are called liberal or radical. Sometimes they are called refreshing. Rarely are they called un-Christian or heretical.

There can be no question that the Christology of the Unificationist, although shaped differently than traditional Christianity, has a high regard for Jesus, comes into close personal fellowship with him, and also brings the Unificationist into the experience of what the Apostle Paul calls living "in Christ."

Unificationists have also been severely censored by Christians for their view of the mission of Jesus. Critics like to quote Unificationists as believing that "Jesus failed in his mission" and that Jesus "did not come to die."

Critics in addition to committing the error of caricaturing the Unificationists' point of view also fail to recall the debate which has been going in biblical circles all during this century. A typical traditional view held by orthodox and fundamentalist Christians is that the purpose of Jesus' mission was to die on the cross to provide atonement for the sins of humanity. A typical point of view held by liberal and radical Christians and by some Jews is that the purpose of Jesus' mission was to establish the Kingdom of God on earth in his lifetime. The Gospel record, according to the latter scholars, is a re-interpretation made on the intention of Jesus by the early Christian community because of what happened at Golgotha. Because he did die, it had to be proposed that Jesus' purpose was to die.

Rudolf Bultmann has suggested the problem with which all critics and theologians must deal: "The greatest embarrassment to the attempt to reconstruct a portrait of Jesus is the fact that we cannot know how Jesus understood his end, his death... What is certain is merely that he was crucified by the Romans, and thus suffered the death of a political criminal. This death can scarcely be understood as an inherent and necessary consequence of his activity; rather it took place because his activity was misconstrued as a political activity. In that case it would have been—historically speaking—a meaningless fate. We cannot tell whether or how Jesus found meaning in it. We may not veil from ourselves the

possibility that he suffered a collapse." ("The Primitive Christian Kerygma and the Historical Jesus")

For the Unificationist, Jesus' cry of dereliction from the cross, "My
God, my God, why have you forsaken me?" (which is the only "word"
from the cross given by either Matthew or Mark), is the expression of
that collapse, that sense of rejection which Jesus totally felt along with the
awareness of the failure of his mission.

Vincent Taylor, when describing the mission of the twelve, wrote:
"What Jesus expected, and what he sent forth the Twelve to announce
was the speedy coming of the rule of God and the setting up of the
messianic community of the Son of Man." Continuing, Taylor concluded, "No small part of the significance of the mission is that it failed."
Before Taylor, Albert Schweitzer described the mission of Jesus in similar
terms and after Taylor, Hyam Maccoby has done the same.

Unificationists are sensitive to the insights of both Vincent Taylor and
Rudolf Bultmann and speak to the death of Jesus as the climax or
consummation of the failure of Jesus' mission to fulfill his avowed intention of establishing the Kingdom of God on earth in his own lifetime. For
these views some American Christians would like to run the Unificationists out of the country. The Germans and French did manage to drive
Albert Schweitzer into Africa where he eventually became more famous
as a medical doctor than he had been as a musician or theologian.

In *Divine Principle* the subject of Jesus' mission is presented under the
heading "The Purpose of the Coming of the Messiah." It warrants a
closer look.

Unlike most of Christian theology which is tied in with the relationship of the mission of Jesus to the fall of man, Unificationism ties the
mission of Jesus in with creation. "God's purpose of creation was to be
fulfilled with the establishment of the Kingdom of God on earth."
Salvation or restoration, then, was to come about through God's Messiah
who would re-establish humankind to a state comparable to that of the
ideal of creation of the pre-fallen state.

The purpose of Jesus, according to this view, had to be to establish the
Kingdom of Heaven on earth. Looked at in another way, "The purpose of
salvation (restoration) history focuses on the fulfillment of the principle
of creation." Jesus came to fulfill the principle of creation. Two texts from
Matthew are used to support this concept: "Be ye perfect as your Father
in heaven is perfect" (5:48), "Thy kingdom come on earth as it is in
heaven" (6:10).

This intention of Jesus is also viewed by the Unificationist in relationship to the mission of John the Baptist. It is noted that the proclamation of John the Baptist and of Jesus is the same. John the Baptist, according to Matthew 3:2, and Jesus, according to Matthew 4:17, proclaim the same message: "Repent for the Kingdom of Heaven is at hand."

The Jewish belief of Jesus' day was that Elijah would come prior to the coming of the Messiah. "Elijah truly shall come first and restore all things (Matthew 17:11)." According to Matthew 11:14 and Matthew 17:13 this was to be the role of John the Baptist. However, according to John 1:21, this is a role which John the Baptist himself rejected. Since the mission of Elijah and Messiah were integrally and imperatively related, with the fulfillment of Elijah's mission vital to the success of the mission of the Messiah in establishing the Kingdom of Heaven on earth, the failure of John the Baptist to accept the role of Elijah was one of the factors which made it impossible for Jesus to fulfill the providence of restoration, i.e., establish the Kingdom of Heaven on earth.

According to *Divine Principle* John's protest that he was not Elijah (John 1:21) was the principal cause blocking the way of the people to Jesus. The mission of John the Baptist as a witness to Jesus ended with his testifying to Jesus and with his baptism of Jesus. For Unificationists, John the Baptist should have assumed his role as Elijah and worked effectively along with Jesus. John the Baptist should have become a foremost disciple of Jesus. This, of course, he did not do. He even continued to baptize separate from Jesus and his disciples, and reference is made to the disciples of John, indicating that his following continued as a movement separate from Jesus' followers.

Thus, betrayed by John the Baptist, Jesus had to wander about the seacoast of Galilee and in the region of Samaria looking for those who would listen to his Gospel. John the Baptist greatly offended Jesus and failed to accomplish his mission although he was greatest among the prophets (Matthew 11:11).

Unificationists note that Jesus was rejected by John the Baptist, his own family (Luke 2:48), by his own disciples (Matthew 26, 27) and by the people. Jesus, then, came to accomplish the will of God for establishing the Kingdom of Heaven on earth in his lifetime but died a reluctant death on the cross due to the disbelief and lack of acceptance of him by those closest to him as well as the populace and nation to whom he ministered.

If Jesus had not been rejected, he would not have been crucified. Unificationists argue that crucifixion could not have been primary to the will of God, since even the Apostle Paul who made the crucifixion central to his own message maintained that Jesus was crucified out of ignorance and disbelief (I Corinthians 2:8). God's will, Unificationists say, is expressed in two texts in the Fourth Gospel. "This is the work of God, that ye believe in him whom he hath sent." (John 6:29) "I come that they might have life, and that they might have it more abundantly." (John 10:10).

In *Divine Principle* a relationship is made between the apparently separate and contradictory concepts of the mission of Jesus: to establish the Kingdom of Heaven on earth, or to die on the cross. It is pointed out that two prominent salvation motifs appear in Hebrew tradition regarding the fulfillment of God's will. God has entered into a covenant relationship with his people, and this is a relationship in which both God and man share responsibility. One motif is the kingdom motif. The other is the suffering motif. The former is primary. The latter is an alternative which comes about due to humankind's failure to carry out its responsibility for bringing about the fulfillment of the first.

The Messianic kingdom motif is to be found in Isaiah 9:6-7 which speaks of a peaceful and lasting kingdom of David, Isaiah 11:4 which speaks of righteousness stemming from Jesus the father of David, Isaiah 60:1-12 which speaks of peace and righteousness and God as light and glory, and Luke 1:30-33 which speaks of the everlasting kingdom of David.

The Suffering Servant motif is to be found in Isaiah 52:13-53:12, which speaks of the individual or nation that suffers as God's servant for others and Mark 10:45 which identifies the mission of Jesus with giving his life as a ransom for many.

The Christian community understood Jesus to have fulfilled the dynamics of Isaiah 52, 53 (Mark 10:45). Jesus originally understood his mission to be the establishment of the Kingdom of Heaven on earth (Mark 1:14, 15) but re-interpreted his own mission to be one of suffering and death (Matthew 16:21). Salvation, then, accomplished by Jesus' mission of his suffering and death on the cross was reconciliation (Romans 1-6) rather than restoration. Since restoration includes renewal both of the spiritual and the physical aspects of humankind's nature, and since reconciliation may be thought of as pertaining to the spiritual aspect of salvation, Jesus in his death upon the cross did provide spiritual salvation for mankind, i.e., reconciliation and forgiveness of sins.

Critics of Unificationism should never fail to take into account another of *Divine Principle's* statements: *"We can never deny and must affirm the magnitude of the grace of reconciliation (or redemption) by the suffering and death of Jesus."*

To all of this still another dimension is given by Unificationists. Jesus' mission of suffering and death, which resulted from the disbelief of the Jewish People and the failure of John the Baptist to unite with Jesus, may be viewed as a consequence to the work of Satan. Satan's work is thought of as having begun at the time of the Monarchy (ca. 1000 B.C.) in terms of Satan's success in corrupting the "ideal of the temple" so that the temple for a millennium did not actualize the presence and the power of God. Malachi, who had prophesied Elijah's return (4:5) had also spoken of "the messenger of the covenant" for the purification of the Lord's Temple. Jesus, as the messenger of the covenant, cleansed the Temple, but because of lack of support from the people accomplished only being brought to the attention of temple authorities and being led down a course that consummated in his death on the cross. By invading Solomon, Satan succeeded in corrupting the "ideal of the Temple." It may be said too that Satan invaded that temple which was Jesus' body (John 2:18-21), i.e., God gave the body of Jesus over to Satan.

The bodies, therefore, of those who believe in Jesus still remain subject to Satan's invasion. Although the eternal penalty for sin has been removed by the death of Jesus, the actuality of sin in the daily lives of believers remains. But since God's predestination to restore the Kingdom of Heaven on earth is absolute and unchangeable, Christ has to come again to fulfill perfectly the will of God, and since sin still works in us, Christ must come again on the earth to accomplish the complete providence of restoration which will include the physical as well as spiritual salvation.

V. ITS ESCHATOLOGICAL PERSPECTIVE

Among the more debatable points of Unificationism is the contention that in Jesus' intention to establish the Kingdom of Heaven on earth, he also intended to marry and to have a family. This conclusion is based on a line of argument based on the Apostle Paul's designation of Jesus as the second Adam. If that is so, then Jesus had to have his Eve and together they were to have had children. Jesus' crucifixion, however, interrupted and changed this course of his life and mission.

Since it is the contention of Unificationists that Christ must come again, it is also their contention that when he does come he will marry and have a family. It is the claim of Rev. Sun Myung Moon that Jesus himself appeared to him on an Easter morning in Korea and challenged him to complete his mission. This was the vision that inaugurated and inspires the mission of the Rev. Moon. Sun Myung Moon's intention is to complete the mission of Jesus by arousing humanity to respond to the will of God and thereby bring about the completion of the providence of restoration, i.e., the establishment of the Kingdom of Heaven on earth. Jesus as Messiah completed the spiritual aspects of the providence of restoration. Jesus has commissioned Moon to complete the physical aspects of the providence of restoration.

In view of this it is striking that Rev. and Mrs. Moon's children number twelve (thirteen at time of publication—ed.), that Rev. Moon speaks of himself as having overcome the dominion of Satan, and that some of his closest followers speak of him as being in charge of the spirit world.

Whatever messianic pretensions these items suggest may be tempered however by the facts that five of his children are girls, he enjoys taking the whole family to Great Adventure in New Jersey, he loves to fish in the Atlantic Ocean for tuna and in the Hudson River for carp, and his magic touch is in business, being especially successful as a major distributor of ginseng tea in the Far East.

Unlike many Christians who believe only in a spiritual kingdom of God, unlike liberal Christians who do not believe in the second coming of Christ, and unlike Christians who believe in the second coming of Christ as the return of Jesus on the clouds, and unlike Jews who reject Jesus as the Messiah altogether and look forward to the coming of another Jewish Messiah, Unificationists believe in a second coming of Christ, who does not come on clouds and who is not a Jew but one who is a believer in Jesus. The fundamental difference between Unificationist eschatology and either Christian or Jewish eschatologies, however, lies in the Unificationists' concept that the fulfillment of the providence of restoration is more dependent upon the people's response to God than it is on the Messiah himself. The Kingdom of Heaven is not so much what the Messiah brings about as what the people fulfill and do.

When I personally asked Rev. Moon what would happen if he and his movement were not instrumental in bringing about a response of humanity to the will of God and should fail in establishing the Kingdom of Heaven on earth, he replied casually and graciously, "Then someone else will do it at another time. God's will will be done."

As startling and controversial as this eschatology may be, it does provide the necessary function of challenging Christians and Jews to think eschatologically. Since the Hebrew Christian scriptures have an eschatological perspective and a strong apocalyptic element, it is incumbent upon both Christians and Jews to take this dimension and element in the Bible seriously. Independently of Rev. Moon, Christian biblical scholars have only recently begun to do so.

Just a decade ago Klaus Koch, Professor of Old Testament at the University of Hamburg, posed a crucial question: "Has biblical scholarship really done everything that it was possible to do by historical methods?" (*The Rediscovery of Apocalyptic*, 1970). He answered the question himself by suggesting that biblical criticism has dealt only sparingly with eschatology and especially meagerly with that special dimension of eschatology, apocalyptic literature. Koch emphasized how apocalyptic concepts formed the final stage in the religion of the Old Testament and provided a determining role for the origins of Jesus as well as primitive Christianity. He outlined in detail his thesis that scholars are still far from an adequate overall grasp of this subject.

Koch pointed out how interest in apocalyptic literature in German theological education practically disappeared during the 1900s through the 1950s. He credits Ernst Käsemann with pointing out how "apocalyptic was the mother of all Christian theology..." and both Käsemann and Wolfhart Pannenberg with engendering in certain of the younger German theologians a positive apocalyptic renaissance and how Martin Noth, O. Ploger and D. Rossler helped to resume research into this area so long ignored in German scholarship.

He also reminds us how Rudolf Bultmann contributed to the neglect of proper treatment of apocalyptic literature. In his essay "The New Testament and Mythology" Bultmann wrote: "The cosmology of the New Testament is essentially mythical in character... The mythology of the New Testament is in essence that of Jewish apocalyptic and Gnostic redemption myths... This mythology is outdated for every thinking person today, whether he is a believer or an unbeliever..."

Koch sketched the rise of interest in apocalyptic literature among British and American scholars signaling the major contributions made by R.H. Charles, George F. Moore, R. Travers Herford, H.H. Rowley, W.D. Davies, and C.K. Barrett.

He also reminds us of Rudolf Otto's judgment: "Jesus' preaching of the Kingdom is manifestly connected with (and yet is... in definite contrast to) an earlier historical phenomenon, i.e., the later Jewish eschatology and apocalyptic... Jesus' preaching both reflects and transforms them."

Koch also allows Ethelbert Stauffer to speak again: "The world of apocalyptic ideas is the one in which the New Testament writers were really at home." But, Koch laments that voices like these became lost in the great chorus of New Testament scholars who view apocalyptic of every kind—even the book of Revelation—with mistrust and discomfort. For some such as Gerhard Ebling apocalyptic suggests a heretical tendency, and many scholars are not unsympathetic with R. Travers Herford's dictum, speaking about eschatology and apocalyptic, "Although both are the children of prophecy, the one is a Jacob, the other (apocalyptic) an Esau."

Koch's conclusion: "The prevailing opinion among German New Testament scholars is still that apocalyptic is a marginal phenomenon which undoubtedly played a certain role in some early Christian circles but which, seen as a whole, is unimportant." However, in spite of the general reluctance of German scholars to give apocalyptic its due and in spite of both English and American theological worlds leaving apocalyptic primarily in the hands of obscurantist sects, Koch insists that Pannenberg and others have helped launch a renaissance of apocalyptic. "Everything suggests that in the coming decades theology will have to concern itself increasingly with the apocalyptic writings."

Apocalyptic literature conveys the conviction that God will save and restore His people and establish His kingdom. This is a message compatible with Unificationism. One of the essential features of apocalyptic literature is that it is not to be interpreted literally and presents a philosophy of history rather than a chronological scheme for history. With this, Unificationists have some difficulty, as do all Fundamentalist Christians, especially sectarian Christians.

One of the most serious limitations to the effectiveness of Unificationism comes in its use of apocalyptic literature. Although Unificationists can ascribe to apocalyptic as a code language presenting a philosophy of history, the founder, the chief interpreter, and numerous Unificationists see in the Apocalypse of John predictions of the coming of Rev. Sun Myung Moon, Unificationism, and Mrs. Moon.

Rev. Moon is seen in Revelation 7:2 to be "another angel ascending from the east having the seal of the living God." The 144,000 (Revelation 7:14) is seen as a symbol of Unificationism, and Rev. and Mrs. Moon are thought to be depicted in Revelation 19:7 as "the Lamb . . . and his wife . . ."

As startling as this use of Revelation may seem to be, however, it should be taken as no more so than Hal Lindsay's contention that the contemporary European Common Market and the current crisis in the Middle East are depicted in Daniel, and that what is in Revelation describes events which are and will be current.

Using the Apocalypse to foresee contemporary events and figures is useful as long as the Unification Movement has no biblical scholars. Such an intepretation is a principal cause for hoping that biblical scholars will soon be forthcoming. When this happens, Unificationism will retreat as an obscurantist cult, and emerge as a viable new religious movement.

BIBLIOGRAPHY

Bauer, Bruno. *Christus und die Casaren*. Berlin: Eugen Grosser, 1877.

Baur, Ferdinard Christian. *The Church History of the First Three Centuries*, 3rd ed. London and Edinburgh: Williams and Norgate, 1878.

Bultmann, Rudolf. "The Primitive Kerygma and the Historical Jesus." In *In Search of the Historical Jesus*. Edited by Harvey K. McArthur. New York: Charles Scribner's Sons, 1969.

Case, Shirley Jackson. *The Historicity of Jesus*. Chicago: The University of Chicago Press, 1912.

Drews, Arthur. *The Christian-Myth*. T.F. Unwin, 1910. The Open Court Publishing Co., 1912.

Hasel, Gerhard. *Old Testament Theology: Basic Issues in the Current Debate*, Grand Rapids: William B. Eerdman's Publishing Company, 1972.

Hegel, George W.F. *Lectures on the Philosophy of Religion*. First published in German in 1832, trans. from the second German edition by Rev. E.B. Speirs and J. Burdon Sanderson. 3 vols. London: Kegan Paul, Trench, Tubner and Co., LTD, 1895.

Hess, Johann Jakob. *Lebensgeschichte Jesu*. Achte, vom Verfasser neu bearbeitete. Zurich: Auflage, 1822.

Hobbes, Thomas. *Leviathan*. Edited by A. Waller. Cambridge: University Press, 1904.

Holy Spirit Association for the Unification of World Christianity. *Divine Principle*. Washington, DC: Holy Spirit Association for the Unification of World Christianity, 1973.

Hume, David. *A Treatise on Human Nature,* (1739, 1740) Edited. by T.H. Green and T.H. Grose. 2 vols. London: Longmans Green, and Co., 1874.

————. *Enquiry Concerning Human Understanding* (1748). Edited by L.A. Selby-Bigge, Oxford: Clarendon Press, 1894.

Kant, Immanuel. *Die Religion Innerhalb der Grenzen der Blossen Vernunft* 1794). *Sammtliche Werke*. Herausgegeben von Karl Rosenkranz und Friedr. Wilh. Schubert, Leibzig: Zehnter Theil, Leopold Voss, 1838.

Kim, Young Oon. *Unification Theology and Christian Thought*. New York: The Golden Gate Publishing Company, 1975.

Koch, Klaus. "The Rediscovery of Apocalyptic," *Studies in Biblical Theology*. London: SCM Press, 1970.

Locke, John. *An Essay Concerning Human Understanding,* Oxford: Clarendon Press, 1894.

————. *A Commonplace-Book to the Holy Bible*. From the 5th London Edition, New York and Boston: American Tract Society, n.d.

Reimarus, Hermann Samuel. *Fragments from Reimarus* Vol. 1. Edited by Charles Voysey. London and Edinburgh: Williams and Norgate, 1879.

Ritschl, Albrecht. *The Christian Doctrine of Justification and Reconciliation,* first German edition 1870-1874, English translation by H.R. Mackintosh and A.B. Macaulay, 2nd ed., Edinburgh: T.&T. Clark, 1902.

Schleiermacher, Friedrich E.D. *Das Leben Jesu,* herausgegeben von R. Rutenik, Berlin: Druck und Verlag von Georg Reimer, 1864.

Schweitzer, Albert. *Von Reimarus zu Werde,* 1906, ET as *The Quest of the Historical Jesus,* 2nd ed., NY: The Macmillan Company, 1926.

Smith, J. Frederick. *Studies in Religion Under German Masters,* London and Edinburgh: Williams and Norgate, 1880.

Strauss, David F. *Das Leben Jesu,* 1835, English translation from the 4th German edition in one volume, Swan Sonnenschein & Co., 1892.

Taylor, Vincent. "The Mission of the Twelve," Chapter 22 in *In Search of the Historical Jesus,* Harvey K. McArthur, NY: Charles Scribner's Sons, 1969.

Volkmar, Gustav. *Jesus Nazarenus und die erste christliche Zeit mit den beiden ersten Erzahlern,* Caesar Schmidt, 1882.

Weisse, Gustav. *Die evangelische Geschichte kritisch und philosophisch Bearbeiter.* Leipzig: Erster Band, Breitkopf und Hartel, 1838.

Wilke, Christian Gottlob. *Der Urevangelist,* Dresden und Leipzig: G. Fleischer, 1838.

Wright, William Kelley. *A History of Modern Philosophy,* NY: The Macmillan Company, 1941.

Theodore E. James

Reason, Revelation, and Romans 1:18–21

The desire to investigate more thoroughly some of the meanings, implications, and interpretations of St. Paul's Letter to the Romans 1:18–21 was aroused and stimulated by the reading of a paper written by Dr. James M. Penton, which he presented at a seminar on Revelation at San Juan, Puerto Rico, January 21–25, 1981.[1] In the paper Dr. Penton states (p. 2):

St. Paul tells us at Romans 1:15–20 (N.E.V.): "For we see divine retribution revealed from heaven and falling upon all the godless wickedness of men. In their wickedness they are stifling the truth. For all that may be known of God by men lies plain before their eyes; indeed God himself has disclosed it to them. His invisible attributes, that is to say his everlasting power and deity, have been visible, ever since the world began, to the eye of reason, in the things he has made."[2] In a similar passage St. Augustine of Hippo remarks: "Let your mind roam through the whole creation; everywhere the created world will cry out to you: God made me."[3] Hence, for nearly two thousand years certain Christians have taken a naturalistic approach to their religion and have tried to understand God through a rational study of the physical universe. Unfortunately this assumes that God's nature is reflected in the universe and that He is not transcendent or "wholly other." Neither does it take into consideration (1) the imperfection of the world since the Fall, (2) the "exceeding sinfulness of sin," and (3) it denies the fundamental Pauline doctrine of the spiritual adoption of the individual Christian and the inner testimony of (p. 3) the holy spirit. (Romans 8) For the above reasons I strongly believe the fundamental rationalism of Roman Catholicism, much of Fundamentalist and sectarian Protestantism and the Unification Church creates important theological problems for them. While I believe that one may admit the truthfulness of Romans 1:20 (in spite of serious philosophical problems), to go from a fundamental assertion that God *is* and *has created* to a determination of His nature is unwarranted. We know that "God is love" not through reason but rather through revelation and the testimony of the spirit. (2) WHAT DO WE KNOW WHEN WE KNOW GOD? Knowing God may mean several things to different persons. Frankly, however, since I firmly believe in the transcendent nature of God and feel that He is "wholly other," I feel that He can be known through revelation only.

Before entering into an analysis and evaluation of the main points of the above, I would like to present my understanding of the positions of the "fundamental rationalism of Roman Catholicism, much of Fundamentalist and sectarian Protestantism and the Unification Church," which do not appear to me to "create important theological problems for them," though they may for Dr. Penton's position, if I understand him correctly.[4]

I will begin with the position of the Unification Church as presented in *Divine Principle* and other related explanatory material. The other points of view will be presented tangentially as I consider appropriate. In the beginning of *Divine Principle* the question is asked:

How can we know the characteristics of God, who is an invisible being?[5] We can know them by observing the world of creation. For this reason, Paul said:

"Ever since the creation of the world his invisible nature, namely, his eternal power and deity, has been clearly perceived in the things that have been made. So they are without excuse." (*Romans* 1:20)

Using the principle of analogy, in Unification Thought, nature is considered to be the work of art produced by the Divine Artist: "Just as the work of an artist is a visible manifestation of its maker's nature, every creation is a 'substantial object' of the invisible deity of God, the Creator. His nature is displayed in each creation. Just as we can sense an author's character through his works, so we can perceive God's deity by observing His creation."[6] There follows a very detailed account of what one may and does learn about God from a study of the physical universe.

The first characteristic of God is positivity and negativity which is revealed in the dual reciprocal relationship of the particles that form atoms and molecules of non-living things, the stamen and pistil in plants, and the male-female relationship in animals (p. 20–21). All things in existence have an external form and an internal character. In the make-up of man there is a body, or "external form" and mind or "internal character" (p. 22). God is understood as the absolute being which is the ultimate cause, First Cause, of all beings, containing the absolute and subjective character and form (p. 23). God's subjective character and form are called His "essential character" and "essential form" (p. 34). These two latter characteristics form a reciprocal relationship with the characteristics of positivity and negativity so that the latter are the attributes of the former essential character and essential form. Positivity and negativity "also have a reciprocal relationship existing between internal and external, cause and result, subject and object, vertical and horizontal."(*ibid.*) The positivity and negativity are also called "masculinity" and "femininity." "... in relationship to the whole creation, God is the masculine subject representing its internal character" (p. 25). God is the Creator and is eternally self-existent, transcendent of time and space so that the fundamental energy of His being is also absolute and eternally self-existent and the source of the energy which enables all things to maintain their existence (p. 27–28). The Universal Prime Energy of God is a vertical power while the power of the give and take action of creatures is a horizontal power. The universal presence of the horizontal power is a means by which the omnipresence of God is known (p. 39). In man there is intellect, emotion and will which are reflections of the knowledge, love and beauty of God. God is a personal being,[7] having all the characteristics of the human person, such as intellect, will, etc., in an analogous way. But the most fundamental characteristic of God is not mind but heart, the essence of His personality.[8] God is a God of heart. "What does this mean? It means that our understanding of God must be based on an appreciation of human feelings. God feels at least as sensitive to what goes on in the world as we do. If He is a God of heart, then He experiences the whole range of emotions from loneliness and intense grief to wonderful joy. If He is forgiving, He is also wounded by pain. God can love and express righteous indignation. Consequently, because God is a God of heart, He must be profoundly affected by everything which takes place in His creation."[9]

There seems to me to be no doubt that *Divine Principle* does accept and utilize the conviction that a natural theology can be developed from an intelligent contemplation of the physical world and that this does not "create important theological problems for them." *Au contraire.* The theology of the Unification Church is presented in *Divine Principle* and elaborated and explained in other official publications.[10] By this I do not mean to say that the theology is entirely natural theology; that it is not is clearly seen in the many references to the writings of the Old and New Testament as well as to the special revelation claimed by Rev. Moon.

As regards the "rationalism of Roman Catholicism" it is quite evident that theologians and philosophers in the general tradition of Catholicism did and do accept Paul's viewpoint. I think that he developed that viewpoint as a result of the personal revelation made to him by Jesus, by the study of the Hebrew Scriptures, and by the comparing of what he understood thereby with the opinions of Stoic and Epicurean philosophers who were familiar with the opinions of Plato and Aristotle.[11] Paul seems firmly convinced that a human person by using natural God-given reason and applying it to the facts of experience could and did reach a knowledge of the existence and basic nature of God. This conviction was strengthened by Paul's knowledge of the Hebrew Scriptures, especially the Psalms and Wisdom, wherein the basic Pauline conviction is anchored.[12]

The tradition in Catholicism can be traced from Paul through Justin Martyr, Clement of Alexandria, John Chrysostom and Augustine, to mention but a few, to Thomas Aquinas and to Vatican Council 1, and to many contemporary theologians and philosophers.[13] In agreement with the Psalms, Wisdom, and Romans 'rationalistic' catholics accepted and developed a substantial natural or philosophical theology in which, from the contemplation of the works of God, His existence and something of his nature can be known.

In his commentary on this passage in Romans,[14] John Chrysostom states that the letter of Paul is contending that the knowledge of God was placed in men from the beginning but that they applied it to 'stocks and stones' (p. 351). It is plain that God placed this knowledge in them because "that which may be known of Him is manifest in them." "Whence was it plain then? Did He send a voice from above? By no means. But what was able to draw them to Him more than a voice that He did by putting before them the creation, so that both wise and unlearned, and Scythian and barbarian, having through sight learned the beauty of things which were seen, might mount up to God. Wherefore he says (v. 20) "For the invisible things of Him from the creation of the world are clearly seen, being understood by the things which are made." What also the prophet said, "The heavens declare the glory of God." (Ps. xix, 1 [xviii, 2]) Again, "all things abiding in order and by their beauty and their grandeur preaching aloud of the Creator." It seems clear that Chrysostom interpreted the passage in Romans as involving the assertion of a natural theology of the existence and attributes of God. God did not express this by a voice of personal revelation in the literal sense but by creating a universe which is a natural voice or natural revelation of the eternal power and Deity of God.

Many people become acquainted with Augustine through the reading of his *Confessions*.[15] In that work he recounts what he considers the most significant stages in his own personal development which led him to an intimate relationship with God. One memorable event was the reading of Cicero's *Hortensius* which, at the age of 18, stimulated in Augustine a deep and abiding love for philosophy. That work of Cicero, which was influenced by the *Protrepticus* of Aristotle, "changed the direction of my mind" and "with an incredible intensity of desire I longed after immortal wisdom. I had begun the journey upwards by which I was to return to You" (*Conf.* p. 45). The one thing "that delighted me in Cicero's exhortation was that I should love, and seek, and win, and hold, and embrace, not this or that philosophical school but *Wisdom* itself" (p. 46). The reading of Aristotle's *Categories* turned out to be a positive help for his knowledge of God later, though his evaluation of it was considered as negative because "Not only did all this (i.e. the explanation of the 9 accidents) not profit me, it actually did me harm, in that I tried to understand You, my God, marvelous in simplicity and immutability, while imagining that whatever had being was to be found within these ten categories" (p. 79).

After Augustine became able to think about God as a spiritual being, through the influence of some books of the Platonists,[16] he realized how Aristotle's *Categories*, which deals with material beings, had impeded his journey of the mind to God. But in the *De Trinitate*[17] he recalls the contents of the *Categories* and employs them *per viam negationis* to illustrate the nature of God.

The next stage in his spiritual journey is preceded by a prayer in which we find echoes of Romans 1:20. "Without ceasing Thy whole creation speaks Thy praise—the spirit of every man by the words that his mouth directs to Thee, animals and lifeless matter by the mouth of those who look upon them: that so our soul rises out of its mortal weariness unto Thee, helped upward by the things Thou has made and passing beyond them unto Thee who hast wonderfully made them; and there refreshment is and strength unfailing" (p. 83). Later in the same context he quotes apparently from memory different New Testament statements incorporating parts of verses from Romans 1:21–23, denying that he followed in the footsteps of the Egyptians and had fixed his mind upon their idols, "changing the truth of God into a lie and worshipping and serving a creature rather than the Creator" (p. 144). He goes on to relate how by turning within himself he was enabled to see that God is " 'I am who am' . . . and there was from that moment no ground of doubt in me: I would more easily have doubted my own life than have doubted that truth is: which is clearly seen, being understood by the things that are made" (p. 145). Here he again cites Romans 1:20. In chapter XV of the *Confessions* Augustine says, "And I looked upon other things, and I saw that they owed their being to You, and that all finite things are in You; but in a different manner, being in You not as in a place, but because You are and hold all things in the hand of Your truth; and all things are true inasmuch as they are" (p. 148). This method of reaching God is expressed in detail when he says:

> I was altogether certain that Your *invisible things are clearly seen from the creation of the world, being understood by the things that are made*; so too are Your everlasting power and Your Godhead . . . Enquiring then what was the source of my judgment, when I did so judge I had discovered the immutable and true eternity of truth above my changing mind. Thus by stages I passed from bodies to the soul which uses the body for its perceiving, and from this to the soul's inner power, to which the body's senses present external things, as indeed the beasts are able; and from there I passed on to the reasoning power, to which is referred for judgment what is received from the body's senses. This too realized that it was mutable in me, and rose to its own understanding. It withdrew my thought from its habitual way, abstracting from the confused crowds of phantasms that it might find what light suffused it, when with utter certainty it cried aloud that the immutable was to be preferred to the mutable, and how it had come to know the immutable itself; for if it had not come to some knowledge of the immutable, it could not have known it as certainly preferable to the mutable. Thus in the thrust of a trembling glance my mind arrived at That Which is. Then indeed I saw clearly Your *invisible things which are understood by the things that are made*; but I lacked the strength to hold my gaze fixed, and my weakness was beaten back again so that I returned to my old habits, bearing nothing with me but a memory of delight and a desire as for something of which I had caught the fragrance but which I had not yet the strength to eat (p. 149–150).

It is evident that Augustine would disagree with Dr. Penton for his contention that "We know that 'God is love' not through reason but rather, through revelation" for Augustine says:

And indeed heaven and earth and all that is in them tell me wherever I look that I should love you, and they cease not to tell it to all men, so that there is no excuse for them... And what is this God? I asked the earth and it answered: "I am not He"; and all things that are in the earth made the same confession. I asked the sea and the deeps and the creeping things, and they answered: "We are not your God; seek higher." I asked the winds that blow, and the whole air with all that is in it answered: "Anaximenes was wrong; I am not God." I asked the heavens, the sun, the moon, the stars, and they answered: "Neither are we God whom you seek." And I said to all the things that throng about the gateways of the senses: Tell me of my God, since you are not he. Tell me something of Him." And they cried out in a great voice: "He made us." My question was my gazing upon them, and their answer was their beauty... Man can interrogate it (the earth) and so should be able clearly to see *the invisible things of God understoond by things which are made* (p. 215–216)

An obvious *proof* of the existence of God is also given in the *Confessions* when Augustine says:

We look upon the heavens and the earth, and they cry aloud that they were made. For they change and vary. (If anything was not made and yet exists, there is nothing in it that was not there before: and it is the essence of change and variation that something should be that was not there before.) They cry aloud, too, that they did not make themselves. "We exist because we were made; but we did not exist before we existed to be able to give ourselves existence." And their visible presence is itself the voice with which they speak (p. 264).

Such a proof is a condensed example of a proof from causality. The heavens and the earth are, they exist (fact of experience); they cry aloud that they were made. Why? Because they change and vary, and whatever changes and varies needs a cause to bring about that change and nothing can cause its own existence.

There are many other places in the writings of Augustine which utilize the text from Romans to substantiate his expressed conviction that one can and does acquire a knowledge of the existence and of the invisible characteristics of God by means of the application of human reason to the facts of experience. In Tractate II, 4 "On the Gospel of St. John" he says:

> "But truly there have been some philosophers of this world who have
> sought for the Creator by means of the creature; for He can be found by
> means of the creature, as the apostle plainly says, "For the invisible things of
> Him from the creation of the world are clearly seen, being understood by the
> things that are made, even His eternal power and glory; so they are without
> excuse." And it follows, "Because that, when they knew God;" he did not
> say, "Because they did not know," but "Because that, when they knew God,
> they Glorified Him not as God."[18]

The same text is quoted by Augustine and the same comments made in
Tractate XIV, 3.

In "On The Spirit And The Letter"[19] there is a lengthy commentary on
Romans and C. 19 is entitled "The Knowledge of God through the
Creation." In it he states:

> For the wrath of God... is revealed from heaven against all ungodliness and
> unrighteousness of men, who hold down the truth in unrighteousness;
> because that which may be known of God is manifest in them: for God hath
> showed it unto them. For the invisible things of Him are clearly seen from
> the creation of the world, being understood through the things that are
> made, even His eternal power and divinity; so that they are without excuse;
> ... Observe, he does not say that they were ignorant of the truth, but that
> they held down the truth in unrighteousness. For it occurred to him (Paul),
> that he would inquire whence the knowledge of the truth could be obtained
> by those to whom God had not given the law; and he was not silent on the
> source whence they could have obtained it: for he declares that it was
> through visible works of creation that they arrived at the knowledge of the
> invisible attributes of the Creator. And, in very deed, as they continued to
> possess great faculties for searching, so they were able to find.

There are many other places in Augustine which attest to his respect
for philosophy and natural human reason as the handmaid of revealed
theology.[20] I think that a careful reading of the works of Augustine show
that he did develop a natural theology which is not only a logical prelude
to his Biblical Theology but a useful instrument, even a necessary one, in
the understanding of the contents of the special revelation contained in
the Word of God. The *De Trinitate*, especially, shows the limitations of
that natural theology regarding the basic dogmas of faith concerning the
Trinity, Incarnation, and Redemption etc. In these areas a special revela-

tion is absolutely necessary for a knowledge of what is to be believed, though human reason is of help in the attempt to understand the content believed.

In the arena of discussion about natural theology the position and weapons of Thomas Aquinas are, perhaps, better known than those of any other antagonist, especially among those on the Catholic side. It is significant that Aquinas begins his presentation of Sacred Science by an inquiry into the problem of "Whether, Besides the Philosophical Sciences, any further Doctrine is Required?"[21] The second argument on the negative side contends that "everything that is, is considered in the philosophical sciences, even God Himself; so that there is a part of philosophy called theology, or the divine science, as is clear from Aristotle. Therefore, besides the philosophical sciences any other doctrine seems superfluous."[22] As Aquinas views the problem, then, it is not whether there is a philosophical or natural theology, but, rather, whether there is a need for a *revealed* theology. His students have already acquired a knowledge of the philosophical disciplines including theology; is there a need for a Sacred Doctrine?[23] In his reply to that question, Aquinas states that "it was necessary for man's salvation that, besides the philosophical disciplines which are investigated by human reason, there be a doctrine according to divine revelation." The basic reason for a revealed theology is that "man is ordered to God as to an end (goal) that exceeds the comprehension of reason." If one does not know this, one may not take advantage of the means necessary to reach that end. Though salvation is not restricted only to those who have accepted a divine revelation, "in order that salvation may come to pass in men more suitably and certainly it was necessary that they be instructed about divine things by divine revelation." And in the reply to the second negative argument Aquinas explains that sciences are distinguished by their different points of view, what is technically called by the scholastics their different "formal objects." Hence there is no prohibition that the same things can be treated by the philosophical disciplines, insofar as they are known by the light of natural reason, and by another science, insofar as they are known by the light of divine revelation. As a matter of fact each discipline should be helpful to the other rather than segregated in unrelated compartments.

With this point of departure let us investigate the contents of Aquinas' natural or philosophical theology. First of all he points out in the *Summa Theologiae* (Q.2) that the existence of God can be proved in five ways, in each case by means of a *demonstration quia*, that is, by a demonstration that begins with what is more known to us, for example an effect, what comes into existence, and proceeds by means of the principle of causality, to a knowledge of the existence of the cause of the effect. This type of demonstration has also been called an inductive demonstration or proof in distinction from a deductive demonstration or proof. For Thomas the first question to ask about something is *an est*, does it exist? If that question is answered affirmatively, then one can inquire about what it is. Being convinced that human reason can and does prove the existence of God as the pure act of existing, from things or events in the realm of human experience, Aquinas proceeds to show that from the same source one can derive many attributes of God.

First he considers the simplicity of God (Q.3). He argues that God is an absolutely simple being, that is, involving no complexity or composition of parts, because wherever there is a composition the parts composed are related as potentiality and act and God is pure act, i.e., contains no passive potentiality. Thus God is not a body, does not have quantitative parts, is not composed of matter and form, His individual substance does not differ from His essence or nature, His essence and existence are the same, God is not in a genus, a class of beings, with others, in God there are no accidents and God cannot enter into composition with anything else so that God is a part of something else or something else is a part of God.

God is shown to be absolutely perfect (Q.4) because a thing is said to be perfect in proportion to its actuality and God is total, complete, pure actuality. God is good (QQ.5,6) because the good is what is desirable, the desirable is such insofar as it is perfect, the perfect is such insofar as it is actual, and God is purely actual as *Ipsum Esse*. God is not just a good but goodness itself in all its perfection. God is infinite (Q.7) because the principles of limitation can be considered either as matter as regards form or form as regards a limit of matter. Again finitude may be considered as related to potentiality: what is finite is potential in some restricted way as regards the potentiality to be or act in a certain way. None of these types can apply to God who is not a body involving matter and form and not involved in potentiality in any way. God is not an infinite magnitude because any magnitude would either be a natural or mathematical one. God is not a natural magnitude because such is a body. He is not a mathematical magnitude because such would have some figure or shape which involves the quantitative. God is "outside" any limitation whatsoever.

Thomas shows that God is not only transcendent as being itself, "outside" and "above" in dignity and perfection all other things, "the wholly other," but He is also immanent, (Q.8) God with us, because He is the agent giving us existence and preserving us in existence. He is the immediate and necessary cause of our being and the being of everything else. An effect depends on a cause in the precise respect in which the cause is the cause. God is the immediate cause of our being. If He left us, we could not continue to be. If God were not immanent to us and all other things, nothing would be in a created world. For the same reason God can be said to be everywhere, not as confined to a place but He is wherever anything is, by His power, by His presence, by His essence. God is immutable because in Him there is no potentiality for change, since He is pure act (Q.9). He is eternal (Q.10) because as First Cause and wholly immutable He has no beginning, no end, and no succession of any kind. God is simultaneously complete and perfect in the possession of unending life. No other thing can be eternal in the sense of being absolutely immutable with no beginning of any kind and no possibility of change.

Aquinas shows (Q.11) that unity can be applied to God because unity involves the notion of being undivided and since God is absolutely simple He is undivided both actually and potentially. There can be only one God, because if there were more than one God, each would be identical in essence, since each is considered as God, and each would differ from the other gods, because each has its own act of existing whereby each would differ, i.e., be more than one. In each one essence would differ from existence. Hence none of the so-called Gods would be God, because in God essence and existence are the same. No created intellect by its natural powers can see the divine essence (Q. 12). There is a discussion in Q. 13 of the names we use to talk about God. Since we know God from creatures by way of excellence and remotion, any name which is originally constructed by human persons to express human knowledge of things, is applied to God in either of two ways. If the name signifies a characteristic which does not involve a limitation in itself, such as wise, that name may be applied to God analogously as indicative of the excellence of wisdom; if a name signifies what is limited in itself, such as mobile or finite, it can only be applied by adding a negative prefix or suffix, such as im-mobile or in-finite or change-less.

Is God personal (QQ.14–20)? Proceeding analogously from our knowledge of what characterizes a human person Thomas understands that immateriality is the basis of knowledge acquired by intellect, and that since God is absolutely immaterial He is intellectual knowledge. God knows Himself and all other things without any discursiveness whatever. Since God is an intellectual being, He also possesses will, which is free as regards all activities related to creatures. Since love in persons is naturally the first act of will and since there is will in God, which is the same as His essence, God is Love Itself.[24]

Hence being personal, as regards God insofar as He can be known by natural reason, means that we can refer truly to God as a Being who possesses life which involves intellectual knowledge and free will and love. God is a personal being. However, any conviction that God is Three Persons in One Being depends upon a special divine revelation. If one stresses knowledge, God may be said to be Truth Itself and the source of all truth; if one stresses will, God may be said to be Love and the source of all good. In the area of distributive justice, which is displayed in the order of the universe, God can be said to be just, but not in the area of commutative justice, which relates to buying and selling, and other kinds of exchange.

Thomas shows that the God he has come to know by natural reason is not a deistic type, an uncaring, absentee God, but one who has care for His creatures (Q.22). Divine providence is the intellectual plan in the mind of God, the model of all creatures as ordered to their ends or purposes. The execution of the order of Divine Providence is called Divine Government. Providence is eternal; government is temporal.

Since power is directly related to an active principle, and since God is pure act, absolutely and without any limitation, He is all-powerful (Q.25). This doesn't mean that He can make a square-circle or donkey-man or any contradiction, because these are absolute impossibles and no-things. God is omnipotent because he can do all *things* that are possible absolutely, i.e. whose characteristics are not contradictory or where a predicate is compatible with the subject. So "whatsoever has or can have the essential elements of a being is numbered among the absolute possibles in respect of which God is called omnipotent." God is known as Creator because He is the First Cause of all beings other than Himself (Q.2). This does not mean that God is first in a line of causes stretching out in time, but that He is First in the order of Being, value, dignity, the Source of all other things and values. The question of God as Creator is taken up later in the *Summa Theologiae* (Q.44) where Thomas employs the notion of participation. "It must be said that every being, that is in any way, is from God. For whatever is found in anything by participation must be caused in it by that to which it belongs essentially... Now it has been shown above, when treating of the divine simplicity, that God is self-subsisting being itself, and also that subsisting being can be only one... Therefore, all beings, other than God, are not their own being but are diversified by the diverse participation of being, so as to be more or less perfect, are caused by one First Being, who possesses being most perfectly." Thomas gives a precise meaning to creation (Q. 45) by pointing out that creation is the emanation of all being from the universal cause, which is God. Such an emanation is not necessary but free. To be more exact about the meaning of creation Thomas emphasizes that the emanation of all beings presupposes *non-being* which is *nothing*. The emanation which is called creation is the free production of something by God from nothing where "from" does not refer to a material cause, something worked on to give it a new structure, but only an order of what is now to its previous non-being. A creature is "made from nothing", i.e., it is not made from anything.

Presented in a very superficial way the above tells us of many of the "invisible things" of God that are contained in the natural theology of Thomas Aquinas. In addition to the references to the *Letter to the Romans* scattered throughout his writings, he also wrote a *Commentary on Romans*. It is considered to have been written sometime between 1259–65 whereas the *Summa Theologiae* Part I is assigned to the years 1269–70.[25] If this is the exact chronology, the contents of the *Summa Theologiae* presented above should be an illustration in detail of the principles expressed in the *Commentary*. Let us see if that is the case.

Thomas comments that when Paul says, "quod notum est" (v. 19), "what is known," he agrees that the wise Gentiles *knew* (my emphasis) the truth about God. Secondly, he indicates from whom they accepted this kind of knowledge, "For God revealed it to them." In the third place, he presents the means by which, the invisibles of God are revealed. Therefore he says, firstly, that rightly (Paul) says that they held back the truth of God, for it was in them insofar as there was a true knowledge of something of God, because what was known of God, i.e., what is knowable by reason about God by man is manifested in them; it is manifested in them from the fact that there is in them an intrinsic light. Therefore we must know that something about God is entirely unknown to man in this life, namely *what* God is... because man's knowledge begins from those things which are connatural to him, namely, from sensible creatures, which are not proportioned to the representation of the divine essence. However, man can from these creatures know God in a three-fold way...indeed in one way *per causalitatem*: because natural creatures are defectible and mutable they must be reduced to an immobile and perfect principle and in this manner it is known that God is;[26] *per viam excellentiae* all creatures are reduced to a first principle not as to a proper and univocal cause as man generates man but as to a common and more excellent cause; *per viam negationis* because the finite and limited characteristics of creatures are denied of God. Just as art is manifested by the works of the artist, the wisdom of God is manifested by his creatures, not by sense or imagination but by the intellect. Then when he says, "God manifested it to them" he points out by what author the knowledge was manifested to them... God, indeed, in a two-fold way manifested something to man: one way by infusing the interior light by means of which man knows... In another way by proposing exterior signs of his wisdom namely sensible creatures. Thus therefore God manifested it to them by infusing the interior light and by proposing exteriorly visible creatures in whom, as in a certain book, the knowledge of God is read. The essence of God is designated in a plural fashion by the word "invisibles" because the essence in itself is not known according to what it is in itself, as it is one. However, it is manifested to us by certain similitudes found in creatures and thus the unity of the divine essence is known under the notions of goodness, wisdom, and the like. Something else is known about God, namely His power as evident by the fact things proceed from Him as from a source. The divinity of God is said to be known insofar as they knew God as the last end toward which all things tend. For the divine good is considered as the common good in which all participate; because of this Paul says divinity, which signifies participation rather than deity which signifies the essence of God... The invisibles of God are known by the way of negation, his everlasting power by the way of causality, the divinity by way of excellence... When it is said, 'a creatura mundi' (v. 20) in one way man can be understood. In another way it can be understood as referring to the whole of creation. In another way it can be understood as the creation of things, as if it were said, 'from the creation of the world' which can be understood that from the creation of the world man began to know God by means of those things which have been made. It is possible that this commentary be taken as a blueprint for the development of a natural theology by Aquinas. The *Commentary* does lack something of the clarity, precision, and detail of the later *Summa Theologiae*, which is characteristic of the difference between these two types of works. Nevertheless the basic point comes over clear that one can know a lot about God by natural reason by means of the way of causality, negation, and excellence.

Vatican Council I is very clear in its statement, in agreement with St. Paul, that God can be known by natural reason:

> Holy Mother the Church holds and teaches that God, the beginning and end of all things, can be known with certitude from created things by the natural light of human reason for the invisible things of Him are seen being understood from the creation of the world through those things which are made. (Romans 1:20)... If anyone has said that the one and true God, our creator and Lord, cannot be known by the natural light of human reason through those things which have been made, let him be anathema.[27]

Some have tried to avoid the obvious meaning and purpose of the declaration by the Council by contending that the Council states that *"Deum certo cognosci posse,"* that God *can* be known with certitude but that the Council does not contend that anyone has ever done so.[28] Such a clumsy attempt at semantical evasion is quite inaccurate when one reads St. Paul carefully and notes that he is quoted by the Council. One of Paul's basic points is not that "the wrath of God is revealed from heaven upon the irreligiousness and unrighteousness" of those men who were just *able* to know God but upon those who "held back the truth of God in unrighteousness." Paul is obviously saying that "they are inexcusable" because "God manifested to them his invisible characteristics even His everlasting power and divinity and they transferred this information to the likeness of the image of corruptible men and birds and four-footed animals and serpents."

It is evident that Augustine and Thomas Aquinas were not just *able* to know the existence of God and some of His attributes, but they actually developed a very formal natural theology. Semantically and logically one cannot conclude from "posse" (can be) to "esse" (to be, is) or from "cognosci posse" (can be known) to "cognoscitur" (is known), but the scholastics generally admitted, as everyone should, that from "esse ad posse valet illatio" (the inference from to be, [is] to, to be able, [can], is valid). Because men have developed a knowledge of the existence of God and of some of His attributes by the use of human reason applied to the facts of experience without any special revelation, it is quite obvious that such knowledge *can* be acquired.

If one consults Martin Luther's interpretation of the passage in Paul's

Letter to the Romans, one finds that Luther agrees with Paul about the actual fulfillment of the natural possibility of knowing the existence of God and His power and Divinity from a contemplation of the created universe. In his *Lectures on Romans* Luther admits the natural knowledge of God and the *real* actual possibility of a natural theology.[29] He states in the "Glosses" that the wrath of God is revealed from heaven "against all ungodliness on account of their turning from the true God, and wickedness, on account of their turning to idol worship..." (p. 9). He adds:

> But that they have had the truth of God and have held it back he now shows. 19. *For what is known of God*, that is, the knowledge of and about God, *is manifest in them*, that is, they have this manifestation about Him in themselves, *because God has shown it to them*, that is, He has shown them amply how they may recognize Him, namely as follows: 20. *For the invisible* things, such as goodness, wisdom, righteousness, etc., *of Him, ever since the creation of the world*, that is, since the act of creation, *by the things that have been made*, that is from the works, that when they see that there are works, they also recognize that a Creator is necessary, *are clearly seen*, perceived not by the senses but by the understanding, *His eternal power also*, His strength, for this His works declare, *and deity*, that is, that He really is God. *So they are without excuse*, as much those who have thus sinned knowingly in the first place as those whom they have made their followers through such great ignorance." (p. 9–10)

Later in the "Scholia" he comments,

> 19. *What is known about God.* This is a Greek way of expressing what might be better translated in our language in an abstract way; "the known things of God," that is, "the knowledge of God,"...20. *From the creation.* Some people (and, if I am not mistaken, also the writer of the *Sentences*, Book I, Distinction II)[30] interpret this to mean: "By the creature of the world," that is, by man, "God's invisible things are seen." But this can be rejected easily on the basis of the Greek text, where we read: "Ever since the creation of the world," or as Matt. 25:34 has it: "From the foundation of the world," or this way: "From the creation of the world" (that is "ever since the creation of the world," not only from the present time on) it has always been true that God's invisible nature is seen and recognized in His works... Therefore the meaning is: Even if the wise of this world did not perceive the creation of the world, they could have recognized the invisible things of God from the works of the created world" (p. 154).

Again Luther:

19. *Because God has shown it to them.* With these words Paul makes it clear that also all gifts of nature must be credited to God as the Giver. The fact that he is speaking here of the natural knowledge of God is clear from the following addition, in which he shows how God has manifested Himself to men, namely thus (v. 20): *For the invisible things of Him ever since the creation of the world are clearly seen in the things that have been made* (these things are recognized in a natural way by their effects), that is, from the beginning of the world it has always been true that the "invisible things of God, etc." He states this so no one should quibble and say that only in our time could God be known. He could be, and can be known from the beginning of the world (p. 156).

In his *Commentary on Romans*[31] the Lutheran Anders Nygren seems to have some ideas of his own on the problem at hand. As I understand his interpretation the natural knowledge of God expressed by Paul refers only to those who are worthy of the wrath of God because they have turned to ungodliness and unrighteousness. A natural knowledge of God does not lead to a positive approach to God. He says:

Romans 1:20 is one of the places in the New Testament which has been subject to the worst misunderstanding. From what Paul says about God's self-revelation to the Gentiles men have sought to educe an entire "natural theology" or "natural religion." But Paul has also been misunderstood by those who deny that there is any natural theology in his thought. We must give further attention to this matter. Is it proper in any sense to speak of a "natural theology" or a "natural knowledge of God" in Paul? Before we can answer that question we must examine the problem which confronts us in the concept of a natural knowledge of God. Belief that man is able to attain to knowledge of God grew up outside of Christianity and in a wholly different climate of thought. When this view is confronted with God's revelation in Christ, the question arises as to the relation between the natural knowledge of God and the divine revelation mediated through Christ... It is clear that he (Paul) cannot be made an advocate for any sort of natural theology or natural religion in the accepted meaning of these terms... They who have thought that he did understood his words thus because they came to him with their own concept of natural theology... We are left in the dark about the apostle's purpose. He tells how God through Christ has, in the new aeon, revealed a new righteousness and thereby bestowed life on us. But, formerly, in the old aeon, the wrath of God was revealed from heaven against all unrighteousness. It is in connection with this declaration about the wrath of God that verse 20 speaks... In so far as he touches the question of a natural knowledge of God, he does not do so with the positive intent of declaring that natural man is possessed of the ability to come to a knowledge of God. As to that his thought is found clearly stated in I Corinthians 2:14; the natural or "psychic" man cannot understand the truth about God (p. 105).

However, it seems to me, the statements in Corinthians here are not concerned with the problem of a natural knowledge of God but with the contrast of a sensual man and the perceiving of the Spirit of God. What Nygren skirts is that man can be without excuse only if he has the ability to know God as God and then makes God into a lesser reality or image of a lesser reality. One must know and misuse before being guilty of the wrath of God.

> Paul *touches* the problem of the "natural knowledge of God." But does he actually get into it? It is certainly not his idea that "the natural man" has the ability to find his own way to God. What is the result when the man who has turned away from God would be pious and Godfearing? Paul answers that such a man searches creation and turns to the worship of idols. Paul never says that the natural man finds the marks of God in nature. That idea, imposed on his words by 'natural theology' is quite opposed to his meaning (p. 106).

It is quite obvious that Nygren's interpretation of Paul hinges on Nygren's conviction that a natural knowledge of God is only relative to the wrath of God or what is deserving of the wrath of God. To be sure it is obvious in Paul that the 'natural man' cannot come to God in the sense of being justified by his own knowledge or acts. But it is difficult to understand how a man "who has turned away from God" could be "pious and Godfearing" and would turn to the worship of idols. If it is true that "Paul never says that the natural man finds the marks of God in nature" I wonder about whom Paul is talking in Romans 1:18–21. Moreover, it seems to me that Nygren's statement conflicts with what Luther says in his treatment of those verses. Nygren continues his understanding of Paul:

> It is thus easy to see why Paul can have no dealings with "natural theol-ogy,"... Natural theology assumes a deistic view. It postulates a God who, after creation, withdrew from the world and concealed himself behind that which He had made. And it looks upon men as left to themselves and desiring nothing more than to find God by means of the evidence of Him

which creation bears; for they worship and serve Him (p. 107).

This is a very poetic view of deism, but I do not agree that all forms of natural theology are deistic. This may be the case with the people whom Nygren knew to advocate a "natural theology," but deism is not essential to natural theology, as is evident in the natural theology of Augustine, Aquinas, and Luther.

Karl Barth's interpretation of a natural knowledge of God is conditioned by his general view of the role of knowledge and of the fallen nature of man regarding his knowledge of God. If human reason were vitiated by the fall, it would be impossible for a man to discover the truth about God through his own efforts. Now such a consequence follows if "the truth about God" is the truth of God revealed in the Scriptures and, especially, in Jesus Christ. But the fact of the fall of man does not destroy human reason so that it can no longer function as reason. If such were the case, Paul would seem to have no justification for his contention that men before and during the dissemination of the "Good News" of Christianity, "from the creation of the world his invisible attributes are clearly seen— his everlasting power and divinity—being understood through the things that are made." Granted that Paul does not contend that these people knew that God is Creator in the precise sense, he does assert forcefully that men can and did know about God "from the creation of the world."

It seems to be a general opinion that Karl Barth did not accept a natural theology. In his work *Anselm: Fides Quaerens Intellectum*[32] he appears to contend that theology is "Faith Seeking Understanding" and thus could not be natural, if by natural one means knowledge preceding Faith. In *Credo*[33] Barth contends that it is "by faith that we understand that the worlds were fashioned by the Word of God" (p. 29) and that "the Reader of the Old and New Testaments remembers that in this book the Church has up to now heard God's Word" (p. 177). If this is the case a natural or philosophical theology is impossible and superfluous (p. 183–186). Barth does not accept the concept of a natural theology because theology cannot be carried on within "an edifice of thought constructed on certain fundamental conceptions which are selected in accordance with a certain philosophy by a method which corresponds to these conceptions. Theology cannot be carried on in confinement or under the pressure of such a construction. The subject of theology is the history of the communion of God with man and of man with God. This history is proclaimed, in ancient times and today, in the Old and New Testaments... The subject of theology is, in this sense, the "Word of God."[34] It is quite clear that "theology" for Barth means "Biblical Theology" and more especially "Christian Theology," and as such cannot tolerate the adjectives natural or philosophical. As he says, "... there would perhaps be no theology at all, unless the Church's task consisted centrally in the proclamation of the Gospel in witness to the Word spoken by God" (p. 11). "If one would trust in... the gods set up, honored and worshipped by men in ancient and recent times: the authorities on whom man relies, no matter whether they have the form of ideas or any sort of powers of destiny, no matter what they are called... Faith delivers us from trust in such gods" (p. 19). Barth further emphasizes that "God is hidden from us outside His Word. But He is manifest to us in Jesus Christ" (p. 20). These statements may be difficult to reconcile with Romans 1:19–20 unless one qualifies "God" with the adjective Christian as referring only to God, Father, Son, and Holy Spirit. Paul seems to say that one can have some kind of accurate knowledge of God prior to and/or distinct from the Christian faith whereas Barth identifies faith and knowledge (p. 23, 25) and qualifies his concept of knowledge of God:

> Of course it is of the nature and being of this object, of God the Father, the Son, and the Holy Spirit, that He cannot be known by the powers of human knowledge, but is apprehensible and apprehended solely because of His own freedom, decision and action. What man can know by his own power according to the measure of his natural powers, his understanding, his feeling, will be at most something like a supreme being, an absolute nature, the nature, the idea of an utterly free power, of a being towering over everything. This absolute and supreme being, the ultimate and most profound, this "thing in itself" has nothing to do with God. It is part of the intuitions and marginal possibilities of man's thinking, man's contrivance. Man is able to think this being; but he has not thereby thought God. God is thought and known when in His own freedom God makes himself apprehensible... God is always the One who has made Himself known to man in His own revelation, and not the one man thinks out for himself and describes as God. There is a perfectly clear division there already, epistemologically, between the true God and the false gods. Knowledge of God is not a possibility which is open for discussion.

I am not contending that, in opposition to Barth, man can know independently of Christian revelation that God is Father, Son, and Holy Spirit. But it is at least possible that man can know "by his own power that there is a supreme being and that that being is not a false god but a being of everlasting power and Divinity and Creator," what Paul states in Romans 1:19–20. Moreover, Paul is stating that that knowledge of God is authentic and can be acquired and, with the exception of God as creator in the strict sense of the source of *creatio ex nihilo*, such knowledge has already been acquired. In contrast Barth says "Knowledge of God is a knowledge completely effected and determined from the side of its object, from the side of God" and "Knowledge of God takes place where divine revelation takes place, illumination of man by God, transmission of human knowledge, instruction of man by this incomparable Teacher" (p. 24).

For Barth the well-known arguments for the existence of God that have been and are still presented in natural or philosophical theology are humorous and fragile (p. 38). "...God is not only unprovable and unsearchable, but also *inconceivable*." (*ibid.*) Such statements may appear somewhat controvertible coming as they do after he states "When we Christians speak of 'God' we may and must be clear that this word signifies a priori the fundamentally Other" (p. 36), and the Biblical references to "God is love" and "God is Creator." It is even more questionable when Barth says, "He whose nature and essence consists, whose existence is proved, in His descending into the depths... " (p. 40). "Once a man has understood 'God in the highest,' it becomes impossible for him to want any imagery in thought, or any other kind of imagery" (p. 41). It is possible that Barth is using the terms "unprovable" and "unsearchable" and "inconceivable," which have a very definite meaning in philosophy, logic, and traditional theology, in an equivocal way. Even so, this does not help in the clarification of the problem.

When dealing with God the Creator, Barth contends, "When we approach the truth which the Christian Church confesses in the word 'Creator,' then everything depends on our realizing that we find ourselves here as well confronted by the mystery of faith, in respect of which knowledge is real solely through God's revelation" (p. 50). If one admits that God the Creator is solely a mystery of faith and if Barth is using 'mystery' and 'faith' in the sense that it cannot be known otherwise, then by revelation, we have an obvious instance of circular redundancy: what is only known by revelation is only known by revelation. The history of philosophy and theology is not so dogmatic in excluding from the Christian Church those Christians who contend that the knowledge of God the Creator is obtained by direct contemplation of the physical universe, including Paul, Augustine, and Aquinas, to mention just a few. Barth would not react very kindly to the statement of Vatican I, "If anyone has said that the one and true God, our creator and Lord, cannot be known by the natural light of human reason through those things which have been made, let him be anathema." In a very poetic way Barth says, "The world with its sorrow and its happiness will always be a dark mirror to us, about which we may have optimistic or pessimistic thoughts; but it gives no information about God as the Creator." (p. 52)

When we turn to Barth's treatment of The Epistle to the Romans we are somewhat amazed because he does not take up the same questions. As a matter of fact he seems to be oblivious of their importance. Verses 19–20 are passed over without any awareness of their controversial contents. After some preliminary asides Barth states, "We know that God is He whom we do not know, and that our ignorance is precisely the problem and the source of our knowledge... The recognition of the absolute heteronomy under which we stand is itself an autonomous recognition; and this is precisely *that which may be known of God*" (p. 45, 46). In regard to v. 20 "For the invisible things of God are clearly seen," he refers to the fact that "Plato in his wisdom recognized long ago that behind the visible there lies the invisible universe which is the Origin of all concrete things" (p. 46). If this statement is compared with the *Dynamics in Outline*, quoted at great length before, it may stimulate a doubt that the author of the former is the same as the author of the latter. Or is Barth attempting by silence to avoid the apparent teaching of the *Credo* and *Dynamics in Outline* as related to Romans 1:19–20?

Hans Küng asserts what he considers some presuppositions for a valid proof of the existence of God.[36]

1. an immediately evident external or internal experience.
2. methodical reflection and strictly logical deductive thinking.
3. a valid universal metaphysical principle.

I grant that the first one is obviously the only valid starting point, because to conclude to the *existence* of God, the existence of something must be given at the very start of the proof. I think that the second point is quite inaccurate, because the procedure is inductive rather than deductive. The existence of God is not deduced from some universal principle, but by applying a valid metaphysical principle to the fact of experience one is logically compelled to conclude that there is a God. A deductive argument is a means of inferring a conclusion contained in certain premises. But *that God is* is not contained in the premises in a way to be deductively inferred. Starting with an instance of something existing, by means of a metaphysical principle, the principle of causality, a bridge is established from this fact of existence to Existence Itself. Since the principle is metaphysically valid it is applicable to all instances of existing. From finite existing to Existence Itself is a valid transition. So a valid proof starts with existence and ends with existence. How can the positively infinite be implied in the finite? There is no deductive thinking here. But granted the validity of the metaphysical principle one can turn away from the finite, as inadequate to explain its existence, to infinite being, Existence Itself, as the only sufficient ground for the existence of finite being.

Küng's main difficulty seems to be in another area. He asserts (p. 529) "There must be a proof that is... obvious to everyone." If such were a general prerequisite for any proof, *any* proof in mathematics, science, and even, everyday living would be a priori impossible. Such a prerequisite is totally unrealistic. Again (p. 531) he says, "If however all these proofs of God... are supposed to be conclusive, why is not any single one of them *universally accepted*?" (emphasis mine). Again (p. 533), "There is not a single proof that is universally accepted." Again (p. 534), "But a supreme goal (or a supreme order) cannot be proved rationally in a universally convincing way..." Again (p.548), "It cannot be proved in a universally convincing way that God exists." All these Küngian dogmatic pronouncements fail to show that the validity of a proof fundamentally and ultimately and necessarily depends upon its universal acceptance. If such were *the* criterion for a valid proof, there would be an absolute skepticism about the validity of any proof in any area of human thought or activity. The criteria for a valid proof of the existence of anything, including the existence of God, are:

1. a contact with existence in the facts of experience.
2. application of valid metaphysical principles.
3. application of the valid laws of logic.
4. application of the valid laws of Epistemology.

If some existence is a fact, if the metaphysical principles are true, if the valid principles of logic are applied correctly, and if the principles of Epistemology are correctly applied, the conclusion must follow and be true. To consider that these points that are intrinsic to a valid proof are ultimately irrelevant to a proof and that a proof is a proof *only* if there is acceptance, universal or otherwise, is to consider that what makes a proof a proof is really extrinsic to the proof and arbitrarily, i.e., without utilizing the factor of experience and the value of metaphysics, epistemology, and logic, conferred on something. Why is this done? There should be some

reason or reasons. They would not be logical, metaphysical, epistemological or experiential, What could they be?

John Hick employs a similar absolute criterion for the validity of any
proof. He says:[37]

> The existence of God can undoubtedly be proved if proof is equated with a
> formally valid argument... This first sense of "prove" is referred to here
> only to be dismissed as an inconvenient and confusing usage. It is much
> better to follow the more normal practice and to distinguish between an
> argument being valid and its conclusion being true. The validity of an
> argument is a purely formal characteristic of the relation between its constit-
> uent propositions, and does not guarantee the truth of any of them. It
> guarantees that *if* the premises are true the conclusion is true also; but it
> cannot guarantee that the premises, and therefore the conclusion, are true...
> A second sense of "prove" is that in which a conclusion is said to be proved,
> not merely if it follows from premises, but only if it follows from *true*
> premises... It is surely the third sense, in which to prove something means
> to prove it *to* someone, that is really in question when we ask whether the
> existence of God can be proved.

First I would like to clarify a point in formal logic. Actually a "formally
valid argument" can be constructed of false premises as well as with true
ones and in either case the conclusion follows necessarily, and must be
true, if the premises are true, but *may* be true or false, if the premises are
false.

It is obvious that Hick and Küng both consider that the main characteristic, the absolutely essential one, of a proof for the existence of God is
extrinsic to the proof itself and based totally on extrinsic acceptance. If
Küng and Hick are attempting to prove that acceptance is essential to any
proof, I think the argument is self-destructive. If I accept what Küng and
Hick say in their argument that acceptance is the essential factor without
which there is no proof, I could refute their argument, in a way they
assert is valid, by merely asserting that I don't accept their argument in
this context and therefore their argument is not universally accepted and
therefore not probative at all. Of course it is a truism to say that if an
argument doesn't convince me, I don't accept it. But then it would be
intelligent to ask why does the argument not convince me. What does
one require in order that a "proof" would convince? Again, the response
could only be in terms of something that is extrinsic to the proof itself,
something extra-logical, extra-metaphyscial, extra-epistemological, and
extra-experiential.

Many of the problems connected with Romans 1:18–21 are directly related to the semantics of the contents and their relation to the overall message of Romans. I would like, therefore, to concentrate a little on the area of semantics, especially v. 18. Paul states that the wrath (*órgē—ira*) of God from heaven is revealed upon all impiety (*asebeian—impietatem*) and injustice (*adikian—iniustitiam*) of those men who hold back or suppress (*katechontōn—detinent*) the truth of God in injustice or unrighteousness (*en adikia—in iniustitia*). The wrath of God is a metaphorical expression of the displeasure of God regarding what some men do and that God has withheld any positive relationship with those who suppress the truth of God "in injustice or unrighteousness." Thus there is introduced the reason why God is angry with some men and why later God allows them to sink to idol worship and immoralities of all kinds (v. 21–23). Note that it is *not* a fact that some men become idol worshippers *because* they develop a natural knowledge of God, as some interpreters contend, but because they suppress the truth of God in ungodliness and unrighteousness. The reason why the wrath of God is revealed upon them is (v. 19) because what is known of God (*quod notum est dei—to gnōston tou theou*) is clear to them, (*Manifestum est in illis—phaneron estin en autois*), for God manifested it to them (*Deus enim illis manifestavit—o theos gar autois ephanerōsen*). Here there is some dispute about the meaning of *what is known (gnōston—quod notum est)*. The Greek and Latin both use the past participle of the verb to know, which indicates that Paul says, "what is known," but, as some contend, this would be redundant in connection with "manifest" (*phaneron—manifestum*) and so it must be rendered as *what can be known*. But it may be that Paul means just what he says. He is not saying that the wrath of God is revealed upon those who suppress the truth in unrighteousness because they were *able* to know God, but that they *knew* God and this was evident to them because God had manifested it to them. God manifested it in the things that He made for they mirror the Divine Artist and by giving man an interior light by which he knew this. So what was known of God is clear to them because God manifested or made it clear to them.[38] And how did God manifest it to them? For his invisible attributes (*aorata autou—invisibilia ipsius*) from the creation of the world (*a creatione mundi—apo ktiseōs kosmou*) are clearly seen (*conspiciuntur— kathoratai*) by means of the things which have been made (*per ea quae facta sunt—tois poiēmasin*), also his everlasting power and divinity (*sempiterna quoque eius virtus et divinitas—ē te aidios autou dunamis kai theiotēs*). So they are inexcusable (*ita ut sint inexcusabiles—eis to einai autous anapologētous*).

To return now to the statements of Dr. Penton quoted at the beginning of this paper, I would like to point out, first, that his use of the word 'naturalistic' as descriptive of the approach of certain Christians to their religion is inappropriate, if one takes the term in its usual meaning in philosophy and religion. The suffixes "ism" and "istic" usually refer to any system, doctrine, theory, etc., that is considered as inferior, disparaged, discredited, belittled. "To disparage is to attempt to lower in esteem, as by insinuation, invidious comparison, faint praise."[38] In philosophy 'naturalistic' involves the denial of the supernatural and spiritual creation; in religion it denies divine revelation and contends that all religious truth may be derived from the natural world.[39]

I do not think that it is true, also, to state that an attempt to understand God through a rational study of the physical universe assumes that "He (God) is not transcendent or 'wholly other.' " The Christians who do attempt to acquire a knowledge of the invisible characteristics of God "from the creation of the world" even God's "everlasting power and deity (divinity)" stress the transcendence of God and the fact that the Divine Artist does mirror something of Himself in His products. God is considered as "wholly other" and also immanent. One does not have to deny that "God is with us" in order to say that God is "wholly other," since the statements consider God from different aspects that are simultaneously true.

I fail to see how a natural theology could not take into consideration "the imperfection of the world since the Fall" providing that the Fall does not vitiate the very nature of the physical universe. The created world is always imperfect both before and after the Fall, since it is created. Yet when it was created God saw that it was good and every creature is perfect in its own kind. The Fall of man from friendship with God does not destroy any natural perfection from the sun, moon, stars, planets, including the earth with its rivers, fish, birds, animals, and men. The grace of personal friendship with God was lost by the Fall, but that is not a natural perfection, but supernatural. The loss of this grace may make it more difficult to see God in his works, but it does not make that impossible.

I am at a loss to understand how one can talk about the "exceeding sinfulness of sin," except in an exaggerated mythological way. 'Sin' is a word that is privative in meaning; it refers to a lack of what should be. How a lack could be full of sin, a lack full of exceeding lacks is a puzzle to me.

I cannot understand how a natural theology "denies the fundamental Pauline doctrine of the spiritual adoption of the individual Christian and the inner testimony of the Holy Spirit."(Romans 8) The doctrine of the spiritual adoption of the individual Christian concerns a supernatural activity of God whereby a Christian becomes an adopted son of God and brother of Jesus Christ. It seems to me that such a situation would make the Christian better able to perceive the "Hand of God" in the formation of the universe and some of the characteristics of the Artist. On the other side the natural knowledge of the "invisible attributes" of God could help man approach closer to a Being of "everlasting power and deity (divinity)." How a natural theology could deny "the inner testimony of the holy spirit" is beyond me, even if one adopts the negative view of some Christians that the natural knowledge of God is that which draws down from heaven the wrath of God, because it leads to ungodliness and unrighteousness. Paul does not say that all people who have known God, from those things which have been made, have suppressed the truth of God in unrighteousness. What he does say is "We see divine retribution revealed from heaven upon all the godless wickedness of men of those who suppress the truth of God in unrighteousness." So it is not all who search for God in nature that are worthy of the wrath of God but only those who have suppressed the truth of God in unrighteousness.

Moreover, though Dr. Penton claims that "we know that God is love not through reason, but rather, through revelation and the testimony of the spirit," we have seen that there are some who know that God is love by contemplating the great gifts that He has given them in the universe. Also, though Dr. Penton may *believe* in the transcendent nature of God and *feel* that He is "wholly other" and *feel* that God can be known only through revelation, there is a strong suspicion that these statements or affections are not compatible with the explicit statements of Paul in Romans 1:18–21.

The discussion of the contents of Romans 1:18–21 and their meaning for or against a natural theology or philosophical theology or a proof for the existence of God and nature of God has been carried on by people who consider that Romans 1:18–21 is an authentic part of the *Good News* of Christianity. It is accepted as part of the word of God. It is considered to be an inspired statement based on faith whose truth is guaranteed by God in some way. It is considered as something to be believed. But if one would bracket this belief and accept the statements of Paul in Romans 1:18–21 as statements of an individual living at a certain time in history expressing his intellectual conviction that one can and does know that there is a God of everlasting power and divinity, some of whose invisible characteristics can be known by intellectual activity, then Paul's statements may be considered to have even greater and broader force and persuasive power for those who do not admit that the Bible contains a special form of revelation to men. I mean that it would no longer be necessary to restrict the force of the argument to those who *believe* in Romans as expressive of the word of God in some special way. If I am a Christian believer I must believe that I do not have to believe that there is a God; I can know it by human reason by contemplating the things in the universe. Armed with the natural knowledge of God I am in a position to evaluate any claim for a special revelation made by that God. Without a natural means to know that there is a God, would any belief in a revelation made by an unknown God be based on a blind act of faith that may entail some serious psychological difficulties as to the way one may distinguish the authentic revelation from a spurious one?[40]

NOTES

1. The conference was sponsored by the Unification Theological Seminary.

2. *The New English Bible: New Testament*, Oxford University Press, Cambridge University Press, 1961, p. 256. In the Revised Standard Version and others these verses are indicated as 18–20. In fact 15 seems to be a typing error.

3. This may be *Confessions* Bk. 10, 6, ff. or 17, 17. John Gibb and William Montgomery in *The Confessions of Augustine*, Cambridge University Press, 2nd ed. 1927, p. 279, note 7, *interrogavi terram* quote Plotinos, *Enn.* v. 1–4 as expressing similar ideas.

4. The basic issues of disagreement between Dr. Penton and me were discussed by us in great detail publicly and privately during the conference. Subsequently (4/22/81) I wrote to him and explained my desire to deepen my analysis and evaluation of *Romans* 1:18–21 and asked him to write me in more detail about his point of view and especially to inform me of what the "official position" of the Jehovah's Witnesses was, if any. So far I have had no reply.

5. *Divine Principle*, The Holy Spirit Association for the Unification of World Christianity, N.Y., 1973. (Scripture quotations are from the Revised Standard Version.) Chap. 1, Principle of Creation, Section 1, The Dual Characteristics of God, pp. 20–64.

6. *Ibid.*, p. 20.

7. Young Oon Kim, *Unification Theology* (NY: Holy Spirit Association for the Unification of World Christianity), p. 66.

8. Holy Spirit Association for the Unification of World Christianity, *Outline of the Principle*, Level 4 (NY: Holy Spirit Association for the Unification of World Christianity, 1980), p. 13.

9. *Unification Theology*, p. 67.

10. In addition to those cited *vide Unification Thought*, Unification Thought Institute, N.Y., 1973. First full translation from the original Korean. Young Oon Kim, *Unification Theology and Christian Thought*, revised ed. (NY: Golden Gate Publ. Co., 1976). Although I agree that a natural theology can be developed by the application of human reason to the facts of experience and that *Divine Principle* and supplementary writings have accepted this, I do not think it is valid to require a univocal or literal one to one correspondence between the facts of experience and the inferences drawn from them. For example, the fact of bi-polarity among things in Nature, their negativity and positivity, their masculinity and femininity does not necessarily require such contrasts in the nature of God. It is necessary to be aware of the literal implications, as well as of the metaphorical/allegorical ones.

11. *Vide Acts* 9:29; 14:7–17; 17:16–31; 20:15–18. It is possible that Paul met and discussed with the Greek philosophers at Miletus and Ephesus as well as with the Epicureans and Stoics, etc., at Athens.

12. E.g., *Job* 12:7–10; *Psalms* 18:2 (19:2); *Wisdom* 13:5–9; 12:23–27.

13. Justin Martyr, "Exhortation to the Greeks," "Discourse to the Greeks," "The Monarchy or The Rule of God," *The Fathers of the Church*, by Thomas B. Falls, (NY: Christian Heritage, Inc., 1948); Clement of Alexandria, *Stromata, Patrologia Latina* VIII-IX; John Chrysostom, *Homily* III. *The Epistle to the Romans, Nicene and Post-Nicene Fathers*, ed. P. Schaff, Vol. XI (Grand Rapids: Wm. B. Eerdmans Publ. Co., 1956), pp. 351–352. Augustine, *Exposition of Romans*; Sermon 71; *On Christian Doctrine* 1.4; *City of God*, passim; *On the Gospel of St. John*, passim; *On Psalms*, 19, 50, 106, etc. Aquinas, *Summa Theologiae* I. 1–26; *Commentary on The Epistle to the Romans, Opera Omnia*, Parma ed., Vol. XIII, (NY: Musurgia, 1949), pp. 15–16. Thomas refers to *Romans* 19 and 20 in many places in the *Summa Theologiae*.

14. *Ibid.* note 13.

15. *The Confessions of St. Augustine*, trans. by F. J. Sheed. (NY: Sheed & Ward, 1943).

16. *De Civitate Dei* VIII, 12.

17. *De Trinitate* V, 4, 5, 8.

18. "Tractate II on St. John," *A Select Library of the Nicene and Post-Nicene Fathers of the Christian Church*, ed. Philip Schaff (NY: The Christian Literature Co., 1888), vol. VII, p. 14.

19. *Ibid.*, Vol. V, c. 19, p. 91, The Knowledge of God Through the Creation.

20. *Ibid.*, *De Civitate Dei*, 8, 12, p. 152; "I have specially chosen them because their juster thoughts concerning the one God who made heaven and earth, have made them illustrious among philosophers...the most illustrious recent philosophers, who have chosen to follow Plato, have been unwilling to be called Peripatetics, or Academics, but have preferred the name Platonists. Among them were the renowned Plotinus, Iamblichus, and Porphyry, who were Greeks, and the African Apuleius, who was learned both in the Greek and Latin tongues." The translator of the books from Greek to Latin is considered to have been Gaius Marius Victorinus Afer, a celebrated rhetorician and theologian. *Vide* Marius Victorinus, *Traités Théologiques Sur la Trinité*, Latin text by Paul Henry, trans. Pierre Hadot, vol. I, Introduction, pp. 7ff, (Paris: Les Éditions du Cerf., 1960).

21. *Summa Theologiae*, I, I, 1.

22. *Ibid.*, Aristotle, *Metaphysics*, V, 1 (1026a 19).

23. In the view of Thomas *doctrina* is the knowledge possessed by the professor while *disciplina* is the knowledge as received by the pupil.

24. In direct opposition to Dr. Penton, Aquinas claims that one can know that God is love without a special revelation.

25. Angelus Walz, *Vide Saint Thomas Aquinas: A Biographical Study*, English translation by Sebastian Bullough (Westminster, MD: The Newman Press, 1951), rear-piece.

26. The word 'reduce', 'reducere' is used in logic to indicate the fact that something is known by indicating that to which it is related for the fact of its existence or its meaning.

27. Vatican Council I (1869–70) Sess. 3, c. 2 (*Denz* 1785).

28. Hans Küng, *Does God Exist? An Answer for Today*, trans. Edward Quinn (NY: Doubleday & Co., 1980), pp. 513, 770. Such a statement by Küng is contradicted by his evaluation of the Vatican statement against Barth "according to Romans 1, it is quite clear that the pagans had a knowledge of the fact of God without any special revelation." This is what Paul stated and Vatican I quoted. In *A New Catholic Commentary on Holy Scripture*, p. 1107, 843f, *re* v. 19, 20 of Romans, "Vatican I (*Denz* 1785) was referring only to the capacity of human reason to acquire knowledge of God."

29. *Luther's Works*, Vol. 25, *Lectures on Romans: Glosses and Scholia*, ed. H.C. Oswald (St. Louis: Concordia Publ. House, 1972).

30. *Ibid.*, p. 154. n. 37 refers to the fact that the reference is to Distinction III, *Patrologia Latina*, CXCII, 529.

31. Anders Nygren, *Commentary on Romans*, trans. C.C. Rasmussen, from *Romarbrevet*, Sweden, 1944 (Philadelphia: Fortress Press, 1967), 9th printing.

32. Karl Barth, *Anselm: Fides Quaerens Intellectum* (Faith in Search of Understanding), trans. Ian W. Robertson (NY: Meridian Books, The World Publ. Co., 1962).

33. Karl Barth, *Credo* (NY: Chas. Scribner's Sons, 1962).

34. Karl Barth, *Dogmatics in Outline* (NY: Harper & Row, Harper Torchbooks, The Cloister Library, 1959), p. 5.

35. Karl Barth, *The Epistle to the Romans*, trans. E.C. Hoskyns (London: Oxford University Press, 1965), 7th imp.

36. *Ibid.*, p. 530.

37. *The Existence of God*, edited with an introductory essay by John Hick (NY: The Macmillan Co., 1964).

38. *Webster's New World Dictionary*, 1966.

39. *Humanist Manifestos I and II*, (Buffalo, NY: Prometheus Books, 1973).

40. There are many other Commentaries on the Letter to Romans 1:18–21 and many other analyses of the significance of the words expressed, but time and space do not permit me to present them in detail. *Vide*:

Ahern, Barnabus M., *The Epistle to the Galatians and Romans; New Testament Reading Guide*, Collegeville, MN: The Liturgical Press, 1960.

Brunner, Emil, *The Letter to the Romans: A Commentary*, London: Lutterworth Press, 1959. First published in 1938. "The denial of such a 'general revelation' of grace in Jesus Christ can appeal neither to Paul nor to the Bible at large... If man did not know God, how could he be responsible? Man cannot excuse himself by pleading that he could not know God prior to his revelation in Jesus Christ; he could very well know him, namely his majesty as Creator and therefore also the fact that he belongs to God" (pp. 17, 18).

Dictionnaire de la Théologie Catholique, Paris: Librairie Le Touzey et Ané, 1937, vol. 13, partie 2, col. 2879: "*Dieu se fait connaître a l'homme par la création... La raison ou l'intelligence, s'exerçant sur los choses crées, permet à l'homme de connaître clairement ce qui est connaissable de Dieu... Saint Paul marque bien la transcendance de Dieu, son indépendance du monde.*"

Dodd, C.H. *The Epistle of Paul to the Romans*, NY: Harper and Bros., 1932, pp. 24–25. "There is no other passage where Paul so explicitly recognizes 'natural religion' as a fundamental trait of human nature... the created universe offers sufficient evidence of its 'divine Original'... Paganism... in Paul's judgment, has not the excuse of ignorance. The truth is there, but the impiety and wickedness of men hinder it."

Franzmann, M.H., "Romans" in *Concordia Commentary*, St. Louis: Concordia Publ. House, 1968, pp. 39, 40.

Hunter, A.M., *The Epistle to the Romans*, introduction and commentary, London: SCM Press, 1955. "Clearly Paul is thinking of what we call nowadays 'a General Revelation' of God independent of the Special Revelation to the Jews," p. 32. Hunter's emphasis is on "the wrath" of God.

Käsemann, Ernst, *Commentary on Romans*, trans. G.W. Bromiley, Grand Rapids: Wm. B. Eerdmans Publ. Co., 1980, pp. 36–43. "A. The Revelation of God's Wrath on the Gentiles (1:18–32)" is the section heading and the main concern. There is an extensive bibliography, mostly in German. There is a great deal of exegesis, e.g. *to gnōston tou theou* is said to be understood as "knowable" rather than "known" because of an apparent tautology. "It still remains questionable... whether it should be translated as 'what is knowable of God' (the commonview) or... 'God in his knowability'... In any case this catchword raises the hotly contested issue of a natural theology in Paul." Käsemann presents something of the popular Hellenistic philosophy, Stoic theology, refers to Pseudo-Aristotle *De Mundo* 399a-b, *Corpus Hermeticum* V, Seneca *Naturales questiones*, Cicero *Tusculanarum*, Epictetus *Discourses*, Philo *De praemiis et poenis*, etc., and though Acts 14:15–17; 17:22–29 draws on the same tradition "and here one surely can and must speak of natural theology," he contends that "would in fact be advocating a natural theology which could scarcely be reconciled with his eschatology and christology." (39–41) Presumably, if Paul said no more than Hellenistic Judaism and Acts, he would be advocating a natural theology but that such would conflict with what Paul maintains in his eschatology and Christology. Käsemann does not substantiate that claim here.

Lenski, R.C.H., *The Interpretation of St. Paul's Epistle to the Romans*, MN: Augsburg Publ. House, 1961, (originally published 1936). "He insists that *to gnōston* must be translated as what is *known* not *knowable*, though many use knowable in order to avoid what they consider a tautology" (p. 95). "Clearly seeing the unseen regarding God is simplicity itself. It is done with the mind or reason (*nous*) by means of a mental act (*noeîn* one that is not abstract speculation but sane and sober thought on the things made by God, all of which advertise his existence and his power and divinity" (p. 97). "We see the things made, see them with our physical eyes, but they convey more to us than their own undeniable existence; having a mind, by mental perception and by means of the visible we fully see the invisible, God's omnipotence and divineness. This is natural theology which is universal in scope" (p. 99).

Lyonnet, Stanislaus, *Quaestiones in Epistulam ad Romanos*, la series, Rome: Pontificio Istituto Biblico, 1962, C. II, De Naturali Dei Cognitone (Romans 1, 18–23) p. 59–88. He contends that although *to gnōston tou theou, quod notum est de Deo* is understood as *what is known* by many of the Fathers and ancient writers and the word *gnōstos* was used in ordinary speaking and in the New Testament for *known*, in classical writing and philosophy it signifies what *can* be known, because there seems to be a tautology. However, *phaneron*, if rightly understood, would not make a tautology (p. 64). Lyonnet's work is scholarly throughout and is recognized in the literature.

Maly, Eugene H., *Romans*, Wilmington: Michael Glazier, Inc., 1979. Though he admits that Paul is speaking of a "natural revelation" and that the knowable of God includes those divine attributes manifested in the creation of the world, he passes over these points in order to stress the wrath of God and God's punishment. (Only a small part of one page is devoted to vv. 18–23 concerning these points).

Murray, John, *The Epistle to the Romans*, vol. 1, Grand Rapids: Wm. B. Eerdmans Publ. Co., 1959. A lot of detailed exegesis.

O'Neill, J.C., *Paul's Letter to the Romans*, Penguin Books, 1975. "20. This is a concise summary of an argument for the existence of God that was already at least 500 years old when Romans was published, having been stated by the Greek philosopher Anaxagoras... The argument had been taken over into Jewish apologetics by Jews who were living scattered in the Hellenistic cities, where they spoke Greek and attempted with some success to win their Gentile neighbours to Judaism... I think the proof here summarized is valid."

O'Rourke, J.J., "Romans 1, 20 and Natural Revelation," CathBiQuart 23 (3, '61), 301–306. He emphasizes the fact that Paul does not say that the human mind of itself can obtain knowledge of God as Creator. The extension of the text is not necessarily universal. *New Testament Abstracts*, vol. 6, (1961–62), Weston, MA: Weston College, p. 200.

Owen, H.P., "The Scope of Natural Revelation in Romans 1 and Acts XVII," NTStud 5 (2, '59) 133–143. *New Testament Abstracts* 3, (3, 59) p. 262. "From the NT, therefore, the theologian will not try to prove by the use of unaided reason the existence of the Creator from *poiemata*, but will see that Paul implies that the knowledge gained by natural revelation constitutes a "point of contact" for the gospel. Finally, although the Apostle is not speaking of philosophers such as Plato, yet even these failed to understand God as the Creator; and this failure only Judeo-Christian revelation could redeem." When Owen states in the body of his article that no Gentile attained the belief in God as Creator of the world, I think that such a statement cannot be objectively verified though it is true that none of the ancient philosophers whose works we possess, attained to this belief. One who would study Genesis, even as a work of literature, may be able to attain a "belief in God as Creator." If Owen is asserting that it is only by faith that one can understand that the world was created in the strict sense of *created*, he would be in direct opposition with many of the great philosopher-theologians of the Christian Church, such as Augustine and Thomas Aquinas.

Robinson, John A.T., *Wrestling with Romans*, Philadelphia: The Westminster Press, 1979. "... Whatever men can know of God they have *en autois*, within them or among them. For God has disclosed it to them... Paul thus specifically contradicts the Barthian denial of any point of contact, any revelation, outside Christ. Brunner convicted Barth here of being unbiblical; mankind has no excuse precisely because there *is* a general revelation through creation. Equally Paul contradicts the Thomist view that man can by his own reason know God apart from revelation. Man does not know some things by reason and some by revelation—but all by revelation. Even the pagan world can know only 'because God himself has disclosed it to them' (verse 19). But while Paul fully allows for a natural revelation he provides little confidence for a natural theology. Here St. Thomas Aquinas is, I believe, clearly unbiblical. He assumes that man's reason working on the natural revelation can build up a coherent and, as far as it goes, entirely correct view of the nature and attributes of God. The whole of his *Summa Theologica* I, up to the doctrine of the Trinity... is grounded on natural reason alone, and this foundation is never subsequently modified or corrected in the light of biblical insights. It need not be, because natural reason is a perfectly adequate instrument as far as it goes. But this is precisely what Paul proceeds to deny" (p. 21–23). There is quite a lot of equivocation in the use of the word "revelation." There is said to be a general revelation through creation, which disagrees with Barth, and a contradiction of Paul with Aquinas because Aquinas claims that men can know God by human reason apart from revelation. This equivocation is again utilized when Robinson asserts that Aquinas thought he could set up a natural theology based on reason *and* a natural revelation. I think that Robinson is not correct when he goes on to imply that Paul considers that human reason itself is perverted because some men who know God refused to honor Him as God. As Robinson adds... "knowledge of God is not just something intellectual: it is an acknowledgement of God *as* God, a recognition which is given only in the true worship of God..." (p. 23).

Rosin, H., "To gnōston tou Theou," *Theolzeit* 17, (3, '61) 161–165, *New Testament Abstracts,* vol. 6, (1961–62), Weston MA: Weston College. The usual translation of these words, as "that which can be known of God," does not suit the context of Romans 1: 18–32.

Schelke, Karl H., *The Epistle to the Romans,* NY: Herder & Herder, 1964. Only a part of a page devoted to our text. He does emphasize that man cannot know "the entire mysterious nature of God with reason alone; nor God as the Father, whom Jesus Christ has revealed."

Taylor, Vincent, "The Epistle to the Romans", *Epworth Preacher's Commentaries,* London: The Epworth Press, 1962. 1:20. This verse implies the truth of what is called "Natural Theology," the belief that God makes known His power and divinity in creation, so that men are "without excuse."

Hae Soo Pyun

Divine Principle and Oriental Philosophy

In this presentation, I shall consider three points.

1. How I feel about the *Divine Principle* in relation to the Chinese philosophical tradition.

2. Whether the *yin-yang* principle adequately explains the creation.

3. What Chinese philosophy offers towards understanding the deeper meaning of *Divine Principle*.

The presence of Chinese thought in *Divine Principle* is thought to be quite pervasive, yet, except in one or two instances, I find it hard to identify specific parts as of Oriental origin. Christianity on the one hand, and Chinese thought on the other, have so much in common that if I adduce an example from the teachings of the Unification Church[1] to show that it is of Oriental origin, someone else may easily prove that it is also to be found in other Christian teachings. We often hear members of the Church respectfully quoting the Reverend Moon: "You must become better than I, you must go beyond Christ." This, I assume, is unmistakably of Confucian origin. In Chinese Buddhism it is often said that a true Buddhist does not walk on the same Path that the Enlightened One had trodden. This belief was influenced by a Confucian maxim: "As blue is extracted from the indigo plant but becomes bluer than its source, so a disciple, learning all from his master, must surpass him." The Bible says the same thing: "Verily, verily, I say unto you, he that believes in me, the works I do shall he do also; and greater works than these shall he do..." (John, 14:12).

This does not mean that the Oriental influence is minimal. Far from it. For our present purpose, I shall briefly explain five[2] examples that I believe are found in the teachings of the Unification Church.

1. "Human nature is *originally* good."

Expounded by Mencius (371–289 B.C.) roughly twenty-three centuries ago, this idea has exerted a powerful influence on the Oriental mind and thought ever since. The Chinese people thought it important enough to make it the opening sentence in their favorite primer for children, *San Tzu Ching (Three Character Classic)*: "At their birth, all men are by nature good."

Mencius elucidates what he means by the original goodness of man in terms of analogies:

a. If someone sees a small child about to fall into a well, he will not debate with himself whether or not to do something about the situation. He'll rush to the rescue of the child first, though not because he wants to be friends with the child's parents, to seek the praise of his neighbors, or to escape an evil reputation if he did nothing. For Mencius, every human being is born with the original impulse toward goodness.[3]

b. Mencius elsewhere uses another analogy to illustrate his point. Originally, Ox-Mountain was covered with beautiful trees, but being near a large population center, its trees had been hewn down with axes and hatchets. But the nourishment from the rain and the dew helped the mountain to sprout new buds. Then cattle came along to graze on the mountain. No wonder Ox-Mountain became so bald. When the townfolk saw how bare the mountain was, they were led to believe that it had never had any beautiful trees. Aren't there, Mencius asks, the seeds of goodness and righteousness in the heart of every man? (The expression, *shim-jung*, heartistic love, comes from Mencius.)

In other words, the fall of man may be compared to that of trees by axes and hatchets. Mencius believed that, like Ox-Mountain, man, too, has the power within himself to restore his lost or fallen human nature with some help from the environment.[4]

Years ago, many Christian missionaries in China thought that Mencius' doctrine on the original goodness of man, so strongly entrenched in the minds and attitudes of the Chinese people, was one of the major stumbling blocks to their willingness to become Christians. This is no longer the case. *Divine Principle* has reconciled the two different views with one stroke.

2. Sometimes the Oriental influence upon the teachings of the Unifica-

tion Church crops up in phrases and sentences rather than in a major theory, such as, "X must be carried out by the individual, family, society, nation and the world." This reasoning is spattered over many speeches of the Reverend Moon. To cite just one recent example, in the Founder's Address at the Seventh ICUS (International Conference on the Unity of the Sciences) in Boston, he said:

> The Absolute Being's ultimate ideal of love is that the ideal individual unite with another ideal individual to form an ideal family, that the family develop into an ideal society, the society into an ideal nation, and the nations into an ideal world.[5]

This thought may be traced to one of the Confucian classics, *Ta Hsüeh (The Great Learning)*:

> The ancient who wished to illustrate his illustrious virtue to the world would first bring order to his own state; he who wished to bring order to his own state would first regulate his family; and he who wished to regulate his family would first cultivate himself... When he cultivates himself, his family will be regulated; when his family is regulated, his own state will be put in order; and when his own state will be put in order, there will be peace and concord throughout the world. From the Son of Heaven down to the common people, all must regard self-cultivation as the root (of social action).[6]

3. Another phrase that is crucial to the Unification Principle is "The Kingdom of Heaven on Earth." This may be ascribed to some Confucian influence. In Boston, I wanted to put to the test the Zen technique called *Mundap (Mondo* in Japanese), consisting of the shortest possible question and answer, so I asked one of our graduates, "Tell me what *Divine Principle* teaches—you have only three seconds!" Startled by this question out of the blue, he could not come up with any definite answer that satisfied me or especially him. He sheepishly challenged me to offer mine, which I gave as follows: "The Kingdom of Heaven on Earth and the Ideal Family."

When I attended the *Divine Principle* seminar for the Korean community in the New York metropolitan area the most attractive idea put forth, for me, was this thunderbolt: "The Unification Church does not preach about the Kingdom of Heaven but intends to erect the Kingdom of Heaven on Earth!" The verb "to erect" (action) and the addition "on

Earth" won me over on the spot. In the jargon of Zen, I thought I almost had a *satori* experience.

If I understand the earlier phrase, i.e., "from the individual to the family all the way to the world," then I may add that the ideal family must precede the Kingdom of Heaven on Earth, which in turn must precede the Kingdom of Heaven in the beyond. This leads us to the crucial role of the "family" in *Divine Principle* and the Church.

4. The emphasis upon the "family" is easily the most obvious Oriental influence on the *Unification Principle*; no one will take it for anything else. Of all the churches and temples, only the Unification Church calls its members "sikku," family members. So it is natural for sikku to call one another brothers and sisters, or to respectfully address the founder "Father" and his spouse "Mother."

The importance of the "family" in the Church cannot be exaggerated. This is too obvious to elaborate. Confucianism teaches Five Cardinal Human Relationships: (1) parents and children; (2) husband and wife; (3) older and younger generations; (4) friend and friend; and (5) the superior and his subordinates. Three out of these five human relationships are in the family. Each relationship is called *lun* (Chinese) or *ryun* (Korean), consisting of two Chinese characters, "human" and "book-binding." In other words, these relationships when put into practice in the right way, bind one human to another, as the loose pages are bound in a book, and that which is binding is humanly "good" (human plus two), while that which puts them asunder is less than "good."

The Unification interpretation of the parent-child relationship on a God-centered foundation, as in the four-position foundation, is significant, and in my view, an enduring improvement over the Confucian *lun*. This puts Confucianism in an entirely different ball park. (In Confucianism I don't see a catcher wearing head gear or a chest protector.)

SECTION 2

I now come to the *yin-yang* principle, on which I will be expected to make extensive comments. In the *Divine Principle* Study Guide, written credit to Oriental thought is given only to this cosmological dimension of Chinese thought (Part I, p. 16).

This *yin-yang* principle, based on the *I Ching (The Book of Changes)*, has gone into the Unification Theory of Creation, and textually, it is the only conspicuous Oriental feature in *Divine Principle*. I am obliged to give to this question a great deal more space than to other Oriental elements in Divine Principle, because even a cursory examination of *yin-yang* philosophy requires volumes, not a few pages. It must be noted, however, that (1) *The Book of Changes* is probably the most difficult, elusive, and obscure text in Chinese thought. Most of the sentences sometimes sound like "abracadabra" to most people. (2) Although it is more often quoted than other texts, it is least understood. (3) Lastly, I have expanded more time and energy on it than on any other single treatise in the Chinese tradition, yet I am least sure of my own footing.

So far, I have given a sympathetic reading of *Divine Principle* insofar as it is influenced by Chinese thought, and I am about to give an equally sympathetic interpretation of the *yin-yang* strand in it. However, my own view on the *Book of Changes* differs considerably from the one adopted in *Divine Principle*. My disagreement has little to do with the substance but a good deal, I am afraid, with the formulation, which may give rise to some logical difficulties. First, let me state my view on the *Book of Changes* and then proceed to some of the implications to which it may lead.

The *I Ching* is sometimes called *Chou-I* or *The Book of Changes* in the Chou dynasty (1111–249 B.C.). *I* is composed of two Chinese characters, the sun (on top) and the moon (below). The Chinese language is pictorial, and when you put these two characters next to each other, you have "light"—the sun and the moon in unison illumine the world. In the character *I*, etymologically considered, the sun stands or sits on top of the moon and they appear to play "hide and seek" in the heavenly orbit. Scholars have ascribed three related but different meanings to the *I*.

1. *Easy or Simple*: *The Book of Changes*, difficult as it is, was considered "easy" and "simple" when compared with the more difficult and arbitrary procedure of divination used in the preceding Shang dynasty (1751–1112 B.C.) by means of boring a hole on the tortoise shell with a burning stylus.

2. *Change*: For the ancient Chinese whose livelihood depended on farming, what could be a more obvious and indisputable proof of "change" than the revolution of the sun (source of energy) and the moon (lunar calendar for farming) in the firmament of Heaven? *I*, then, means "change"—a cyclical conception in the *Book of Changes*.

When the sun sets, the moon appears; when the moon is down, the sun rises. The sun and the moon alternate, and thus, light is produced. When cold departs, heat arrives; when heat goes away, cold comes. Cold and hot seasons alternate, and thus, the year completes itself.[7]

These are instances or illustrations of the dynamic processes of change in nature. But for the Chinese thinkers, change is not to be confused with "flux," patternless flow of events, because four seasons come and go with regularity, the sun and the moon play "hide and seek" with regularity or according to determinable "rules of the game."

Hence, "change" ultimately points beyond itself, it implies predictable "patterns," laws, "principles," "regularities," etc., in a scientific sense.

3. *Permanence*: *I*, therefore, signifies non-change, permanence. The sun and the moon, four seasons come and go, but they all come and go always in accordance with the eternal, unchanging laws of nature. The laws of change, of which the revolution of the sun and the moon is an instance, are not themselves subject to change. These laws are also called *I*.

Let's pause for a moment and examine carefully what we have discussed.

(1) *I* in the second sense of change refers to the *visible* world. We daily can see the sun and the moon in their tireless traversing on the heavenly orbit; we "feel" the comings and goings of four seasons. We enjoy the flowers in spring and multi-colored leaves in the fall. (2) But in the third sense of permanence, the laws that govern and regulate these processes of change in the universe are *invisible* to us. If you throw a stone up in the air, it will fall—an instance of change. Spinoza's stone would say it is falling of its own free will. A stone that speaks the language of the *I Ching* will admit reluctantly: "I'm falling but I'm obeying the law of gravity. That's all." The law of gravitation is not subject to change, nor is it visible to us. (3) According to the *Book of Changes*, we seek to know the *invisible* through the *visible*, as in *Divine Principle* we desire to know the nature of God through His creation. (4) In the etymology of *I*, we already have the germs of *yang* (sun) and *yin* (moon). According to the *Book of Changes*, *yin* and *yang* are invoked as universal principles to explain the fact of *change*. In other words, when they interact with each other—male and female principles—change takes place. Within the framework of *yin-yang* philosophy, there would be no change without the interaction between these complementary opposites, *yin* and *yang*.

After there are Heaven (this symbolizes Male, Father, or *yang* principle) and Earth (Female, Mother, *yin* principle), there comes into being individual things. After individual things come into existence, there are interactions between the two complementary opposites, *male* and *female*. After there are male and female, there is the relationship between husband and wife; after the relationship exists between husband and wife, there is the relationship between parents and children...[8]

But where and how did Heaven and Earth themselves come from? When the *yin-yang* principles are employed to answer this inconvenient question, they go beyond the implication of the fact of change and propose to tackle the problem of the *origin* of all things. Here, however, the Chinese philosophical tradition suddenly becomes a little less eloquent and more reticent. It says: There was the beginningless Beginning, the Primeval Beginning as it were, sometimes called *Tai Chi* (Korean, *Taeguk* or *Wu Chi* (Korean, *Muguk*).

One (*Wu Chi*) begets *Tai Chi*, which in turn gives birth to two (*yin* and *yang*); they in turn, bring forth four, and then ten thousand things. If pressed harder, the *I Ching* and Chinese thinkers like Lao Tzu, who quotes from the *I Ching*, would spell out their own version of the Cosmological Argument, which ultimately depends on the impossibility of the *actual* infinity in the causal nexus or change of beings. This chain must stop somewhere, must come to an end, must go back to the First Member, the Uncaused Cause; a watch cannot be nor can be conceived without a Watchmaker.

Now, I have explained very cursorily the meanings of *yin-yang* principles in the hope of throwing some light on *Divine Principle*'s theory of God and His creation. I cannot at this moment determine to what extent this *yin-yang* business is essential or indispensable to Unificationism's interpretation of the creation and its Creator, God. As the text stands, its presence appears important, but its formulation, as applied to the nature of God, may lead to some logical dilemmas. For the moment, I'll consider Mr. Young Whi Kim's statement or formulation of the *yin-yang* as it stands in the the *Divine Principle Study Guide*:

Oriental Philosophy understands God as a being who only has the dual characteristics of Positivity (yang) and negativity (yin). It does not know that God is a being of *Sung-Sang* and *Hyung-Sang*, which are more fundamental than Positivity and Negativity. By having Sung-Sang and Hyung-Sang, God becomes the God of will, feeling, heart, and character.[9]

Two questions come to my mind:

1. *Invisibility of God*: On page 12 of the *Study Guide*, under the heading of "5. The Relationship between *Sung-Sang* (Internal character) and *Hyung-Sang* (External form)," we find:

Sung Sang	Hyung Sang
Invisible	Visible
Internal	External
Vertical	Horizontal
Cause	Effect
Subject	Object

However, on page 15 of the same *Study Guide*, we have God, Invisible Subject, represented by a large circle within which we find both *Sung-Sang* (invisible) and *Hyung-Sang* (visible attribute). This formulation requires a considerable dialectical ingenuity to keep God invisible. If the *Study Guide* identifies God with the visible world—I doubt that this is its intention, this horn of dilemma is just as painful—there would be no difference between the Creator and Creation; the distinction between Cause and Effect, Subject and Object would be specious. If it takes the other horn of the dilemma, God's *Hyung-Sang* (visible attribute) must be re-defined or radically modified to insure God's invisibility.

The Book of Changes might be able to hint at a possible way out. It would identify *Wu Chi* with God's Original *Sung-Sang* and Divine Law (*I* in the third sense; governance of all things in the universe or God's invisible Act) with God's Original Hyung–Sang (still invisible, as the law of gravity is invisible to us).

If this assumption be correct, then its implications are very simple yet lead to no dilemma. Oriental philosophy could understand *Sung-Sang* and *Hyung-Sang*, but in the case of God, Uncaused Cause, *Sung-Sang* and *Hyung-Sang* are co-extensive and identical—they are one, indivisible and invisible. In the language of Western philosophy, God's Being and God's Act are one and the same thing. For our limited understanding due to the Fall of Man, we need this conceptual distinction between *Sung-Sang* and *Hyung-Sang* when we talk about God. God is One—in Him, Subject and Object are not two but one, the dichotomy between External and Internal does not hold, Cause and Effect are One. For God, then, His Original Hyung Sang,[10] Divine Law that operates in the universe, operates invisibly through the forces of *yin* and *yang* and at the same time, He is One. The Logical consequence of this argument is that to speak of *yin* and *yang* as applied to God is to make a distinction between Subject and Object in God, which is contradictory to affirm.

2. *Eternal, Unchangeable Nature of God:* As I have already indicated, the distinction between *yin* and *yang* does not hold in the case of God, only in the case of his creation. One inescapable implication of this position is that God being One and without parts, without *yin* and *yang* or agencies of change, He is subject to no change. In his speech at the 1976 Washington Monument rally, Rev. Moon spoke of one eternal, unchanging God who loves us all. So I take it that this is the position of Unification Theology.

a. If God's Original *Hyung-Sang* be identified with Divine Law, which is invisible to us as well as eternal, of which the Law of Gravity constitutes but a small part, then there would be nothing in His nature that is subject to any modification, change or mutation.

b. Should God contain *yin* and *yang*, forces through which God's *Hyung-Sang* operates invisibly to effect the creation and operation of His creation, then God, insofar as He is composed of *yin* and *yang*, would Himself be subject to change.

The question boils down to this: The *Study Guide* formulation must steer clear between the Scylla of the concept of changeable and changing God composed of *yin* and *yang* and the Charybdis of the concept of unchanging and unchangeable God with no *yin-yang* forces or agencies of change as part of His being.

a. If God is eternal and changeless, the rest of the *Divine Principle* stands.

b. If God, with *yin* and *yang* agencies of change, is subject to change, then the logical implications for the rest of *Divine Principle* are far reaching, indeed. Theories of indemnity, of responsibility of man, of restoration or salvation, and many other key notions must be radically modified beyond recognition. The formulation adopted in the *Study Guide* and the *Divine Principle* must face this horn of the dilemma. For change always implies that X, the subject of change, goes from state A to state B, such that A and B are different. For instance, the indemnity that we have in mind to pay may be good enough at stage A or B to earn our salvation or to restore our fallen nature, but it may carry a different price tag—due to spiraling inflation as at present—at C, D . . . *ad infinitum*. We may not be able to catch up with the changing God at all. We may not be able to determine precisely where God is now or in the foreseeable future—at D, or O or G.

SECTION 3

I now come to the last part of this paper: whether Chinese philosophy has anything to offer to help us to understand *Divine Principle*. It is not my intention to Orientalize *Divine Principle*, but only to Orientalize my own approach to it.

In the Founder's address at the Boston ICUS, Rev. Moon stressed practice or praxis more than a mere cerebral exercise. He said, "Absolute values then must be pursued not through knowledge but through love."[11] This point has been reiterated countless times. At the first faculty meeting of 1978, a message from Rev. Moon came to Barrytown from across the Atlantic Ocean: "Things taught at the UTS are too theoretical..." This fatherly rebuke, if you call it that, I took personally in good part. I should like to have Chinese philosophy illustrate what I surmise Rev. Moon might have meant.

As you must have noticed, I have attempted to understand *Divine Principle* from the standpoint of Chinese philosophy, but I might as well own at this point that my own understanding of Chinese thought has been considerably influenced in the last two years or so by *Divine Principle*.[12] I should like now to present this feedback to amplify what I judge to be the long term implications of Rev. Moon's fatherly remarks.

No matter what scholars, both East and West, think or say about the Chinese philosophical tradition, one historical, economic, and social fact cannot be ignored: the overwhelming majority of the Far Eastern peoples had been farmers until recent times, generation upon generation, and this fact has colored the content and the manner of their thinking. To a hard-nosed pragmatist like a farmer, an idea must be a seed that bears fruit, for fruits are "practical." In one sense, then, *Divine Principle*, too, must serve as a seed that with proper care should bear fruits: the Kingdom of Heaven on Earth and the Ideal Family.

But what does the word "practical" signify in the Chinese tradition? The etymological meaning of "practical" is a picture of the kernel of a fruit stone. Fruits are delicious, nourishing, and practical, when you eat them. But in a second and higher sense, the kernel of the fruit stone is said to be more practical—more than one fruit you have eaten. However, the seed does not normally bear the ideal fruits without proper and loving care by man. In other words, the "practical" implies, on the third and still higher level the practical know-how, and requires "blood, sweat, and toil" to bring the original seed to its complete fruition.

The Church has the seed; it has the land to till, the world; it also has the people to work on it. Yet do they really have the know-how? Maybe we are here to find something along this line and share it with others.

But what does the so-called know-how involve? In what does it consist? What does it boil down to?

The venerable Chinese philosophical tradition teaches that things thought and things done must go hand in hand. To this end-in-view, theory and practice must be engaged in a *yin-yang* dialogue. According to one fundamental principle of *yin-yang* philosophy, there is no such thing as pure *yin* or pure *yang*. *Yang* contains a little of *yin* and vice versa. Male has a tiny amount of female hormone, female a little of male hormone. Theory seeks to ask practical questions, while practice learns to question theory on a new and higher theoretical level. There is, then, nothing in theory that does not issue in practical consequences. There is always something in praxis that further clarifies theory from deeper understanding.

You may ask now what this *yin-yang* dialogue is supposed to lead to. In other words, what does the unity of theory and practice consist in? If I understand correctly some ramifications of Rev. Moon's remarks, he may very well mean that we must learn to transmute the "practical" brass into the "concrete" gold, the "practical" on the fourth and still higher level. The know-how must map out the highway step by step, and post roadsigns on it, toward the end-in-view. In the case of *Divine Principle*, it means, first, the Ideal Family and then the Kingdom of Heaven on Earth.

Many fruitful steps have been taken since the founding of the Unification Church. Some of these steps have been the paying of costly indemnities, indemnity being a necessary condition for restoration. But indemnity in itself, indemnity as a concept or theory is empty. Its true meaning comes only through intelligent praxis. To accept this praxis may turn out to be part of the indemnity package.

Let me suggest one step as part of this indemnity: I don't know how close we are—how many more steps we must take—to the Kingdom of Heaven on Earth. For this end, we must first have the Ideal Family full of heavenly soldiers called *sikku*. The good old Confucius seems to hit the mark, so let me close my own discussion with one of his less appreciated aphorisms:

In the Ideal Family, "people near are happy, and then people far away wish to come and join."[13]

NOTES

1. In this paper, the "teachings of the Unification Church" is used to include *Divine Principle*, *The Way of God's Will*, Rev. Moon's speeches to the public or to the family members. Sometimes, I use "Unification Principle" to denote the same.

2. There could be more than these. In certain cases, any comparison may be misleading. For instance, the theory of indemnity is related to the Buddhist doctrines of *Karma*. Yet it is a moot question whether the former is influenced by, let alone derived from, the latter.

3. Mencius, Book II, Part I, Chapter 6.

4. *Ibid.*, Book VI, Part I, Chapter 8.

5. Moon, Sun Myung, "The Re-Evaluation of Existing Values and the Search for Absolute Values," Nov. 24, 1978, p. 2, last paragraph.

6. Confucius, *The Great Learning*, 3rd paragraph.

7. *I Ching*, "The Great Commentary," Part II, Chapter 5.

8. *Ibid.*, "Sequence" to the 31st Hexagram, Hsien.

9. *Divine Principle Study Guide*, p. 16. *Sung-sang* and *Hyung-sang* are very ingenious concepts in *Divine Principle*. They have no equivalents in Oriental or Western Philosophy. However, in Oriental Philosophy, *yin* and *yang* are applied to "creation" but never to "God," "Heaven," etc. In this respect I beg to differ with Mr. Kim's position on this question.

10. Some contemporary theologians argue that they cannot "experience" God, so they remain atheistic or at best agnostic theologians. In this newly suggested formulation, our answer to these skeptical theologians is very simple and clear. We experience, and more important, we cannot but experience, God's *Hyung-Sang*, but not his *Sung-Sang*. Without this "partial" experience of God, partially due to the Fall of Man, our experience of anything—experiencing natural phenomena, for instance—would become completely unintelligible 'gobbledygook.' However, we must admit that our experience and hence, our knowledge of God's *Hyung-Sang* is not perfect in the sense of being complete and whole.

11. Moon, *Op. cit.*, page 3.

12. I consider what follows to be the most important part of this paper. I must admit that Part 2 of this paper is an instance of a "cerebral exercise."

13. Confucius, Analects, XIII, 16.

James Michael Lee

John Dewey and the Unification Church; Some Points of Contact

At first glance there seems to be a very minimal number of contact points between the philosophy of John Dewey and the Unification Church. A few molar instances could be adduced to shore up this contention. For example, John Dewey strongly maintains that there are no absolutes; everything is relative.[1] This unifixing of the absolutes certainly goes against the core and spirit of the Unification Church.[2] Dewey also believes that truth is determined instrumentally on the basis of what works productively for the individual or group.[3] Such a belief is definitely rejected by the Unification Church.[4] Dewey holds that values come about progressively by experimentation; he also comes out strongly against external authority insofar as it is external authority.[5] Dewey's writings are none too flattering to organized, supernaturally-based religion. In short, there seems at first blush to be very little in common between the educational philosophy of John Dewey and the Unification Church.

SCHOLIUM: THE UNIFICATION CHURCH

A word or two is in order about the way in which I conceptualize the Unification Church. By Unification Church I mean that portion of the people of God which shares and lives a particular or special type of faith, hope, and love. In this conceptualization, the Unification Church is not coextensive with the *Divine Principle*. In other words, the *Divine Principle* constitutes only one dimension—albeit a pivotal dimension—of the Unification Church. Further, in my conceptualization, the *ecclesiasticum* (and the Unification Church, like all institutional churches, does indeed have an *ecclesiasticum*) *is not coextensive with the Unification Church. The ecclesiasticum* constitutes one dimension, a dimension which existentially interacts and interpenetrates the Unification Church's *ecclesia*, and vice-versa.

In terms of the present little article, my conceptualization of the Unification Church means that the sources which I adduce will be drawn not only from the seminal *Divine Principle*, but also from the *ecclesiasticum* as well as from the thoughts of Church members, the affects of Church members, and the lifestyle of Church members individually and collectively.

RELIGION

Prior to the intrusion of the scholium, I observed that there seems at first blush to be very little in common between the philosophy of John Dewey and the Unification Church. Yet a closer examination of Dewey's writings reveals that there are quite a few points of contact between his thought and the Unification Church. Let us use Dewey's views on religion as one example. To be sure, Dewey is opposed to all specific supernaturally-oriented and institutionally-based religions. He essentially shares a Comtian view of supernaturality, a view which regards man's belief in a supernatural religion as the lowest and most primitive stage of the human quest.[6] He stands against sectarianism in any form, that is to say the specific beliefs and practices of a particular church or denomination.[7] In Dewey's view, an elitist exclusivist social group like an institutional church is highly constricting to the personal and social growth not only of its members but also of the wider community as well. Dewey maintains that each person and each group must be essentially and structurally wide open for all sorts of new experiences, experiences which may reinforce or even flatly contradict presently-held beliefs, practices, and structures. The institutionalism of religion, especially when such institutionalism is both based on and directed toward the supernatural, fundamentally requires religion to be anti-human. Thus Dewey asserts that "the association of religion with the supernatural tends by its own nature to breed the dogmatic and divisive spirit." History proves this contention, Dewey forthrightly declares.[8]

As I have experienced the Unification Church in its worshipping/ fellowshipping/ministerial/studying/here-and-now living *ecclesia*,[9] I have been favorably impressed by the openness and by the kindly accommodation which the Church seems to have toward the person and the belief-system of others, including those with whom the Church members might disagree. Thus it appears, to me at least, that it is only natural for the Unification Church to appreciate the points of contact it might have with Deweyism and with those who hold this philosophy in greater or lesser degree. Contact enables dialogue and promotes fellowship. Such dialogue and fellowship can help prevent the Unification Church from falling prey to the all-too-frequent temptation of religious doctrinairism and insularism. In stating this, I am in no way minimizing the many basic differences in the fundamental views held by the Unification Church on the one hand and by John Dewey on the other hand. Rather, my statement is intended to highlight the fact that despite basic differences, there are still points of contact which can be made and which can be productively utilized.

Let me very briefly deal with one major point of contact between the Unification Church and John Dewey on the issue of religion.

Dewey emphasizes the importance of the *religious* in men's lives even though he rejects religion in its concrete specific institutionalized sense. By religious Dewey means that personally-experienced processive wholeness which constitutes one's effective and living relationship to the universe. Dewey states that the religious and the moral are the two most fundamental dimensions in all human experience and in all education. Thus it was no accident that he gave the first major address to the newly-founded Religious Education Association in 1903, an address entitled "Religious Education as Conditioned by Modern Psychology and Pedagogy."[10]

Dewey's emphasis on the religious and the moral as central in human experience certainly represents a major point of contact for the Unification Church. To be sure, every dimension of the Unification Church, ranging from Sun Myung Moon's deeply-felt experience of Jesus in his early days [11] to seminary life to fundraising activities, has the religious and the moral at the center. To be sure, the Unification Church's religious and moral centralities are supernatural while Dewey's religious and moral centralities are nonsupernatural. Nonetheless, Dewey's conceptualization of the religious and the moral, while not being nearly as full or as rich as that of the Unification Church, still is contained within the

Unification Church's conceptualization as a necessary aspect.

In talking to Unification Church members, especially past and present seminarians, I have found that these individuals do indeed make the religious and moral dimension a major point of contact with those non-Unificationists whom they encounter. Some of these non-Unificationists were never attracted to a supernaturally-oriented and institutionally-based religiousness or morality. Others of these non-Unificationists left one or another supernaturally-oriented and institutionally-based religion because these individuals came to believe that there was insufficient religiousness and morality (in John Dewey's sense) present and active in these religions. From what the Unification Church members tell me, they frequently use a particular non-Unificationist's Deweyistic deep sense of religious and moral centrality as the initial and indeed abiding axis around which to build a relationship and then to evangelize.

Very early in my career, before the mellowing influence of Vatican II, I taught in a small insular New England Catholic girls' college run by nuns. In the summers the college ran a very modest graduate program in which most of the students were nuns. I would frequently suggest to these nun-students that as Christians, their first and paramount concern was not to convert everyone to Catholicism, but to assist each individual to become a more religious person and to wholeheartedly serve God according to the exigencies of his own personality. Surprisingly for those pre-Vatican II days, many of the nun-students did not become upset at what might initially seem to be heresy or at least Catholicism of a suspicious sort. John Dewey's notion of the religious has something similar to say to the Unification Church as I said to those nun-students many years ago. Some persons most likely can serve God best by not becoming members of the Unification Church, and by remaining in the processive religious situation in which they presently find themselves. God meets and greets and works with persons according to the developmental state of each individual's personality. So it seems to me that in his evangelization endeavors, a Unification Church member would serve God and persons best not by trying to convert everyone to Unificationism, but by attempting first to help the individual to learn how God speaks personally to him, and then to assist him to be further empowered to authentically respond to that present revelation.[12]

SCIENCE AND THE RELIGIOUS

A second major point of contact between John Dewey and the Unification Church is that of the relationship of science and the religious. Though Dewey asserts that the religious cannot be found in religion, and the Unification Church maintains that religion is the highest embodiment of the religious, nonetheless both agree that the relationship of science to religion is of paramount importance in today's world.

In Dewey's view, the term "science" refers not only to natural science but to social science as well. While he devotes considerable attention in his writings to natural science, nonetheless he is even more concerned with social science. Though natural science and social science both aim at controlling the world for human benefit, nonetheless both kinds of science are autonomous and not simply dimensions of the selfsame science. [13]

The spectacular progress of science in the past few centuries, Dewey declares, has spawned a crisis between science and the religious. Dewey puts it this way:

> The crisis is due, it is asserted, to the incompatability between the conclusions of natural science about the world in which we live and the realm of higher values, of ideal and spiritual qualities, which get no support from natural science. The new science, it is said, has stripped the world of the qualities which made it beautiful and congenial to men; has deprived nature of all aspiration toward ends, all preference for accomplishing good, and presented nature to us as a scene of indifferent physical particles acting according to mathematical and mechanical laws.[14]

Dewey believes that the clash between science and the religious is a productive one for the religious because the procedures and rationale of modern science open up fundamentally new avenues for the religious. The religious went as far as it could in ancient and medieval times precisely because it was inextricably linked, more than its devotees realized, to a primitive and outmoded science. With the onset of modern scientific experimental procedure and empirically-verified conclusions, the religious has become freed from the bondage brought on by a relatively impoverished view of the world. (Science and the religious both represent explorations and interpretations of reality). Modern science substitutes experimental procedure for blind authority, data for objects, and verified truths for mere speculative opinions.[15] Such a substitution enables the religious to be based on and interpenetrated with that which is real, and as a result bestows a wholesomeness and an enriched form of qualitative experience on the religious. Science enables individuals to accurately ascertain those human wants and needs which are genuinely religious and productively human. The truly religious and genuinely moral must satisfy scientific conditions because the truly religious and the genuinely moral must be grounded in what is demonstrably real.[16]

For Dewey, then, the religious is most real and most fecund when it is tethered to and directed toward this world. It is here that modern science has its critical role to play, since science gives us reliable knowledge and productive interpretation of this world.[17]

The religious is at bottom a process, a procedure, as Dewey sees it. The religious is a special *way* in which an individual interprets, feels, and lives his experiences. Thus the contribution which science makes to the religious is not just in the area of empirically-verified conclusions but even more importantly in the area of procedure. This is a central point in Dewey's philosophy. For Dewey, the scientific procedure also constitutes the way in which an individual thinks—and the general way in which an individual thinks is axial to the way an individual thinks religiously and acts religiously. In a celebrated passage Dewey describes the five stages of thinking—stages which are always present but not necessarily in the order given below.

1. suggestions, in which the mind leaps forward to a possible solution;

2. an intellectualization of the difficulty or perplexity that has been *felt,* directly experienced into a *problem* to be solved, a question for which the answer must be sought;

3. the use of one suggestion after another as a leading idea, or *hypothesis*, to initiate and guide observation and other operations in the collection of factual material;

4. the mental elaboration of the idea or supposition as an idea or supposition *reasoning*, in the sense in which reasoning is a part, not the whole, of inference; and

5. testing the hypothesis by overt or imaginative action.[18]

Though limitations of space prevent a thorough or even adequate explanation of this seminal passage, three points are worth briefly mentioning. First, thinking productively about the religious must begin with and always work through a personally-experienced and personally-felt difficulty. If the religious does not become a recurring problem for the person, then any thinking about the religious will most likely be superficial and purely cerebral (as opposed to personal). Second, religious truth must be sought not by means of an authoritative external statement or set of authoritative external statements, but rather as a fruitful hypothesis to be pursued. Only in the freedom and tentativeness generated by hypothetical thinking (as opposed to authoritative thinking) can there eventuate an open and genuine solution to the problem. Third, the truth of any proposition and experience can only be ascertained by careful empirical experimentation in conjunction with the guiding hypothesis. Any a priori truth simply lacks empirical verification and so is only an opinion.

While it is obvious that the Unification Church does not subscribe to all of Dewey's views on the relation of science and the religious, still there do exists major points of contact. These major points of contact are useful not only in the evangelization efforts of Church members, but also in expanding vertically and horizontally[19] the life of the Unification Church in general and the meaning of the *Divine Principle* in particular.

Like Dewey, the Unification Church believes that the reconciliation of science and religion constitutes a particularly pivotal area of modern times. The annual science conference sponsored by the Church is an eloquent affirmation of Unificationism's commitment to this reconciliation. The *Divine Principle's* "Introduction" asserts that the mission of the new truth will be "to present the eternal truth that religion has pursued and the external truth searched for by science under one unified theme."[20] O that other Christian religions would adopt such a similar and prophetic view of the intimate relation of science and religion! The unification of religion and science is central to Sun Myung Moon's religious view of reality, a view which is radicated in the reciprocal dynamic unity of Sung Sang (internal character) and Hyung Sang (external form). Of course, Sung Sang and Hyung Sang stand in opposition to Dewey's monism. Still, Dewey would applaud the Unification Church's tendency (while differing with its specifics) to see the religious (and the irreligious) dimension of the world and the worldly dimension of the religious.[21]

It seems to me that in the fruitful seeds of its Sung Sang and Hyung Sang theology/philosophy/psychology/cosmology, the Unification Church might further explore the way in which religion and indeed the Unification Church is itself scientific and proceeds scientifically. I suspect that John Dewey might advise this course of action; at the very least I suspect he would countenance it. Furthermore, it seems to me that the Unification Church could profit from John Dewey's recognition that science is social science as well as natural science. One gets the distinct impression that social science is neglected to a certain extent in the thought and concern of Unificationists when they deal with the reconciliation of science and religion. If the twentieth century has been the age of natural science, the twenty-first century in all probability will be the age of social science. The Unificationists would be well advised not to miss the import of this likely eventuality.

There seems to be a major point of contact between Dewey's stress on the empirical verification of truth in action and the living doctrine of the Unification Church. To be sure, Church members have told me on innumerable occasions over the years that there is heavy emphasis in their movement on empirically-verified results. For example, members have told me that even though the Church leadership does not smile with especial warmth on the Oakland procedures of evangelizing because these procedures are not in accord with the culturally-conditioned peda-gogical practices used in Korea in the early days of the movement, nonethe-less the Church leadership has not moved against the Oakland proced-ures because these practices have produced beneficial empirically-verified results. Church members have also told me that the worthwhileness of activities such as Home Church, Ocean Ministry, Protracted Intensive Workshops and the like are all ultimately judged in terms of the empirically-verified degree to which they yield desired results. Indeed, the truth of the Unification Church itself seems to many members to be verified on the basis not just of the converts it is winning but also on the basis of the beneficial religious effects which this conversion and its aftereffects have on the lives of the converts.[22] The *Divine Principle* is replete with empir-ical verifiers.[23] Thus, for example, the *Divine Principle* judges that John the Baptist failed in his mission of strengthening the Lord's path because the DP interprets the empirical evidence presented in the Bible as suggest-ing that John shirked his sacred duty of following Jesus.[24] There is even a sense in which the Unification Church empirically verifies that the *Divine Principle* is a verbal formulation of divine inspiration.[25] Narratives of the deep spiritual life of Sun Myung Moon, accounts of the profound religious effects which his captivity and post-captivity ministry had on various persons, and the deep religious results which the *Divine Principle* has had on the lives of Unificationist converts—all these and other empirical supports are adduced to verify the contention made by Moon and the Church that the *Divine Principle* is an authentic verbal formula-tion of divine inspiration.

Another major point of contact between Dewey and the Unification Church is the notion of the religious as directed to this world. While the

Divine Principle unmistakably indicates that a Unificationist should live fully in the invisible substantial world, it also teaches that the same Unificationist should dwell fully in the visible substantial world.[26] To be sure, the Unification Church has been criticized by unfriendly voices as living too successfully in the visible substantial world—effective fishing ventures, skillful real estate dealings in the nation's largest city, a well-constructed newspaper venture, a herbal import company, a fast-food restaurant, and the like.

Yet another major point of contact between the philosophy of John Dewey and the Unification Church is the view of the religious as process. The Unification conceptualization of the religious in the world is a highly processive one, beginning with creation and moving slowly but inexorably toward the second coming and the final restoration. Dewey regards natural science and social science as revealing the structure and coloration of process. The Unification Church, it seems to me, could profit considerably from Dewey's view without having to embrace this view in the total and particular way in which Dewey does. Science for Dewey is not an accumulation of facts. Rather science is above all a set of procedures, a method for interpret*ing* reality and for construct*ing* a fruitful life for self and for others. Science is not a collection of conclusions; it is the way or method of constructing human endeavor so that conclusions are reached as a result of the process.[27]

In both the *Divine Principle* and in everyday Unification living, the Church places considerable verbal emphasis on process and on coming to grips with the scientific structure of process.[28] Yet it seems to me that the Church has only begun to scratch the surface of its efforts in exploring the scientific structure and operation of process. Let me illustrate this point by giving an example of some of the Unification Church's efforts to date in the religious education process. By religious education I mean those instructional and guidance processes which deliberatively facilitate desired religious outcomes in people, e.g. conversion experiences, evangelistic outcomes, and the like. By and large the Unification Church still uses the religious education principles (cognitive structures) and practices (operations explained by cognitive structures) employed in the early Korean days of the movement. I am not aware of any major serious scientific effort within the Church to satisfactorily explain and systematically test the structure and operation of this Korean religious educational process as used either in Korean or in non-Korean settings. Sometimes the Korean process-paradigm is looked at and slightly modified, but generally not from a serious and careful scientific perspective. Johnny Sonneborn, for example, reports that Ken Sudo once operated a training program designed to devise and implement new procedures for more effective religious education in an evangelistic mode.[29] However, from what I can learn, Sudo's admirable efforts, together with the piecemeal efforts by Unificationists here and there, typically are not intentionally grounded in a careful detailed analysis of the social-scientific structure of the teaching-learning process. Nor does a sizeable portion of the Church seem very interested in learning or operationalizing the scientific structure and functions of the teaching-learning process (e.g. evangelization activities) in order to better understand and significantly improve its all-important religious education ministry. Members greatly enjoy recounting their personal experiences about what they perceptually regard as successful religious education processes; often these members adduce personalistic hip-pocket data rather than scientific evidence to support their feelings of effectiveness. Only rarely have I found that these members are interested in deeply exploring the scientific structure of their perceived successes, or in painstakingly working to put their future religious education processes on a sound scientific footing.

To those Unificationists who might object to my gentle criticism in the previous paragraph on the grounds that it is unwritten Unificationist bad form to provide anything but the most positive reinforcement, including frequent undeserved personal praise, I must reply that give and take constitutes one of the cardinal principles of the Unification religion. Furthermore, Proverbs 13:24 states that a person freely chastises those whom he loves. A person who does not truly love others will not take the time or the effort—or the subsequent opposition—to chastise them.

What does Deweyism (or neo-Deweyism) have to offer the Unification Church in terms of helping the Church unify social science and its religious education activities in such a manner that these activities are thereby rendered optimally effective? Several suggestions come to mind. First, establish a central research and training facility for the social-scientific analysis of the process of religious education in its various forms. This facility comprises two parts, namely research and training. In the research area, the effort of the staff would be directed toward careful social-scientific analysis of the structure and operations of religious education endeavor. This analysis could then be interfaced with Unification thought (e.g. *Divine Principle*), Unification affect (e.g. the feeling dimension of the Unification prayer life), and Unification life-style, so as to bring an added dimension to the social-scientific analysis of the religious education act. In the training sector of the facility, attention would be given to intensive development and preparation of Unification-ists highly skilled in religious education processes. Second, establish regional bands of educational process consultants to assist state and local Unificationists in becoming more educationally successful. These pro-cess consultants would be trained at the Church's national research and training facility, and then move about a designated region systematically upgrading the efforts of Unificationist religious educators (CARP work-ers, State Leaders, etc.) on the pedagogical firing line. Third, establish and publicize national conferences devoted to the social-scientific exploration of the religious education process. The Unification Church sponsors an annual conference on science and religion, as well as several national theology conferences. The major seminary sponsors and hosts its own theology conferences. In order to place social-scientific thinking about the religious education process at the heart of the Unification movement, both the Church and the seminary should establish religious education conferences of a scope and stature comparable with their theological conferences. Fourth, send on a representative portion of seminary grad-uates for doctoral studies in the social-scientific dimension of religious education. At present I know of only one student who ever was sent on for doctoral studies in this area. Fifth, place religious education in the seminary more at the center and more in an integrational matrix than is presently the case. At present, those courses offered in the social-scientific basis and operation of religious education are, in the perceptions of most students with whom I have talked over the years, closer to the periphery than to the center of the seminary's educational endeavor. Also, religious education does not seem to presently serve as the integrational matrix for the seminary curriculum, even though the diploma awarded to successful graduates is a religious education one. The theoretical understanding of the Church's essential religious education mission, and the practical success of the Church's religious education efforts could be significantly enhanced by making religious education more central and more integra-tional in the curriculum and the perceptions of the students.

RECONSTRUCTION THROUGH EDUCATION
THAT IS RELIGIOUS

A third major point of contact between John Dewey and the Unification Church is their common emphasis on reconstruction that is religious. This reconstruction embraces both the person and society.

A leitmotif, and quite possibly the leitmotif of Dewey's thought is that of reconstruction. This theme runs constantly throughout Dewey's major writings, minor articles, speeches, and other activities. Thus Dewey is an unabashed utopian: he wishes to make a better world, one in which the religious and the moral hold sway. The task of philosophy, in Dewey's view, is not to engage in idle speculation for speculation's sake. Rather the task of philosophy is to illumine human action in a dialogical manner so as to more effectively enable the reconstruction of persons and of society. Dewey's whole system of philosophy can only be appreciated if it is viewed as a philosophy of reconstruction.[30]

For Dewey, reconstruction is no superadditum to experience. Nor is reconstruction an end external to experience or a goal extrinsic to human functioning. Rather, reconstruction lies at the very essence of the processing person. This point can be succinctly illustrated by examining one of man's most basic processes, namely that of learning. Dewey asserts that learning is fundamentally an ongoing personal reconstruction of experience. When a person is learning, he is reconstructing his knowledge and his experiential world because he is acquiring new data and new interpretations in such a manner that his former data and interpretations are slightly or greatly changed (reconstructed) in the process. Each act of learning is thus an act of personal reconstruction. Learning is the process in which various data and explanations are reconnected and reconstructed from their former anchorages and placed into newer and larger wholes.[31] Man's reconstruction in and through learning is the reason why he does not become bogged down in the particular sense data or the cognitive facts which he experiences, but is able to reconstructively combine and re-form these data and facts into new personally-held views.[32] "There is no intellectual growth without some reconstruction, some remaking, of impulses and desires in the form in which they first show themselves," writes Dewey.[33]

Learning is a process of personal reconstruction because it involves the whole processing person. Learning is not just passive experiencing. Learning is also active experiencing such as that which occurs in both overt and nonovert activity. As Dewey once remarked, "We cannot speak of an idea and its expression; the expression is more than a mode of conveying an already formed idea; it is part and parcel of its formation."[34]

Commenting on this and a related passage from Dewey, Melvin Baker writes: "This means that just as act and ideal or technique and content are interacting elements, each reconstructing the other, so too are these two kinds of images reconstructing each other in imagination. This permits the extension of experience beyond the bounds of present sensibilities; it is growing intelligence."[35]

Reconstruction is essential to making the individual and society more religious because reconstruction lies at the heart of productive personal development and societal growth, according to Dewey. Thus he contends that true religiousness, like true faith, is the processive and progressive reorganization and reconstruction of reality in such a fashion that ennobling moral values and ideals are experimentally fashioned and empirically tested. Without ongoing essential reconstruction, the religious will in all likelihood be transmogrified into a fixed doctrinal apparatus which limits human growth and impedes the flowering of the religious.[36] For Dewey, ultimate moral motives are nothing more and nothing less than social intelligence,[37] an intelligence which is quintessentially reconstructive.[38]

In Dewey's view, the process and goal of genuine and fecund reconstruction must be grounded in science and proceed along scientific lines. Any reconstructionist effort which is not scientific in foundation and practice will surely fail, because no genuine reconstruction of humanity or morality is possible without a thorough scientific foundation and process. Conversely, the nature and operations of science are themselves fundamentally reconstructive; a nonreconstructive science is only a self-enclosed isolated entity devoid of any significance, fruitfulness, and life. If reconstructionism is to flourish, the contextual, living, and institutional conditions into which it enters and which determine its human and religious consequences must be subjected to that kind of serious and systematic inquiry worthy of being designated scientific.[39]

If people are to be re-formed and/or to re-form others, then they must first re-construct themselves and/or others. For Dewey, the content and goal of philosophy is to reform and reconstruct persons and society. To be a philosopher, to be a religious person, is to be a reformer, that is to say a reconstructionist. Verbally and existentially, reform and reconstruction are very close indeed.[40]

Dewey looks to educational endeavor, especially focussed intentional education as it exists in the school, as a prime engine and dynamic locus for effecting personal and societal reconstruction. For Dewey, the school is an ideal educational society precisely because it is, or at least should be, a living laboratory for democratic living. Like a genuine laboratory, the school should feature firsthand experiences and experimentation which are constantly imbued with the scientific spirit and constantly subjected to scientific test.[41] The school, that living social laboratory, enables each learner to continuously and experimentally reconstruct his own personal value system and his own individual way of encountering reality. The school is, above all, a social group where students as a social group learn to share their selves, their ideals, and their experiences in order to individually and collectively reconstruct their own society as well as external society. [42] The school curriculum should properly arise from the pressing personal problems and social concerns of the learners individually and collectively. In order to do this, the curriculum must change its axis from inert subject matter to living human experience. "Hence", Dewey writes, there exists "the need of reinstating into experience the subject-matter of the studies, or branches of learning. It must be restored to the experience from which it is abstracted. It needs to be psychologized; turned over, translated into the immediate and individual experiencing within which it has its origin and significance."[43] The teacher's pedagogical method is student-centered in that it seeks to help the student engage in an ongoing reconstruction of his experiencing by engaging in the scientific process of thinking discussed earlier in this essay.[44] In Dewey's own words:

> It thus becomes the office of the educator to select those things within the range of existing experience that have the same promise and potentiality of presenting new problems which by stimulating new ways of observation and judgment will expand the area of further experience. He must constantly regard what is already won not as a fixed possession but as an agency and instrumentality for opening new fields which make new demands upon existing powers of observation and of intelligent use of memory. Connectedness in growth must be his constant watchword.[45]

It is apparent from my analysis of some of Dewey's views on reconstruction through education that certain of his concepts are not in keeping with the living teachings of the Unification Church. For example, in neither word nor deed does the Church subscribe to the process of education as one of reconstructing a student's basic moral and religious values through experimentation. However, there are a great many major points of contact between Dewey and the Unification Church on reconstruction in general and reconstruction through education in particular.

Reconstruction is a central truth and axial fact in the Unification Church. The Unification Church typically calls reconstruction by another name, namely restoration. There is a process of restoration and a goal of restoration all within the general providence of restoration. This restoration pertains to both the history of the world and the history of each individual person. The history of the world can only be truly viewed, in the Unificationist way of thinking, as an ongoing reconstruction, an ongoing restoration. Reconstruction and restoration are part and parcel of the same process.[46] Furthermore, the history of each individual can be most fruitfully viewed as a process and a product of reconstruction or restoration. A person's religious conversion to the Unification Church is regarded as a major reconstructional axis in the member's life, an axis which enhances the possibility of authentic restoration. Indeed, the Unificationists conceptualize salvation not as being justified unto God, but as restored unto an ongoing reconstruction or perfecting of self with and unto God. Statements of three Unificationists on this matter will reinforce the point I am making. Jonathan Wells remarks: "So salvation—actually we tend not to use this word in Unification theology; we talk more about restoration—becomes the work of the Holy Spirit through my physical body here on earth."[47] Tirza Shilgi observes as follows: "I think there is an essential difference between what we in the Unification Church define as the goal of salvation and the understanding of the goal of salvation in evangelical Christianity, in that we see the goal of salvation as being perfected man, whereas the Evangelicals would define their goal of salvation as forgiveness of sin."[48] Franz Feige puts the whole reconstructionist tone, coloration, and axis of restoration in clear perspective when he states:

> Salvation is a process of restoration. Hence, it doesn't necessarily have anything to do with Christianity or with our movement. It can work in everyone's life; even an atheist can participate in the process of restoration, even though he doesn't know it, through paying indemnity. What is indemnity? If something has lost its original status or position, for example a stone has fallen down, then that can be restored by bringing the stone back to its original position. Paying indemnity means paying back, reversing. The energy that I put into getting the stone back into position is called indemnity. Through indemnity I am able to restore... Now, restoration in the Unification Church is not just entering into a relationship with Jesus and the Holy Spirit, but involves being engrafted into the second advent family. This engrafting is both spiritual and physical.[49]

Unification Church members with whom I have conversed over the years explicitly or implicitly affirm that the convert work and evangelization work in which they are actively engaged are important aspects of helping to restore the world. Of course, conversion is a major form of personal and social reconstruction. It is a reconstruction of the way in which a person thinks, feels, and lives. V. Bailey Gillespie, an astute student of religious conversion, regards this phenomenon as a process of reconstructing oneself in order to gain integrity and completeness[50]—what the Unificationists would call restoration to the path of perfection.[51]

Though the Unification Church would not go as far as Dewey in making science virtually the sole basis for the moral and religious reconstruction of the world, still the Church does indeed place science in an axial and central place in the restoration for which it is striving. Here, then, we have another important point of contact between Dewey and the Unification Church. In the Unification perspective, science and religion are in each other as Hyung Sang and Sung Sang.[52] In the restoration of the world, science and religion have both indispensable and intertwining roles to play. The leadership of the Unification Church seems deeply aware of this. For example, the rallies at which Sun Myung Moon spoke were typically orchestrated in a manner which deliberatively embodied the finest in social-scientific theory and research. The rank-and-file Unificationist pays a great deal of lip service to the unification of science and religion both in the forging of the restoration and as the fruit of the restoration. The lack of existential appreciation of the structure and operations of science on the part of so many Unificationists—a failure which can only delay and impede the coming of the restoration according to Unificationist thought—must be regarded simply as a lag between belief and action, a lag which has been the bane of virtually every religion. (Such a lag, I should note parenthetically, is also characteristic of Dewey-based educational reform.)

The place and shape of education in reconstructing the world represents one of the most fertile major points of contact between John Dewey and the Unification Church. In Dewey's view, the highest form and most fruitful area for doing philosophy and doing religion is the educational endeavor. Education is purposive experience and so is capable of producing optimal growth. Education, then, is the process and the product of living, a living which is soaked with the moral and the religious.[53] The school typically represents the ideal and most effective form of education because the school provides that special environment in which education can best take place. In the school, facts which were torn away from their original place in one's overall experience are rearranged with reference to some general organizing principle, an organizing principle which grows out of and is in harmony with both the logical and psychological conditions of subjec : matter and learning.[54] Schooling is not discontinuous with wider educational endeavor; rather, schooling is a more purposeful way of approaching educational endeavor, a way which uses as its starting point the needs and interests and modes of expression acquired in wider educational activity.

Crucial to John Dewey's vision of schooling is his conceptualization of the school as a laboratory. In Dewey's view, the school is a laboratory for democracy in which students could learn in a first-hand immediate way. In Dewey's view, the reason why so many schools fail to properly educate their students unto growth is because what is given in school is second-handed and mediated through symbols rather than experienced in first-hand manner.[55] Effective schooling is a laboratory in which the students test in terms of their personal educational value the varieties of experiences and subject matters available. Effective schooling is also carefully planned and executed and evaluated by a teacher who is well trained for the pedagogical task and who tethers every phase of his pedagogical activity to scientific structures and operations.

The Unification Church can meaningfully contact Dewey's views of education on most of the areas mentioned above. From my own conversations with the Unification Church leadership, successful major workshop leaders like David Hose, and rank-and-file Unificationists engaged in a variety of apostolates, there seems to be enormous stress placed on education by the Church. To be sure, the schooling sector of educational endeavor seems more highly valued by the Unification Church than almost any other religion. An uninformed outsider visiting either the World Mission Center in New York City or the Church headquarters might come away with the impression that church life consists in an endless series of workshops.

As far as their social-scientific knowledge and skills permit, the workshop leaders strive to make this school experience a laboratory for Unification living. A wide variety of cognitive, affective, psychomotor, verbal, nonverbal, and lifestyle elements are programmed into the workshop/laboratory experience to make it as personally religious and meaningful to the learners as possible. If perhaps many of the workshop leaders (especially the weekday-night ones and the short weekend ones) are not too proficient in the social-scientific structure and operations of the workshop as laboratory, nonetheless the commitment on their part and on the part of the leadership of the workshop as laboratory is very clear and very strong. Unificationists could learn much from Dewey on how to make their laboratories for enriched Unification living more effective. I have little doubt that such an awakening will occur, because in my experience I have found the members of the Unification Church very open to new ways of looking at things and doing things, especially things which they regard as having a ready and demonstrable payoff either in terms of attracting new recruits to the Church or in terms of spiritually enriching the lives of the members.

CONCLUSION

In 1897 John Dewey published one of his most personal and most passionate statements, *My Pedagogic Creed*. The last affirmation of *My Pedagogic Creed* is:

> I believe that in this way the teacher always is the prophet of the true God and the usherer in of the true kingdom of God.

There are probably not too many Unificationists alive who could write a sentence more in harmony with Unificationism than this one. Surely this sentence, like most of the affirmations made in *My Pedagogic Creed*, suggest many major points of productive contact between John Dewey and the Unification Church.

NOTES

1. On this point, see Henry W. Stuart, "Dewey's Ethical Theory," in Paul Arthur Schilpp, ed., *The Philosophy of John Dewey*, 2nd edition (NY: Tudor, 1951), pp. 293–333.

2. See, for example, *Divine Principle*, 5th ed. (NY: Holy Spirit Association for the Unification of World Christianity, 1977), pp. 46–52. As a non-Unificationist, a nonexegete of the *Divine Principle*, and a nonhermeneuticist of the *Divine Principle*, I would like to make two observations about the use of this document. First, a more intelligent, more in-depth, and more

helpful use of the *Divine Principle* would be greatly facilitated if Church officials subsidized both in finances and in personnel the development of a concordance to the *Divine Principle* in its present form or in any future form it might take. Concordances of the Bible such as *Strong's Exhaustive Concordance and Nelson's Complete Concordance* have been of inestimable assistance not only to Biblical Scholars but also to serious laypersons and clergy who wish to use the Bible fruitfully. Indeed, there are even some Protestant Bibles which have a mini-concordance right in the Bible itself for the use of laymen and clergy who read such an edition. The onset of computer technology makes the development of a complete concordance of the *Divine Principle* relatively easy compared to the painstaking handwork of pre-computer days. Second, a more intelligent, more in-depth, and more helpful use of the *Divine Principle* would be facilitated if Church officials preferable in consultation with Sun Myung Moon, divided the *Divine Principle* in its present or possible future form into chapters and verses as is the case with the Bible. Such a procedure would also assist international scholarly and nonscholarly use of the *Divine Principle*, since people in diverse lands would thereby know precisely which text is being cited by a person from a different country.

3. John Dewey and James H. Tufts, *Ethics*, revised ed. (NY: Holt, 1921), pp. 364–367.

4. *Divine Principle*, pp. 25–27.

5. Thus Dewey remarks: "Men still want the crutch of dogma, of beliefs fixed by authority, to relieve them of the trouble of thinking and the responsibility of directing their activity by thought. They tend to confine their own thinking to a consideration of which one among the rival systems of dogma they will accept." John Dewey, *Democracy and Education* (New York: Macmillan, 1916), p. 394.

6. Dewey, *A Common Faith* (New Haven: Yale University Press, 1934), pp. 29–57.

7. *Ibid.*, pp. 7–10.

8. Dewey "Experience, Knowledge, and Value: A Rejoinder," in Schilpp, *The Philosophy of John Dewey*, p. 595, italics deleted.

9. In my experience, the studying aspect of Unification life, at least in its Barrytown seminary, seems to be less developed and less wholeheartedly embraced by the members than the other aspects of its ecclesial life which I mention in the body of the text. The Korean leadership of the Church appears to be enthusiastically supportive of deep and painstaking scholarly activity for each member in proportion to that particular member's ability. However, among the seminary students at least, the idealized role model which they have somehow taken seems by and large to be that of activist-student rather than scholar-student.

10. Dewey, "Religious Education as Conditioned by Modern Psychology and Pedagogy," in Dewey, *The Middle Works*, Volume 3, edited by Jo Ann Boydston (Carbondale, Il.: Southern Illinois University Press, 1977), pp. 210–215.

11. Thomas Carter and Linda Corrigan, "Life of Sun Myung Moon from 1920 to 1960," unpublished manuscript, 1979, p. 3.

12. Though I am in no way a specialist in Unificationist theology or learned in other aspects of Unification thought, there does appear to be at least one passage in the *Divine Principle* which seems somewhat in accord with what I have written in this paragraph. "The spirit men who in their lifetime did not believe in any religion but lived conscientiously, also come again at permitted times in order to obtain the benefit of resurrection through the second coming". (*Divine Principle*, p. 190, lines 10–12). Also another contextually-related passage states: "...the spirit men who believed in religions other than Christianity while on earth will have to come again, like the spirit men of Paradise, in order to receive the same benefit of resurrection through the Second Advent, though the time of their visitation may differ according to their spiritual positions" (*Divine Principle*, p. 180, line 30; p. 181, line 2). An ecclesiastically-approved commentary on the *Divine Principle* has this to say: "...although people capable of spiritual communication communicate with the same spirit world, since the spiritual level, circumstances, and individual character are different in each spiritually open person, the level of the spirit world with which they communicate and the contents of the revelations they receive differ from one another" (*Outline of The Principle, Level 4* [New York: Holy Spirit Association for the Unification of World Christianity, 1980], p. 82). (See also *ibid.*, pp. 33–37).

13. See Dewey, "Social Science and Social Control," in *New Republic*, LXVII (July 29, 1931), pp. 276–277. I should note in this connection that some social scientists have vitiated their procedures and conclusions by attempting to slavishly pattern their work on natural science.

14. Dewey, *The Quest for Certainty* (New York: Minton, Balch, 1929), p. 40.

15. *Ibid.*, pp. 98–139.

16. Dewey, *Logical Conditions of a Scientific Treatment of Morality* (Chicago: University of Chicago Press, 1903).

17. On this point, see Hans Reichenbach, "Dewey's Theory of Science," in Schilpp, *The Philosophy of John Dewey*, pp. 159–160.

18. Dewey, *How We Think* (Boston: Heath, 1933), p. 107.

19. My choice of these two adverbs here is deliberate, and is intended to intersect with the vertical and horizontal relationships discussed in the *Divine Principle* and by Unification Church members.

20. "Introduction" in *Divine Principle*, p. 10.

21. Dewey, naturally, would reject the dichotomy of world and religious. For him as a monist, the world is religious and religious is the world. However, in contrast to most Christian theologies which have set the world over and against religion, Dewey would be sympathetic to the Unification Church's tendency to see world and religion as unified dimensions of the same reality—the same "new truth."

22. This theme runs throughout the testimony of converts as recorded in Richard Quebedeaux and Rodney Sawatsky, *Evangelical-Unification Dialogue* (NY: Rose of Sharon, 1979).

23. The Bible, too, is full of empirical verifiers of all sorts. The most famous New Testament passage in this connection is Mt. 7:20 ("By their fruits you shall know them"). The miracles which Jesus performed can be viewed as empirical verifiers of his message.

24. *Divine Principle*, pp. 343–348.

25. I am not altogether pleased with my use of the term "divine inspiration" as this term might unintentionally evoke controversies in Protestant and Catholic circles about the nature and object of divine inspiration. My point in using this term is to indicate that for the Unification Church, the revelations which Sun Myung Moon experienced are claimed to be of divine origin. To be sure, the Unification Church seems to understand the *Divine Principle* as one incomplete verbal formulation of Sun Myung Moon's revelations. The *Divine Principle* is regarded as one formulation because it might well be that Moon might redictate another version of the same revelations that covered in the *Divine Principle*. This document is regarded as an incomplete verbal formulation because it only includes some of the content which Sun Myung Moon says he received in his encounters with God. Speaking as a fervent religionist, I can only hope that Moon does dictate more of the contents of his revelations in addition to the *Divine Principle*. New documents will not only enrich the Unification Church, but also will act as a fertile source of theological speculation and religious activity among non-Unificationist religions.

26. *Divine Principle*, pp. 57–64.

27. Dewey, *Essays in Experimental Logic* (Chicago: University of Chicago Press, 1916), pp. 13–18.

28. I would expect that despite molar differences on some basic issues, Unificationists would greatly enjoy and profit from continuing major dialogue with process philosophers and theologians, not only those from the Whiteheadian tradition but also those from the Teilhardian tradition as well.

29. Johnny Sonneborn, "Statement," in Quebedeaux and Sawatsky, *Evangelical-Unification Dialogue*, p. 91.

30. Dewey, *Reconstruction in Philosophy,* enlarged edition (Boston: Beacon, 1948), pp. v-viii.

31. Dewey sets the stage for his later and richer formulations of this basic principle in "Psychology" in John Dewey, *The Early Works,* Volume 2, edited by Jo Ann Boydston (Carbondale, Il.: Southern Illinois University Press, 1967), pp. 83–89.

32. See Dewey, *Reconstruction in Philosophy,* pp. 77–102.

33. Dewey, *Experience and Education* (NY: Macmillan, 1938), p. 74.

34. Dewey, "Imagination and Expression," in *Kindergarten Magazine,* IX (September, 1896), p. 63.

35. Melvin C. Baker, *Foundations of John Dewey's Educational Theory* (NY: King's Crown, 1955), p. 21.

36. Dewey, *A Common Faith,* pp. 26–28.

37. Dewey, *Moral Principles in Education* (NY: Greenwood, 1959), p. 43.

38. Dewey, *Reconstruction in Philosophy,* pp. 161–186.

39. *Ibid.,* pp. xxiii-xxix.

40. *Ibid.,* p. xii.

41. On these points, see Dewey, *The School and Society* (Chicago: University of Chicago Press, 1900).

42. Dewey, *Democracy and Education* (NY: Macmillan, 1916), pp. 81–178.

43. Dewey, "The Child and the Curriculum," in Dewey, *The Middle Works,* Vol. 2, p. 285.

44. Dewey, *Democracy and Education,* pp. 193–211.

45. Dewey, *Experience and Education,* p. 90.

46. An official Church commentary on the *Divine Principle,* with the accompaniment of attractive and illuminating charts and diagrams of diverse sorts, devotes considerable space to the interpretation of world history from the viewpoint of the dispensation for and in restoration. See *Outline of the Principle, Level 4,* pp. 101–115.

47. Jonathan Wells, "Statement," in Quebedeaux and Sawatsky, *Evangelical-Unification Dialogue,* p. 294. Insertion of the words "reconstructive and reconstructing" before the word "work" in Wells' statement would bring his point more to salience, I believe.

48. Tirza Shilgi, "Statement," in *ibid.* Again, to heighten the salience of Shilgi's remark with respect to the point I am making in this paragraph, the word "reconstructed" could fruitfully be substituted for her word "perfected".

49. Franz Feige, "Statement," in *ibid.*, p. 298.

50. V. Bailey Gillespie, *Religious Conversion and Personal Identity* (Birmingham, Al: Religious Education Press, 1979), pp. 44–123.

51. In view of the Unification Church's heavy emphasis on convert making and convert preserving, I am ceaselessly amazed by how few Unificationist members seem to be scientifically knowledgeable in the psychology and pedagogy of religious conversion.

52. *Outline of the Principle, Level 4*, pp. 6–14.

53. Dewey, *Democracy and Education*, pp. 49–62.

54. Dewey, *The Child and the Curriculum*, pp. 273–276.

55. Dewey, *Democracy and Education*, pp. 271–274.

56. Dewey, "My Pedagogic Creed," in Dewey, *The Early Works*, Vol. 5, p. 95.

Kurt Johnson

The Unification Principle and Science; Promise, Paradox and Predicament

As a scientist,[1] I want to address some issues concerning the relation of the Unification Church movement's "Unification Principle"[2] and science. There is already some volume of literature on this relatively new subject, and the reader is referred to it for basic discussions.[3] Because of the breadth of science, and the problem of topical selection for this kind of compilation concerning Unificationism, it has been important for me, first of all, to decide what subject area should be addressed. One attractive option would be to present an example of how the Unification Principle can be applied to a particular scientific problem. Though this requires a detailed and precise application of aspects of "The Principle" to a particular scientific discipline (which might be useful in demonstrating the potential value of the Unification ideology in science) this approach is probably unnecessarily limited for a publication of more general interest. However, for the sake of example, one particular application of Unification Principle to an ecological problem is summarized in Figure 1 and its explanation.[4] For the present compendium of essays, it seems more useful and probably more interesting for a scientist to address a larger range of issues regarding science. For such a discussion I have chosen to consider how the Unification Principle, in its role as a particular ideological viewpoint, will be required by history to have an interesting interplay with science. Such a dialogue with science, with the latter having open inquiry as its nature, will include not only the present situation of Unificationism as an emerging ideology but also Unificationism's potential for creating a sociological environment in which a potential Unificationist society will have to relate to science on a more extensive level.

Science is by definition an area of open inquiry concerning reality and how it works.[5] A relevant question, then, is how science relates to ideologies which by definition have variously fixed points of view. Ideologies arise because they hope to provide new information or new insights to already existing societies and their information systems. An ideology aspires to make this contribution in an organized fashion which can exert influence on the already existing system. In the interplay of an emerging ideology and an existing system it can be expected that the new ideology will make some contributions which are constructive and important, some which suggest paradoxes in their relationship with the norms of inquiry in the existing system, and others which will create predicaments or problems. The predicaments caused by the interplay of the new ideology and the existing system arise because the new ideology either seeks to change particular basic directions or content in the views of the existing system, or proposes to do so by means that may not be considered appropriate by the existing system. Without doubt, the aim of an emerging ideology is to add new information to a given system or, at least, to rearrange some information in that system. This is especially true when the source of the new ideology, as with Unificationism, is religious or metaphysical and seeks to dialogue with a society that is basically secular and technological.

Within the above-mentioned dialogue, an ideology (if it is serious at all) must come into a multi-faceted dialogue with science. This is because science functions on numerous levels in a society. One is the "higher" level of its educational research, and technological institutions; another is a "lower" level, a popularized substrate involving the elementary education in a society (that is, early education) and the popular media. There is within every modern secular and technologically-oriented society a popular "scientific mythology", or popular science, propagated by the necessities of elementary levels of education and the popularized media. As will be seen below, this popular scientific mythology is, in every society, quite different than the positions actually held by scientists or by "science." The popular invasion of mythologized science into the world view of peoples within various societies creates an inevitable clash and confrontation in the information-rich arena of world media. One has only to think of the basic differences in world view of a communist youth, a fundamentalist Christian youth, and a fundamentalist Moslem youth to understand this reality. It can be taken for granted that not only does each of these persons or views participate in its society (be it by guns, votes, or by simply being a statistic) but that none of them could be expected to have a particularly fruitful discussion concerning world-views with the educated elite of their respective nation.

The importance of examining the breadth of this problem as regards a new ideology and science is twofold: (a) the new ideology confronts the world arena of competing world views and (b) the nature of science and the nature of the new ideology are both elucidated by examining their potential interplay. The world is an open market for information, whether it be propaganda or empirically demonstrated thought. It must be recognized that any ideology will, by nature, clash with the nature of science as open inquiry and this clash will probably be characterized by a mix of promise, paradox and predicament.

Unificationists should be comfortable with this confrontation for two reasons. Firstly, Unificationists can hardly be expected to abandon any of the views they claim are derived from revelation. These impose arbitrary opinions on certain matters of world view. Secondly, Unificationism (or any ideology) shares with science a general method of dealing with reality. This includes the setting up of certain pre-supposed conditions and from these developing logic and concepts. Both science and ideologies, therefore, are bound to have untested "sacred cows." These will rise and fall only with much conflict and trepidation. History has seen nothing so far in science or religion that has ever survived in a consistent conceptual form.

Because of the juxtaposition of science as open inquiry and the nature of ideologies as variously arbitrary, discussion of Unificationism and science by one scientist can obviously be biased. This bias can favor either the point of view of the ideology or the many possibilities open to science as open inquiry. In this essay I will try to avoid this potential bias by placing emphasis on suggesting problems rather than describing solutions. Since the topic involves Unificationism as an emerging ideology, it is expected that all of the areas addressed in the paper will find their eventual solution only through the historical development of actual events.

Scientific Information in Societal Groups and Other Systems

In order to understand what science is and how accumulated scientific information comes into dialogue within and between societies, it is first important to understand how scientific information is placed into and subsequently circulates within a given social system. Science itself is an organ for gathering information and carefully discerning modes and ways in which this information can be conceptualized and applied. As such it is a strict discipline. Science, however, has no mechanism to control the use of its information as it "trickles down" to the popularized levels of societies. At the popular level, scientific information is used not only in the creation and selling of sensationalized ideas, but in the various coercions of politics which seek to use scientific information to sway the populace to causes, fears, promised solutions and their associated political enfranchisements. Very often, much of the scientifically based information involved in the latter processes is either distorted or incorrect. This problem is a difficult one simply because the misuse of scientific information within a society is most often inadvertent. For instance we have a "fight to cure cancer" though within science cancer can hardly be considered one "kind" of disease. We have classified various behavioral abnormalities as "mental illnesses" implying that they are "diseases" that one can "get." We have popular concepts of "ecology" and "evolution" which have little to do with what ecologists and evolutionary biologists actually study. We have "arms races" based on technological arguments and billions of dollars spent on "illegal" activities (such as alcohol, drugs, gambling, prostitution, and firearms) though by sociological definition these activities are seen as deviant.

Far from the disciplined work of research laboratories and the so-called institutions of higher learning, popularized scientific books are written and bought by the millions, propaganda prepared and distributed with zeal, and media money-makers produced and viewed by the masses. All of these form world views, and their reality, no matter how far from actual reality, takes on a very powerful reality of its own. If popular institutions cannot be expected to produce constructive world views that have any basis in scientific reality, the education system is no less promising. In a strict appraisal, there is actually no education before the doctoral level which can in any field hope to include a real sensitivity to how information is derived, how it can be used to draw conclusions, and how it relates or does not relate to what one wants to know. The emerging new ideology cannot escape from this reality in which the gap between science as discipline and science as popular myth is great.

The relevant evaluations concerning an emerging ideology, then, are these: (a) how is science used in the new ideology? and (b) what kind of position is predicted for science in the sociological context implied by the new ideology? The question is even more complex if the new ideology is "religious." This is because not only does the realm of religion include all the dynamic interplay concerning accuracy and popularization which have been mentioned above concerning science, but because by nature the "religious" ideology will have a particular and inevitable clash with science.

As with other sources of information, religions vie for adherents and territories of control and influence in a society. Within the various sects and denominations a few thousand to several millions of adherents hold this or that set of information as the most basic and true. Some feel called to convert others to their beliefs whether by educational, economic or political means. Some feel that pluralism is good, others that they are destined to assimilate everyone else. Outside of established religions, in the realm of popular myth and fantasy, salesmen promote everything from space-alien origins and cleansing of the body with supposed "non-chemical" organic substances to various apocalyptic promises. Yet within all this, mankind as a species is still made up of individual persons who search for truth and in this search come to believe that this or that view of life, no matter how disparate or varied, is true. Within societies it is the basic mode of popular belief that dominates the economic, political and day-by-day circumstances of man. Learning, or the tested learning characteristic of science, holds little sway.

It is upon this complex stage that the Unification Movement emerges as another group with saleable information, that is, potentially persuasive information. It is characteristic of the Unification Movement to want some of this information accepted as "new" and other parts of it as at least a preferable rearrangement. Working within an evangelistic framework, the Unification Movement has the potential to envision and attempt to create a sociological structure characterized by aspects of its beliefs. Its claim is that such a structure will make things "better" for mankind, and even "better" for God. This kind of claim goes far beyond the realm of science, for science is simply groups of people studying reality within a certain disciplined framework of inquiry. It is useful, then, to inquire about science within such a megaphenomenon as apocalyptic movements and the societies they predict.

Science Within Unificationism Itself

How is science used within Unification Principle itself? Does or can science as science exist within the framework of a particular ideological world-view? Is such science, and can it remain real science? Or is it quasi-science, or doomed to be pseudo-science?

A brief and objective look at Unification Principle indicates that it is characterized by theism (a belief in a supernatural being, in this case one also seen as active in the contemporaneous world) applied through a theistically modified dialectical ontology. According to Unificationism, the theism hopes to address religion with a unifying potential, or at least be capable of generating a new platform for productive inter-religious dialogue. The dialectical ontology hopes to bring to bear the persuasive powers of Marxism, but without necessary atheism. Through theistically modified dialectics (e.g. modify the basic Marxist mechanics by discarding the ontology of contradiction and process of negation, replacing them with mutuality and cooperation toward a common purpose), Unificationism hopes to embrace science and technology within one unified world-view. By removing the atheism, Unificationism hopes to avoid the negation of the individual so common to the history of Marxist political regimes and replace it with reverence for the individual based on a religious view of God as the common parent of all mankind. By this distinctive theistic feature Unificationism hopes to address the problems of disunified and fragmented societies which have become dysfunctional through internal splitting along racial, economic, and other self-interest lines.

At face value the combination of theism and theistically dialectical ontology is promising. Theism has the promise of imbuing a transcendant view of reality with a reverence for the value of the individual, while dialectics promises to allow a view of the material universe which is compatible with sciences very general understanding of complementary particles and principles and hierarchies of order based on the elaboration of these. As a dialectical theism, Unificationism seems to rid itself of several of the pitfalls of dialectical materialism. Rudimentally, the presupposed relations of the complementary components in Unification ontology do not relate through struggle based on inherent contradiction. Progress does not occur through negating the integrity of one componnent by aggressive action and the assumption of superiority by the other. Rather, a more humane ideal of progress is suggested by having the complementary model of all relations, and the basis for resulting hierarchies, in the context of a larger complementary model including a transcendent dimension and a complementary physical dimension. This complementarity of the transcendent and physical dimensions of reality in Unificationism allows for the reality and claims of religion while proposing a set of mechanics which can include science, both as an area of open inquiry and a social arena for applying technological knowledge. For the scientist, the most interesting feature of such an ideological proposition is whether it predicts something new or promising as regards methodologies in science which may be a counterproposal to reductionism.

A problem occurs, however, both in Unification Theology as a revealed religion and in its dialectical ontology as a basis for science. The problem is inevitable but remains to be solved all the same. Unificationism's religion is allegorical, that is, it presents one accepted interpretation of scripture, and for only one of the world's religious traditions at that. Unificationism's ontology is presented as a series of assumptions based less on philosophical principles than on allegorical arguments of creation by design. The ontology grapples with a mythological framework limited to the symbolic imagery of creation stories from one near eastern people—the ancient Israelites. This theology, based on a particular allegorical interpretation of certain scripture, is seen as inevitably assimilating all other previously revealed religions. The science is seen, at least so far in the history of Unificationism, as an adjunct to the theology. Since the theology is apocalyptic, the ontology predicates a deterministic view of history based on the same principles that are offered for subjective science.

As a result there are two disparate kinds of science involved in the presentation of Unificationism thus far in its history: (a) the more or less valid mobilization of selected scientific facts to buttress the Unificationist's allegorical theological argument of creation by design and its resultant historical determinism and (b) Unification ontology as applied to philosophy and science which as a conceptual model offers itself as one potentially encompassing more intellectual territory than others to date. To scientists with some awareness of (a) science as various systems models and paradigms of assumptions and logic and (b) science as a deductive process in which statements about reality are tested and discerned according to criteria of veracity, consistency, parsimony, repeatability, predictability, and utility, it is the latter part of Unification science that is attractive. This part, however, is nearly completely undeveloped. Rather, the former approach, of attempting scientific proof-texting of arguments for creation by design, is currently dominant in Unification education. One cannot expect all adherents of any religion to have intellectual pursuits as a prime value. However, as noted before, it is the creation of the popular myths of a world view within a society that actually hold sway, and so it is in Unificationism.

Despite this current historical problem, Unificationism still stands as a potential basis for significant development of non-reductionist views of reality (that is, views which limit causality to purely material or physical bases). Reductionism seems at its heart more congruent with the nature of scientific inquiry. However, it must be entertained that if the cosmology of the universe is non-reductionist in nature and contains a transcendent dimension, the reductionist paradigm is necessarily frustrating and inadequate. Unificationism offers a system based on a gigantic complement of transcendent and physical dimensions. The realities of input, information flow, and output in such a system offer a unique philosophical dimension. Unification's model of Sung Sang and Hyung Sang, as metaphysical complements including a transcendent and physical dimension, allows the introduction of new information, control, or management from somewhere other than within or below the sums of the parts in a physical system. Certainly, such a model cannot be scientifically applied simply within reference to its unscientific transcendent claims. However, it is possible that the assumption of such a cosmology as a basis for framing methodologies may have some demonstrable value. For instance, based on Unification Principle, some methodology which is within itself scientific may make some significant contributions in two areas:

a. molecular biology, genetics, biochemistry, and theoretical biology where the study of systems might be better approached through a cosmology allowing input of information from more than just the bottom or within the sum of the parts.

b. offering a progressive creationism that could possibly address the transcendent and value-laden nature of man in a context of the overwhelming evidence supportive of the continuing origin of biotic and inorganic diversity through the various natural evolutionary processes accompanying the historical process of time.

However, even a successful non-reductionist paradigm has problems.

If allowing input of information from a transcendent dimension is placed into the methodology a priori, no more reason is apparent for expecting consistency in relation to the scientific criteria of veracity, parsimony, testability, repeatability, predictability or utility than would be expected when reductionism is posited a priori. There are paradoxes in this view because it is questionable to what extent a purely Unification-ist methodology could be developed without imposition of the Unifi-cation model as a doctrine. If, however, results in a coherent and scientific system based on the allowance of the Sung Sang/Hyung Sang assump-tion were more veracious, parsimonious and internally consistent, or allowed higher incidence of predictive value, this might lend credence to considering that the assumptions of a Sung Sang/Hyung Sang cosmol-ogy are more satisfactory than the reductionist one. To science, it would simply be a matter of which lended itself more to the goals of scientific inquiry. The development of workable methodologies based on the Sung Sang/Hyung Sang cosmology, which could compete with other world views, would have to involve specialists who prefer the viability and usefulness of the Unificationist view. It is not known how soon such persons will be available or even understood within present Unification-ism. Certainly the application of the idea of input of information from the transcendent component in relation to a claim of progressive creation-ism is characterized by gaps between the major biological groups. The Unificationist view, in this regard, is attractive and compatible with current salient features of information in evolutionary biology. It is reminiscent of the kind of view that Catholicism has developed with Teilhardian evolutionism. But Unification Principle adds a problem to exclusive claims when it understands that the Sung Sang and Hyung Sang metaphysical components act simultaneously. If, as stated in Unifi-cation Thought, the actions of Sung Sang and Hyung Sang are simultan-eous, Sung Sang action leaves a "trail" (or a reconstructable record) in the Hyung Sang. The paradox of this is that it presupposes that purely physical explanations of the activities of the Hyung Sang, based on the trail (e.g. the fossil record, biologically retrievable diagrams of evolution-ary, spatial and geological divergence, etc.) would in themselves be quite persuasive. Hence, modern evolutionary biology does claim that all of the major features of biotic diversity and its inter-relations can be account-ed for by the explanations of the mechanisms within the biosphere itself. Similarly, over half of the world seems to have found materialistic views persuasive. It remains to be seen whether the eventual value of the cosmology based on Sung Sang and Hyung Sang will be determinable by Unificationist scholars coming forward with arguments, models, and methodologies acceptable to the scientific community to others. Another alternative for Unificationism is to press itself onto science as a doctrine through religious, economic, or political activity. This is one area in which the paradox of the situation will only be resolved through seeing the actual course of Unificationism. Marxism has had all of these problems and more, so the parallel is well taken. Marxism established itself as a doctrine and then attempted to work out the problems of its methodologies.

In conclusion it can be stated that within the Unificationist ideology there are several aspects which imply potentially useful scientific models. It remains to be seen whether these can be developed into comprehensive contributions which would achieve acceptance by establishment scientists. In a parallel situation, Marxist models of phenomena have not necessarily been viewed as successful or preferable by scientists outside Marxist dominated countries. They are preferred only within the arenas where Marxism has itself been established through economic or political means as a social doctrine. Still, there are areas within Unificationism which have particular promise for science. These have interest in themselves and their potential value should not be denegrated.

Science Within A Unificationist Society

Science in Education and Religion: There are purely utilitarian evaluations which are relevant to the relations of ideology and science. It is quite possible that some societies will choose to emphasize ideological doctrines and prefer these more than those prompted by rational inquiry. For instance, a religious society might choose to balance its scientific aspect (especially as to what it teaches children) by favoring a progressive creationism model of natural process (regardless of its testability). This is because the society feels that a materialistic view of man leaves the children possibly devoid of a basic appreciation of values. Such a position by a society is certainly not scientific *per se*, but it must be recognized that many groups and societies favor untested beliefs as opposed to ideas derived from open inquiry. Further, the same society or particularly a movement might choose progressive creationism based on an Adam and Eve story (with commitment to this story either as literal truth or symbolic truth) because it feels the problem of racism can only be solved through man's embracing the concept of God as a common parent.

Historically, societies have a poor record for relating testable truth to what is claimed by their social or religious points of view. Unification-ism, to the extent that it has doctrines, shares this same sociological potential. How science would function in such a doctrinaire society is questionable. Interplay between Unificationism (as allegorical religion) and science (as open inquiry) would take extreme sensitivity. A society with fixed religious assumptions may not be open to a freedom to falsify its own religious claims. Also, its usages of scientific information to support its religious ontology may result in an unrecognized but chronic pseudoscience. This is the predicament of a religion when its teaching involves some science and some religion. On the other hand, we must entertain the historical possibility that some group might come up with "*the* Truth", perhaps by revelation as is claimed by Unificationism. If certain positions expressed by Unificationism are indeed true per se—one might expect the inevitable clash between its science and its religion would somehow be avoided or at least be less protracted. Marxism does not seem to be in much different a position historically. It is quite possible that if Unificationism would adopt the profile of a religion capable of creating persons of high moral character, civic virtue, and altruistic motivation in a free society, as opposed to the organization of an authori-tarian society around its ideology, science could function as science. The historical issue is whether science within one particular ideological frame-work is actually science or inevitably becomes pseudo-science. Even if science could function as science in a Unificationist society, in many areas of scientific pursuit (like the individual disciplines) it is hard to imagine why an individual scientist would adopt a Unificationist model for explaining his information if another model was just as or more satisfac-tory. It seems he would only do so if Unificationism was the assumed ideology, as in the case in many Marxist explanations of phenomena.

The above comments suffice concerning some conditions confronting science at the professional level in a Unificationist society. The other aspect of science in societies, that of the substrate of popular belief and early education, also requires comment. With Unificationism, the consid-eration is important because it is expected that a Unificationist society will exhibit the kinds of problems characteristic of societies with a monolithic world view. The agenda of restoration in Unificationism implicitly implies that the Unificationist view is to be taken as a guideline for a sociological system. In such a society there would be one preferred religion requiring particular educational norms. Since, as has been noted, there is a distinct gap in the nature of scientific information operating at public levels and that operating in professional sciences, a Unificationist society could not be exempt from this problem. Hence, it can be expected that the norm of education in a Unificationist society, at least before the doctoral level, would be that reinforcing the allegorical religious views of Unificationism. We can consider some contemporaneous comparisons to enlighten this view. In the United States a majority of persons are taught from birth that there is a God and that God created the universe. These persons generally begin to confront alternative views of the universe when they enter the secular educational realm. In a Unificationist society there would be no separation of church and state. Hence, there is an open question about what kind of creationism would be taught in the schools: would it be a creationism based on a literal interpretation of Unificationist scriptures similar to that of fundamentalist Christianity, or would it involve a more open teaching based on the more scientific views and possibilities in Chapter One of the *Divine Principle*, "The Principle of Creation." As has been noted earlier, there is not necessarily a conflict between the teachings of Chapter One of Divine Principle and the demonstrations of modern science. The contradiction only arises when the view of creationism in Unificationism is placed totally within the allegorical context of Unificationist religion. To date it is the latter kind of creationism that is taught in Unificationist education, that is, the literalistic fundamentalist approach. However, the fact that the other variety has been emphasized to some extent at the Unification Seminary evidences some sensitivity to the problem. It may be that Unificationism may evolve a situation similar to Christian denominations. Here, theological students, entering seminary to study for the ministry, discover a different view of the scriptures and theology from their professors than what they had been taught in the home or in the Christian preparatory schools. Even if this latter situation were the case, however, it would be expected that the normative view of science in the Unificationist society would still be that typical of other societies, that is, the popularized view. The major question is that posed before: would the Unificationist society opt for a simplistic short cut to the enfranchisement of its world view, that is, an authoritarian structure in which the creative portions of its theology were subordinated. In such situations, common throughout the world, ideals are taught only as abstract ideas. Or, would Unificationism successfully experiment with sociological models based on its professed ideology—one that clearly sees the integral balance between the components and the integrity of the parts. It is clear in the parallel of Marxism that Marxism has opted in most cases for the former counter-productive short cut. Marxist ideals of equality and egalitarianism exist in the professed beliefs of Marxist systems, but are contradicted by the actual praxis of most of their societies.

Science in Unificationist Social Structures: The most salient advantage of a projected Unificationist society based on the best parts of its ideology would be a theistically oriented society providing a unified and mutualistic emphasis. This would be characterized by the utopian aspect of Marxist goals but without the denigration of the individual so often seen in Marxist political regimes. Unificationism in a westernized framework could at least provide a cohesive world view that would be less prone to split along the lines of racial, economic, and self-interest groups. The difficulty is whether such a unified world view in context of actual political and bureaucratic institutions could actually be enfranchised without itself becoming intolerant of pluralism. Though pluralism is a healthy characteristic of societies which claim to be open and governing in the best interest of human beings (since someone is always bound to disagree) it is precisely what dedicated practitioners of one belief often find most objectionable. It has already been stated that within Unification principle per se there is no problem of an unbalanced view of the positions and integrity of the parts. There is, in fact, an extreme sensitivity to this problem such that the issue of priority and posteriority (the sense of which side needs to win out over another) is addressed in a manner definitely eclipsing that in Marxism. Yet such idealistic world views are often very difficult to put into practice. Such general ideals of freedom, equality, egalitarianism are also present in most of the world's great religions, in Marxism, and even in the Soviet constitution. That such ideals exist is no promise that they can actually be fulfilled. The short cut of a controlled rigid society, along with the compelling political nature of human beings and their interests in power and social control, are always tempting historically and have most often won out. A challenge to Unificationism will be to experiment with its ideology in ways that can try to put its ideal view of relationships into actual practice. It is precisely on this point that Unificationism needs to be extremely careful. This is because its general characteristics—religious world view, allegorical theology, historical determinism, and apocalyptic eschatology—all fit the categories that have been least successful historically in approximating their world views with actual concomitant systems of praxis. If

Unificationism successfully argues that Marxism, as dialectical materialism, has failed to deliver the egalitarianism it promised, what guarantee
can it offer that dialectical theism will do any better? This question can
only be answered in time, but in the meantime it is useful to sketch out
what Unificationists should be wary of and where they should be skeptical and sensitive. As a modern-day colloquialism aptly states: if you do
not know where you are going, you may end up somewhere else.
Unificationists should be aware that a wise way to proceed would be as if
no amount of historical determinism could magically solve the gravity of
the kinds of problems -which have been reviewed in this paper. The
position of science in the society is determined to a great extent by the
relative openness of the society. This problem of science and arbitrariness
is not simply limited to pure science. It is even more important to
technology. Technology can survive in societies which are basically
intellectually closed, but usually it only survives as a mimic of technolo-
gies that are being developed elsewhere in creatively open societies. The
resources for the creative development of technology, which certainly
must be a part of a scenario of world restoration, lie in the creativity of
pure science and an environment for pure intellectual pursuits.

Summary and Conclusions

This paper has reviewed a number of issues that will confront Unificationism as it approaches its inevitable dialogue with science. It also has
examined some characteristics of Unification science itself, and some
aspects of Unification science which are predicted by Unification Principle and Unification praxis to date. These have concerned the present role
of science in Unificationism, Unificationist teaching, and the position of
science expected to occur when Unificationism has established a society
of its own guided by its ideology. Certain problems concerning science as
a realm of open inquiry and the inevitable arbitrariness of ideologies have
also been reviewed. Numerous examples have been given concerning
potential value in certain Unificationist concepts in regard to science.
The direction that some of these might be pursued and developed has
been suggested. The general purpose of the paper has been to suggest
aspects regarding science and Unificationism which might best be resolved if anticipated in advance. As stated, it remains to be seen what
direction Unificationism will take in dealing with the above-mentioned
challenges.

Explanation of Figure

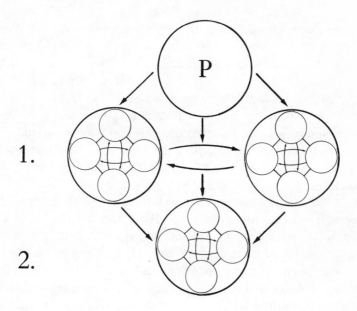

Example of Unificationist ideology applied to one specific scientific problem. The Unificationist "Four-Position Model" was used to illustrate the following content from the text of an ecological publication by the author: "The native vegetational communities comprising true prairie, mixed prairie, and the short grass disclimax prairie were *closed* communities. Each was composed of a characteristic species diversity, with correspondent percentage admixtures and population densities varying with environment conditions of particular localities. On a larger scale, however, they replaced each other in a broad geographic transition. Their basic nature was a dynamic 'two-tier' variance. Herein, an evolutionarily stable, but dynamic flora was in evidence, suited to an equally dynamic climate, and providing natural rhythms suited to adjust to broad transitions through space or environmental variations in particular localities through time. Hence, the 'entire' character of this native environment at any one time was an almost random assortment of ecological situations providing the spectrum of niches for supported fauna, both broadly and specifically adapted. In this context, the micro-climax of specific localities at any one time recapitulated the macro-climax of the region which was based on a co-dominant system of plants. These plants had dispersed into the region from different evolutionary origins following the Pleistocene epoch and established the dynamic co-dominant climax pattern." The Four Position Model was chosen because it allowed the illustration of co-existing dynamic levels contributing to a larger dynamism distinguished by a distinct recapitulation of certain general characteristics. The diagram consists of a Four Position Foundation containing the inner action of other Four Position Foundations (see *Unification Thought*). The top of the Four Position Foundation (P) represents the purpose: to explain the epiphenomenon. The two interacting elements beneath it (at level 1 in the diagram) represent the "Division" stage of "Origin-Division-Union" action in Unificationism. At this interactive level, the two complementary components are as follows. (1) at the left the inner Four Position Foundation represents the interacting factors of the macro-climax characteristics of the environment based on geographic transition. These are: 'purpose' being to model the macro-climax characteristics; components of the 'division' level being (left) macroclimactic factors across an east-west transition of several thousand miles at mid-latitude in North America in the subjective position and (right) the admixture and species diversity of flora and fauna available in all possible combinations for the region; resolution at the "union" level being the macro-climax factor available at any particular locality to influence interaction with local conditions. (2) at the right the inner Four Position Foundation represents the interacting factors of the micro-climax characteristic of the particular geographic locality based on moisture versus slope. These are: purpose being to model the micro-climax characteristic of any one geographic locality; components of the "division" level being (left) availability of ground water at any location based on moisture versus slope and (right) the admixture and species diversity of flora and fauna available in all possible combinations at the locality; resolution at the "union" level being the micro-climax factor available at any particular locality to influence interaction with regional conditions. The characteristics of the macro-climax are seen in the subjective position at the interactive level because they determine local parameters generally; the characteristics of the micro-climax are seen in the objective position at the interactive level because they determine local parameters generally; the characteristics of the micro-climax are seen in the objective position at the interactive level because they limit the regional parameters specifically. At the resolution ("union") level of the entire diagram (level 2) the general "two-tier and recapitulating" nature of the plains and prairie co-dominant evolutionary system is illustrated. It is characterized by a pattern that is random at any one point in space and time but specifically systematized within its larger context. The ability of the plains and prairie closed ecological community to maintain its entire regional character without any specific local structure at any one period in time had hitherto been difficult to understand. Also understood by this modelling is that opening of the community leads to its destruction. This is because the introduction of any non-random phenomenon across the broad geographic transition or at the specific geographic locality "breaks a link in the chain." Once a factor is taken out of the ability of this community to shift and adjust at random, it quickly breaks down. The demise of the closed co-dominant climax community took place in the United States within sixty years of man's initial interference.

NOTES

1. The author is, by training, an evolutionary biologist.

2. Generally, the theological content of Unificationism is referred to in the movement as "The Principle." Various books have appeared concerning this thought, including those called "Divine Principle" and outlines or explanations of "The Principle." "Unification Thought," "Unification Theology," and "Counterproposal to Marxism" are used for respective philosophical, theological, and other specialized applications of "The Principle." For the sake of discussing aspects of "The Principle" and science, in this paper I will use the term "Unification Principle." This is chosen because it is many of the non-theological attributes of "The Principle" (such as the world view presented in Chapter 1 of *Divine Principle*) that bear most upon its relation to science. A detailed analysis of the relation of Unificationist ontology to aspects of science would require a broad comparison over numerous areas of science, as has been attempted to some degree in *The Scientific Basis of Divine Principle* (see footnote 3). In this paper such a comparison is impossible because there is not ample space to review the precise details of Unificationist ontology itself. To date this topic is best explored in *Explaining Unification Thought*, a publication of the Unification Thought Institute.

3. There has been little development of Unificationist science to date. Issues of *The Journal of the Society for Common Insights* (NY: SCI Press), vols. 1 and

2 (1976, 1977) included several articles concerning the Unification Principle and science. An informal book entitled *The Scientific Basis of Divine Principle* was developed by me and several other contributors for a course in science and religion at Unification Theological Seminary. This was not an official publication of the Unification Church and cannot be considered authoritative. Several dialogues on science and Unificationism have been sponsored by the New Ecumenical Research Association but their contents have not been published to date.

4. Adapted from my "Prairie Plains Disclimax and Disappearing Butterflies in the Central United States" *Journal of Invertebrate Conservation*, 1983 (in press).

5. A broad definition of science is difficult because of the methodological spectrum between the so-called hard sciences and soft sciences. For purposes of this essay I consider science any activity that studies phenomena through some process of testing either in an inductive or deductive mode.

BIBLIOGRAPHY

Holy Spirit Association for the Unification of World Christianity. *Divine Principle*. NY: Holy Spirit Association for the Unification of World Christianity, 1973.

Johnson, K. "Plains and Prairie Disclimax and Disappearing Butterflies in the Central United States." *Journal of Invertebrate Conservation* (1983) (in press).

Johnson, K. and Johnson C., *et al. The Scientific Basis of Divine Principle*. NY: The SCI Press, 1981.

Society for Common Insights. *The Journal of the Society for Common Insights*. Vols. 1 and 2. NY: The Society for Common Insights, 1976 and 1977.

Unification Thought Institute. *Explaining Unification Thought*. Barrytown, NY: Unification Thought Institute.

Tyler Hendricks

Voluntary Association, Intermarriage and "The World of the Heart"

The United States is often popularly conceptualized as a nation which exalts individualism, where "human affairs should be thought of in terms of the individual,"[1] and in which progress has been made chiefly through the achievements of heroic individualists. Recent scholarship however is revealing a discrepancy between Americans' conception of the individual *qua* individual and the way that people in reality lived and worked. Paul E. Johnson, for example, in his study of the origins of the city of Rochester, New York, found that the economic foundations of the city were laid through family and friendship networks, networks often bolstered through intermarriage. Mary P. Ryan, in her study of Utica, New York, found that conversion through evangelical revivals, once generally thought of as a supreme example of individualistic behavior, occurred in and was mediated by family networks, with mothers and wives responsible in a significant number of cases for the conversion of their children and husbands. Johnson's study indicates that the majority of the subjects and supporters of revivals were gathered from stable, well-established elements of the community. Anthony F. C. Wallace uncovered community solidarity and mutual support among the leading families in an early industrial community in Pennsylvania, and demonstrated that the economic unit of society in the working class was not the individual but the nuclear family.[2]

People in association with each other, not rugged individualists, established the functioning social world of the United States. People formed associations in order to travel west in wagon trains. Donald G. Matthews argues that the lasting contribution of the Second Great Awakening was not revivalism per se but was its effect as an "organizing process," a grand social movement which knit communities and eventually the nation together. Carroll Smith Rosenberg provides a fine example of how a maternal association forged in the fires of a Finney revival served to unite women of the cities and the far-flung western communities. Gregory A. Singleton argues that this associational development in the first half of the nineteenth century provided the experiential and attitudinal basis for the corporate society which later emerged in industry, government and media, shaping America on the national level in the latter half of the century.[3]

This data suggests that the tradition of "American as rugged individualist" may be even more a romanticization than we have generally heretofore realized. We must place a new emphasis upon the motif of family and community cooperation as a hermeneutic for understanding the American experience. The primary mode through which people of the nineteenth century achieved this group solidarity was "voluntary association."

Voluntary association, although it may involve exceptional individuals, does not lend itself to the promotion of individualism or of individual independence. Alexis de Tocqueville noted what he called "the tyranny of the majority" which characterized the social world of the 1830s in America. At least on the level of "moral beliefs," he said, "there is a passive, though a voluntary, obedience... In the moral world, everything is classed, adapted, decided, and foreseen."[4] H.D. Thoreau escaped to solitude at Walden Pond, writing that most men "live lives of quiet desperation," mentally chained to store, farm, church and political party. Orestes Brownson spoke of this same problem when he noted that one could not go to sleep, get up, eat a meal or kiss his wife without consulting some society or association. Thus it seems clear that American society of the nineteenth century rewarded unity and cooperation more than it did non-conformity and strict individualism. This period was a time of tumultuous social, ideological and technological change, and the United States was composed of a fast-developing population of divergent and often discordant races spread over unpopulated territory or crowded into "instant cities." It is not surprising that such a society would not highly value nor greatly reward, as a rule, the non-conforming individualist. Treatment of minority or deviant social groups, such as blacks, Catholics, Mormons or immigrants from southern and eastern Europe, testifies that this pressure to conform, to "Americanize," did not play only upon individuals.

I introduce this issue because I think that it is an important factor in the historical context within which we are to understand the future of the Unification Church in the United States. At issue on the theoretical level is the relationship of the individual to society; the balance between the rights of individuals and the duties of individuals. Historically the myth and rhetoric of America has tended to emphasize the rights and opportunities of the individual over against societal norms and traditions. However, in historical reality it has been behavior oriented by family and group which has been rewarded. This tension between rhetoric and reality was not a serious problem for most people in the nineteenth century. I would cite two factors responsible for this: one, the existence of the frontier in terms of both geography and economics, and two, that of which de Tocqueville spoke, the general consensus of opinion which guided individuals to exercise their independence for the purpose of forming social groups, voluntary associations, benevolence and moral societies, churches and nuclear families. With the turn of the twentieth century, however, the frontier closed geographically, and from the 1930s it began to close economically. More important has been the breakdown of what I consider was a general consensus of opinion concerning the relationship of the individual to society. The strong nineteenth century emphasis upon the rights of individuals has persisted, but it has done so without the persistence of the consciousness of the duty of the individual toward society.

We can find two major suggestions for resolution of this tension, both of which portray themselves as the legitimate legate of the American tradition. These two are represented roughly by groups known as the Moral Majority and the People for the American Way. I am using these groups in a very general and perhaps stereotypical sense. After discussing their prescriptions I will turn to a third alternative, which also has its claim to the American tradition, although it calls upon other traditions as well, the Unification Church.

The Moral Majority emphasizes the notion of the individual's responsibility toward society. One has a duty to one's family, one's community and nation, and this is the primary basis for one's action. This duty is oriented by a transcendent moral law, a law consistent with Protestant

Christianity, especially in its Anglo-American formulations. Obedience to this transcendent moral order will guarantee God's blessing upon the nation, family and individual. Therefore, morality is considered a social duty. The interpretation of this transcendent order is roughly consistent with the mores of the nineteenth century evangelical culture in America; it calls for an internalized discipline necessary for maintenance of Christian industrialism and commerce and for sanctification of the family circle around the hearth.

The People for the American Way organization, on the other hand, emphasizes the rights of the individual over against society, in particular over against the perceived imposition of antiquated social and personal norms, specifically those norms advocated by the Moral Majority. In the People's view there may be a transcendent moral law but each person must be free to interpret it by him or herself, particularly in the realm of personal morality. People for the American Way sees imposed morality as a threat to pluralism and to the freedom of the individual, and perceives the continued upholding of nineteenth century values to be an absolutization of culturally relative norms, an absolutization which has the potential to lead to social coercion or even totalitarianism. People for the American Way calls upon the traditional American mythos of the individual's to pursue happiness as he or she best sees fit.

These two opponents are actually calling upon same world view, that view of nineteenth century liberalism which believed in an "invisible hand" active in the world. The theory was that if individuals are left to their own "enlightened self-interest," an invisible force, perhaps God, or natural law, would coordinate their various enterprises, creating a prospering and harmonious society. The assumption of many Americans was that as soon as they could free themselves from the superstition and bad habits of the past, all individuals naturally would come to see evangelical morality and "Christian industrialism" as the absolute truth of the universe. Those who made this assumption in the nineteenth century often got a good return on their investment. Moral Majority continues to make that assumption and feels that our problem is that not enough people are making it with them. People for the American Way rejects the absolute claim of nineteenth century evangelical morality, but nonetheless seems to believe in an invisible hand which will insure that the optimum situation will obtain through the decisions of individuals made based upon their own desire for happiness. Thus they, with the Moral Majority, accept the basic doctrine of enlightened self-interest and an immanent natural law. The free desires of adult individuals, short of criminal ones, take precedence over any traditional or theoretical morality, and are the foundation for healthy society.

Both these alternatives ultimately frame their answers in terms of the individual: the duties of the individual in a morally monistic world, or the rights of the individual in a morally pluralistic world. The People for the American Way criticizes the Moral Majority for denying pluralism, and they in turn are criticized for denying the existence or relevance of absolute norms.

At this point I would like to bring out the Unification position. Unificationism admits of valid considerations on both sides of the argument. Agreeing with People for the American Way, Unificationism sees serious problems with the nineteenth century world view associated with the Moral Majority position, specifically in its historical tendency to racial, religious, cultural and national exclusivity. However, Unificationism would agree with the Moral Majority that there exist absolute norms in terms of morality and social ethics, at least in principle, and that these norms do emphasize the duty more than the rights of the individual, in relation to family, society, nation, world and God. There are many agreements also between Unification and the Moral Majority position concerning family and social morality taken in more detail. However, Unification rejects the idea that this morality is to be enforced through political action, which boils down to the making of laws. Morality is rather the normative outgrowth of the establishment of proper relationality, involving all degrees of relationship between individuals, families, social and national structures, earth and heaven.

Unificationism agrees with the People for the American Way acceptance of pluralism and with that which pluralism implies: a qualified cultural relativism. (The qualification here would enter into the area wherein cultural relativism leads to moral relativism.) Further, Unification recognizes that human beings are more subtle and complex than the evangelical norms of the nineteenth century might give them credit as being; this applies particularly to the realm of creativity, individual freedom in artistic expression, and the definition of work and productivity. In these areas, as well as others, Unification would tend to view nineteenth century norms as restrictive and narrow. Further, it is clear that in order for the human race to survive, not only socially but ecologically, new understanding of the human relationship with God, each other and the created order must come to the fore. The liberal attitude represented by People for the American Way has more openness to the expression and exercise of such novelty of world view than does the Moral Majority. Ergo the paradoxical situation of the Unification movement attracting as the greater part of its constituency people from a liberal and often radical background (at least in America) and yet espousing a fairly conservative "moral majority" type personal and family morality.

I mentioned above the Unification proposal of "establishing proper relationality." This establishment has a religious origin and center to it; it is established, from the viewpoint of Unificationism, through the mediation of the Messiah. This may sound like a radical and disjunctive solution, and on one level it is. But on the large scale social level it need not be. Reverend Moon's message, properly understood, has great potential to gain the approval of many Americans, especially in light of the American tradition of cooperation and association for the sake of social advancement. This is so because that message dovetails in an important way with certain aspects of the American tradition, aspects brought out by the Moral Majority and/or People for the American Way but treated implicitly by these groups as discordant or mutually exclusive. These aspects are, on the one hand, pluralism and, on the other, an absolute moral standard or transcendent moral law. To these must be added another significant dimension of the American tradition not brought out by either of the groups dealt with above, that being the cross-fertilization in the American tradition of Judeo-Christian millennialism and the belief in America's special historical role or destiny. This translates in real terms into the belief that, as put by Ralph Gabriel, "progress is normal and the future promises more than has been realized in the present."[5] To explicate the significance of these points I will refer to the teachings of Reverend Moon.

The *Divine Principle* states that God's desire for America was that through the practice of Christianity there would develop here the unity of all races, cultures and religions. Unification would agree, then, with the traditional American "whig" view of providential history, which viewed the Puritans as carrying the purest seed of the Protestant Reformation faith to the New World in order to establish here a people and nation in a covenantal relationship with God. This nation was to become, in God's eyes, a nation which would be a home for people of all the nations of the world. I will refer to "God's Hope for America," a major address delivered by Reverend Moon at Yankee Stadium in 1976, for elaboration on this point.

He said that there were two motivations for colonists to come to America: the desire for wealth and the desire for "God and freedom," i.e., "to build a new nation centered upon God." If those motivated by wealth "had become the mainstream of America, there would have been far greater strife, division, and struggle between the different races and national groups. The United States would have been filled with unrighteousness and injustice." However, the godly motivation inspired a sufficient condition of Christian practice to enable God's hope to reside with the United States. Therefore there accrued great blessing from God in terms of physical prosperity and relative peace. The purpose of the blessing was and is not for the sake of the United States itself but for the sake of the world.

What does America have to offer to the world? Reverend Moon says that it is not Christian doctrine, and not wealth; it is rather the ideal of international and interracial harmony that America is to share, in substance and symbol, with the world.

If your lineage has been in America for some time, it probably unites many different nationalities. In your bloodstream many kinds of blood are blended together. Nations who used to be enemies have united in your blood. When the individuals and the families which transcend racial and national barriers gather together to create a church, a society and a nation, that nation will become God's ideal nation for all peoples.

This reduces to very practical terms. God's strategy, as envisioned by Reverend Moon, is to unite black, white and yellow, Arab and Jew, Catholic and Protestant, by bringing them to America and allowing them to harmonize here—ultimately through intermarriage. This harmonization is to be lubricated by the working of a broadly based "civil religion" in a voluntaristic society. The present admixture of European races in America would be expanded to the world level.

This is actually, I believe, a "post-modern" way of thinking, in that it presupposes sensitivity to the power of cultural conditioning, sensitivity to the degree to which one's consciousness is shaped by the social world into which one is born. Given such conditioning, it is apparent that there are cultural and personal differences which reach beyond language into areas of epistemology, or the way we variously interpret the world, which simply are beyond anyone's capacity to resolve. The solution is to "blend " our blood through intermarriage, through God-centered, interracial and international families, and in so doing blend our cultural and hermeneutical frames.

Reverend Moon observes that the United States has been the proving ground for this development, development with a limited scope (confined mainly to European races) but on a large scale. Thus he sees the existence and potential of the United States as a work of God: "There is only one nation like this in all history. It is apparent that this unique nation of America is the creation of God." Christianity is the basis for the "spiritual revolution" to begin, though Christianity in its present form does not constitute the ideal.

> To do this, Christianity of the world must unite. The church must liberate herself from sectarianism. She must undergo a drastic reform and achieve an ecumenical and inter-religious unity. For this, we need a spiritual revolution. We need a new ideology, and this new ideology must incorporate Oriental philosophy, uniting the cultures of the East and the West.
>
> This new ideology will also be capable of unifying all the existing religions and ideologies of the world. Therefore, it has come in the form of a new religious movement. The Unification Church Movement has been created by God to fulfill that mission. This spiritual movement must first succeed here in America in order to spread throughout the world. The new ideology which the Unification Church brings is "Godism," an absolutely God-centered ideology. It has the power to awaken America, and it has the power to raise up the model of the ideal nation of God upon this land.

Thus Reverend Moon is saying that a new ideology will be at the basis of a spiritual revolution which in turn will give rise to the coming together, on the most fundamental basis, of races and nations. "True Americans," he continued, "are those who are proud of such international families, churches and of the nation which consists of all peoples."

How does this relate to the earlier question concerning the problem of the relationship between the individual and society in America today? The answer is simply that unity between the individual and the whole is brought about when individuals accept common ideals or goals around which they can unite. The cultural ideals and principles of evangelical Protestantism, for example, served to unite the major portion of the United States population in the early part of the nineteenth century. Those ideals, however, were limited to the level of one race, culture, religion and nation. When racial differences were bridged, as in the abolition movement, it was done so only to the extent of the principle that all should have equal treatment under the law. Evangelical Christianity did not effect a unity of love or heart between whites and blacks. Therefore the tradition represented by Moral Majority is open to severe criticism for its inability to undergird a pluralistic society. Reverend Moon's ideology is directed exactly at that point. Individuals, he teaches, will join together when they perceive common, mutually beneficial ideals and purposes. The ideals of which he is speaking, as summarized in the Yankee Stadium speech, are so broad as to include people from every racial, cultural and national background. Therefore the problems inherent with a pluralistic situation are mitigated to the extent, at least, to which we allow our common ideals to outweigh our concern for whatever frictions our differences create. At the same time, those ideals constitute the basis for us together to go beyond moral relativism, to find common standards for our lives and society.

These ideals, of course, must be rooted in God; they can have no other origin. The purpose motivating the "spiritual revolution" cannot be individual gain (as in capitalism), the nation or race (as in fascism), the mythical proletariat (as in communism); it can only be God. Only God, the ultimately mysterious, ultimately personal, ultimately transcendent, ultimately powerful, can undergird such a spiritual revolution.

Because Reverend Moon's message is to a significant degree consistent with, as well as a development of, the American tradition, it need not be seen as calling for a radically disjunctive social change. The American consciousness is in many ways prepared, by everything from our general "civil religion" ideals, to Sesame Street, to the civil rights movement, to assimilate such an ideal vision of the world. (Even the strong admonitions, in some sectors of society, of parents to their children to beware of the "brainwashed Moonies" may have an unexpected effect, for does not the rising generation often tend to adopt that about which their parents warned them?)

Corresponding with this general cultural development must be a more "internal" or small scale development of an intentional community, a "seed culture," to set the pattern around which the general, universal culture will ultimately shape itself. This is the "leaven which leavens the whole lump." The external, general development, which might be seen as the work of God immanent in history, is ultimately futile without this corresponding internal development, which is the result of God's inbreaking into history in a radical, unexplainable and unexpected way. This inbreaking, in turn, has no meaning and will have little effect outside the context of a culture prepared to receive and nurture it.

This internal or seed community, which expresses traits which will come to typify the whole culture, is termed in Unification "the world of the heart." What are the dimensions of this "heart," and how is the "world of the heart" to be brought about?"   The *Divine Principle* gives only general answers to these questions. The *ideal family* is the center of heart, and family relationships—those of parent and child, husband and wife, brother and sister, centered upon God—set the basic standards of relationship within the larger society. *Divine Principle* calls for the expansion from the individual's relationship to God, to relationships within the family, between families, between social groups and structures of society, and between nations. Thereby 'heart,' an invisible, ineffable quality associated more closely with God's grace than with human effort, finds its place in the human social world. It does so, as I understand Unificationism to be saying, through the establishment of proper relationality, centered upon God. Thus, social amelioration grows out of the factors of heart and relationship.

Heart and relationship are intertwined in Unificationism. Heart is given from God, but it is mediated, even "liberated," by the establishment of proper relationship. This heart, or power of love, is the only power which can overcome the historical resentments associated with race, nation, religion, culture and, ultimately, gender. The mediator of this, of God's heart, is the Messiah. The social structure mediating this heart is that structure of relationships centered around the Messiah, or in "attendance" to the Messiah, and that social structure itself would then be the Messiah, the mediator of God's heart, to the general society, nation and world. Within that structure would occur a model of interracial, international marriages, as is indeed being attempted in the Unification Church. Such a development can come only voluntarily, on the basis of religious faith. With the acceptance of the norms of the "new age ideology" such voluntary desires of people would become commonplace, and intermarriage could occur naturally on a large scale.

I hope not to be overly prosaic about this. Unificationism calls for revolutionary changes in the consciousness structure of all people, races and cultures. It calls for a harmonization of beliefs and norms which are logically and/or emotionally in many instances impossible to harmonize. The new world view and social practice which might accomplish such harmonization—or abet the transcendence of the need for it—has to emerge out of the "seed culture" itself, that social network which incarnates the ideal, at least in a formative or tentative way. The Unification

Church family is attempting to be that social group, and the enduring basis for the "world of the heart" must be strongly evident in the minds and lives of its children.

NOTES

1. Ralph Henry Gabriel, *The Course of American Democratic Thought* (NY: The Ronald Press, 1940), p. 4.

2. Paul E. Johnson, *A Shopkeeper's Millennium: Society and Revivals in Rochester, NY, 1815–1837* (NY: Hill and Wang, 1978), pp. 21–28, 33. Mary P. Ryan, *Cradle of the Middle Class: The Family in Oneida County, New York, 1790–1865* (NY: Cambridge University Press, 1981), pp. 75–83. Anthony F.C. Wallace, *Rockdale: The Growth of an American Village in the Early Industrial Revolution* (NY: W.W. Norton and Company, 1972), pp. 44–69.

3. Daniel Boorstin gives a fascinating account of the associational life on wagon trains in *The Americans: The National Experience*. Donald G. Matthews, "The Second Great Awakening as an Organizing Process," *American Quarterly*, XXI (1969), 23–42. Carroll Smith Rosenberg, "Beauty, the Beast and the Militant Woman: A Case Study in Sex Roles and Social Stress in Jacksonian America," *American Quarterly*, XXIII (1971), 562–584. Gregory H. Singleton, "Protestant Voluntary Associations and the Shaping of Victorian America," in Daniel Walker Howe, *Victorian America* (University of Pennsylvania Press, 1976).

4. de Tocqueville, Alexis, *Democracy in America* (NY: Schocken Books, 1961), unabridged, vol. 1, p. 33,.

5. Gabriel, *op.cit.*, p. 4.

The booklet "God's Hope for America" and the textbook *Divine Principle* are both available from the publisher, Holy Spirit Association for the Unification of World Christianity (Unification Church).

Henry O. Thompson
Therese Stewart

The Unification Theological Seminary

At the entrance to the chapel of UTS—the Unification Theological Seminary—a bronze plaque has been fastened to the wall as a new cornerstone. The plaque is a gift of the class of 1978. It indicates that the seminary was founded by Rev. Sun Myung Moon on September 20, 1975. The first class graduated in 1977 and the second, represented in the bronze plaque, graduated in 1978. So much for beginnings, in the formal sense of the term.

The real beginning is somewhat earlier. The UTS catalogue describes the beginning as going back to at least 1954, when in a small dwelling in Seoul, Korea, the founder of this Seminary drew up the outline for the association now known as the Unification Church International, which today has "daughter churches in more than 120 nations."

Another beginning is the purchase of the defunct Christian Brothers Academy in Barrytown, New York, 90 miles north of New York City, on a bluff overlooking the beautiful Hudson River, ten miles north of Kingston. The Academy is itself a part of this story as is the land on which it, now UTS, stands.

An officer of the American Revolution, Major John R. Livingston, built a home here in 1796. He called his place Massena House, after a French Marshal in the armies of Napolean Bonaparte. Tradition says that in 1868, nine-year-old Teddy Roosevelt spent several months visiting in this Massena House. The building burned down in 1885 but it was replaced by a smaller and different style of house which still stands today opposite the chapel and its plaque, across the circular drive which is now part of the main entrance to the school. This new Massena House, now nearly a century old, was extensively repaired and refurbished in the Fall of 1982, restoring it, if not to its pristine glory, at least to serviceability, and to its ability to withstand the sun and the rain, the snow and the cold of this lovely area. The House serves today as the home of several UTS families.

John Baptiste De La Salle (1651–1719) was born in Rheims, France. At the age of 16, he was a canon in the Rheims church, a position held by four different popes. Instead of the Papacy, John turned to education. He and Adrien Nyel started the first school for poor boys, offering them an education hitherto reserved for the rich who could afford tutors. John went on to found the first professional school for teachers. He started a Normal School for boys who wanted to become part of the Brothers of the Christian School ("Fraters Scholarum Christianarum") which he founded. At the age of 53, he started yet another school, for the middle class, where he taught practical skills such as commerce and math. His use of French instead of Latin stirred up a storm of protest. While education is taken for granted today, La Salle and his Christian Brothers suffered for daring to educate outside the proscribed tradition of their day.

By the time St. John (canonized in 1900) died, his order had 274 Brothers teaching 9,000 pupils in 26 houses across the face of France. In 1843, the movement spread to the United States. In 1950, St. John became the Patron Saint of Teachers. A Christian Brother, Jeffrey Gros, was elected director of the Commission of Faith and Order of the National Council of Churches in 1983, after serving as acting director for a year and a half.

The Christian Brothers acquired land at Pocantico Hills, NY, in the late 1880s. They started a novitiate there in 1905 and in 1909 imported 16 stained glass windows from France. John D. Rockefeller bought their land in 1928 for $850,000. He gave them a gift of one million dollars. They bought the 250 acre property at Barrytown and in 1930 finished building the present Seminary structure, shaped like an "H" in ground plan. The wings are four stories high while the cross-bar has two stories. The chapel, on the second floor of the cross-bar, was built to include the

16 French windows. Eight of these tell the story of De La Salle's life. One pictures Brother Joseph who directed the American work in 1900. The French cathedrals of Notre Dame and St. Sulpice (where La Salle went to school as a child), and St. Peter's in Rome, are included.

The chapel was the spiritual center for the Christian Brothers and it remains so for UTS. Worship services each morning are led by students, faculty, and visiting clergy and speakers. Sunday services are held in the chapel though students also attend services in local churches. Prayer and study groups are both spontaneous and sponsored by the Seminary. "Central to the fulfillment of Seminary goals is the creation of a climate in which the development of a rich personal relationship with God is respected as the most important aspect of life. Prayer and worship are seen as an integral part of Seminary life, and a relationship with God is seen as a foundation for deepening relationships with others."[1] The chapel is always open for individual prayer and meditation.

In 1965, the school was renovated. In the chapel, inlaid lights replaced the chandeliers. The stone altar was installed, to symbolize the Old and New Testament. The metal circle over the altar is said to define the sacred space, the Holy of Holies. A new steel girder was placed across the kitchen ceiling to hold up the altar. A stone holy water font was placed in the foyer.

Silence and class separation were the rule in St. Joseph's Normal School. The high school students ate in what today is UTS' main dining room on the ground floor at the east end of the cross-bar of the "H," while the novices ate in today's student lounge at the west end of the cross-bar, beneath the chapel. The faculty and retired Brothers ate in the smaller rooms parallel to the lounge, along the hallway to the kitchen. The novices stayed in the northwest dorm, today's women's dorm. High school students were housed in the east wings while the other Brothers were in the southwest wing, today's staff and guest rooms. The novices' common room for study and classes is today's Lecture Hall II, in the northwest wing. Below it, the Do Jang, the training room for the martial art of Wonwha-do, used to be a meeting room, barber shop, tailor shop and audiovisual room. Today's typing room in the east wing was the chem lab for the Brothers. The high school student's common room is today's Lecture Hall I on the second floor over the main dining room.

The Christian Brothers Institute closed in 1970. In 1974, the Unification Church bought the property. In October, 1974, Rev. Moon appointed David S.C. Kim to start a Seminary here. The history of the Holy

Spirit Association for the Unification of World Christianity (HSA-UWC), or simply, the Unification Church, is shared in earlier sections of this text. Here it needs to be noted that education was a part of Rev. Moon's vision and dream from the earliest years of his ministry. In his inaugural address at the Seminary's founding he referred to the Seminary as the Cornerstone of the Kingdom of Heaven. The Seminary's President, Mr. David S. C. Kim, was one of the first Unification missionaries to the United States (Portland, Oregon, 1959). One of the Seminary's first faculty, Dr. Young Oon Kim, is also one of the first missionaries to the U.S. (Eugene, Oregon, 1959). Earlier, Dr. Kim was a professor at Ewha University in Seoul. A Methodist with strong interest in the work of Emmanuel Swedenborg, Dr. Kim joined the Unification movement in 1954. She remains the only full time faculty person at UTS who is a Unificationist. She teaches theology and in a sense is not only the theologian for UTS, but for the entire movement, a living example of the tradition that a seminary is called to be a "think tank" for the church. Her work in world religions has prepared her in a unique way for the world-wide concerns of the Unification movement.

The faculty has grown somewhat from its beginnings in 1975. It now includes as full time staff an Orthodox Jewish rabbi teaching the Hebrew Scriptures and Judaism, a Greek Orthodox teaching Church history, a Korean Confucianist scholar teaching oriental philosophy and the philosophy of religion, a Roman Catholic psychologist teaching counseling and the psychology of religion, a United Methodist teaching religion and society (homiletics, world religions, ethics, ministry), an evangelical scholar teaching the Greek Scriptures. Adjunct faculty include United Methodists, Roman Catholics, Dutch Reform, Presbyterian, and Unificationists at both the graduate and post-graduate stages. Visiting lecturers have come from across the spectrum of human traditions of East and West, North and South.

The students also come from a cross section of the American and the human scene. They come initially to a two-year diploma program in Religious Education, which in time will hopefully be a Master's degree (M.R.E.). In 1980, a new three-year diploma program was begun which hopefully will in time be a Master's in Divinity (M.Div). Each Fall, about 50 new students arrive and each June since 1977, about 50 students graduate. The Alumni Association now numbers over 300 women and men, many in the United States, but others scattered over the continents of Africa, Asia, Europe and Latin America, as well as Australia and the islands of the seas. Several dozen alumni are pursuing graduate studies in various universities from Massachusetts to California.

The diversity of faculty and students is a part of the purpose of the Seminary as it "seeks to promote interfaith, interracial and international unity." Part of this purpose is also sought through a variety of conferences sponsored by UTS on ministry, life styles, doctrine, religious freedom, and interfaith dialogue in general. The main focus of the school, like any other, is of course its academic program. Courses are taught in Biblical studies, Jewish history, theology, world religions, ministry, religious education, philosophy, psychology, and related areas such as pastoral counseling, Biblical archaeology, the Kingdom of God, ethics, and Home Church. The last is a general program of the Unification movement which involves visitation in neighborhood homes, assistance to the elderly and other neighborhood services such as youth centers, day-care centers, clean-up campaigns, raising money for C.R.O.P. through walk-athons. Visitation includes sharing the program and teachings of the Unification movement as well as service and entertainment and simply being a good neighbor. UTS participates actively in this general program.

The students are on work-scholarships, which means they provide much of the effort in serving meals, washing dishes, cleaning and maintaining the building and grounds, staffing the post office, bookstore and information booth, and caring for many of the other necessities of life normal to any school. There are several extras, however, such as taking care of the horses, digging and maintaining a pond, planting trees, developing nature walks, stocking the pond with golden carp rescued from the polluted Hudson River. Some of the land has been farmed, primarily for vegetables for the Seminary but also for distribution to people in need in the area. Students assisted in the repair of Massena House and in the building of the soccer field and tennis courts, and the new library. Such "Peace Corps" type activities have been valuable in post-graduate work in the U.S. and the Third World. Some of it was directed by former Peace Corps volunteers.

Besides serving as missionaries to various parts of the world, UTS graduates serve in the Unification "Ocean Church" program which includes commercial fishing and establishing worship and teaching centers. Some work in, or as directors of, state centers in each of the 50 states of the U.S. Numbers of them are in the program on college campuses known as the Collegiate Association for the Research of Principles (CARP). Some work is with the Unification newspapers and other publications, fishing and boat building companies, and other commercial activities either of the Unification movement or their own, parallel to what Protestants call a "tent-making ministry" or the "worker-priest movement" of Roman Catholicism.

Life is not all work and no play. The usual run of school activities include tennis, baseball, volleyball, soccer, intramural basketball, boating, fishing, swimming, horseback riding, cross-country skiing, plays, entertainment nights, movies, music, art, photography and debates. One particular activity noted earlier is Wonhwa-do, a martial arts developed by former UTS faculty member and administrator, Dr. Joon Seuk, now the Director of CARP. The martial arts sometimes appear to be a form of exercise or alternately a way of self-defense in a day of high street crime and home burglaries. Dr. Seuk, however, explains Wonhwa-do as a spiritual discipline which brings unity to body and mind. Such a unity of body, mind and spirit seems singularly appropriate to a school and a movement dedicated to the unity of humanity.

Local activities are supplemented by individual, class or Seminary trips to museums, art galleries, churches, religious communities, and the many attractions of New York City—"The Big Apple." Here the Unification movement also has its national headquarters, three newspapers— The New York Tribune, Noticias del Mundo, and The Unification News (a fourth is the Washington Times in Washington, D.C.), a symphony orchestra and various other musical and theatrical groups. Seminarians also participate heavily in such programs as the annual International Conference on the Unity of the Sciences sponsored by the International Cultural Foundation. At "home," the students produce "The Mid-Hudson Tide," a monthly community-service newsletter for and about local activities included in the Home Church areas, and "The Cornerstone," a monthly newsletter about UTS and Unification programs. "The Mid-Hudson Tide" is produced in the Seminary's own print shop operated by students. The shop also prints special bulletins and other programs.

The New ERA—The New Ecumenical Research Association—is a program that developed at UTS under the direction of Head Librarian, John Maniatis. New ERA has held over 50 conferences in many parts of the world and published over a dozen books based on the papers presented on theological issues, religious freedom, life styles, etc. It was formally founded in March, 1980, after preliminary conferences over the previous three years. The Global Congress of the World's Religions (GCWR) is another "spin-off" of UTS. It was begun by former UTS faculty, Dr. Warren Lewis, with the support of President Kim, to encourage interfaith dialogue among the religious traditions of the world. Three preliminary annual meetings (San Francisco, Boston, Los Angeles) led to a formal founding in November, 1980, at Miami Beach. Subsequent meetings include Seoul and Philadelphia besides regional meetings in England, India, Sri Lanka and Pakistan. Four volumes of proceedings have been published.

No description of UTS would be complete without reference to the library. It began as shelves or "stacks"in one of the two gymnasiums in the east wing of the building. In 1980, the opposite gym at the northeast was remodeled with a main floor added, to provide new stacks, new study areas, an attractive well-lighted air conditioned periodical and reading room, microfilm and office space. The library now subscribes to almost 500 periodicals, and has over 20,000 volumes. Academic committees visiting UTS for charter and accreditation review have commented on its strength, surprisingly high for a new school, as they have also positively reviewed the entire academic program. The library was specifically cited by these committees when they recommended to the Board of Regents that the Seminary be granted the Provisional Charter for which it applied in April, 1975.

NOTES

1. *Unification Theological Seminary Catalogue 1982/83.*

SOURCES

Kopacz, Kasia and Martin, Chad. "Welcome: The Unification Theological Seminary." No date. Their sources for the Christian Brothers and the Barrytown property include personal conversations with Brothers Bernard Peter, Peter Drake, Thomas Scanlon, Andrew Winka, Augustine Loes, and Mr. Morrison, a Barrytown teacher at the Institute. Written sources include: Brother Leo Kirby, *I, John Baptiste de la Salle* (Winone, MN: Saint Mary's Press, 1980); Martin Dempsey, *John Baptiste de la Salle* (Milwaukee: Bruce Publ. Co., 1940); Edward Fitzpatrick, *La Salle, Patron of All Teachers* (Milwaukee: Bruce Publ. Co., 1951); and Angelus Gabriel, *The Christian Brothers in the United States, 1848–1948* (Declan X. McMullen, 1948).

Quebedeaux, Richard. "Korean Missionaries to America," *New Conversations* 6, No. 3 (Spring '82), pp. 6-15.

Unification News, 2, No. 6, (June '83), p. 2.

Unification Theological Seminary Catalogue 1982/83. This or a later edition is available from the Office of the Dean, 10 Dock Rd., Barrytown, NY 12507. The catalogue includes complete information on admission requirements, fees, course work and community life.

Personal communications from faculty, staff, students and friends.

Those Who Contribute

Dr. Thomas Boslooper is a retired minister in the Reformed Church of America and Professor of Biblical Studies at UTS. He holds the Ph.D. from Columbia University in Religion and New Testament. Among his published works is *The Image of Woman*.

Mr. Lloyd Eby is Lecturer in Philosophy at UTS. A Unificationist for nine years, he is a doctoral candidate at Fordham University.

Dr. Josef Hausner is Associate Professor of Biblical Literature and Judaic Studies at UTS. His Ph.D. in Religion and Society is from Columbia University.

Dr. Tyler Hendricks is Adjunct Assistant Professor in Church History at UTS. He holds the Ph.D. from Vanderbilt University. He joined the Unification family eleven years ago.

Dr. Theodore E. James taught philosophical ethics at UTS. He holds the Ph.D. from Columbia. He is Professor Emeritus of Philosophy, Manhattan College, NYC; Lecturer, Fairfield University and Adjunct Professor of Philosophy, Sacred Heart University, Fairfield, CT. He is the author of numerous works, scholarly and popular.

Dr. Kurt Johnson has been Lecturer in Science and Religion at UTS. He holds the Ph.D. from the City University of New York. His special research interest is in butterflies.

Mr. David S.C. Kim is President of UTS. He was one of the first Unificationists in the United States. He was appointed by Rev. Sun Myung Moon to initiate the establishment of UTS in October 1974. He has guided its growth and development throughout its history.

Dr. Young Oon Kim is Professor of Theology at UTS. She is a graduate of the theological school of Kwansei Gakuin University in Japan, took three years of graduate study at Emanuel College, University of Toronto, and taught at Ewha Women's University in Seoul, Korea. She holds the H.L.D. from Ricker College. Among her published works are: *World Religions, Unification Theology, Introduction to Theology,* and *Types of Modern Theology.*

Dr. Jan Knappert has lectured at UTS on Islam and African religions. He teaches at the University of London, School of African and Oriental Studies. He holds the Doctor Litt. et Phil., the highest degree obtainable in the Netherlands.

Dr. James Michael Lee has served as adjunct Professor of Religious Education at UTS. He holds the Ed.D. from Teachers College, Columbia University. Among his published works are *The Flow of Religious Instruction.*

Dr. Joseph J. McMahon is Associate Professor of Education and Philosophy. He holds the Ph.D. in Philosophy from St. John's University. Among his published books is *Between You and You.*

Dr. Hae Soo Pyun is Adjunct Assistant Professor of Oriental Languages and Oriental Philosophy. He holds the Ph.D. from Columbia University in Philosophy. Among his published works is *The Metaphysics of E.J.E. Woodbridge.*

Dr. Richard Quebedeaux is lecturer in Religion and Society at UTS and a Consulting Coordinator for Ecumenical Conferences. He teaches ecumenics at UTS. He holds the D.Phil. from Oxford University. Among his published books are *The New Charismatics* and *By What Authority.*

Dr. John Andrew Sonneborn is Lecturer in Religion and Society. He holds the D.Min. from N.Y. Theological Seminary.

Dean Therese Stewart is Academic Dean and Lecturer in Religious Education at UTS. She holds the M.Ed. from the University of Minnesota and has completed course work for the doctoral program in education at Teachers College.

Dr. Henry O. Thompson is Associate Professor of Religion and Society. He holds the Ph.D. from Drew University in Old Testament and Archaeology. Among his published works are *Mekal the God of Beth-Shan* and *Ethics in Nursing*. The latter is co-authored with Joyce Beebe Thompson.

Mr. Jonathan Wells is Lecturer in Theology. He holds the M.A. from Yale in theology and is a doctoral candidate in theology at Yale.

Dr. Yaqub Zaki (James Dickie) is from Scotland. He has taught Islam at UTS. and has held teaching posts at the University of Lancaster and other schools in England and Scotland.